Environmental Governance in Europe

*For Alison, Ita and Susan, for their love, tolerance
and quite a bit of patience*

Environmental Governance in Europe

A Comparative Analysis of New Environmental Policy Instruments

Rüdiger K.W. Wurzel

Professor of Comparative European Politics and Jean Monnet Chair in European Union Studies, Department of Politics and International Relations, University of Hull, UK

Anthony R. Zito

Reader in Politics, School of Geography, Politics and Sociology, Newcastle University, UK

Andrew J. Jordan

Professor in Environmental Politics, School of Environmental Sciences, University of East Anglia, UK

Edward Elgar

Cheltenham, UK • Northampton, MA, USA

© Rüdiger K.W. Wurzel, Anthony R. Zito and Andrew J. Jordan 2013

All rights reserved. No part of this publication may be reproduced, stored in a retrieval system or transmitted in any form or by any means, electronic, mechanical or photocopying, recording, or otherwise without the prior permission of the publisher.

Published by
Edward Elgar Publishing Limited
The Lypiatts
15 Lansdown Road
Cheltenham
Glos GL50 2JA
UK

Edward Elgar Publishing, Inc.
William Pratt House
9 Dewey Court
Northampton
Massachusetts 01060
USA

A catalogue record for this book
is available from the British Library

Library of Congress Control Number: 2012951744

This book is available electronically in the ElgarOnline.com Social and Political Science Subject Collection, E-ISBN 978 1 84980 472 1

ISBN 978 1 84980 466 0 (cased)

Typeset by Columns Design XML Ltd, Reading
Printed by MPG PRINTGROUP, UK

Contents

List of figures and tables	vi
List of abbreviations	vii
Preface	xii

PART I   INTRODUCTION

1	Environmental policy: from government to governance?	3

PART II   CONTEXT

2	Governing by policy instruments: theories and analytical concepts	23
3	Changing institutional contexts for the use of policy instruments	46

PART III   GOVERNING BY NEW INSTRUMENTS

4	Governing by informational means	77
5	Governing by voluntary means	107
6	Governing by eco-taxes	133
7	Governing by emissions trading	158

PART IV   EMERGING PATTERNS OF GOVERNING

8	Changing patterns of environmental policy instrument use	189
9	Out with the 'old' and in with the 'new'? Governing with policy instruments	219

Bibliography	241
Index	273

v

Figures and tables

FIGURES

8.1	Items of EU environmental legislation 1972–2009	201

TABLES

1.1	Governance and policy instrument typologies compared	11
1.2	Different policy instrument typologies	14
2.1	Different environmental policy instrument typologies	26
2.2	Types of environmental policy instruments analysed in this book	29
2.3	Theorising the adoption and adaption of policy instruments	44
3.1	A framework for characterising jurisdictional contexts	47
4.1	Number of EU eco-label licences 1995–2011	87
4.2	EU eco-label licences and leading product groups in 2010	89
4.3	Organisations registered with EMAS compared to ISO 14001 certifications	97
4.4	Ranking order EMAS uptake in EU member states	98
5.1	Voluntary agreements in EU member states in the mid-1990s	108
5.2	UK negotiated agreements	120
6.1	Total eco-tax revenues as a share of GDP and aggregate totals	134
7.1	Installations and allowances in the first trading phase (2005–2007)	170
8.1	Innovators, followers and laggards for different NEPI types	208
8.2	The use of different NEPIs and environmental regulations since the 1970s	213
9.1	A simple governance-cum-government typology	226

Abbreviations

ACEA	*Association des Constructeurs Européens d'Automobiles* (European Automobile Manufacturers Association)
ALARA	As Low as Reasonably Achievable
BAT	Best Available Technology
BP	British Petroleum
BPM	Best Practicable Means
BDI	Federal Association for German Industry (*Bundesverband der Deutschen Industrie*)
BImSchG	Federal Air Quality Control Act (*Bundes-Immissionsschutzgesetz*), Germany
BMGU	Federal Ministry for Health and Environment (*Bundesministerium für Gesundheit und Umwelt*), Austria
BMI	Federal Interior Ministry (*Bundesministerium für Inneres*), Germany
BMLFUW	Federal Ministry for Agriculture, Forestry, Environment and Water Management (*Bundesministerium für Landwirtschaft, Forstwirtschaft, Umwelt und Wasserwirtschaft*), Austria
BMU	Federal Ministry for Environment, Nature Protection and Reactor Safety (*Bundesministerium für Umwelt, Naturschutz und Reaktorsicherheit*), Germany
BMUJF	Federal Ministry for Environment, Youth and Family (*Bundesministerium für Umwelt, Jugend und Familie*), Austria
BRC	British Retail Consortium
BS	British Standard
BSI	British Standards Institute
CBI	Confederation of British Industry
CDA	Christian Democratic Appeal (*Christen-Democratisch Appèl*), the Netherlands
CDU	Christian Democratic Union (*Christlich Demokratische Union*), Germany
CEC	Commission of the European Communities

CEU	Commission of the European Union
CCL	Climate Change Levy
CCLA	Climate Change Levy Agreements
CSU	Christian Social Union (*Christlich Soziale Union*), Germany
CECED	European Council of Domestic Appliance Manufacturers (*Conseil Européen de la Construction d'Appareils Domestiques*)
CUEP	Central Unit on Environmental Pollution
CFCs	Chlorofluorocarbons
CO_2	Carbon dioxide
D66	Democrats 66 (*Democraten 66*), the Netherlands
DAU	German Accreditation and Admission Association (*Deutsche Akkreditierungs- und Zulassungsgesellschaft für Umweltgutachter GmbH*)
DDT	Dichlorodiphenyltrichloroethane
DEFRA	Department for Environment, Food and Rural Affairs, UK
DEHSt	German Emissions Trading Authority (*Deutsche Emissionshandelsstelle*)
DG	Directorate-General (of the European Commission)
DIN	German Industry Standard (*Deutsche Industrienorm*)
DoE	Department of the Environment, UK
DTI	Department for Trade and Industry, UK
EAP	Environmental Action Programme
EC	European Community or European Communities
ECOFIN	Economic and Finance Minister Council
ECJ	European Court of Justice
EEA	European Environment Agency
EEB	European Environmental Bureau
EFTA	European Free Trade Agreement
EMAS	Eco-management and Audit Scheme
EMS	Eco-management Scheme
EMU	Economic and Monetary Union
EP	European Parliament
EQOs	Environmental Quality Objectives
ETG	Emissions Trading Group, UK
ETS	Emissions Trading Scheme
EU	European Union
FDP	Free Democratic Party (or Liberal Party) (*Freiheitliche Partei Deutschlands*), Germany
FFSR	Farm Films Recovery Scheme

FoE	Friends of the Earth
FPÖ	Freedom Party of Austria (*Freiheitliche Partei Österreichs*)
GATT	General Agreement on Trade and Tariffs
GHGE	Greenhouse Gas Emissions
GMO	Genetically Modified Organism
HCFCs	Hydrochlorofluorocarbons
HLG	High Level Group of Independent Stakeholders on Administrative Burdens, EU
HOLSCEC	House of Lords Select Committee on the European Communities
ICC	International Chamber of Commerce
IGBCE	Mining, Chemical and Energy Industrial Union (*Industriegewerkschaft Bergbau, Chemie, Energie*), Germany
IPPC	Integrated Pollution Prevention and Control
ISO	International Organization for Standardization
JAMA	Japanese Automobile Industry Associations
JI	Joint Implementation
KAMA	Korean Automobile Industry Associations
LTA	Long-term Agreement
MBIs	Market-based Instruments
MEP	Member of the European Parliament
Mt	Million Ton
mWh	Megawatt Hour
NAP	National Allocation Plan
NEPIs	New Environmental Policy Instruments
NEPP	National Environmental Policy Plan, the Netherlands
NEPP+	National Environmental Policy Plan Plus, the Netherlands
NGO	Non-governmental Organisation
OECD	Organisation for Economic Co-operation and Development
ÖVP	Austrian People's Party (*Österreichische Volkspartei*)
OMC	Open Method of Coordination
PSPS	Pesticides Safety Precautions Scheme
PVSs	Public Voluntary Schemes
PvdA	Labour Party (*Partij van de Arbeid*), the Netherlands
QMV	Qualified Majority Voting

RAL	German Institute for Quality Assurance and Labelling (*Deutches Institut für Gütesicherung and Kennzeichnung e.V.*)
RCEP	Royal Commission on Environmental Pollution
RIVM	National Institute of Public Health and Environmental Protection (*Rijksinstituut voor Volksgezondheid en Milieuhygiene*), the Netherlands
SCCM	Foundation for the Co-ordination of Environmental Certification Systems *(Stichting Coordinatie Certificatie Milieuzorgsysteem)*, the Netherlands
SEA	Single European Act
SEM	Single European Market
SPD	Social Democratic Party (*Sozialdemokratische Partei Deutschlands*), Germany
SPÖ	Social Democratic Party of Austria (*Sozialdemokratische Partei Österreichs*)
SMEs	Small and Medium Enterprises
SRU	German Environment Expert Council (*Sachverständigenrat für Umweltfragen*)
SOx	Sulfur Oxides
TA	Technical Instructions (*Technische Anleitung*)
TC	Technical Committee
TFEU	Treaty on the Functioning of the European Union
UBA	Federal Environment Agency (*Umweltbundesamt*), Germany
UBA GmbH	Federal Environment Agency (*Umweltbundesamt GmbH*), Austria
UGA	German Eco-management and Audit Scheme Advisory Board (*Umweltgutachterausschuß*)
UK	United Kingdom
UN	United Nations
UNCED	United Nations Conference on Environment and Development
UNEP	United Nations Environmental Programme
UNFCCC	United Nations Framework Convention on Climate Change
US EPA	United States Environmental Protection Agency
USA	United States of America
VAs	Voluntary Agreements
VDA	Association of the German Automotive Industry (*Verband der Deutschen Automobilindustrie*)

VKI	Association for Consumer Information (*Verein für Konsumenteninformation*), Austria
VNO-NCW	Confederation of Netherlands Industry and Employers (*Verbond van Nederlandse Ondernemingen – Nederlands Christelijk Werkgeversverbond*)
VOC	Volatile Organic Compounds
VROM	Ministry for Housing, Physical Planning and the Environment (*Ministerie van Volkshuisvesting, Ruimtelijke Ordening en Milieubeheer*), the Netherlands
VVD	People's Party for Freedom and Democracy (*Volkspartij voor Vrijheid en Democratie*), the Netherlands
WBCSD	World Business Council for Sustainable Development
WIFO	Austrian Institute of Economic Research (*Österreichisches Institut für Wirtschaftsforschung*)
WTO	World Trade Organization
WWF	World Wide Fund for Nature

Preface

This book constitutes the culmination of our research efforts, offering an integrated theoretical approach bringing together the literature on (environmental) policy instruments and (environmental) governance as well as institutional theory and policy learning and transfer. It aims to fill a gap in the existing literature, by using new empirical research to bridge the new policy instrument literature with the new governance literature. In other words, this book assesses whether new environmental policy instruments constitute important touchstones for a critical assessment of widely made claims that traditional (tools of) government has been giving way to new (modes of) governance in Europe (and other highly developed regions) over the last decade.

This book provides a critical assessment of the use of 'new' environmental policy instruments in European (environmental) governance across five different European jurisdictions – Austria, Germany, the Netherlands and the United Kingdom (UK) as well as the European Union (EU) – over a period of four decades starting in the early 1970s. But it also focuses on wider theoretical debates in public policy, particularly policy learning and policy transfer. While much of the existing environmental policy instrument literature tends to examine only one level of governance, this book systematically assesses the member state level and the EU level, whilst also taking into account important (policy instrument) developments on the international level.

It is based on original research which was undertaken between 2000 and 2012. This approximately one decade long period of research should not be interpreted as a misunderstanding of Paul Sabatier's advice that public policy should be studied over a period of at least one decade. Rather it is the fortunate result of additional funding which we received to continue our original research on 'new' environmental policy instruments (NEPIs). The original project was funded (project number L216252013) by the Economic and Social Research Council (ESRC) under its Future Governance Programme with its highly supportive director, Professor Edward Page. Our understanding of European environmental governance in general and environmental policy instruments in particular has greatly benefited from our ability to undertake additional

xii

Preface xiii

work in Austria, Germany, the Netherlands and the UK, as well as in Brussels. Rudi Wurzel gratefully acknowledges funding from the Anglo-German Foundation (project number 1493) and the British Academy (reference number SG-46048) as well as University of Hull internal funding. Anthony Zito would like to thank Newcastle University for travel funding that proved instrumental in completing this manuscript. Finally, Andrew Jordan is grateful to the Leverhulme Trust (FOO 204 AR) for funding his Major Research Fellowship.

Over the years we have received a great deal of support and guidance from a wide range of individuals and organisations. The list of names would simply be too long to be stated in this preface. We are enormously grateful to all interviewees in Austria, Germany, the Netherlands and the UK as well as in Brussels – many of whom we interviewed several times over the years. Moreover, we would like to thank all of our academic colleagues who either commented on various draft publications and/or provided extremely useful information from which this book has benefitted. Finally and most especially we would like to thank our families for their patience over the last decade.

Rudi Wurzel, Anthony Zito and Andrew Jordan

PART I

Introduction

1. Environmental policy: from government to governance?

INTRODUCTION

Since the 1990s there has been a huge upsurge in scholarly interest in governance and the new modes of governance with which it is associated. The governance 'turn' has produced a wide range of books (for example, Héritier and Rhodes, 2011a; Kooiman, 1993a, 2003; Rosenau and Czempiel, 1992), journal articles (for example, Rhodes, 1996; Héritier and Lehmkuhl, 2008; Risse and Lehmkuhl, 2007) and special issues of leading journals (for example, Lascoumes and Le Galés, 2007; Kassim and Le Galés, 2010; Schuppert and Zürn, 2008), as well as handbooks (Benz et al., 2007) and anthologies (for example, Bellamy and Palumbo, 2010). Schuppert (2008: 14) estimates that the use of the term governance in scholarly publications rose by a factor of about 20 between 1990 and 2003 (see also Zürn, 2008: 553). For Palumbo (2010: xii) it 'is another of those pivotal words endowed with a virus-like ability to spread across research fields in a remarkably short time'. It is therefore legitimate to ask whether there is anything important to say about governance that has not already been said.

Our argument is that while governance is undoubtedly a term in good currency, the debate about its scope is often conducted at too high a level of abstraction. By descending the 'ladder of abstraction' (Sartori, 1970: 1040) to look at how governance plays out in relation to specific modes and instruments of governing, it is not only possible but important to say something new about governance. It is indeed the case that there is still no widespread agreement on its precise meaning. But there is sufficient agreement on one important thing – that governance is associated with governments' declining ability to steer and direct societal actors in a hierarchical top-down fashion while using 'command-and-control' regulation (Bellamy and Palumbo, 2010; Pierre and Peters, 2000: 83–91; Genschel and Zangel, 2007; Rhodes, 1996; Schuppert and Zürn, 2008). Governments' reduced steering capability chimes with other prominent governance themes such as the increasing importance of multi-level decision-making arenas (Bache and Flinders, 2006; Hooghe and Marks,

2003; Marks, Hooghe and Blank, 1996) and the formation of policy networks and networked governments for arriving at policy decisions (for example, Jordan and Schout, 2006; Schneider, 2004).

It is the ambiguity and vagueness of the term governance which made it an important 'bridge term' and that encouraged its wide use amongst scholars from different disciplines such as political science, sociology, economics and law (see Benz et al., 2007; Schuppert, 2008; van Kersbergen and van Waarden, 2004; Zürn, 2008). However, the lack of a widely accepted and clear definition of the exact meaning of governance has come at a price. Jachtenfuchs (2001: 258) has argued that the governance perspective 'offers a *problematique*', not a theory (but see Stoker, 1998). Palumbo (2010: xiii) suggests that 'governance theory since its inception roughly two decades ago ... is a conceptual device that helps rationalize and articulate the changes that have been undertaken by liberal democracies since the late 1980s' (however, see Stoker, 1998). However, governance can be said to encompass a series of interrelated social phenomena including: (1) the dispersal of policy-making powers amongst a wide range of public and private actors which often coordinate their actions in policy networks; (2) the increasing importance of multi-level governance decision-making structures due to the loss of powers by the state upwards (for example, to the supranational EU level and international organisations such as the World Trade Organization – WTO), downwards (for example, regions and municipalities) and sideways (for example, to corporations and non-governmental organisations – NGOs); and (3) the rise of new modes of governance that rely heavily on horizontal decision-making or 'self-steering' instead of hierarchical top-down command-and-control regulation (Pierre and Peters, 2000; Schuppert and Zürn, 2008) although in order to be effective they normally need the 'shadow of hierarchy' in the form of a credible threat of government intervention (Héritier and Rhodes, 2011). It is in relation to this third category – modes and instruments – that we believe new empirical analysis can and should profitably focus.

This book tries to explore the changing relationship between new (environmental) policy instruments and new modes of (environmental) governance. The concept of modes of governance is derived from early work by German scholars, particularly Scharpf (1994, 1997). This literature sought to understand the underlying dynamics of relations and decision-making powers among political actors in governing systems in highly developed states. The concept of mode allows us to differentiate various forms of social co-ordination, and to better distinguish between governing as an activity and the effects of that activity (Mayntz, 1993: 11–12). As will be explained in the following pages, some scholars have

Environmental policy: from government to governance? 5

sought to better understand how actors govern by studying the use of policy instruments, which are tools that governors use to steer society. Héritier and Rhodes (2011b: 163) have argued that '[n]ew modes of governance... come in various guises, aim at various objectives, are based in numerous different instruments and are linked in varying ways to governmental action'.

The more fuzzy concept of new governance modes is usually defined more widely than that of policy instruments which, as will be explained below and in Chapter 2, constitute more specific governing tools. Our analysis grounds the governance concept empirically by focusing primarily on the more concrete and narrower concept of policy instruments. While, as was explained above, 'governance' has been called a bridge term, the term 'new modes of governance' has been referred to as a 'frame concept' (Bartolini, 2011: 6). Helpfully, the governance literature typically demarcates three distinctive modes of governing society: hierarchical (associated with government), market and networks (for example, Bähr, 2010; Frances et al., 1991; Powell, 1991). This book has the wider aim of building an analytical bridge between studies of (new modes of environmental) governance and (new environmental) policy instruments. Chapter 2, which advances a threefold classification of policy instruments, explains in more detail how different types of policy instruments relate to different modes of governance.

Critical statements about the need to promote 'better government' through new modes of governance have gravitated towards calls for practical tools. For example, the World Bank started to demand 'good governance' from the early 1990s onwards. One decade later, the European Commission promoted new modes of governance as an alternative (for example, the so-called open method of coordination (OMC) to the traditional Community method (for instance, legally binding regulations proposed by the Commission and adopted by the Council of Ministers and the European Parliament (EP)) in its White Paper entitled *European Governance* (CEC, 2001b) which also calls for new policy instruments and better regulation.

As has already been suggested, the academic debate about governance tends to be 'over-theorised' and 'under-empiricized' (Jordan et al., 2013). In contrast, much of the policy instrument literature tends toward under-theorisation (Jordan et al., 2012a). This book tries to make a significant contribution by linking these literatures and analytical perspectives. To that end, it aims to contribute towards governance theory-building efforts by developing a robust and empirically relevant analytical framework (see, in particular, Chapter 2) which provides a sound basis for the assessment of the alleged transition from government towards governance in environmental policy. More specifically it surveys the use of new environmental policy instruments across five different European jurisdictions, namely Austria, Germany, the Netherlands and the United Kingdom (UK) as well as the European Union (EU), over a relatively long period of time – roughly four decades starting in the early 1970s. We believe that this wide geographical scope and long timeframe is necessary to understand the transition to governance. In the past, studies of governance have tended to be based on small 'n' studies of specific jurisdictions covering a relatively short period of time (Salamon, 2002); by contrast, the policy studies literature emphasises the importance of studying change and learning over a decade or more (for example, Sabatier, 1999).

Environmental policy is a particularly suitable policy sector for a critical analysis of the alleged rise of new policy instruments for the following two main reasons. First, since their early beginnings in the late 1960s, modern-day (Western) European environmental policies have been widely perceived as inherently *regulatory* in nature (Weale, 1992b: 154–82). This strong regulatory legacy would make any rapid and widespread uptake of new environmental policy instruments across five different European jurisdictions all the more significant (see also Jordan, Wurzel and Zito, 2005, 2007). Second, environmental policy constitutes a classic cross-cutting policy sector whose requirements need to be taken into account also in a wide range of other (non-environmental) policies including agriculture, economic, energy and transport policies (for example, Jordan and Lenschow, 2008). New environmental policy instruments may therefore have an impact also on non-environmental policy sectors. For example, emissions trading schemes for greenhouse gas emissions (GHGE), which have been set up with the aim of reducing the threat of climate change, have a significant impact on not only on national energy policies but also on economic and financial policies too (for example, Wurzel, 2008a).

This book examines the adoption and use of three different types of environmental policy instruments (suasive, market-based and regulatory instruments) in five different jurisdictions since the early 1970s. For reasons explained in more detail below (and in Chapter 2), it argues that the transmogrification in environmental policy instruments and policy instrument mixes provides valuable empirical touchstones of the alleged shift from traditional *government*, which consisted primarily of hierarchical top-down 'command-and-control' regulations, towards *governance* that relies more strongly on instruments which encourage societal self-organisation and/or market solutions. We reflect on what any shift from one to the other says about governing in the late 20th and early 21st centuries. We empirically assess also the degree to which this shift reflects a wider pattern of convergence or divergence in the approaches to governing in Europe.

The next section traces the origins of the debate about governance. Chapter 1 then links the (new) governance debate to the renewed interest in policy instruments. In doing so, our empirical study of policy instruments seeks to inform and is informed by the more theoretical study of governance. Chapter 2 explains the policy instrument typology which we use and then sets out the key theoretical arguments that will help us track both the degree of changes in modes of governance and government over time.

GOVERNING: FROM GOVERNMENT TO GOVERNANCE?

The Governance Turn

The term governance has a long tradition in the study of politics and public administration (Bellamy and Palumbo, 2010; Benz et al., 2007; Héritier and Rhodes, 2011a; Kooiman, 2003; Schuppert and Zürn, 2008). According to Jessop and Sum (2006: 249), its use in the English language dates back to the 14th century (see also Mayntz, 2008: 45). In the past, political scientists have often treated the terms governance and government as synonyms (Mayntz, 2008: 45; Stoker, 1998: 17; Zürn, 2008). Palumbo (2010: xiii–xiv) has pointed out that '[e]tymologically, both terms [for instance, governance and government] derive from the Latin root *gubernare* (which, in turn, derives from the Greek word *kubernãn)*'. Finer's (1970) seminal *Comparative Government* constitutes one important example for the interchangeable use of the terms government and governance.

Governance: different meanings

However, as the use of the term governance grew it quickly took on many new meanings (Mayntz, 2008: 45). However, since at least the 1990s there has been a growing tendency for scholars to accept that it signifies a move away from hierarchical (tools of) *government* towards more horizontal (new modes of) *governance.* Palumbo (2010: xiv) therefore pointed out that 'political analysts have all come to perceive governance as a departure from traditional, state-centred styles of governing'.

The discussion of blurred boundaries and complex interactions between government and governance certainly attracts scholars from many disciplines. For example, some legal scholars have accepted the possibility that new modes of governance and traditional tools of government may cohabit although this does not rule out conflicts between certain types of new modes of governance and traditional legal approaches. For example, de Búrca and Scott (2006), Trubek et al. (2006) and Trubek and Trubek (2007) have articulated the notion of 'hybridity' where the new modes of governance and traditional tools of government operate in conjunction.

To confuse matters still further, many governance scholars have moved beyond positive analysis to adopt (implicitly or otherwise) more normative interpretations (for a review, see Jordan, 2008) by arguing that state intervention in the form of hierarchical command-and-control regulations is inefficient and *should* be supplanted (or at least supplemented) by new policy instruments and new modes of governance which are more effective and rely more heavily on horizontal self-steering. The multiplicity of different definitions led Kooiman (2003: 5) to conclude that the study of governance is still in a 'period of creative disorder'.

Analysing governance empirically

Rather than argue for one conception over the other, we contend that it is best to treat these competing and evolving typologies as part of a long-term governance research agenda which requires more intensive empirical research (see also Eberlein and Kerwer, 2004: 122; Héritier and Rhodes, 2011a; Hood, 2007; Jänicke and Jörgens, 2004: 301; Kooiman, 2003: 4–5; Lascoumes and Le Galés, 2007; Marinetto, 2003: 605–6; Schuppert, 2008; Zürn, 2008).

Clearly, there is an urgent need for better cross-comparative empirical data to allow for an assessment of the putative shift from (traditional tools of) *government* towards (new modes of) *governance* from a *governing* perspective which focuses on the overall pattern of change and possible interactions between 'new' and 'old' policy instruments. This book aims to make such a contribution by providing both new empirical findings and novel analytical insights. We use our new empirical findings to 'test' the proposition which has become prevalent in comparative public policy, namely that there is a convergence in policies and therefore also in governance over time (DiMaggio and Powell, 1983; Knill, 2005).

Much of the governance literature has emphasised a strong dichotomy between *government* and *governance*. Although this dichotomy should not be over-stated, it remains a standing hypothesis, or even the 'orthodoxy', in much of the recent literature (Marinetto, 2003: 597). If the 'strong state' characterised the extreme form of government in the era of 'big government' (Pierre and Peters, 2000: 25; Kitschelt and Streeck,

2003), then the equally extreme form of governance is the 'autopoetic self-referential system' which can no longer be influenced, let alone steered, by top-down government intervention (Luhmann, 1984). This is a juxtaposition that many mainstream political scientists reject, pointing out that governance and government are inextricably bound up in what is often referred to as *governing* processes (Van Tatenhove et al., 2006; Holman, 2006).

In this book, we use *governing* as the generic term which subsumes both traditional (tools of) *government* and new (modes of) *governance*. We agree with Kooiman's (1993b: 2) definition of governing as 'all those activities of social, political and administrative actors that can be seen as purposeful efforts to guide, steer, control or manage'. This definition enables us to subsume both 'old' tools of government and 'new' forms of governance under one analytical umbrella term. Although modes and tools both form part of governing, they represent different levels of analysis. Our use of the term governing therefore differs significantly from Tömmel and Verdun's (2009a). Tömmel (2009: 12) delineates governing as 'strategic actions of the state or public authorities in order to intervene in the economic and social sphere' while she defines governance as 'providing common goods or establishing public order as a result of interactions between various categories of actors and the coordination of their behaviour'. While Tömmel equates governing with governmental activities, in this book we use the term *governing* to subsume both hierarchical top-down *government* and horizontal modes of new *governance*. The use of governing as the generic term for government and governance allows us to differentiate between analytically different policy instrument types which may co-exist in one particular policy field (such as environmental policy).

How new is governance?
There is a group of scholars who argue that governance represents a substantial break from the past (for example, Stoker, 1998: 26). Rhodes, a key proponent within this group, argues that governance is a '*new* process of governing; or a changed condition of ordered rule; or the *new* method by which society is governed' (Rhodes, 1996: 652–3). The narrative often evoked here is that in highly industrialised liberal democracies' hierarchical, top-down structures of *government* have increasingly given way to new modes of *governance* which encourage self-organisation by societal actors. In other words, traditional tools of government are said to have been *supplanted* by new modes of governance.

10 *Environmental governance in Europe*

Other scholars have, however, argued that new modes of governance still require some form of steering from public actors (for example, in the form of regulation) or necessitate co-governing arrangements in which public and private actors cooperate (Bähr, 2010; Kooiman, 2003; Hey, Jacob and Volkery, 2008; Jänicke and Jörgens, 2004; Jordan, Wurzel and Zito, 2005, 2007). Indeed many of the new policy instruments and new modes of governance flourish in the shadow of hierarchy (Héritier et al., 1996; Héritier and Rhodes, 2011a; Börzel, 2010). Importantly, Zürn (2008) argues that the 'shadow of hierarchy' (Scharpf, 1994), which promotes self-regulatory measures by societal actors on the national level, finds its equivalent in the 'shadow of anarchy' that encourages the adoption of cooperative measures by states (and societal actors) on the international level in the absence of a world government. The key thing therefore is to focus on the interactions between 'new' and 'old' policy instruments (Jordan et al., 2005), as this will – we hypothesise – illuminate the changing relationship between government and governance. The next section explains how we intend to assess this empirically.

Governing by Multiple Instruments?

Eberlein and Kerwer (2004: 136) distinguish the following four forms of interactions between traditional tools of government and new instruments of governance: (1) government and governance instruments complement each other without one of them being supplanted by the other (*co-existence*); (2) government and governance tools merge with each other (*fusion*); (3) government and governance instruments compete with each other (*competition*); and, (4) one form (for instance, government or governance) supplants the other and thus replaces it (*replacement*).

Streeck and Thelen (2005b) have put forward a slightly different but equally well known typology covering: (1) *displacement* (for instance, slowly rising salience of subordinate change relative to dominant institutions); (2) *layering* (for instance, new elements attached to existing institutions gradually change their status and structure); (3) *drift* (for instance, neglect of institutional maintenance in spite of external changes resulting in slippage in institutional practice on the ground); (4) *conversion* (for instance, the redeployment of old institutions to new purposes); and, (5) *exhaustion* (the gradual breakdown of institutions over time). Streeck and Thelen's typology gives a greater sense of how the governing process develops and how, over time, the interaction between particular government and governance tools may transform into something else. For example, the co-existence of government and governance tools may have an underlying dynamic where the governance tool gains in salience and

Environmental policy: from government to governance? 11

gradually erodes the traditional tool of government. The next subsection introduces some of the main concepts in the policy instruments literature.

PINNING DOWN GOVERNANCE: POLICY INSTRUMENTS AS AN ANALYTICAL FOCUS

We have demonstrated that there is a potentially large overlap between the new (modes of) governance literature and the new policy instrument literature. This is unsurprising as the analytical focus on policy instruments is examining the same kind of 'governing' dynamics operating at the sub-systemic, sectoral scale.

Table 1.1 Governance and policy instrument typologies compared

Governing type	Main policy instrument type	Main type of interaction between 'governing' actors and 'governed'	Instrument type and core content
Hierarchy	Regulation	Coercion: 'Governance by government'	Sticks: top down government intervention
Market	Market-based/ economic instruments	Competition/fiscal incentives: 'Governance with government'	Carrots: fiscal incentives
Network	Suasive instruments	Societal self-regulation: 'governance without government'	Sermons: information and appeals

Source: Own compilation which draws, amongst others, on Bemelmans-Vldec et al. (1997) and Zürn (2008).

The recent upsurge in the study of policy instruments (for example, Lascoumes and Le Galès, 2007; Kassim and Le Galès, 2010) led Christopher Hood, whose pioneering book *The Tools of Government* was published in 1983, to argue that 'the analysis of policy instruments is ... as central an issue in public management and public policy today as it was two decades ago' (Hood, 2007: 142–3). Hood also pointed out that

12   *Environmental governance in Europe*

there has been a long tradition in the analysis of policy instruments which can be traced to the Enlightenment era (Hood, 2007: 128; see also Kassim and Le Galès, 2010). In continental Europe 18th century cameralism and German *Polizeywissenschaft* ('police science') had already focused on the effectiveness of different policy instruments and their interplay (for example, Hood, 2007: 1; Maier, 1980; Tribe, 1984).

However, policy instrument studies have ploughed an independent furrow (for example, Jordan et al., 2013), often excluding an explicit research focus on the effects that different policy instruments have on the relationship between the governed and the governing. They often treat the selection of policy instruments merely as technical choices rather than political decisions although there are notable exceptions (for example, Hood, 2007: 128; Howlett, 1991; Howlett, 2011; Lascoumes and Le Galès, 2007; Kassim and Le Galès, 2010).

This book uses a modified institutional analysis to bridge the gap between the policy instrument literature, which is often focused on technical questions behind instruments, and the wider literature on new modes of governance. As Chapter 3 explains in more detail, the historical context and evolution of particular policies is fundamental for an understanding of policy instrument selection and usage. It provides for a better understanding of the role of governance.

In the most general sense policy instruments constitute the 'myriad techniques at the disposal of governments to implement their policy objectives' (Howlett, 1991: 2). In other words, policy instruments are the tools that policy actors use to attain their policy goals (de Bruijn and Hufen, 1998: 12–13; Howlett, 2011). Kooiman (2003: 29–30, 44–5) argues that policy instruments are the crucial bridge between the policy frame or 'image' that informs how policy makers act and their actual governing action. Policy instruments usually embody particular policy philosophies, goals and outlooks while providing concrete manifestations of policy actions (Hall, 1993). As will be explained in more detail in Chapter 2, the analytical framework which we will use for our book draws heavily on Peter Hall's (1993) threefold framework of policy change when trying to assess whether traditional tools of government have been supplanted (or merely supplemented) by new policy instruments and/or new modes of governance. In his seminal work, Hall (1993) differentiates between the recalibration of existing policy instruments (first level change), the adoption of new policy instruments (second level change), and a more fundamental paradigm or goal change (third level change).

For Lascoumes and Le Galès (2007: 11), the study of policy instruments can be seen as a particularly promising approach for uncovering deeper

Environmental policy: from government to governance? 13

underlying societal and governmental changes because '[p]ublic policy instrumentation reveals a (fairly explicit) theorisation of the relationship between the governing and the governed. In this sense, it can be argued that every public policy instrument constitutes a condensed and finalized form of knowledge about social control and ways of exercising it'.

Given that policy instruments have such a central position in encapsulating the connection between governing objectives and the actual activity of governing (including its impact on the governed), our empirical differentiation between different policy instrument types should capture different governing arrangements and modes that are reflected in the use of particular policy instruments. The categorisation of policy instruments into particular types, though essential, nonetheless constitutes an analytical challenge because '[t]he variety of instruments used in governance is almost unlimited and will vary from 'soft' ones such as information and advice to 'hard' ones such as taxes and regulations' (Kooiman, 2003: 45). Indeed the policy instrument literature has become rather obsessed with the matter of definition. Table 1.2 lists influential policy instrument typologies by important public policy scholars. As can be seen from Table 1.2, the typologies differ significantly in terms of the main types of modes of governance and/or tools of government as well as the jurisdictional focus that the individual authors are seeking to understand. We acknowledge these differences in definitional approach and use it to inform our own typology in Chapter 2.

In Table 1.2 (which does not provide an exhaustive list of different tools of government) it is worth highlighting in particular Hood's (1983) classic fourfold typology of policy instruments which focuses on the range of resources available to those who govern. Hood's typology is not intended to identify differing degrees of imposition which policy instruments may exert. However, Hood identifies specific instruments which governments may use to instigate societal changes.

Howlett (1991) helpfully reviews three different theories of instrument choice, represented by a British scholar (Hood), and various American and Canadian scholars. In contrast to Hood, Howlett's typology offers a continuum based on the 'degrees of legitimate coercion', with self-regulation being the minimum scale and public ownership/seizure reflecting the maximum value. However, the larger point of Howlett's analysis is to argue that Doern and Wilson (1974) as well as the British and American typologies, purport to be general theories of instrument selection but instead have been greatly shaped by the specific political context in which they were used. Howlett calls for (1) greater efforts to understand the link between instrument selection and policy styles and (2) comparative research that brings more cases into the analysis.

14   Environmental governance in Europe

Table 1.2   Different policy instrument typologies

Author(s)	Main types of modes of governance and/or tools of government	Generic, national, EU or international focus
Hood (1983, 2007)	1. Nodality 2. Treasure 3. Authority 4. Organisation	Generic/national
Howlett (1991) (Canadian typology)	1. Private behaviour (self-regulation) 2. Exhortation 3. Expenditure 4. Regulation 5. Public Ownership	Generic
Howlett (2011)	1. Organisational instruments 2. Authoritative implementation tools 3. Financial implementation tools 4. Information-based tools (NB: Tools 1–4 exist as both substantive and procedural tools)	Generic
Kassim and Le Galès (2010)	Following Lascoumes and Le Galès (2007), see below	EU
Lascoumes and Le Galès (2007)	Legislative and regulatory 1. Economic and fiscal 2. Agreement based and incentive-based 3. Information-based and communication based 4. *De facto* and *de jure* standards	Generic/national
Tömmel (2009) in Tömmel and Verdun (2009a)	1. Hierarchical 2. Competition 3. Cooperation 4. Negotiation	EU

As Chapter 3 demonstrates, the policy instrument literature tends to divide its analytical focus between core internal characteristics of the instruments and the wider political context that shapes their usage. In his 2011 work, Howlett tries to combine these two approaches by emphasising both context and core instrument characteristics. Lascoumes and Le Galès (2007, which bears a heavy influence on Kassim and Le Galès,

Environmental policy: from government to governance? 15

2010) also seek a similar synthesis of external drivers, instrument characteristics and instrument context.

The chapters in Tömmel and Verdun's edited volume emphasise the importance of process in the act of governance, focusing particularly on how actor behaviour is co-ordinated. There is no expectation that mapping policy instruments can be done on a continuum; rather co-existence and hybrid mixes feature strongly (Tömmel, 2009: 12–13).

Our short literature review of different policy instrument typologies suggests that any analytically useful policy instrument typology has to consider whether to emphasise particular core elements (for example, substantive output versus process) and whether such a characterisation fits on a continuum (for example, from hard to soft policy instruments) or requires distinctly separate instrument categories. Clearly, most of the policy instrument research emphasises the need for contextualisation in order to understand the selection, use and implementation of policy instruments.

Hence this book takes a more wide-ranging approach of examining how governing manifests itself through 'new' and 'old' policy instruments. Our approach takes into account the existence of policy instrument mixes and allows for the possibility of hybrid relations between different types of instruments. Given the spectrum of possibilities, we develop an analytical framework which examines both particular policy instrument mixes within different political jurisdictions and the governing types which they signify. Using governing as our generic concept allows us to identify and assess hierarchical top-down and societal bottom-up governing as well as the degree and nature of their co-existence in a policy sector such as environmental policy.

The review of some of the key policy instrument typologies alerts us to the need to contextualise any given policy instrument. While allowing for the possibility of co-existence in different modes of governing (for instance, the simultaneous use of traditional tools of government and new policy instruments as well as new modes of governance), we opt in Chapter 2 for a threefold policy instrument typology that differentiates between suasive, market-based and hierarchical policy instruments.

Following the strong emphasis given to contextualisation and the role of institutions in the policy instrument literature, this book uses an institutionalist approach. First, it seeks to examine the wider political institutional factors which shape policy instrument choice, use and implementation. Major research questions which we address include: How much does the EU and international relations level matter for policy instrument choices? How much do the national institutional structures and policy styles within a given European jurisdiction matter?

Secondly, we acknowledge the importance of understanding the nature of a particular type of policy instrument for a specific policy problem and within a certain institutional context, where meanings may differ for the same instrument types. In order to assess how particular types of instruments morph within a particular jurisdiction and/or a particular policy sector/sub-sector, it is helpful to use a generic category of policy instrument types which can serve as a baseline for cross-country and cross-sectoral comparisons. Furthermore, such analytical distinctions allow us to see how policy instrument mixes relate to each other.

We first review existing policy instrument categorisations before we present our threefold instrument categorisation and put forward the analytical framework we use to examine the evolution of NEPIs as well as broader modes of governance in five different European jurisdictions.

Third, we identify the drivers of and barriers to policy instrument change. We examine whether the nature of policy instrument change, if it has taken place at all, is a revolutionary paradigmatic type of change or an incremental shift in a particular policy instrument or policy instrument type for context-specific purposes. A related dimension involves the potential variation in approach to the policy goals versus the specific instruments. Hood (2007) argues that policy actors sometimes find it easier to agree on the policy tools than the policy goals. Similarly, the choice of certain policy instruments may foster the achievement of certain policy goals while constraining others.

Moving beyond conceptualising the nature and process of instrument change, a fourth ambition of this book is to understand the evolution of environmental governance by trying to explain how the dominant environmental policy instrument mixes have changed over a period of four decades. It is only then that the underlying dynamic of governing becomes clearer. Do 'new' environmental policy instruments actually lead to a significant change of the traditional policy context or are they more like a superficial gloss or a useful adjunct to the dominant modes of governance in a given context? In addition to the jurisdiction specific contextual analysis over time, our analysis of European environmental governance also acknowledges the importance of the EU multi-level decision-making arena for the selection and use of environmental policy instruments. Explaining both the temporal and multi-level dimensions of governing with 'new' and 'old' environmental policy instruments are key theoretical and empirical challenges to which our book endeavours to make a significant contribution.

THE GOVERNANCE OF ENVIRONMENTAL PROBLEMS

As mentioned above, environmental policy constitutes a particularly crucial case for an assessment of the putative shift from government towards governance because it has been widely seen as an inherently regulatory policy sector with cross-cutting characteristics (Weale, 1992a). The traditional approach to pollution control in (Western) Europe initially relied heavily on the adoption of command-and-control regulations in which national governments and/or the EU stipulated in law detailed environmental standards with which the governed had to comply with within a certain deadline. Cost-effectiveness considerations and/or the concerns of policy actors who later had to implement these policy instruments on the ground often played only a secondary role during the adoption process of traditional command-and-control regulations (for example, Gunningham, Grabosky and Sinclair, 1998; Stavins and White-head, 1992: 8–9; Weale, 1992a).

Traditional textbook distinction is made between top-down pollution control regulation and NEPIs, which are said to pay greater attention to cost-effectiveness considerations and allow stakeholders more involvement in the formulation of environmental policy goals as well as more flexibility in achieving them. This book will take these ideal types and relate them to the various ways in which instruments are *actually* being adopted and used in practice (see also Jordan et al., 2011). This will allow us to also interrogate the claim that, over time, regulatory instruments have become 'smarter' and have taken on the form of 'light touch' regulation at least when compared with much of the command-and-control environmental regulation of the 1970s (Gunningham, Grabosky and Sinclair, 1998). We show that many typologies are a poor guide to what is happening in practice. Scholars of governance must therefore be alert to the links between different types of instrument: for instance, the possibility that 'old' and 'new' environmental policy instruments coexist or form hybrids through the fusion of (elements of) traditional regulation and (elements of) new modes of environment governance (see also, for example, de Búrca and Scott, 2006; Gunningham, Grabosky and Sinclair, 1998; Schuppert, 2008: 24; Hey, Jacob and Volkery, 2008).

PLAN OF THIS BOOK

This book assesses the spatial, temporal and sectoral patterns of environmental policy instrument change in five different jurisdictions while drawing on empirical examples from a range of sub-sectors. It analyses

whether significant policy instrument change has taken place over an extended period of about four decades. Such a long time period is widely seen
as sufficient for detecting policy (instrument) changes (for example, Sabatier, 1999: 3). Our book identifies the spatial patterns of NEPIs uptake by assessing whether policy instrument convergence or continued divergence has taken place across different jurisdictions (and sub-sectors). This book investigates whether there has been a significant move from traditional tools of government towards new policy instruments (equating to a shift from government towards governance) or whether some kind of hybrid form of governing has emerged. Finally, our book assesses whether the uptake of NEPIs has occurred primarily in one particular sub-sector (for example, energy/climate change policy) or whether it is more widespread. Lowi (1972) makes the important argument that the characteristics of the policy sectors themselves can shape the nature of politics and the decisional processes.

To fully understand policy instrument innovation and convergence/divergence, we must identify its main drivers and barriers (Knill, 2005: 765–9). Our institutional approach examines the possibilities for policy transfer and learning, which might explain policy (instrument) convergence. In order to establish causalities, policy analysts must disentangle internal (for instance, the intra-territorial) from the external (for instance, extra-territorial) variables which may drive policy instrument convergence and or lead to continued policy instrument divergence. This book therefore focuses on environmental policy instrument pioneers that may shape changes in environmental policy instrument usage. We also assess whether policy instrument learning and/or transfer has occurred between the different jurisdictions.

Chapter 2 explains the overall theoretical framework while Chapter 3 identifies the main institutional context that has shaped new environmental policy instruments in the five different jurisdictions (for instance, Austria, Germany, the Netherlands, the UK and the EU). The chapters in Part III are deliberately ordered in such a way that the analysis starts with those instruments which should theoretically best support the claim that there has been a wide-ranging shift towards a new governance paradigm. Chapters 4 and 5 focus on informational means (eco-labels and environmental management schemes) and voluntary agreements respectively thus on relatively 'soft' environmental policy instruments which in theory require no or only relatively little direct government intervention. Chapters 6 and 7 analyse the use of two important market-based instruments, namely eco-taxes and emissions trading schemes. Eco-taxes have been

Environmental policy: from government to governance?

widely used in some European jurisdictions for a long period of time while emissions trading is an innovative policy instrument which is new to Europe.

In these four chapters the analysis starts with the jurisdiction that adopted a pioneering role and then examines the followers. In doing so, we explore whether there are institutional or policy learning factors that lie behind the policy instrument adoption pattern. We also assess whether policy instrument learning and transfer have occurred between the pioneering jurisdictions and those that followed.

In Part IV, Chapter 8 focuses on the temporal pattern of change (for instance, has there been a significant change in the direction of governance?), the spatial patterns of uptake and use (for instance, is there significant, long term convergence?) and any significant sectoral biases (for instance, does governance via new instruments emerge more strongly in some sectors (for example, transport, agriculture, etc.) than others?). It also assesses the role of regulation in its evolutionary context, allowing direct comparisons to be made with the growing use of NEPIs and efforts to make 'command-and-control' regulation smarter (Gunningham, Grabosky and Sinclair, 1998). In short, it assesses the empirical evidence for and against the well-known claim that the traditional tools of government have been usurped by new policy instruments. The chapter finally assesses the role of policy learning and policy transfer in explaining the usage patterns.

Finally, Chapter 9 reviews the more general conclusions which our findings have for the government versus governance debate that has attracted much attention amongst political scientists as well as scholars from other disciplines. What do the selection and characteristics of the policy instruments in question suggest about the nature of governing? It also assesses the wider implications for studies of governance and for environmental policy studies.

PART II

Context

2. Governing by policy instruments: theories and analytical concepts

INTRODUCTION

This book investigates the extent to which environmental policy has undergone a transformation from (traditional tools of) *government* towards (new instruments of) *governance*. Although much of the general governance literature claims that there has been a decisive shift from traditional government (namely, command-and-control regulations) towards new modes of governance (for example, Rhodes, 1996), many of the more empirically minded NEPIs studies have argued that traditional regulation has not disappeared but simply become 'smarter' (for example, Gunningham, Grabosky and Sinclair, 1998). However, very few NEPIs studies have tried to systematically assess the wider political and governing implications of this alleged shift (for exceptions, see Bähr, 2010; Holzinger, Knill and Lenschow, 2009; Jänicke and Jörgens, 2004; Jordan, Wurzel and Zito, 2003a, 2005, 2007, 2012b).

The rest of our argument unfolds as follows. Chapter 2 starts with an explanation of the typology of environmental policy instruments used in this book. We then turn to broader public policy approaches to understand the underlying forces behind the selection and use of policy instruments at the EU and member state level. The next section explores the core elements and arguments of the mainly historical institutionalist approach which provides the central theoretical focus for this book. The case is then made for widening the notion of policy change found in institutionalist approaches with more exogenous forms of learning, including notions of policy transfer. Both the policy learning and policy transfer related concepts seek to enrich the book's cross-temporal, cross-territorial and multi-level approach to policy (instrument) change.

COMPETING TYPOLOGIES

Following on from Hood (2007: 133–7), Linder and Peters (1998) and others, we differentiate environmental policy instrument typologies into two overarching approaches. The first is interested in the nature of the policy instruments while the second is more interested in the political dynamics which shape specific policy instrument mixes.

Linder and Peters (1998) articulate four different schools of thinking about policy instruments: (1) 'instrumentalists' who highlight and champion a particular instrument and its characteristics; (2) 'proceduralists' who tend to focus on how a concrete problem leads to the development of a tool; (3) 'contingentists' who study the goodness of fit between the instrument and problem; and (4) the 'constitutivists' who emphasise the importance of the context in which a tool is adopted as well as how the tool is adapted and interpreted (Linder and Peters, 1998: 40–1). Hood (2007) rightly differentiates a separate fifth category of those approaches mainly seeking to develop generic categorisations of instruments which assess the trends in the environmental policy instrument literature. There is also arguably a sixth approach that is more focused on external political dynamics, particularly 'drivers' of innovation.

Keohane, Revesz and Stavins' (1998) rationalist equilibrium model presents a 'drivers' outlook to understanding policy instruments irrespective of specific policy problems. Their study focuses on how lawmakers balance their own priorities and constituency benefits with the demands for particular instruments by various interest groups. Knill and Lenschow's (2000) edited volume contextualises the drive towards NEPIs within wider efforts by policy makers to make EU environmental policy more effective and efficient within the context of globalisation. Mol, Lauber and Liefferink (2000) are more 'constitutivist'; they assess how both deregulation and ecological modernisation pressures are channelled through domestic institutions in three EU member states (Austria, Denmark and the Netherlands) and three policy sub-sectors (industrial energy efficiency, packaging waste and labelling of organic food products) for one specific type of policy instrument which they label 'joint environmental policy-making'. Heinelt and Töller (2001) offer a somewhat similar comparison while focusing on the implementation of two EU informational instruments (namely, environmental impact assessment and the EU eco-management and audit scheme (EMAS)). Their explanation for the national differences in implementation centres mainly on the nature of the diverse policy content and style which can be found in different national administrative and legal structures, the economic structure (for example, the size of firms) and interest group representation.

Economists, who contributed much of the early literature on, in particular, market-based environmental policy instruments (see, for example, Baumol and Oates, 1988; Common, 1988; Endres, 2000; Wicke, 1989), focused primarily on the cost-effectiveness of different

Governing by policy instruments: theories and analytical concepts   25

instruments (see also Howlett and Ramesh, 1993: 7; Jordan et al., 2011). Their work generally fitted the category of 'instrumentalists' who postulate that they have a clear idea about how a particular policy instrument works and what likely effect it will have (Linder and Peters, 1998: 37).

Environmental economists usually downplayed the role of contextual factors (such as institutional constraints) when advocating market-based policy instruments as the most cost-effective instruments. They often also failed to realise that the use of environmental policy instruments in practice often differs considerably from textbook economics (for example, Jordan et al., 2011). Of course some of this work, including a number of OECD studies (for example, 1994, 1999b), have put forward a more nuanced assessment that takes into account institutional context variables. Moreover, not all instrumentalist approaches adopt an economists' approach. Andersen (1994), who offers a meticulous comparative four country public policy study of the use of eco-taxes, finds evidence that instrument choice can have a significant independent impact on environmental outcomes.

Due to space constraints we review only some of the most important competing policy instrument typologies which are of direct relevance for our overall analytical framework and/or empirical research (see Table 2.1). Given our interest in governance, we pay particular attention to the importance of contexts and institutions for determining the adoption and use of instruments. Our earlier work took a somewhat different stand, focusing more on the main drivers for and barriers to the use of NEPIs as well as categorising the instruments (for example, Jordan, Wurzel and Zito, 2003b, 2003a). Other scholars have used our categorisation of policy instruments to advance their own arguments. Taking a more constitutive approach, Bailey (2003) gives a positive assessment of the role that NEPIs have had in shaping the implementation of EU environmental policy. He highlights the importance of political and economic capacities for the use of NEPIs.

One of the earliest typologies was Majone's exposition of environmental policy instruments which provided an early 'constitutive' understanding of policy instruments. Majone grounded his instrument typology in an institutional framework and emphasised that bargaining and politics defines the meaning that these instruments take (Majone, 1976: 610–2). Majone's fivefold environmental policy instrument classification bears some resemblance to the more generic policy tool typology which Hood (1983) later put forward in his influential *Tools of Government*. The focus on institutional organisation as an environmental policy instrument can also be found in other policy instrument typologies (for example, Howlett, 1991; Kern, Jörgens and Jänicke, 2000).

26　　　*Environmental governance in Europe*

Table 2.1　Different environmental policy instrument typologies

Authors	Main types of instruments identified	Main focus (i.e. generic, national and/or EU); instrument school of thought
Bähr (2010)	Command-and-control Economic Suasive	EU; constitutive
Bemelmans-Videc, Rist and Vedung (1997)	Regulation Economic Informational	Generic/national; constitutive
De Bruijn and Hufen (1998)	Regulation Financial Information transfer	Generic/national; notes several schools, mainly categorising
Golub (1998)	Taxes and subsidies Voluntary agreements Eco-audits Tradable permits Traditional regulation	EU and national level; categorising
Gunningham, Grabosky and Sinclair (1998)	Command-and-control regulation Self-regulation Voluntarism Education and information instruments Economic instruments Free market environmentalism	Generic/national; instrumentalist
Halpern (2010)	Legislative and regulatory Economic and fiscal Agreement-based and incentive-based Information- and communication-based *De facto* and *de jure*/best practice	EU; constitutive
Holzinger, Knill and Schäfer (2003, 2006)	Interventionist Economic Context-specific	EU; constitutive/ categorising
Holzinger, Knill and Lenschow (2009)	Hierarchical Competition Cooperative Negotiation	EU; constitutive/ categorising

Authors	Main types of instruments identified	Main focus (i.e. generic, national and/or EU); instrument school of thought
Jordan, Wurzel and Zito (2005, 2007)	Market-based Eco-labels Environmental management systems Voluntary agreements Regulation	EU and national level; constitutive
Majone (1976)	Regulation, direct public action, and subsidies Effluent charges Contract and redefinition of property rights Organisation	Generic; constitutive

Golub (1998) and de Bruijn and Hufen (1998: 17–8) offer examples of the categorising approach suggested by Hood. De Bruijn and Hufen's threefold typology differs from both Majone and Golub in placing policy instruments along a continuum of the degree of coercion which these instruments exert. According to de Bruijn and Hufen (1998: 18), regulations generally have a coercive and reactive character because they are often adopted and/or implemented only after undesirable behaviour has been detected. In de Bruijn and Hufen's typology, financial incentives (for example, charges and taxes) have a more limited coercive character because they leave the targeted actors with a degree of choice (for example, either to alter their behaviour or to pay (more) for the pollution which they cause). Information transfer instruments produce the least amount of coercion (de Bruijn and Hufen, 1998: 18–9).

Holzinger, Knill and Schäfer (2003, 2006) differentiate between: (1) interventionist; (2) economic; and (3) context-oriented policy instruments. Their studies, which focus only on EU policy instruments, conclude that despite the hype about new modes of governance 'there is a broad gap between the political and scientific advocacy of new ideas and their actual implementation through corresponding changes in underlying policy instruments' (Holzinger, Knill and Schäfer, 2006: 419). The approach taken by Holzinger and colleagues best fits the constitutivist and categorist schools. Bähr (2010) also puts forward a threefold typology for EU policy instruments which are assessed from a constituvist analytical perspective. Bähr differentiates between command-and-control, economic and suasive policy instruments in EU environmental policy. The threefold classifications put forward by both Holzinger and colleagues (2006) and Bähr (2010) are similar to the policy instrument categorisation that will be used in this book which, however, focuses not only on EU policy instruments but also on member state instruments.

While drawing on Tömmel and Verdun (2009b), Holzinger, Knill and Lenschow (2009) offer the following fourfold typology for EU environmental policy instruments: (1) hierarchical; (2) competition; (3) cooperative; and (4) negotiation mode. Importantly, Holzinger, Knill and Lenschow (2009: 60–2) conclude that:

> [t]here is indeed a decrease in the relative importance of hierarchical governance ... Even though hierarchical governance clearly remains the dominant approach in EU environmental governance. The introduction of these new modes has been characterised by uneven speed and scope, partially lagging behind the respective political discussions about their introduction.

Halpern's (2010: 54) constitutive study of policy instruments in EU environmental policy since the late 1960s makes a similar point when concluding that 'genuine innovation remains scarce at EU level' (but see Jordan, et al., 2012b). Importantly, Halpern (2010: 54) argues that the EU has 'a tendency to import policy instruments from other political systems in order to legitimise its environmental policy competence'. Gunningham, Grabosky and Sinclair (1998) take a different, more instrumentalist tact, with a more complex policy instrument typology and a recognition that the nature of regulation itself may be evolving. Gunningham and colleagues (1998: 4) contend that they 'demonstrate how environmental regulation could be redesigned so that it would perform "optimally"'.

This very brief literature review has flagged up different typologies and assertions about NEPIs. However, there remains a real dearth of systematic comparative research both spatially and across different policy instrument types. This book is less concerned with 'optimally' designed policy instruments although we also acknowledge the growing importance of policy instrument mixes to achieve better effectiveness and greater cost-efficiency. Instead our book's main aim is to assess whether there has been a decisive shift from (traditional tools of) government towards (new instruments of) governance and, if so, whether this shift could be the result of much deeper political and societal changes as we will explain in more detail in the following.

POLICY INSTRUMENTS: A TYPOLOGY

As Chapter 1 already flagged up, our book adopts the following threefold environmental policy instrument typology: (1) *suasive instruments*

Governing by policy instruments: theories and analytical concepts 29

(including informational measures and voluntary agreements (VAs)); (2) *market-based instruments* (including eco-taxes and emissions trading); and (3) *regulatory instruments* (including 'command-and-control' regulation and 'smart' regulation). We are aware of the fact that our threefold typology (see Table 2.2) is not entirely free of ambiguities because it is sometimes difficult to establish the exact demarcation between different policy instrument types. One of the analytical aims is to explore whether our threefold typology provides useful conceptual boundaries.

Broadly speaking, the fewer the policy instrument categories the more difficult it will be to group neatly all of the different policy instruments which can be found in EU and member state environmental policies. We have tried to address this analytical problem by introducing the six sub-categories (see Table 2.2) which are not meant to be exclusive although they are typical for the main policy instrument category.

The threefold policy instrument typology developed for this book has the advantage of being more parsimonious than the more complex earlier fivefold typology that we employed previously (Jordan et al., 2003a; 2005). The threefold categorisation of the main types of policy instruments allows for a better constitutive assessment of the alleged shift from government towards governance.

Table 2.2   Types of environmental policy instruments analysed in this book

Types of environmental policy instrument	Subtypes of environmental policy instrument
(1) Suasive policy instruments	(1.1) Informational measures (1.2) Voluntary agreements
(2) Market-based instruments	(2.1) Eco-taxes (2.2) Emissions trading
(3) Regulatory instruments	(3.1) Traditional command-and-control regulation (3.2) Innovative regulation

In the empirical chapters which follow (Chapters 4 to 8), we further differentiate our three main policy instrument categories into sub-categories. As can be seen from Table 2.2, informational measures and VAs can be subsumed under the category suasive policy instruments (see Chapters 4 and 5), eco-taxes and emissions trading are both market-based instruments (see Chapters 6 and 7), and regulatory instruments can be differentiated into traditional command-and-control regulation and innovative regulation (see Chapter 8).

Our threefold policy instrument categorisation resembles the above mentioned typology put forward by Bähr (2010) and de Bruijn and Hufen (1998) as well as the categorisation which can be found in Bemelmans-Videc, Rist and Vedung's (1997) influential book *Carrots, Sticks and Sermons: Policy Instruments and Their Evaluation*. Bemelmans-Videc and colleagues' constitutivist study focused primarily on the nature of constraint which a particular type of policy instrument exerts within different institutional and sectoral contexts; regulations ('sticks') are highly choice constraining, economic instruments ('carrots') are moderately choice constraining and informational instruments ('sermons') are 'soft' policy instruments which are barely choice constraining.

Our book's constitutivist aim is to assess what types of policy instruments and instrument mixes have been adopted in different jurisdictions (and policy sub-sectors) since the late 1960s with the aim of finding out whether and, if so why, a shift has taken place from (traditional tools of) government towards (new modes of) governance. Our book is clearly unable to assess all of the different types of environmental policy instruments which have been adopted in Austria, the Netherlands, Germany and UK as well as EU environmental policies since the late 1960s. We have therefore opted for a detailed assessment of only the most important policy instruments sub-categories which are representative of our three main policy instrument types (see Table 2.2). This allows us to get to the core governing characteristics of these instruments. Examples of policy instruments that had to be excluded from a more detailed assessment include unverified VAs which companies put forward in a self-declaratory manner and subsidies (see, for example, Gunningham, Grabosky and Sinclair, 1998).

Suasive Instruments: Informational Measures and Voluntary Agreements

Within our threefold environmental policy instrument typology, suasive instruments constitute the 'softest' policy instrument type. The degree of coerciveness which they exert is low because suasive instruments are characterised by horizontal non-hierarchical features. The suasive instrument category, under which we subsume informational measures and VAs, arguably includes the largest number of different policy instruments – too many to cover in this book. We therefore focus primarily on eco-labels and eco-management schemes (EMSs) (Chapter 4) and VAs (Chapter 5).

Informational measures

Informational measures include a wide variety of tools which can range from the publication of environmental data and the staging of environmental days to more complex suasive instruments, such as the setting up of eco-label schemes and EMSs including the EU's EMAS and the International Organization for Standardization's (ISO) environmental management schemes (for example, ISO 14001). Chapter 4 focuses on eco-labels and EMSs as important examples of informational measures.

Eco-label schemes can take very different forms. The OECD's widely used typology differentiates between three types of eco-label schemes. As will be explained in more detail in Chapter 4, our book focuses on multi-issue eco-label schemes which are independently verified. This type of eco-label scheme was 'invented' in Europe before its usage spread across the globe (Kern, Jörgens and Jänicke, 2000; Jordan et al., 2003c).

Both the EU's EMAS and the ISO's 14001 standard require companies to audit their environmental impact, establish internal environmental management systems to monitor and (where possible) reduce these impacts while providing regular public statements. EMAS is a more challenging scheme compared to ISO 14001 (Jordan, Wurzel and Zito, 2007). We have grouped EMAS into the category of suasive policy instruments because it is a voluntary scheme which provides businesses with independently verified environmental data about their impact on the environment. The acquired environmental data can be used for both internal purposes (for example, to improve processes and procedures) and external marketing (for example, to advertise a positive environmental image).

Voluntary agreements

The definitions of VAs vary greatly. Börkey and Lévèque (1998: 4) provide the following incomplete list of terms which have been used interchangeably: 'self-regulation, voluntary initiatives, voluntary codes, environmental charters, voluntary accords ... co-regulation, covenants, negotiated environmental agreements, *accords de branche, programme cooperative e volontari'*. They identify the following variants as the most important types of VAs: negotiated agreements, public voluntary schemes (PVSs) and unilateral commitments (Börkey and Lévèque, 1998: 4–10). Our book does not focus on PVSs (because they are relatively rare in Europe) or unilateral commitments (because they are widely seen as ineffective (for example, EEA, 1997)).

The OECD (1994: 4) has defined VAs in a very broad manner as: 'voluntary commitments of the industry undertaken in order to pursue actions leading to the improvement of the environment'. A narrower definition was put forward by the European Environmental Agency (EEA) which defined them as 'covering only those commitments undertaken by firms and sector associations, which are the result of negotiations with public authorities and/or explicitly recognised by the authorities' (EEA, 1997a: 11). Similarly, the EU Commission has defined VAs as 'agreements between industry and public authorities on the achievement of environmental objectives' (CEC, 1996a: 5). Our book adopts the definition put forward by the EEA (see in particular Chapter 5).

Market-based Instruments: Taxes and Tradable Permits

The OECD has for a long time propagated the increased use of market-based instruments on cost-effectiveness grounds. It subsumes eco-taxes, emissions trading schemes, deposit-fund schemes and subsidies under the category market-based instruments (OECD, 1994, 1999a, 1999b). The EU Commission differentiates eco-taxes into emission levies, which command payments directly linked to the real or estimated pollution, and product levies which are directed at the raw materials, intermediate inputs (for example, fertilisers) and/or the final consumer products (for example, batteries) (CEC, 1997a). Another important distinction can be made between different eco-taxes depending on their purpose and the use of the revenue which they generate (Ekins, 1999: 42–3). Furthermore, eco-taxes can be differentiated according to their degree of embeddedness (or aloofness). An eco-tax may target only a specific product (for example, petrol) and/or service (for example, transportation by air). It may, however, also be embedded within a wider ecological tax reform which constitutes 'a reform of the national tax system where there is a shift of the burden of taxation from conventional taxes, for example on labour, to environmentally damaging activities such as resource use or pollution' (EEA, 2006a: 84).

The theoretical foundations for emissions trading schemes were laid by the Canadian economist John Dales (1968) in his book *Pollution, Property and Prices* (Hansjürgens, 2005: 5; Lafeld, 2003: 44; Wurzel, 2008a). The principle idea behind emissions trading is to allocate emission allowances to companies (or countries) which they can then sell to other actors. In other words, a market is created for emission allowances. Emissions trading schemes are meant to bring about emission reductions in the most cost-efficient manner. It was the United States (US) which set up the first emissions trading schemes in the 1980s (Ellermann et al., 2007a; Wurzel, 2008a). The first emissions trading

Governing by policy instruments: theories and analytical concepts 33

schemes in Europe were set up in Denmark and the UK in the late 1990s. The EU's emissions trading scheme, which became operational in 2003, is the world's first supranational scheme.

Space constraints limit us to focus only on eco-taxes (Chapter 6) and emissions trading (Chapter 7) which are widely regarded as the most important market-based instruments. Our book does not assess other market-based instruments such as deposit-fund schemes and subsidies. The degree of coerciveness represented by market-based instruments is difficult to generalise. The OECD (1980: 8) has continually emphasised the flexibility of such instruments and their ability to motivate actors through financial incentives rather than regulatory constraint. However, the imposition of price on environmentally damaging activities can be done in such a way that it removes flexibility. This alerts us to the possibility that the use of market-based instruments may not necessarily constitute a clear shift from government towards governance in the way that is expected by some governance theories (see Chapter 1).

Regulatory Instruments

Often derogatively labelled 'command-and-control' instruments, regulation has played a central role in environmental policies at both the EU and member state level and must feature in any assessment of the evolution of governing the European environment. At the core, regulation involves an authoritative action by the state or a public body to steer public and/or private actors towards a particular goal, normally backed by sanctions (Howlett, 2011). Regulatory action typically involves some form of prescriptive rule about how actors ought to conduct themselves and/or set targets (such as emission limits) within a certain timeframe.

Coercion and sanctions are one dimension that differentiates regulations from other instruments. De Bruin and Hufen (1998: 17) emphasise that regulatory instruments 'also possess a normalizing and guaranteeing function', which standardises government behaviour. Regulations tend to be reactive and require monitoring and enforcement. They can take different forms including bans and prohibitions, design and production norms, executive orders, licences and permits, standards, use restrictions and zoning (Majone, 1976: 593; Mickwitz, 2003: 419; Howlett, 2011). Both the policy instrument and governance literatures view command-and-control regulation as the 'hardest' policy instrument because it usually generates a high degree of coerciveness.

However, regulations do not necessarily have to remain static and inflexible. As systems of governing evolve, regulatory instruments will also evolve. Proponents of suasive and market-based instruments often conveniently overlook that, over time, traditional regulation has become more 'innovative', 'light handed' or 'smarter' (see, for example, Gunningham, Grabosky and Sinclair, 1998; Rengeling and Hof, 2001). For example, in the UK, the national integrated pollution control regime (namely, regulation) shares many similarities with what is described in continental states as negotiated agreements underpinned by law (for example, the Dutch covenants). Most European countries never adopted the rigid American-type of environmental command-and-control regulation which made use of the 'technology forcing principle' that triggered a highly adversarial environmental policy-making style (Wurzel, 2002: 93). As Chapter 3 explains, the national policy styles of our four European case countries as well as the EU policy style are characterised by a higher level of consensus.

To more fully understand the policy instrument selection process, we turn now to the core theoretical explanation, institutionalism. It is through an institutional theoretical framework that we conceptualise the processes that select and define the nature of instruments, moving beyond categorisation. Given the explicit effort in this book to contextualise both the empirical response to new governance ideas and new thinking about policy instruments, as well as the need to see how different types of instruments interact, an institutional dimension is essential.

INSTITUTIONAL APPROACHES

Institutional theories are usually based on the assumption that policy instrument choice is dependent upon the wider institutional context in which they are selected and used. This particular view characterises many of the 'new' institutional theories. Institutional approaches can be differentiated into historical, rational and sociological institutionalism (Hall and Taylor, 1996; Aspinwall and Schneider, 2001). March and Olsen (1998: 948) define an 'institution' as 'a relatively stable collection of practices and rules defining appropriate behaviour for specific groups of actors in specific situations'. This definition includes more than just explicitly identified organisations in the public (for example, ministries and agencies) and private sectors (for example, corporations and environmental groups); actors depend on socially constructed rules to orientate their actions within the complex social environment; rules backed by some form of sanction will make actor predictability even stronger (Scharpf, 1997: 39).

National institutions contain 'standard operating procedures' and preferred policy instruments that are often only modified after becoming

Governing by policy instruments: theories and analytical concepts 35

manifestly dysfunctional; any institutional change is likely to be incremental (Rose, 1993). Actors' preferences are derived endogenously on the basis of what is appropriate (in other words, politically acceptable and can be implemented on the ground) in a given institutional context (March and Olsen, 1998). Therefore the policy aim is to satisfice, rather than maximise (Hall and Taylor, 1996). Institutionalist approaches highlight the fact that institutions will vary across a political system (Scharpf, 1997: 41).

Given these tendencies, it is not surprising that scholars have deployed these approaches to explain why policy inertia prevails and change is constrained and at best incremental: accordingly, institutions form and adapt slowly, investing in certain norms, values and cultures. Institutions are stable and resistant to large scale change. Once norms and procedures have become institutionalised they are not changed easily unless there are sudden, external shocks. 'Revolutionary policy learning' (Kitschelt, 1991) is rare, usually occurring in the environmental policy field after an ecological catastrophe or spectacular policy failure. When confronted with challenges (such as the selection of the most appropriate policy instruments), actors prefer to refine what they have already before searching for novel approaches. The tendency to cling to what they know they are good at (for example, policy instruments that appear to 'work') rather than innovate with new instruments, ensures that institutions endure long after they cease to be optimal – for example, competency traps (March and Olsen, 1989: 53–67).

When policy change occurs, past decisions will constrain it (path-dependence). In other words, institutions are 'sticky' in the sense of persisting beyond the historical moment and condition of their original design ('the stickiness of adaptation' – see March and Olsen, 1989: 169). Institutions refract the pressure for change in a way that perpetuates or only gradually reforms existing arrangements. Thus, 'the common imposition of a set of rules will lead to widely divergent outcomes in societies with different institutional arrangements' (North, 1990: 101).

THE ANALYTICAL PROBLEM OF POLICY CHANGE

Although the emphasis on stickiness has been the traditional understanding of the role of institutions, there has been an academic move towards using institutional approaches to understand how policy change and learning can occur (Pedersen, 2006). Part of the premise of this argument rests on the idea that path-dependency does not fully explain the evolution of institutions (for example, Streeck and Thelen, 2005a).

Pierson (2000) argues that part of the reason that institutional mechanisms adhere to particular decisional tracks is due to the fact that institutions (the establishment of which involve substantial efforts of learning and co-ordination) may generate increasing returns for actors, thus enhancing their resilience.

In a similar fashion, Mayntz and Scharpf's (1995) 'actor-centred institutionalism' approach suggests that institutions not only facilitate and constrain a range of choices but also define how the choices will be evaluated by actors operating within the institutions, altering actor perceptions and therefore actor preferences/interests. Institutions will shape how actors engage with each other in the policy context. Learning can be stimulated through these engagements in a way that parallels the viewpoint of the policy framing and other ideational approaches.

Historical institutionalist scholars, although still emphasising the resistance of institutions to change, have been seeking to insert more nuance in the understanding of policy change and the factors which trigger it. Streeck and Thelen (2005b: 6–8) note the dichotomous thinking in the path-dependency assumption that sees change as being: (1) either extremely minor yet continuous; or else (2) sudden and at best episodic if not rare. Streeck and Thelen (2005b: 9) flag up the possibility of 'incremental change with transformative results'. In other words, the long-term impact of the uptake in new modes of governance may be more fundamental (or transformative) than becomes apparent by a superficial survey of governing techniques. As already noted in Chapter 2, Streeck and Thelen (2005b) offer five analytical categories for explaining the process of gradual transformative institutional change: (1) *displacement* (namely, slowly rising salience of subordinate change relative to dominant institutions); (2) *layering* (namely, new elements attached to existing institutions gradually change their status and structure); (3) *drift* (namely, neglect of institutional maintenance in spite of external changes resulting in slippage in institutional practice on the ground); (4) *conversion* (namely, redeployment of old institutions to new purposes); and (5) *exhaustion* (the gradual breakdown of institutions over time). Broadly speaking, these analytical categories for institutional change can be used to highlight different patterns of instrument selection and use.

This newer approach accepts that institutional change can be abrupt and dramatic in its consequences – the model of 'punctuated equilibrium' best summarises this argument (for example, True, Jones and Baumgartner, 1999) – as well as quite incremental and moderate in its

Governing by policy instruments: theories and analytical concepts 37

consequences (Thelen, 2004: 30–1). How institutions make both incremental and non-incremental changes to policy instrument usage is the central focus of policy learning theories.

Policy Learning

One of the key scholars examining public policy, institutions and policy change is Peter Hall. Hall (1993) offers an extremely useful bridge between the study of policy instruments and the overarching developments in the policy process. His attempt to understand how states can engender enormous shifts in public policy leads him to conceptualise the role of policy learning.

Hall's policy change framework encapsulates both institutional and ideational (namely, changes in belief systems and world views) processes which drive public policy change. Following on from Heclo (1974), Hall (1993: 278) defines social learning as the 'deliberate attempt to adjust the goals and techniques of policy in response to past experiences and new information'. Hall (1993: 278) disaggregates the process of learning into three elements of policy which can change and reflect learning: 'the policy goals that guide policy in a particular field, the techniques or instruments used to attain those goals, and the precise settings of these instruments'.

Hall's (1993: 278–80) analytical framework for policy change distinguishes between change in the use of existing instruments (first level change), the adoption of new policy instruments (second level change), and paradigm or goal change (third level change). When first level change takes place existing policy instruments are recalibrated which may happen at frequent intervals. This usually involves learning from new information or trial and error experience, but will not involve changes in the types of policy instruments used or the overarching policy goals. Second order change leads to the adoption of novel policy instruments, but not the overarching policy goals. Only third level policy change also involves a change in the overarching policy goals. These goals will be driven by a core set of ideas which Hall (1993: 279) terms as a policy paradigm: 'a framework of ideas and standards that specifies not only the goals of policy and the kind of instruments that can be used to attain them, but also the very nature of the problems they are meant to be addressing.' Because first and second level changes occur regularly and incrementally they are associated with 'normal' policy-making. A paradigm shift of seismic proportions is required for a third order change. Such shifts take place only periodically as new problems emerge, and anomalous or 'unexplainable' events accumulate.

In the face of challenges to the existing paradigm, policy-makers search for alternative explanations. This process widens the number of actors (such as pressure groups, journalists, intellectuals and academic analysts), who compete to alter the prevailing policy discourse. Policy learning thus takes place at all three different levels. Crucially, first and second order changes do not automatically result in third order change, which requires an evolving societal debate and reflection – social learning – regarding the overall direction of policy. Over time, supporters of the new paradigm become entrenched in bureaucratic structures and alter the instruments to reflect their ideas. A third advantage of Hall's framework for policy change is that it allows us to take into account both endogenous policy (instrument) learning as well as exogenous policy (instrument) transfer the latter of which will be discussed in more detail below. Traditional policy instruments may be modified, supplemented or even supplanted by NEPIs due to endogenous pressures (such as dissatisfaction with existing policy instruments). Alternatively policy instruments may be modified, supplemented or even supplanted by NEPIs due to exogenous pressures (such as competitiveness pressures and policy instrument transfer). This could include national and transnational networks of actors seeking to promote particular paradigms and associated instruments.

Much of the environmental policy instrument literature has primarily focused on what Hall called first and second level change; while much of the general governance literature has paid attention mainly to level three changes although some governance authors have also considered level two changes. This book assesses all three levels of policy (instrument) change. Moreover, it offers a multi-level study of the use of NEPIs on both the member state and EU level; this is something very few environmental policy instrument studies have done up to now.

Learning is an important aspect for policy makers in the instrument selection process: assessments of how well particular policy instruments have performed in their own jurisdiction in the past together with new knowledge about how novel policy instruments are functioning in other jurisdictions may lead to challenges of well entrenched perceptions about the suitability of certain types of policy instruments. Normally, policy instruments are simply recalibrated and fine-tuned to reflect changing circumstances and political demands, but occasionally sudden, unforeseen (external) events de-stabilise a policy area (such as an environmental catastrophe), triggering a sudden search for new policy instruments and/or explanatory frameworks.

Policy Learning and Transfer

Policy learning and transfer concepts identify the possibility for policy (instrument) convergence. Explanations for policy (instrument) convergence are of interest to our study which assesses the degree to which changes in governing operate across our four case countries as well as the EU. The policy transfer literature, which focuses on both learning and institutional dynamics, offers useful insights into how ideas about policies (for example, Dolowitz and Marsh, 1996, 2000; Padgett, 2003; Stone, 2004) and policy instruments (for example, Kern, Jörgens and Jänicke, 2000; Kern et al., 2001; Tews, 2002; Tews, Busch and Jörgens, 2005) spread across political systems.

The policy transfer literature usually focuses on the process by which knowledge at a particular time and place is used in another time and\or place (Bennett, 1991; Dolowitz and Marsh, 1996, 2000). It isolates the agents of transfer within broader political structures. The knowledge they transfer could relate to policy goals (or paradigms), policy content, policy instruments or to administrative arrangements. There has been substantial criticism of the policy transfer argument (for a review, see Benson and Jordan, 2011; 2012). In particular, James and Lodge (2003) note that the policy transfer approach's tendency to synthesise policy change explanations in a way that makes it hard to disentangle from other policy dynamics at work, such as bounded rationality. This monograph places its central focus on institutional and learning dynamics to avoid some of these pitfalls.

In synthesising various concepts in their policy transfer framework, Dolowitz and Marsh (1996, 2000) distinguish between voluntary and involuntary processes. They define 'lesson drawing' as a 'voluntary' policy transfer process which occurs when one political system freely borrows from another a policy or policy instrument; they contrast voluntary policy transfer with coercive policy transfer which involves some degree of (direct or indirect) coercion. Voluntary and coercive policy transfers are therefore perceived as two extremes on a continuum (Dolowitz and Marsh, 2000).

One of the core questions for European public policy (including the study of environmental policy and its instruments), is the role which the EU plays for member state public policies. Some of the literature has viewed the EU as a 'massive transfer platform' (Radaelli, 2000: 6) or a 'supranational idea hopper' (Bomberg and Peterson, 2000: 7). Padgett (2003: 243) suggests 'a more nuanced evaluation of the transfer capacity of the EU', while highlighting the importance of 'the penetration of *feedback* of the European policy process into the domestic arena'.

40 *Environmental governance in Europe*

Pursuing this argument a little further, Bulmer and Padgett (2005: 104–7) combine notions of governance structure with an institutionalist understanding of the EU policy process to differentiate various types of transfer. They identify 'hierarchical governance' as the typical EU governance mode associated with the single European market; here EU institutions can exercise supranational authority, which can invoke coercive forms of policy transfer. Bulmer and Padgett (2005) label the second EU mode of governance as 'negotiation', where EU actors agree rules by common assent or majority decision. Finally they define 'facilitated unilateralism' as the type of transfer which happens when member states agree some form of unilateral and voluntary rules/norms within the EU (in other words, the EU has an intervening role as a facilitating arena).

This more structured institutionalist approach is the basis for Bulmer and Padgett (2005: 105–6) to more closely differentiate the nature of policy transfer. Coercive transfer occurs when states are required to adopt a policy idea as a condition of membership or some conditional benefit (for example, financial assistance). Negotiated transfer involves governance ideas and/or instruments originating in one or more member states being incorporated into EU rules and instruments. This fits with Padgett's (2003) differentiation between 'uploading' (where ideas are transferred from the member states to the EU) and 'downloading' (where ideas are made to fit with domestic institutions and interests) of policy (Padgett, 2003: 228–9; see also Börzel, 2007, 2010; Héritier, 1996; Knill, 2001). Voluntary transfer fits under Bulmer and Padgett's notion of facilitated unilateralism but it can take two forms: one is analogous to the open method of co-ordination (OMC) where a loose institutional setting creates benchmarks while the other takes the form of member states shopping for ideas within the framework of EU processes.

Finally Bulmer and Padgett (2005) modify Dolowitz and Marsh (1996: 106) to flesh out the conceptual categories underpinning policy transfer: (1) 'emulation/copying', where a policy is transferred from one political system to another without alteration; (2) 'synthesis', which involves combining elements of policy from two or more different jurisdictions; (3) 'influence', which is a weaker form of transfer involving a policy system taking inspiration from an external system but creating an entirely home-grown version or building on existing domestic forms; and (4) 'abortive' transfer, where an attempt to transfer is blocked by actors in the domestic context. Bulmer and Padgett hypothesise that hierarchical governance will produce the stronger form of transfer. Negotiated governance will tend to trigger weaker forms of transfer, perhaps some synthesis and influence while facilitated unilateralism at best will lead to

Governing by policy instruments: theories and analytical concepts 41

some weak form of mutual influence (Bulmer and Padgett, 2005: 106). Padgett's (2003: 242–3) empirical findings suggest that the EU institutional dynamics may lead to substantial policy emulation, but this will often result in weaker forms of hybrid transfer (for instance, policies seeking to be uploaded must survive the bargaining process and then in turn must be adopted at the national level where they may constitute inexact transposition).

Although the policy transfer literature takes a broader view of the elements of public policy which may be transferred across jurisdiction and/or time, it shares similarities in focus to the policy instrument literature which centres on 'drivers' and 'context'. The scholarly policy transfer debate about the importance of causal forces versus the institutional 'goodness of fit' maps onto the discussion of policy instruments. Radaelli (2000: 38) points out that:

> [a]ccording to new institutionalism, actors follow rules, shared interpretations, symbols, schemata and meanings. Policy transfer, instead, assumes that policy diffusion is a rational process wherein imitation, copying and adaptation are the consequences of rational decisions by policy-makers.

However, Radaelli (2000: 38–9) also warns that 'this stark contrast should not be overemphasised'.

EXPLAINING INSTRUMENT SELECTION

The institutionalist and policy learning approaches help us to formulate propositions about the selection of policy instruments. Institutional approaches have focused more strongly on divergence in the selection of policy instruments (leading more to influence at best or an abortive attempt at worst). This chimes with the constitutivist explanations of policy instrument selection. Even if we build the potential for institutional change over time, the scenarios in Streeck and Thelen (2005b) emphasise the contingency of outcomes and the complex interaction of institutional rules, political interests and external context. In terms of how policy instruments are understood, institutional approaches tend to place instruments in a secondary role, being defined by the larger (national and/or EU) institutional context. Those institutional structures, beliefs and principles define the 'goodness of fit' that determine which policy instruments are selected and how they are incorporated into the political system.

A key expectation of this approach is that divergence is likely to be a strong phenomenon in any comparison of environmental policy instruments in different jurisdictions. Policy makers within institutions prefer incremental policy change. They also prefer to have instruments that work with the grain of their institutions. Majone (1991) contends that one of the most important criteria used by policy makers when choosing between instruments is administrative feasibility – for instance, 'can it be implemented back home?' (see also Rose, 1991; 1993). Proponents of 'intelligent imitation' also realise that 'any policy idea, whether original or derived, is bound to be modified by the concrete political and institutional conditions in which it is carried out' (Majone, 1991: 80). Therefore 'discordant' instruments are less likely to be adopted and those that are adopted will be shaped to fit more closely with national traditions. This institutional dynamic can be expected to produce a fairly heterogeneous pattern across Europe.

For example, Waltman (1987: 269) identifies the importance of 'policy inheritance' (the way past policy was made) in maintaining divergent patterns of policy adoption. Bennett (1988) highlights the powerful impact of 'domestic constraints' in hindering policy convergence, manifesting themselves as *inter alia* 'policy legacies', foreordained instruments, and entrenched resistance from bureaucracies. Similar concepts appear in the environmental policy literature including 'institutional fit' (Knill, 1998, 2001) and 'institutional design' (Aguilar Fernández, 1994). Finally, Linder and Peters (1989: 49–50) identify national style as an important determinant of policy instrument choice: countries with a strong statist tradition (such as Germany) are more likely to employ intrusive instruments (such as regulation). Howlett (1991: 15) claims that 'different national propensities' favour certain instruments, which Anderson (1971: 122) describes as national 'policy repertoires'.

In Hall's combined institutional and ideational approach to learning, ideas and theories drive the policy makers' instrument selection and usage. Policy instruments have a secondary, instrumental role in underpinning deeper beliefs and philosophies. Howlett and Ramesh (1993) argue that such forces can account for rapid and wide-ranging shifts in the instrumentation of a policy area, and view the instrument selection as one aspect of the wider policy process, in which social learning is a dominant motive. Instrument selection is only one aspect of the wider policy process where learning occurs, and learning is essential for extensive change (Howlett and Ramesh, 1993). Policy transfer and policy learning encompass the possibility that there may be some convergence about policy instrument selection. A lot of weight is placed on exogenous drivers pushing for instrument convergence. Much of the institutional literature also credits exogenous factors with being key instigators for policy change but focus more on the continued divergence due to the

Governing by policy instruments: theories and analytical concepts 43

logics of appropriateness. However, as was mentioned above, institutionalists do not reject the idea of policy (instrument) change. They nevertheless flag up prominently policy (instrument) divergences which occur due to institutional constraints.

CONCLUSION

This book seeks to move beyond over-theorised governance studies which are not grounded in empirical research. It does so by using environmental policy instruments as empirical touchstones to measure the putative shift from traditional (tools of) government towards new (modes of) governance. The policy instrument and governance literatures can offer important insights that could advance the debates in both fields. Much of the existing policy instrument literature focuses on categorising instruments in a manner useful to policy analysis. Some of this literature does attempt a more explicit overarching policy narrative, focusing on constitutivist approaches. This book speaks to both approaches, as it offers a threefold policy instrument categorisation (suasive instruments, market-based approaches and regulation) with relatively sharp conceptual boundaries. The expectation of the governance literature is that less prescriptive (i.e. suasive and market-based) instruments will follow from a more conscious effort to pursue a more governance form of steering. However, as mentioned above, it is important not to associate market-based instruments necessarily with 'softer' forms of instrumentation. Calibration of the actual instrument in practice may give a particular policy instrument type a widely varying policy impact.

In order to speak more closely to the governance versus government debate outlined in Chapter 1, we embrace a much more expansive analysis of the policy processes. Part of that leads us to consider the role of policy learning in addition to the institutional explanations. Policy learning offers a much broader public policy explanation; one that tends to focus on instruments and policy techniques as more secondary conceptual elements to any policy action (see Table 2.3 for a comparative summary of the analytical approaches).

An added benefit of Hall's framework and the policy transfer literature is that there is a greater expectation that instruments will have a more primary role in exchanges and possible policy transfer that may take place between different policy systems. Both the institutional literatures and some of the learning approaches tend to view instruments as secondary policy features that are shaped by wider political forces.

44 *Environmental governance in Europe*

Table 2.3 Theorising the adoption and adaption of policy instruments

	Institutional Approaches	Policy Learning
Themes	Institutions shape the selection and implementation of policy instruments	Instrument choice driven by conflicts between competing actors who hold different beliefs
Role of instruments	Mainly instrumental, embedded in institutional settings which shape the policy development/ search process	Secondary to the policy paradigm; they implement dominant ideas
Key agents of the process	National and/or supranational policy actors who are constrained by institutional structures	Experts, networks, government departments and societal actors
Search process	Path dependency (to achieve 'goodness of fit') unless unusual circumstances (e.g. major policy failure) but rationality will tend to be bounded	Goal directed
Scope for innovation	Potential for innovation is small when goodness of fit poor; high if the fit is good, but endogenous and/or exogenous shocks may trigger rapid innovation	Potentially large
Examples of key proponents	March and Olsen, Streeck and Thelen, Pierson	Heclo, Hall; Mayntz and Scharpf
Policy instrument transfer and convergence	Continued divergence likely as transferred policy instruments are adapted to fit dominant institutional requirements	High degree of policy instrument convergence through emulation and (voluntary and/or coercion) policy transfer

The policy learning and transfer literatures tend to expect a relatively high degree of convergence in the use of policy instruments. Institutional explanations emphasise the primacy of the goodness of fit for policy instruments within a particular institutional setting. They are therefore sceptical about the ability of (new tools of) governance to transform policies in a way that leads to policy (instrument) convergence. The modifications of the policy transfer literature by Bulmer and Padgett (2005) hypothesise that, unless some fairly strong hierarchical incentive

Governing by policy instruments: theories and analytical concepts 45

is asserted in the EU decision-making process, policy transfer is only likely to involve some superficial or even rhetorical borrowing.

Part of the value of Hall's (1993) framework is that it attempts to meld the learning and institutional processes, while at the same time encapsulating the relationship between instruments and wider policy process. Accordingly Hall's synthesis plays a strong structural role in our analytical framework. Chapter 3 explicitly uses Hall's conceptualisation to assess the detailed institutional context in each of the four member states and the EU, as well as how they have shaped core ideas concerning environmental policy. Our case studies will then enable us to assess the actual role and usage that particular policy instruments have in Europe.

3. Changing institutional contexts for the use of policy instruments

INTRODUCTION

In Chapter 2 we critically examined the policy instruments literature and its most important typologies. At the core of the contemporary instruments debate is the question of how the wider institutional context, in a particular jurisdiction, shapes (and is shaped by) policy instruments. In order to explore this question, Chapter 3 examines the institutional characteristics of four national jurisdictions (namely Austria, Germany, the Netherlands and UK) and the EU. As mentioned in Chapter 2, Hall's (1993) analysis provides an important bridging role between instruments and institutions because his analysis of policy change captures both policy learning and the important characteristics of state-society relations. In addition to Hall's (1993) policy change framework, we draw on Richardson's (1982) policy style concept to better explain the interactions between policy styles and policy instruments in five different jurisdictions. The policy styles concept identifies and explains the interaction between the national government's approach to problem solving and the relationship between the government and core societal actors (Richardson, Gustafsson and Jordan, 1982; Richardson and Watts, 1985).

Table 3.1 presents the combined elements of this comparative jurisdictional approach. It formulates them as propositions according to the different hypotheses put forward by *government* and *governance* hypothesis theories (discussed in Chapters 1 and 2). Accordingly, the third column lays out the scenario that would be expected if the institutional and instrumental elements reflect more traditional notions of command-and-control governmental steering. The fourth column proposes the kind of interactions that would exist in a more ideal-type governance scenario. The first row of jurisdictional elements focuses on the more permanent organisational characteristics of each political system, normally found in the constitutional and other legal statements of the rules of the game. The governance propositions suggest that such an organisational structure should reflect a polycentric array of actors that

Table 3.1   A framework for characterising jurisdictional contexts

Policy level	Operationalisation of the concept	Government pole	Governance pole
Organisational structures	Formal rules, constitutional mandates	Authority is hierarchically structured and exercised in top-down fashion	Authority is diffused over a relatively wide range of policy actors who prefer non-hierarchical modes of interaction
Policy style	Less formal but constant interaction between state-society actors. May include rules and principles that have wider application than merely for the specific problem	Governmental actors and rules define the scope of access and exchange of resources; they steer the interactions between state and societal actors in a hierarchical fashion	A wide range of societal actors are involved in policy-making. They define their own input and practice a considerable degree of self-steering
Policy goals	Development of a strategy and system of more specific responses to tackle framed problems; may involve specific policy principles	Governmental actors define the main policy goals and strategies; top-down and hierarchically	Wide set of actors and interactions, reflecting wider societal capabilities to set/change goals and adopt/change strategies, largely in a bottom-up fashion

Source: Adapted from Hall (1993) and Richardson and Watts (1985).

participate in the governing; the governance propositions emphasise less hierarchical modes of interaction and communication. The government pole expects a more top-down, hierarchical government steering process.

By differentiating between organisational structures, policy styles and policy content we partly draw on the analytical framework of our earlier work which tried to identify the main drivers for and barriers to the adoption of NEPIs (Jordan, Wurzel and Zito, 2003a and, 2003b). Jordan and Liefferink (2004) developed further the analytical differentiation between structures, styles and content for the analysis of the Europeanisation of member state environmental policies. However, while Jordan and Liefferink (2004) aimed to gain a more fine grained analysis of changes in national environmental policies induced by Europeanisation, we focus in this book primarily on policy instrument changes. In terms of the role of policy structures, styles and content, these variables can 'determine' the shape and use of policy instruments. However it is not simply a one way process since choices of policy instruments can change policy structures, styles and content. This is a more complex two-way process where institutional variables can constrain instruments but where instruments may also transform institutions.

The second row examines the more informal style of interaction between public and societal actors. The government-oriented policy style under the government pole suggests a more hierarchical core of governmental actors (and rules) which will actively steer policy and state-society relations; in contrast the governance pole suggests a more reactive policy style in which societal actors are dominant. Richardson's policy style framework also examines the question of how anticipatory policy makers are in dealing with policy problems (Richardson, Gustafsson and Jordan, 1982; Richardson and Watts, 1985). Because this dimension cuts across *government*-oriented top-down steering and *governance*-oriented societal self-steering it is not highlighted in Table 3.1: it is theoretically possible for societal steering to be anticipatory. Nevertheless this dimension can be important to both the choice and calibration of policy instruments.

Policy goals are reflected in the overarching strategy and policy instrument repertoire that a particular political system deploys to steer policy and society. The government pole predicts a more top-down, prescriptive strategy defined by a more limited set of (primarily governmental) actors whilst the governance type expects a more horizontal (as opposed to top-down) development of policy strategy involving more societal actors.

The remainder of this chapter uses the broad analytical framework outlined in Table 3.1 to examine the five jurisdictions in the following order: Austria, Germany, the Netherlands, the UK, and the EU. Because an analysis of the detailed history of the evolution of environmental policy in these five jurisdictions is beyond the scope of this book, Chapter 3 instead provides a comparative summary analysis of the organisational structures, policy styles, policy goals and policy instruments as they have developed since the early 1970s.

ENVIRONMENTAL POLICY STRUCTURES AND INSTRUMENTAL STRATEGIES

Austria

Organisational structures

The organisational structure for Austrian environmental policy has evolved substantially over the years. Nevertheless, a core feature remains its relatively high degree of fragmentation which is the result of important environmental competences being distributed amongst several ministries (horizontal fragmentation) and across different levels of government (for instance, the federal and provincial levels) within the Austrian federal system (vertical fragmentation). Since the early 1970s a moderate horizontal and vertical centralisation has occurred within environmental policy organisational structures (Lauber, 1997c, 2004; Pesendorfer, 2007; Pesendorfer and Lauber, 2006). The Environment Ministry has received additional environmental competences, while the federal government has accrued additional powers from the provinces. In terms of ministries, the Environment Ministry as well as the Ministries for Transport, Agriculture and Economics have traditionally shared important environmental competence. The Economics Ministry holds important competences governing environmental issues which are linked to industry, tourism and energy. The Agriculture Ministry is responsible for most water management issues. The Austrian Environment Ministry, which underwent numerous name changes over the years, has evolved significantly since it was established in 1972 under the name Ministry for Health and Environment *(Bundesministerium für Gesundheit und Umwelt* – BMGU).

The Environment Ministry was initially not a very effective political force because of its limited competences and staff resources (Lauber, 1997a, 1997b; Pesendorfer, 2007: 72). In 1987, the Austrian government transformed the BMGU into the Ministry for Environment, Youth and Family *(Bundesministerium für Umwelt, Jugend und Familie* BMUJF), while substantially boosting its competences and staff resources (Lauber, 1997a, 2000; Pesendorfer, 2007). In 2000, a newly elected conservative, right wing coalition government made up of the conservative Austrian People's Party *(Österreichische Volkspartei* (ÖVP) and the right wing Freedom Party *(Freiheitliche Partei Österreichs* (FPÖ)) merged the Environment and Agriculture Ministries, creating the Ministry for Agriculture, Forestry, Environment and Water Management *(Bundesministerium für Land- und Forstwirtschaft, Umwelt und Wasserwirtschaft* –

BMLFUW). It called itself *Lebensministerium* ('Life Ministry') although many environmental NGOs and Workers Chamber representatives think that agricultural interests dominate the Ministry (Interviews, 2011). Academic studies have also argued that the Environment Ministry was effectively swallowed up by the Ministry of Agriculture (for example, Pesendorfer, 2007). The merger certainly reflected the diminished importance of environmental issues for the ÖVP-FPÖ coalition government (Interviews, 2001; *ENDS Europe Daily* 7 March, 2000) which adopted a 'neoliberal minimalism' (Lauber, 2001) that downgraded the political importance of environmental issues. However, Austrian EU membership in 1995 enhanced the relative political importance of the Environment Ministry on the domestic level both horizontally vis-à-vis other ministries and vertically vis-à-vis the provinces – *Länder* (Interviews, 2000; see also Falkner and Müller, 1998; Lauber, 2004; Pesendorfer, 2007). An amendment to the Austrian constitution in the 1990s enhanced the importance of environmental protection, making it a general constitutional aim (*Staatsziel*) which the state has to respect (Lauber, 1997b; OECD, 1995a: 23).

In 1985, the Austrian government set up the Environment Agency (*Umweltbundesamt* – UBA) in order to provide the government with technical scientific expertise. The Austrian UBA has retained a highly circumscribed role which excludes an explicit political role (which stands in contrast to the German Environment Agency, which will be discussed in the following). Consequently the UBA rarely makes detailed policy recommendations and concentrates instead on research. In 2000, the Austrian government privatised the UBA although this did not have a significant impact on its already restricted role.

The federal dynamic is important for understanding Austrian multi-level environmental policy-making. The provinces maintain significant environmental policy competences in areas such as nature conservation, wildlife protection, air emissions from heating systems and non-hazardous waste (Lauber, 1997a, 1997b; OECD, 1995a). However, compared to the German states (*Länder* – see the following), the environmental competences of the Austrian provinces are much more limited. Constitutional amendments in 1983, 1988 and 1993 increased the powers of the federal government in relation to the provinces within the environmental policy arena (Lauber, 1997a: 84; OECD, 1995a). The provinces further lost influence in environmental policy-making as a result of the high degree of Europeanisation of Austrian environmental policy (Lauber, 2004; Pesendorfer, 2007). There is also a third level of government, namely the municipal authorities which wield significant competences for sewage treatment and non-hazardous waste management.

Policy style

In terms of the national policy style, Austria has traditionally been characterised as a classic corporatist state with a close tripartite relationship involving the government, unions and employers (Scruggs, 1999, 2001). In the 1970s, Social Democratic Party *(Sozialdemokratische Partei Österreichs* – SPÖ) governments adopted an economically highly successful 'Austro Keynsianian' policy style (Pesendorfer, 2007: 45). Since the 1970s, however, Austrian corporatism has waned and given way to more pluralistic forms of policy-making at a time of rising unemployment and a spiralling budget deficit (for example, Crepaz, 1995; Dachs et al., 1997; Gehrlich, 1992; Lauber, 2001; Luther and Müller, 1992a, 1992b; Pesendorfer, 2007). Nevertheless, since the end of the Second World War, the Austrian political style has exhibited a high degree of consensus.

The corporatist features became institutionalised in the Chamber of Business *(Wirtschaftskammer)* and the Chamber of Labour *(Arbeiterkammer)*, which have remained important veto players within the Austrian policy-making process although their influence has waned in recent years. The Business Chamber has traditionally maintained close links with the conservative Austrian ÖVP while the Labour Chamber has strong affiliations with the Social Democratic Party of Austria. The SPÖ and ÖVP (in other words, the two largest parties in parliament) served together in so-called grand coalition governments for much of the 1950s and 1960s as well as the 1990s. The formation of a coalition between the ÖVP and the Freedom Party (FPÖ), which under its demagogic leader, Jörg Haider, transformed into an extreme right wing party, triggered the temporary exclusion of Austria from certain EU meetings. The exclusion was lifted only after Haider stepped down as the FPÖ's leader. The ÖVP FPÖ coalition government (2000–07) seemed to signal an end to Austrian consensus politics but it was relatively short-lived. In 2008 another grand coalition made up of the SPÖ and ÖVP took office. The ÖVP-FPÖ pro-liberalisation coalition programme had only a moderate impact on domestic Austrian environmental policy because the ÖVP, which was by far the larger coalition partner, continued to field the Environment Minister who propagated an eco-social market economy *(ökosoziale Marktwirtschaft)* – a concept which the ÖVP had already developed in the 1990s (Pesendorfer, 2007).

The SPÖ, which was a partner in many post-war coalition governments (1945–66, 1983–2000 and since 2007) and governed on its own from 1970–83, was particularly known for its proactive policy stance. It emphasised the importance of the social partnership (*Sozialpartnerschaft*) between the unions and employers. While a proactive approach in economic policy-making was the result of Austro-Keynesianism, the institutional and ideational context was much less favourable for proactive environmental policy-making. Importantly, the new social movements and environmental groups which emerged in the 1970s were not represented in the *Sozialpartnerschaft*. These new groups, which were initially largely shunned by the SPÖ and ÖVP, organised unconventional mass protests against a large hydroelectric power station on the banks of the Donau (Hainburg) and the Zwentendorf nuclear power station (Lauber, 1997a, 1997b, 2001; Pesendorfer, 2007). The success of the protests by environmental groups and the rise of the Green party surprised the traditional catch-all parties (*Volksparteien*).

With the exception of the Green party, which entered the Austrian parliament in 1986, the main parties and the social partners initially perceived environmental concerns as being in conflict with economic objectives, to which the SPÖ, ÖVP and FPÖ as well as the unions and employers gave a greater priority (Lauber, 1997a, 1997b). However, by the late 1980s, the Social Democrats favoured 'the ecological restructuring of industrial society' while the Austrian People's Party campaigned for an 'eco-social market economy' (Lauber, 1997b: 613). Ironically the 'greening' of the SPÖ and ÖVP took place largely against the background of worsening economic conditions and the need for Austria to bring under control its spiralling budget deficit in order to qualify for the EU's Economic and Monetary Union (EMU).

Policy goals and strategies
Although the 1811 Civil Code already stipulated laws for the protection of forests against excessive felling (Lauber, 1997a: 81), the first modern-day environmental regulations were adopted only in the early 1970s. Austrian environmental policy has always been characterised by a heavy reliance on command-and-control regulations, although a limited number of market-based instruments (in particular environmental subsidies and some eco-taxes) were already adopted in the 1970s (Lauber, 1997a: 87, 1997b, 2000, 2003; OECD, 1995a, 2001a; Pesendorfer, 2007).

The precautionary principle (*Vorsorgeprinzip*), which was first invoked in the 1980 steam boiler emission law, served to legitimise government action where significant risk to the environment was believed possible even in the face of scientific uncertainty (Lauber, 1997b: 610). The principle provided an important source of legitimisation of ambitious environmental regulations: many of which stipulated the *Stand der Technik* (best available technology – BAT) principle, which was imported from Germany where it played a central role in domestic environmental policy (see the following). Throughout the 1980s, the Austrian government adopted a considerable number of detailed and ambitious environmental policy measures, most of which consisted of command-and-control regulation (Lauber, 1997a, 2001; Pesendorfer, 2007). Austria is therefore best described as 'a latecomer which became a pioneer' (Lauber, 1997a).

However, the centre-right wing ÖVP-FPÖ coalition government (2000–07) tried to avoid the adoption of unilaterally more stringent environmental standards (Interviews, 2001–02). It adopted a deregulation law in 2001 which triggered the revision of important environmental laws (Pesendorfer, 2007). Moreover, the ÖVP-FPÖ coalition decided that EU environmental laws should no longer be 'gold plated' – in other words, that Austria should not go beyond what was stipulated in the EU environmental laws (Interviews, 2001; Pesendorfer, 2007).

Broadly speaking, Austria was an environmental latecomer in the 1970s. It belatedly transformed into an environmental pioneer in the 1980s (Lauber, 1997a) but fell behind again on certain environmental issues (such as climate change) in the early 2000s (Interviews, 2002 and 2011).

Germany

Organisational structures
The institutional structures of the German environmental policy system have remained remarkably stable since the early 1970s (Pehle, 1998; Jänicke and Weidner, 1997; Weale, 1992a; Wurzel, 2008b). Some observers have argued that the German environmental policy system is characterised by a 'static core' (Knill, 2001: 135–63) which has exhibited a preference for interventionist approaches and 'regulatory rules [that] are highly specified and leave comparatively little flexibility and discretion for the administration' (Knill, 2001: 137). The core environmental policy structures were set up by a centre-left (Social Democratic Party (SPD) – Free Democratic Party (FDP)) coalition government which came to power in 1969. The adoption of a relatively progressive environmental policy formed part of a much wider reform agenda which the SPD-FDP coalition government tried to implement in the early 1970s (Hartkopf and Bohne, 1983; Müller, 1986).

The Interior Ministry *(Bundesministerium für Inneres* – BMI) was allocated the most important environmental policy competences in 1969. An independent Environmental Ministry *(Bundesministerium für Umwelt, Naturschutz und Reaktorsicherheit* – BMU) was set up only in 1986 shortly after the Chernobyl nuclear reactor meltdown and before an important state *(Land)* election. The BMI and BMU have strongly favoured traditional regulation derived from the BAT principle. In particular, the Interior Ministry was dominated by officials with law degrees. Economists are a relatively rare species even in the Environment Ministry (Interviews, 2007).

The Federal Environmental Agency *(Umweltbundesamt* – UBA) was set up in 1974 to provide the government with technical and scientific advice. In the mid-1990s, the UBA reformed its internal organisation from a media-centred (namely, air, water and soil) structure into a sector-oriented administrative structure. The BMU failed to follow this example and instead experimented with cross-media working groups and interdepartmental working groups such as the interdepartmental working group on greenhouse gases *(Interministerielle Arbeitsgruppe Klimagase)*. In 1972, the German government established the Environmental Expert Council *(Sachverständigenrat für Umweltfragen* – SRU) which acts as an independent advisory body. The SRU, which was headed by an economist at the time, propagated the widespread use of eco-taxes in German environmental policy already in the 1970s (SRU, 1974, 1978; Wurzel et al., 2003a).

Germany has a long federal tradition. In environmental policy, the states *(Länder)* have guarded their constitutional competences by insisting on the application of the principle of subsidiarity. In the 1970s, the *Länder* successfully defended their competences for water management and nature protection by blocking a constitutional amendment which would have given the federal government powers similar to those which it had acquired for air pollution, waste management and noise pollution control. A major reform of the German federal system in 2008 did little to bring about a decisive change to the asymmetrical environmental policy competences between the federal government and the *Länder* (which gives the former significantly more powers on air pollution issues compared to water management issues). The horizontal division of environmental competences within the federal system has complicated efforts to adopt cross-media and cross-sectoral approaches including the adoption of environmental policy instruments which cut across different levels of government. For example, there have been lengthy negotiations about eco-taxes which affect the revenue allocation between federal and state levels (Wurzel et al., 2003a).

The 1971 Environmental Programme stipulated the following three action guiding principles (Hartkopf and Bohne, 1983: 1) polluter pays principle (*Verursacherprinzip*); 2) precautionary principle (*Vorsorgeprinzip*); and 3) co-operation principle (*Kooperationsprinzip*). These three principles still inform German environmental policy. The precautionary principle, which aims to prevent pollution from occurring, requires an active role by the state/government. The co-operation principle was intended to encourage horizontal co-ordination between different government departments and improved vertical co-ordination between different levels of government (for example, within the federal system and between the federal government and the main societal groups). However, important structural barriers (such as the federal system, coalition government and relatively independent ministries) made its implementation difficult. The polluter pays principle should have encouraged the early adoption of market-based environmental policy measures. However, the 1976 waste water levy remained for a long time the only significant eco-tax on the federal level (Wurzel et al., 2003a).

Policy style
Germany is generally seen as preferring a moderately active policy style while relying heavily on consensus and consultation (Dyson, 1982, 1992; Weale, 1992b; Wurzel, 2008b). The traditional German policy style exhibited some corporatist features because most post Second World War German governments have consulted closely with both employer groups and unions. However, it is also informed by ordo-liberal ideas according to which the state determines merely the framework conditions (*Ordnungspolitik*) within which market forces reign. Emphasising both ordo-liberal and state interventionist ideas, Germany's managed capitalist system developed into a social market economy (*soziale Marktwirtschaft*) (Dyson, 1982, 1992; Dyson and Goetz, 2003; Dyson and Padgett, 2005). The social market economy has been compatible with the German policy actors' preferences for traditional command-and-control regulation (which reflected state intervention) and VAs, which are often adopted in the 'shadow of the law' as industry seeks to pre-empt government legislation (Scharpf, 1994).

Germany's policy style developed in an incremental fashion. Since the late 1990s, the principle of sustainable development has gained increasing if belated influence in German policy (SRU, 2002). With its equal emphasis on environmental, economic and social considerations, it fosters the idea of shared responsibility amongst different stakeholders rather than the reliance on active state intervention. However, initially many Environment Ministry officials raised concerns that the concept of

56   *Environmental governance in Europe*

sustainable development might be used as a tool for rolling back relatively ambitious environmental regulation (Interviews, 2001 and 2010; Wurzel, 2008b).

The concept of sustainable development was seen by some German environmental policy actors as a challenge to the concept of ecological modernisation which assumes that ambitious environmental policy measures (including command-and-control regulations) can be beneficial for both the environment and economy. In the 1990s, Klaus Töpfer (Christian Democratic Union – CDU) became the first German Environmental Minister who explicitly advocated the concept of ecological modernisation as an action guiding norm (Töpfer, 1989). Töpfer also strongly argued that ambitious traditional command-and-control regulation ought to be supplemented with market-based instruments such as eco-taxes. However, Chancellor Helmut Kohl (CDU) vetoed the adoption of a unilateral domestic ecological tax reform while supporting demands for EU-wide eco-taxes. A domestic ecological tax reform was adopted only by a Red-Green (SPD – Greens) coalition government (1998–2005) in 1999.

In the 1990s, Germany lost some of its environmental leader ambitions due to the huge costs of German reunification, the recession of the early 1990s and the debate about Germany's future as a production and investment location within the global economy – known as the *Standort Deutschland* debate (Weale et al., 2000; Wurzel, 2000, 2002).

Kitschelt (1986) argued that the German environmental policy system is characterised by closed opportunity structures and a high degree of juridification which is largely the result of a strong state law (*Rechtsstaat*) tradition. However, as will be shown in the empirical chapters of this book (Chapters 4–8), Kitschelt's argument only really applies to a particular time period and certain sub-sectors (for example, nuclear power, but not the adoption and implementation of the German eco-label scheme). It also ignores the fact that the SPD-FDP coalition government actively encouraged the founding of environmental groups during the 1970s while also involving them in the eco-label scheme (Hartkopf and Bohne, 1983).

Policy goals and strategies

Since the early 1970s, German environmental policy has relied heavily on command-and-control regulation and VAs. The Association of the German Automotive Industry (VDA) already proposed VAs to reduce automobile emissions in the 1960s. However, Germany has been widely classified as a 'high regulatory state' because of its large number of environmental regulations (for example, Héritier, Knill and Mingers,

1996). Müller-Brandeck-Bocquet (1996: 130) estimated that the number of domestic environmental regulations was as high as 35 000 in 1996 – although this total included various *Länder* legislation as well as relatively minor technical amendments.

Broadly speaking, Germany adopted progressive domestic environmental policy measures (including a small number of eco-taxes) in the 1970s and became an environmental leader on the EU and international level in the 1980s. Post-unification Germany became a more cost conscious environmental leader whose main environmental regulatory philosophy (namely, command-and-control regulations derived from the BAT principle) came increasingly under pressure from the EU which propagated procedural measures (such as the eco audit and management system (EMAS) that were initially resisted by many German environmental policy makers).

The Netherlands

Organisational structures

The post-war Dutch political system has traditionally sought political consensus among societal groups (Cohen, 2000). While the system builds state-society linkages, the state's organisational structure (including the executive and ministries) is segmented (van Waarden, 1995: 341). The Dutch proportional electoral system enhances the role of small parties and inclusive coalition governments. The system spreads responsibilities and power across several government layers: central, provincial and municipal (Eberg, 1997).

Van Tatenhove (1993: 20–1, 33) argues that a process of 'fragmented institutionalisation' shapes Dutch environmental policy at the central level. Roles and powers are located in different organisations, and five ministries have had long-term involvement in environmental instrument selection. This has made policy co-ordination difficult although there is an increasing interministerial co-ordination for EU policy (van den Bos, 1991; Liefferink and Wiering, 2011). The Dutch created the Ministry for Housing, Physical Planning and the Environment (VROM) in 1982. After initially promoting a strong regulatory approach it increasingly sought, during the 1980s, to build a consensus approach towards interest groups (Giswijt, 1987; van Tatenhove, 1993: 42–5; Liefferink and Wiering, 1997: 223). Until 2010, four other ministries shared responsibility with VROM for instruments and for integrating environmental policy into economic activities: (1) the Rijkswaterstaat, DG under the Ministry of Transport and Public Works, managed the state waters and was heavily involved in any instruments affecting water quality and automobiles (Weale et al., 2000: 220); (2) the Finance Ministry has a significant role in designing and operating key eco-taxes; (3) the Ministry for Economic Affairs, with its business sector relationships and its control of the energy and energy conservation portfolio; and (4) the Agricultural Ministry (Hanf and van de Gronden, 1998: 171).

In the evolution of Dutch environmental policy since 1973, the centre-right Christian Democratic Appeal (CDA) party has had the longest stint in power, essentially governing in coalition from 1977–94, and then 2002–10. Many of the major innovations in governing and instruments occurred within the coalitions between the CDA and the conservative-liberal VVD (People's Party for Freedom and Democracy) party and the social democratic PvdA (Labour) and progressive liberal D66 (Democrats 66) in the 1980s and early 1990s. The CDA was displaced in 1994 leading to a period (up until 2003) where PvdA had the upper hand in alliance with D66 and VVD. It is arguable that environmental policy and ambitions have dwindled with a party political shift to the right – excluding a brief renewal between 2007–10 (Liefferink and Birkel, 2011: 150–3; Liefferink and Wiering, 2011).

October 2010 saw another rightwards shift under the minority rightist government (VVD and CDA supported by the anti-immigrant Freedom Party or PVV). This new government, which unravelled when the PVV pulled out of budgetary negotiations in April 2012, shifted away from highlighting environmental and policy issues, particularly as the minority coalition found it politically difficult to force change (Liefferink and Wiering, 2011). The coalition agreement made repeated references to a 'level playing field in Europe' regarding emissions (Government of Netherlands, 2010: article 7). This political orientation has shaped the Dutch selection of instruments and led to the possibility of additional domestic environmental targets being linked to other countries' targets.

Another shift is institutional (Algemene Bestuursdienst, 2010). The 2010–12 government merged the Ministry of Transport and Public Works with VROM to create the Ministry of Infrastructure and the Environment. It also combined the Ministries of Economic Affairs and Agriculture to create the Ministry of Economic Affairs, Agriculture and Innovation.

While the central government generally has the key role in defining standards and targets, establishing national legislation and regulations as well as instrument design, provincial and municipal authorities have considerable responsibility for implementing environmental policy (Weale et al., 2000: 201; Bressers and Plettenburg, 1997: 117). The 12 provinces are responsible for implementing national legislation in their territories, for developing environmental policy and water management plans for their territory, for granting licences under the national Environmental Management Act and for helping manage water quality in provincial waters (Hanf and van de Gronden, 1998: 172). The scope of the provincial role varies, depending on the province and the policy sector. There has been a trend to integrate environmental policy efforts by decentralising policy efforts via the greater use of integrated planning at the more local level (RIVM, 2004); the current national focus away from environmental issues gives a greater role to environmental planning at these lower levels (Liefferink and Wiering, 2011). The 27 water boards have an important role in provincial waters and are responsible for sewage policy (Weale et al., 2000: 222–3; Hanf and van de Gronden, 1998: 173).

Policy style
The Netherlands is the classic consociational system in which significant societal social cleavages have been bridged by consensus seeking elites (van Waarden, 1995: 335–6; Middendorp, 1991). The Dutch public system has numerous policy responsibilities and objectives but uses private sector organisations and objectives to help fulfil these goals (van Waarden, 1995: 338–47). The general policy approach emphasises building consensus with a variety of actors, through consultation and cooperation (often established on a formal basis). Particularly notable in environmental terms is the focus on planning and encouraging private sector self-regulation (Weale, 1992a: 137).

In the 1970s, the Dutch government took a relatively interventionist environmental stance. The increasing orientation towards self-regulation since the 1980s was an important shift away from top-down thinking (Bressers and Plettenburg, 1997: 116). This shift in policy approach occurred under the Lubbers/conservative CDA led coalition government, with a strong innovative push by VVD politicians. Government emphasis on involving actors from the target groups defined by the agricultural, transport, energy and refinery sectors ensued (Weale et al., 2000: 174–5). Considering the reactive/proactive dimension of the policy style matrix, the Dutch policy style became anticipatory with the emergence and evolution of long-term environmental plans involving government and the target groups in the 1980s and 1990s (Weale et al., 2000). These elements placed the Netherlands between the law-based, standards-oriented approach of Germany and the more discretionary British approach of policy goals and instruments (Liefferink and van der Zouwen, 2004: 140–1). The concept of target groups is a prevalent one in Dutch environmental policy and has significant implications for the design of

60 *Environmental governance in Europe*

such instruments as VAs. It is an explicit categorisation of both individuals and organisations within civil society that share characteristics and connections to a particular policy area; the notion of target expresses that they are subject to policy instruments – in other words, they are the target of the instrument (Eurofound, 2010).

The policy style that saw the Netherlands take an active, interventionist approach to domestic policy setting, and which also made it a pioneer in EU negotiations (Andersen and Liefferink, 1997; Liefferink, 1997), waned in the early 21st century. As one EU Council Secretariat official observed (Interview, 2011) 'the Dutch no longer act as an environmental leader in the Council'. Partly this mirrors a political shift to the right at the national level, but it also reflects an administrative recognition of the difficulty of implementing some of the past ambitious targets (Liefferink and Wiering, 2011).

Policy goals and strategies
The Dutch have had a longstanding tradition of using decrees and licencing systems to address industrial hazards, that dates from the 1970s (Bressers and Plettenburg, 1997: 113–4). In 1972, the Dutch government published a memorandum detailing the key environmental problems and numerous measures. A number of environmental laws, mainly organised in terms of sectors (for example, water) or particular problems (for example, noise pollution), followed throughout the 1970s. The acts normally consisted of a government decree issued under the cabinet aegis (Liefferink, 1997: 219–20). The act provided framework legislation setting out general objectives, issues of responsibility and possible instruments (Hanf and van de Gronden, 1998: 162–3). Actors seeking to conduct activities within the regulated area had to secure licences from the appropriate authorities. These licences were conditional on the actors taking certain measures to mitigate pollution.

Since the early 1970s, this legal framework evolved gradually, with an increased focus on: (1) integrating and harmonising the various regulations and licence specification; (2) shifting the environmental strategy towards more preventative and sustainable solutions; and (3) emphasising the handling of problems in a cross-sectoral fashion (Hanf and van de Gronden, 1998: 162–3). This process eventually produced the 1993 Environmental Management Act; it simplified the permit system to allow installations to confront the key environmental priorities in one licence (Bressers and Plettenburg, 1997: 113–4).

The Dutch planning system is also an important post-1970s development for understanding the framework in which instruments operate. The

Dutch environmental plans by 1989 had become large strategic documents involving all levels of government and societal target groups; these documents guide environmental policy, set broader objectives and long-term programmes of action to achieve these objectives (Hanf and van de Gronden, 1998: 162–3).

Dutch environmental policy includes a number of guiding policy principles; it is difficult to label one as being dominant. Weale et al. (2000: 171–2) argue that two key principles operated in traditional regulation: the more significant best practicable means (BPM) and the higher standard of best technical means (BTM). The reforms of the 1993 Environmental Management Act added the 'as low as reasonably achievable' (ALARA) principle focusing on the largest possible protection with the BMP qualification (Faure and Ruegg, 1994: 45–6). The BTM acts as the test for the ALARA principle; where the costs of using the principle are deemed 'unreasonable', BMP can be substituted (Faure and Ruegg, 1994: 45–6).

A further set of important principles for the NEPI innovation are the principles of internalisation and target groups. Internalisation requires co-ordination between the various national ministries which have different societal networks (van Tatenhove, 1993: 47). In the 1980s these concepts were elements of an increasing effort to build new relationships between the state and society that fit the Dutch policy style. The 1990 National Environmental Policy Plan Plus (NEPP+) extended the developments of the planning approach to thinking about policy goals, with an explicit focus on policy instruments and implementation questions.

In terms of types of instruments used, the command-and-control approach of the 1970s, with its framework legislation and licencing, has remained a key aspect of Dutch environmental policy in the early 21st century. The 1989 National Environmental Policy Plan still contains the traditional more onerous regulatory procedures at its centre (Liefferink, 1999: 264). Thus the Dutch policy instrument philosophy has promoted a mix of instruments. Since the 1980s, NEPIs have gained in importance but tended to supplement and extend traditional instruments.

The United Kingdom

Organisational structures

At the dawn of modern environmental policy in 1970, the UK contained some of the oldest and most innovative policy structures in the world. In 1863, the UK created the first industrial permitting agency in the world known as the Alkali Inspectorate (which has since been merged into the national Environment Agency). In 1969, the Government decided to concentrate many of the most important central government-level environmental structures into one department known as the Department of Local Government and Regional Planning. The Minister of this new department, Anthony Crosland, created a central coordinating unit in the Cabinet Office, known as the Central Unit on Environmental Pollution (CUEP). Crosland also created an independent scientific advisory board known as the Royal Commission on Environmental Pollution (RCEP).

This period of innovation continued through to early 1970, when the new Department was combined with the transport portfolio and re-christened the Department of the Environment (DoE), which at the time of its creation was the first environmental ministry in the world (Jordan, 2002). Significantly, the Environment Ministry[1] took the CUEP under its wing, where it has stayed ever since. This period of innovative administrative concentration stopped in the early 1970s, when economic recession struck. In 1976, the transport portfolio was hived off into a separate Department of Transport. Subsequently, another short-lived experiment was conducted in fusing environment with transport (1997–2001), but, since 2001, environment work was attached to agriculture in a new department called the Department for Environment, Food and Rural Affairs – DEFRA.

There have been some notable institutional changes over time. There was a push within the 'New Labour' government to highlight issues such as climate change more strongly. This culminated in the Labour government creating the Department of Energy and Climate Change (DECC), removing the climate change portfolio from the Environment Ministry (Interview, DEFRA official, 2011). The Conservative-Liberal Democratic Coalition government, which came into office in 2010, took the step of purging a number of advisory bodies, including the RCEP which had a record of publishing highly influential environmental reports.

Neither the UK Environment Ministry nor the RCEP was able to command its own, internal environmental economic expertise to develop ideas for new market-based instruments. The UK civil service has traditionally been composed of generalists rather than technical specialists. The RCEP has traditionally been composed of eminent environmental scientists.

Although these structures of government have changed since 1970, their guiding philosophy has remained largely unchanged. The dominant philosophy is that central government should only ever set the broad legislative or policy framework, leaving the detailed aspects of policy fine-tuning and implementation either to specialist agencies or to local/regional government bureaucracies. It is primarily because of the Europeanisation of decision-making since 1973 that senior civil servants and

Ministers spend much of their time discussing detailed emission reduction plans and implementation timetables.

This division of responsibilities fitted the UK policy style and the 'constitutivist' paradigm, according to which the finer policy details could not possibly have been worked out by generalist bureaucrats working in London and in the devolved governments. In the 1990s, many of the more localised technical agencies were brigaded into a national Environment Agency in order to deliver simpler, more cost-effective regulation. The Environment Agency inherited a long legacy of regulatory control from its predecessors dating to the mid-19th century. However, in the 1990s it began to explore the potential of NEPIs (Pearce et al., 2000).

Finally, the legal structures of environmental policy are consistent with the UK's common law legal traditions, its unwritten constitution and the tendency for few legal disputes to reach court. However, the Europeanisation of policy has introduced a 'new formalism' to UK environmental law (Macrory, 1991), which takes the form of clear targets, specific rights and responsibilities, binding timetables and much greater transparency.

Policy style
Voluntarism, discretion and practicability characterised UK environmental policy throughout the 1970s and 1980s (Weale, 1997). Weale et al. (2000: 180–1) see the UK environmental policy style as embodying a strong commitment to co-operation, administrative discretion and technical specialisation. Thus, as new problems became important, new laws and new agencies were established to administer them. As it was sold to foreigners by UK politicians, 'the British approach' (Waldegrave, 1985) was predominantly reactive rather than anticipatory, tactical rather than strategic, pragmatic rather than ambitious, and case-by-case rather than uniform (see also: RCEP, 1984). The UK actors made a virtue of the need to be eternally pragmatic in designing policy. UK environmental policy is often characterised as a 'trial and error' search for the most cost effective (to business) solutions to policy problems.

Policy elites in the UK believed that 'muddling through' was inherently superior to strategic, long term planning, which they viewed as too abstract and too rigid (Ashby and Anderson, 1981). This attitude fitted neatly with the UK's legal system (which relies heavily on common law – in other words, case law which develops general principles from precedents rather than Roman law which applies general principles to case law), its informal and constantly evolving constitution, and the widespread desire to optimise pollution rather than minimise emissions regardless of their environmental impacts (see the following).

64 *Environmental governance in Europe*

Pragmatic opportunism has traditionally coincided with a particular style of operating, described as being informal, reactive, gradualist and accommodative. The style emphasised consultation and negotiation, rather than imposition and confrontation (Weale et al., 2000: 180). In operational terms, regulation proceeded on the basis of courteous negotiation between polluters and regulators operating in exclusive policy communities of experts (what Weale et al., (2000: 181) term 'club government'). Regulators working in specialised agencies preferred not to set standards which could not be complied with (the philosophy of 'practicability'). This style of working had many similarities with the way in which a limited number of contemporary agreements (see Chapters 2 and 5) are currently negotiated in the UK. Critics, however, claimed that this pragmatic approach inevitably led to regulators adopting the norms of those that they were supposed to be regulating.

Policy goals and strategies
It is quite difficult to identify an overall UK policy philosophy or paradigm other than that pollution should be optimised by limiting its effects in the environment rather than reduced at the source (Weale et al., 2000: 177; Jordan, 2002). This approach characterised UK policy content in 1970, and continued to do so afterwards. Lowe and Flynn (1989) concluded that UK policy was little more than a pragmatic 'accretion of common law, statutes, agencies, procedures and policies'. Lowe and Ward (1998: 18–9) argued persuasively that 'Britain's "traditional" approach' was not even completely homespun; it 'came to be defined in reaction to the incursions of EC environmental policy.'

Traditionally, the underlying policy principle has been that standards should be 'reasonably practicable', tailored to reflect local conditions, the economic costs of abatement and the current state of technical knowledge (Jordan, 1998a: 180–1). This approach was assumed to be more effective and more economically efficient than forcing all polluters to attain the same (namely, harmonised) statutory standards. On various occasions different parts of the scientific and political establishment in the UK staunchly defended this pragmatic, case by case style of working (Ashby and Anderson, 1981; RCEP, 1984; Waldegrave, 1985).

The UK has traditionally been reluctant to set long term policy objectives, especially whose achievement could not be guaranteed. The preference was for targets to be negotiated incrementally between industry and technical agencies. The BAT principle, on which German policy relies heavily, has never taken root in the UK. Where long term goals were set, they tended to be associated with distinct geographical areas as opposed to the emission limits favoured by many continental European states.

In terms of the range of policy instruments used in the 1970s, regulation was generally preferred to taxes, subsidies and the kind of sectoral covenants that began appearing in the Netherlands, France and Germany during this decade. Crucially, UK regulatory instruments differed somewhat to those used in continental European states and the EU. Whereas the latter preferred fixed legislative standards and deadlines to ensure comparability of effort and simplify the process of monitoring and enforcement, Britain usually opted for unwritten agreements with polluters, general legal guidelines and standards and flexible implementation systems.

Policy elites were immensely 'proud' of these arrangements (Hajer, 1995). An Environment Ministry guide to national policy in the late 1970s concluded that the UK was 'at an advanced stage in the development and adoption of environmental protection policies' (DoE, 1978: 1). In reality, environmental imperatives were (and largely still are) subservient to the (perceived) need to address the country's long-term economic and industrial decline as a world power. Finding cost-effective solutions to problems is regarded as a key policy objective. The UK has never been a particularly 'green' Member State. More often than not, the UK has passively 'taken' policies shaped elsewhere in the EU, rather than 'shape' EU environmental policy in its own image (Jordan, 2002, 2004; Jordan and Liefferink, 2004).

The history of UK environmental policy reveals one potentially puzzling contradiction between a clear preference for regulation, and the marked absence of clear targets and rules. This contradiction is actually more apparent than real. It arises largely from the UK's legal and bureaucratic culture of consensual negotiation. So while there were rules, they tended to be widely framed and interpreted informally by specialists operating in closed policy communities using unwritten codes and non-statutory administrative 'rules of thumb'. These inherited characteristics are at odds with market-based instruments (for example, Sorrell, 1999), but they should, at least in theory, have favoured VAs. Depending on how one defines a VA, the UK could even be said to have pioneered the use of voluntary approaches (see the following). Yet, UK VAs have generally been relatively small in number, informal (namely, non-legal) in nature, secretively negotiated, local in their implementation and highly flexible in their execution. In principle, eco-labels and other instruments of moral suasion generally go with the grain of UK practice, but market-based instruments (at least those set centrally and transparently

66 *Environmental governance in Europe*

by civil servants working in central government) are alien to the guiding precepts and organising structures of UK policy.

The European Union

Organisational structures

It is a truism that the EU is 'less than a federation, more than an international organisation' (Wallace, 1983: 403). In creating the EU, a group of like-minded states tried to address their common problems more effectively by working together following two world wars. While realising the benefits of collaboration, some have remained wary of surrendering their sovereignty to a supranational entity. Consequently, the EU displays elements of both intergovernmentalism and supranationalism, although its founders strongly believed it would evolve into a federal structure.

In some policy areas (for example, the internal market), the Treaties allow the EU to operate like a quasi-federal state, whereas in others (for example, defence and crime) decisions are reached after inter-governmental bargaining following the doctrine of unanimity in international organisations. Some have likened the EU to an 'upside down federation', where states hold powers that most federations vest in higher level bodies (for example, defence), while the EU oversees the more seemingly mundane activities (for example, environmental policy). Similarly, the EU's power tends to be stronger in the adoption and agenda setting stages of the policy cycle, but states retain a tight grip over financial resources. Compared to states, the EU has a relatively small budget of its own, having no general powers of taxation. Thus, while the EU stands alone among supranational organisations in enjoying the ability to adopt binding legislation (so-called Directives) that requires no review or ratification at the national level, the member states firmly retain implementation of EU laws.

A number of important points flow from this observation. Firstly, the EU is a 'regulatory state' (Majone, 1994), having very limited resources of its own and virtually none in the environmental sector (Jordan et al., 2012). If it wants to get anything done, it has to rely heavily on regulations. Its ability to use NEPIs to achieve environmental goals is remarkably weak. Second, because states dominate the implementation of EU regulation (Jordan, 1999) the EU struggles to put into effect those policies that it has adopted. Some have even argued that this positively encourages states to agree to regulations that they have no intention of ever fully applying (Majone, 1994: 86). Thirdly, even within a single (cross-cutting) sector such as the environment, the vertical allocation of

Changing institutional contexts for the use of policy instruments 67

tasks can be highly illogical. Given that the underlying motive for developing EU environmental policies is to deal with (pollution) problems that spill over borders, one might reasonably assume that member states would deal with sub-national public goods and the EU would concentrate on cross-border, international public goods. However, Weale et al. (2000: 460) point out that the EU spends a considerable effort regulating sub-national public goods such as bathing water and urban air quality, while simultaneously lacking the power to regulate cross-border issues such as energy policy. One of the primary reasons for this arrangement is the open structure of the EU policy process, which allows actors to insert ideas from different directions.

The Treaties are the nearest thing to an EU constitution. As these have been amended periodically, effectively the EU has been engaged in a continuous constitutional debate about its powers. The Treaties provide a set of principles and procedures that guide environmental policy development. Successive Treaty amendments have greatly affected' the power of particular environmental policy actors.

Although Treaty amendments are important, one could not understand EU environmental policy simply by reading the Treaties. In fact, EU environmental policy was already over 25 years old when an explicit reference to the environment was first inserted in the Treaties. The nearest things that the EU has to a blueprint for environmental policy are the Environmental Action Programmes (EAPs) of which the Sixth EAP ran from 2002–12. However, Treaty-based restrictions decisively influence the selection of environmental policy instruments. For example, the EU has no explicit Treaty-based powers to adopt its own VAs. The Treaty requirement for unanimity voting on all tax matters has effectively thwarted the Commission's eco-taxation plans. The Treaty explicitly mentions only the use of regulatory tools (namely, regulations, directives and decisions) and legally non-binding so-called opinions. In practice, the EU has side-stepped this problem by using regulation to create NEPIs such as eco-labels, emission trading and certain types of VAs (Jordan, Wurzel and Zito, 2006).

Another highly significant implication of the Treaties is that the four main EU institutions are heavily involved in the policy-making process. This creates institutional complexity: the Commission shares executive powers with the Council of Ministers and certain implementation functions with the member states while the Council shares the traditional legislative functions and accountability with the directly elected EP and national parliaments. The Commission, with its various Directorate Generals (DGs), initiates environmental policy and acts as the 'guardian of the Treaties,' ensuring that member states comply with the obligations made in primary law (in other words, the Treaties) and secondary law (namely, EU laws to implement the Treaties). In order for Commission proposals to be accepted, it requires approval from the Council of Ministers and, increasingly, the EP. Another crucial EU institution is the European Court of Justice (ECJ). The ECJ's role in interpreting supranational law has given it the opportunity to decide the scope of EU environmental laws and how they have to be implemented by member states. The European Council, which is made up of the heads of states and governments, normally does not get directly involved in the law-making process although it adopts the EU's wider goals and strategies (for example, what level of cuts in GHGE the EU should offer in international negotiations).

Within the Commission, DG Environment has to co-operate with other DGs in taking decisions on environmental policy because the College of Commissioners decides by common consent on Commission proposals. This has been further complicated by the Barroso Commission, in February 2010, carving out the climate change portfolio from DG Environment and creating the DG for Climate Action, a move similar to the one in the UK.

Policy style

There has been a substantial debate about the EU's dominant policy style (for example, Mazey and Richardson, 1993a/b). Dismissing early neo-functionalist predictions that European peak associations increasingly would dominate EU policy-making, Streeck and Schmitter (1991: 159) claimed that channels of interest representation at the supranational level would remain pluralistic, and not move towards the German, Austrian or Scandinavian neocorporatist model (Streeck and Schmitter, 1991: 159). They offered 'American-style pattern of "disjointed pluralism" ... characterised by a profound absence of hierarchy and monopoly among a wide variety of players of different but uncertain status' as a more appropriate analogy. Others (Greenwood et al., 1992; Greenwood and Cram, 1996) argue that there are neocorporatist-type relations in some EU sectors but not in others. In characterising the EU's policy style or *styles*, Mazey and Richardson (1993a/b, 1996a/b) refer to the 'European polity' model developed by Heisler and Kvavik in 1974. This model stresses the importance of regularised access, bargaining and consensus. It views the dominant style as neither pure corporatism nor totally unstructured pluralism, but something in between.

These definitional issues indicate the numerous problems inherent in applying the policy style concept to the EU. First, Richardson, Gustafsson and Jordan (1982: 2) originally developed the matrix to compare different *states'* 'standard operating procedures for making and implementing policies', not those of different sectors. Cross-sectoral variation would have to be ruled out if one were to stick rigidly to the founding premise of the 'policy style' literature which is that national differences are more enduring than sectoral variations. Secondly, one can debate whether the EU has its own 'policy style', or whether the EU's dominant operating procedures are simply an amalgam or 'patchwork' (Héritier, 1996) of national policy styles. The environment is not a discrete policy sector. Instead it cuts across many others sectors (for example, transport and energy) because these are often where the driving forces of environmental damage are located.

If we accept the limitations and examine EU environmental policy in relation to the policy style matrix, several noteworthy points emerge. Starting with the consensual-impositional dimension, much of the existing literature portrays the EU in terms of openness, pluralism and a strong desire to achieve consensus. This is a natural corollary of the EU's structure, where the main policy functions are divided amongst a wide range of actors (namely the Commission, Council, EP, and ECJ as well as the European Council), producing many possible 'veto points' (Weale, 1996). Overcoming potential choke points and getting policy adopted requires consensus which often demands complex compromises which reflect the main priorities of the veto actors. It is difficult to adopt EU policy by imposition – or at least consistent imposition. However, EU actors have sometimes resorted to imposition to achieve their objectives, which is why early European integration has been characterised as 'integration by stealth' (Hayward, 1996). In terms of the reactive-anticipatory dimension, the EU (and the Commission and EP in particular) has been a consistently strong advocate of anticipatory environmental problem-solving. Anticipation and prevention are found already in the first EAP in 1973 and every one since. Partly through the efforts of DG Environment, the EU now has a Treaty-based commitment to long-term, anticipatory problem-solving informed by the precautionary and preventative principles. That, of course, is the objective; in reality, less environmentally minded EU actors often succeed in ensuring that many of the EU's environmental policies are developed in a very ad hoc, incremental and reactive manner. There are examples where the EU has acted in a precautionary manner (for example, climate change). Analysts have explained the EU's tendency to flip from a reactive to an anticipatory mode of operation, by appealing to contingent factors such as sudden crises, the presence of committed and powerful individuals or sustained pressure from particular states (for example, Wurzel, 2002).

70   *Environmental governance in Europe*

Policy goals and strategies

Over the years, DG Environment has sought to develop a coherent policy paradigm around the inter-linked notions of ecological modernisation and sustainable development. A battery of policy principles (such as polluter pays, precaution, anticipation and environmental policy integration) are now codified in the Treaties and/or the six EAPs which the EU has adopted since 1973.

In 2001, the EU adopted a Sustainable Development Strategy. In practice, the sustainable development paradigm is not applied consistently or coherently across all aspects of EU environmental policy-making. This is partly a consequence of the unpredictable nature of EU policy-making, which generates sudden and comprehensive bouts of policy development in some areas, whilst leaving cognate areas relatively untouched. It is also because sustainable development is a cross-sectoral paradigm developed and advocated by environmental actors. In the past, 'non'-environmental actors and sectors have objected and taken active steps to subvert it.

Turning to environmental policy instruments, only a handful of EU laws which took into consideration environmental and/or public health issues existed prior to the early 1970s. McCormick (2001) argues that the first piece of EU environmental legislation focused on ionising radiation within the nuclear safety sector, but one can also look to the 1967 directive on the labelling of dangerous substances, which was adopted in reaction to similar legislation in the US. When identifying command-and-control regulations, it is worth clarifying the legal status of EU legislation. As mentioned above, primary legislation consists of the Treaties while secondary legislation consists of Regulations, Directives and Decisions that the EU adopts to implement the Treaties. Directives were the standard tool of the EU's environmental policy in the 1970s and continue to be so today. They set legally binding common objectives and deadlines but leave to the member states the choice of form and methods to transpose and implement Directives.

In the 1980s doubts began to be expressed about the effectiveness and economic efficiency of EU environmental regulation. Industry actors, seeking less intrusive and economically burdensome forms of control, increasingly advocated new tools such as VAs and eco-taxes. In the 1990s, this relatively technical debate became increasingly entangled in the more openly political debate about the respective powers of member states and the EU. The subsidiarity debate provided industry with an opportunity to push for new policy instruments. Meanwhile, some

Changing institutional contexts for the use of policy instruments   71

member states pressed for the wholesale revision of older EU environmental laws or even their repatriation to the national level, although none were scrapped.

The Commission's 2001 White Paper *European Governance* (CEC, 2001b) presented the most comprehensive strategic statement on new policy instruments. It conceded that EU legislation 'often includes an unnecessary level of detail', is time consuming to revise and update, rarely is implemented fully, and lacks transparent negotiation processes (CEC, 2001b: 18–9). The Commission promised to improve 'the quality, effectiveness and simplicity of regulatory acts'. These included: (1) using regulation as a last resort; (2) using more framework directives, which define only the essential elements of a policy but leave out the technical details that can be implemented via secondary rules; (3) employing co-regulation which links regulation to other tools such as VAs; and (4) increasingly using the open method of co-ordination (OMC), whereby states exchange information about best practice and benchmark their activities, thereby encouraging more informal cooperation and co-ordination (CEC, 2001b).

There are obvious limits to the applicability of these four objectives in the environmental policy sector. Firstly, because the EU remains a regulatory state (Majone, 1994), it is not altogether surprising that NEPIs are used only sparingly at the EU level. Put starkly, in the early 2010s, EU environmental policy comprised roughly of 1000 pieces of regulation (Haigh, 2011), about one dozen VAs, a flagging eco-label scheme and an eco-management and audit scheme (EMAS) which suffered from a low take-up (see also Chapter 8). The EU's main NEPI innovation is the emissions trading scheme (ETS) for greenhouse gases. But there are no EU-wide eco-taxes. This uneven NEPIs pattern has arisen because the EU does not possess explicit Treaty-based authority to adopt certain types of NEPIs (for example, VAs) or requires their unanimous adoption (for example, eco-taxes). Second, EU environmental policy has developed into a fairly mature area of EU activity, not well suited to soft policy instruments such as the open method of coordination (OMC) which relies largely on identifying best practice across member states and has been applied mainly in areas (such as employment and social policies) where EU competences are weak or non-existent.

CONCLUSION

Chapter 3 has sought to explain the key contextual features (namely, organisational structures, policy styles and policy goals and strategies) of

72   *Environmental governance in Europe*

the five political systems assessed in this book. By organising these concepts in this contextual framework, we can isolate some of the constitutive constraints that shape the adoption and usage of NEPIs, and the governing patterns that underpin this usage. This conclusion examines the contextual dynamics in Table 3.1 in turn.

Examining first the organisational structure in place in the 1970s, we find in Austria a small federal state that has policy-making powers fragmented on a vertical level (between the federal government and the provinces) and horizontal level (across different ministries). The other small state in the study, the Netherlands, has also divided environmental competences across ministries and levels of government (although it is not a federal system). In terms of the two large case countries, German environmental policy at the federal level has become somewhat more centralised although strong ministerial independence remains while the *Länder* recently tried to claw back some of the powers which they lost as a result of the Europeanisation of German environmental policy.

The organisational structures and norms for all five political systems have remained relatively stable. This is in line with what historical (and sociological) institutionalist theories would expect. In both Germany and Austria, we have identified moderate changes to some of the key contextual features since the 1990s. In Austria, the organisational environmental policy structures have changed significantly while in Germany they have remained highly stable despite the setting up of an independent Environment Ministry in 1986. There have also been some moderate changes to the Austrian and German policy styles and core environmental policy goals. In the Netherlands, despite the recent rearrangement of some of the ministries, the shared responsibility for aspects of environmental policy remains. The evolution of the EU treaties has brought about significant changes in the 'balance of power' between the main supranational institutions (for example, the EP has become a more powerful player). The various EU accessions have made the EU's power structures more complex, partly because they increased the number of veto points. Up to the 1990s, the UK perhaps faced the most significant adjustment pressures to EU environmental policy although, since the 1990s, it has been able to develop from a policy taker to a policy shaper (Jordan and Liefferink, 2004).

The different institutional features and histories have shaped the different (environmental) policy styles in each political system. Policymakers in Austria, Germany, the Netherlands, the UK and the EU all have emphasised the need for consensus although to various degrees across countries and over time. Arguably the EU has always had a relatively open process in formulating environmental policy. However, the EU has seen increasingly stronger demands for the involvement of a wider range of stakeholders in environmental policy-making resulting in increased consultation prior to the adoption of formal proposals. In this sense we do see a more inclusive dynamic with private actors and environmental NGOs having a stronger voice in shaping the EU environmental policy-making process.

Germany shares with Austria a more strongly interventionist policy style and a heavy reliance on BAT-derived command-and-control regulations. The Netherlands has had a relatively interventionist style concerning the environment. Its dependence on command-and-control regulations has evolved into a greater reliance on policy mixes and elements of discretion. While power was more centralised in the UK system, the traditional British environmental policy style has been less interventionist and more incremental and ad hoc in approach. The EU is arguably characterised by the most diffused power relationships with four central supranational institutions (Commission, Council, EP and ECJ) which are directly involved in the EU environmental policy-making process. The EU has only a very small budget which restricts its ability to adopt certain types of NEPIs (such as subsidies). Moreover, its member states are responsible for the implementation of EU environmental laws.

The anticipatory versus reactive policy style dimension has been relatively stable in all five systems although the Austrian political system exhibited probably the largest degree of change (from waning neo-corporatist to neo-liberal minimalism) during the ÖVP-FPÖ coalition governments (2000–07). The Netherlands and Germany have tried to continue with a sustained anticipatory approach to environmental policy although their national approaches vary significantly. Germany has become more cost-conscious since unification in 1990. Since the early 2000s the Netherlands frequently adopted a 'cost free leadership' position which amounted to little more than rhetorical leadership (Liefferink and Birkel, 2010). The EU Commission has sought to push an anticipatory environmental policy strategy but the EU's complex decision-making structure which contains many access points for veto actors and/or unanimity thresholds has to produce a reactive and incremental environmental policy style.

Changes in government in Austria and the UK as well as in the Netherlands have resulted in significant alterations to the dominant regulatory philosophies and the consequent overarching policy goals. For example, the ÖVP-FPÖ coalition and the Thatcher governments brought about the strong endorsement of neoliberal ideas. Clearly these changes in government have affected national environmental policies but perhaps

74 *Environmental governance in Europe*

not as significantly as one would have expected. Concerns about economic growth have played a strong role in limiting the anticipatory style in particular in Austria and the UK as well as the EU. German and Dutch environmental policy makers have also become more cost-conscious although changes in government in these two countries manifested themselves less in changes to the dominant policy style and more in changes to the policy instrument mixes (see also Chapters 4 to 7).

When comparing the organisational structures and policy styles of the five political systems with the expectations generated by the governance literature, one would expect Germany and Austria to be more reluctant to innovate with NEPIs. The generic governance literature expects the EU Commission to be interested in the adoption of a wider use of governance tools approach despite the political/institutional constraints. The traditional emphasis on flexibility and close partnerships in the UK suggests a strong potential for NEPIs.

However, Chapter 3 suggests that the picture is more complex and varied. First, in the 1970s only some of the five political systems assessed in this book became early environmental pioneers that adopted innovative environmental policy instruments (that conform to the expectation of the governance ideal type). For example, Germany adopted a range of VAs and a waste water levy in the 1970s. Similarly, the Netherlands innovated early on with VAs and eco-taxes while the same cannot be said about Austria, the UK and EU.

This complex picture suggests the need for a closer examination of the uptake and use of NEPIs and traditional policy instruments (in other words, command-and-control regulation) within the five different political systems to which we will turn in Part III (Chapters 4 to 7).

NOTE

1. The DoE/Environment Ministry has been re-organised and re-named several times since 1970. For the sake of convenience, we use the generic name 'Environment Ministry' in the remainder of the book to cover the entire period since 1970.

PART III

Governing by new instruments

4. Governing by informational means

INTRODUCTION

This chapter assesses informational policy instruments by focusing on eco-label schemes and environmental management schemes (EMSs). While eco-labels and EMSs constitute different schemes, they are both relatively soft informational tools which allow participants to review and publicise their environmental performance (for example, Gunningham, Grabosky and Sinclair, 1998; Heinelt et al., 2001; Jordan, Wurzel and Zito, 2005, 2007; Taschner, 1998; see also Chapter 2). Both eco-label schemes and EMSs are voluntary policy instruments schemes that encourage a self-regulatory process in which the participants adhere to environmental performance criteria (in the case of eco-label schemes) or environmental audits (in the case of EMSs).

Informational policy instruments are often also labelled 'moral suasion instruments' because they provide citizens and consumers with standardised information about the environmental impact of certain products, production processes and/or services (for example, Jordan et al., 2004; Wicke, 1987). Companies which operate in markets with a high level of public environmental awareness and 'green consumerism' usually have strong incentives to join eco-label schemes and/or EMSs in particular if their competitors have already done so (for example, Jordan et al., 2004: 163; Micheletti, Follesdal and Stolle, 2004).

Out of the policy instruments assessed in this book, informational policy instruments match most closely the ideal-typical notion of horizontal self-coordination (see Chapter 1). If there has indeed been a shift from traditional tools of government (namely, top-down command-and-control regulation) towards new modes of governance (in other words, soft policy instruments which encourage horizontal self-coordination), then we should expect to see an increase in the uptake of informational policy instruments at the member state and/or EU level.

The next section of Chapter 4 defines the core features of eco-labels and EMSs. Chapter 4 then assesses eco-label schemes before analysing EMSs. Within the eco-label schemes and EMSs sub-sections we track the chronology of the adoption of these two sub-types of informational policy instruments, marking out the 'pioneers' and 'followers' as well as those states which relied merely on the EU's eco-label scheme and/or its eco-management and audit scheme (EMAS) instead of adopting their own national schemes. Chapter 4 will also assess whether international developments have influenced the European use of eco-labels and EMSs.

Germany adopted the world's first national eco-label scheme (Blauer Engel, 2010; Jordan et al., 2004; UBA, 1996, 2010a). Austria (1990), the EU (1992) and the Netherlands (1992) were next in adopting eco-label schemes. Policy instrument diffusion of eco-label schemes occurred in many different countries, but not all of the EU's member states (notably the UK) pursued their own national schemes (Jordan et al., 2004; Kern et al., 2001; OECD, 1991, 1997). Compared to the uptake of eco-label schemes the adoption of EMSs in Europe followed a different leader-follower pattern. Competition took place between rival national, EU and international EMSs. Here again we look at the possible dynamics of transfer and learning versus more constitutivist questions of institutional fit.

DEFINING ECO-LABEL SCHEMES AND ENVIRONMENTAL MANAGEMENT SCHEMES

Eco-labels

Eco-label schemes are soft policy instruments which rely on moral suasion: they provide consumers with standardised information about the environmental impact of particular products and services (Jordan et al., 2004; OECD, 1991, 1997). Eco-label schemes are meant to encourage informed comparisons and, ultimately, more environmentally sustainable purchasing decisions by consumers. In markets with high levels of 'green consumerism' businesses have an economic incentive to apply for eco-labels to avoid competitive disadvantage. Eco-label schemes tend to be less effective at making producers take environmental considerations more seriously in markets with a low degree of 'green consumerism' although they may help to raise public environmental awareness (Jordan et al., 2004).

The OECD (1991, 1997) differentiates between the following three sub-types of eco-label schemes (see also UBA, 1998b): Type I – externally verified, multi-issue schemes; Type II – unverified self-declaratory schemes by manufacturers and/or retailers; and Type III – single issue schemes which are based on quantified product information on life-cycle impacts (for example, the product profile of a particular product model). Type I eco-label schemes were first designed in Europe (namely, in Germany) where they have become relatively widely used although their popularity varies considerably between different European jurisdictions. Externally unverified Type II schemes are also widely used by corporate actors but they have a poor reputation in terms of their environmental ambition and implementation (Jordan et al., 2004; OECD, 1997). Single issue Type III eco-label schemes are usually narrowly focused (for example, on forestry products) and not particularly widely used in Europe. For these reasons and space constraints, this book focuses only on Type I eco-label schemes, many of which are established under private law to avoid breaches of international competition rules under the World Trade Organization/General Agreement on Trade and Tariffs (WTO/GATT) (Jordan et al., 2004: 162; OECD, 1997).

Environmental Management Schemes

The original EU regulation establishing EMAS, which has become known as EMAS I, defines EMSs as 'that part of the overall management system which includes the organizational structure, responsibilities, practices, processes and resources for determining and implementing the environmental policy' (Council of the European Communities, 1993: 2). EMAS I came into force in 1995 and has since been revised twice. EMAS II became operational in 2001 and EMAS III in early 2010.

EMSs establish basic principles of environmental practice that guide how enterprises produce and market their goods and services (Zito and Egan, 1998). The aim is to push for continuous improvement on a voluntary basis: the EMS expects participant organisations to constantly review their environmental impact, create a management system that is accredited by independent environment verifiers, and carry out regular audits (CEC, 2001a).

The idea for EMSs originates from auditing practices which corporations in the US developed in the 1970s. Despite increased environmental regulation there was a rise in the number of major industrial accidents (often resulting in liability) which in turn created an interest in 'compliance audits', a voluntary audit process set up by companies to better control their internal processes (Malek and Töller, 2001: 43). The International Chamber of Commerce (ICC) published an influential document on environmental auditing in November 1988 (Holmes, 1995). In the 1980s, corporate interest in auditing spread to Europe, facilitated by the ICC's document (Malek and Töller, 2001: 43).

EMSs such as the EU's EMAS and the International Standard Organisation's (ISO) 14001 standard tried to encourage industry to adopt

80   *Environmental governance in Europe*

procedures and processes for reviewing their environmental impact. Although their specific requirements differ, EMAS and ISO 14001 both require companies to audit the environmental impact of their activities, establish internal environmental monitoring schemes and reduce, if possible, the negative environmental impact. Companies registered for EMAS and/or ISO 14001 must provide regular public environmental audit and management statements. For reasons which will be explained below, EMAS III incorporated parts of the ISO 14001 requirements to make EMAS a global voluntary policy instrument. Companies which achieve the required EMAS and/or ISO 14001 standards are granted an official confirmation by a competent national authority (as is the case for EMAS) or the ISO (as is the case for ISO 14001), which can be used for marketing purposes. Although the EU's EMAS and the ISO's 14001 are voluntary policy instruments, market and public pressure may push firms to participate to avoid losing out to competitors. Moreover, some governments have linked the successful participation in EMSs to a lighter environmental regulatory regime (see the following).

ECO-LABELLING SCHEMES

Germany: The Pioneering Blue Angel Eco-label Scheme

Germany became an environmental policy instrument pioneer when it set up the world's first national eco-label scheme in 1978. Spray cans free of chlorofluorocarbons (CFCs) became the first products which were awarded the German eco-label in 1978 (UBA, 2008: 2). The symbol used for Germany's eco-label scheme was derived from the UN's environmental logo, which the public nicknamed 'Blue Angel' (*Blauer Engel*). Germany's eco-label quickly developed into a well-known, highly successful scheme which became a reference point or even a model for national eco-label schemes elsewhere (Jordan et al., 2004; Kern et al., 2001; OECD, 1991, 1997; Schwar, 1999).

The popularity of the Blue Angel achieved a peak in the 1990s when the scheme was widely known amongst German consumers and present on more than 4000 product groups (Jordan et al., 2004: 166; UBA, 1998a: 9). Its popularity moderately declined in the late 1990s when it was overtaken by the Nordic Swan, which is a multi-national eco-label scheme created by the Nordic Council states (namely, Denmark, Finland, Iceland, Norway and Sweden), as Europe's most widely used eco-label scheme. However, public relations campaigns and an increase in the number of eligible product and service groups have reversed the decline of the Blue Angel scheme in the late 2000s. The number of Blue Angel eco-label licences granted to products/services was 3385 (from 492 suppliers) in 2006 and rose to 3786 (from 990 suppliers) in 2007. This meant that almost 10 000 products and services carried the Blue Angel label in 2007 (UBA, 2008: 2). By 2010 the number of Blue Angel labelled products and services had further risen to 11 500 (from 1050 suppliers) (UBA, 2010b: 2). In 2011 more than 11 500 products and services (from about 90 product categories) carried the Blue Angel label (Blauer Engel, 2011).

The Blue Angel eco-label is a voluntary third-party scheme organised under private law and licenced by the German Institute for Quality Assurance and Labelling (*Deutches Institut für Gütesicherung and Kennzeichnung e.V.* – RAL). RAL undertakes the testing of products and services which are awarded with eco-labels and prepares and signs contracts. It is a self-financing agency which charges eco-label holders relatively low one-off evaluation and licence fees that are set according to the product's annual turnover. Reduced rates and technical support are offered to applicants from developing countries to ensure that German business cannot use the eco-label for protectionist purposes (Interview, 2002; Jordan et al., 2004: 164).

The German Environment Agency (UBA) and eco-label jury are the other key actors in the Blue Angel scheme. The Environment Agency collects and assesses suggestions for new product and service groups from which the jury selects the products and services for the Blue Angel eco-label award. The eco-label jury guarantees the scheme's independence from undue industry influence because it is made up of a wide range of stakeholders including representatives from consumer and environmental groups (OECD, 1997: 50). The Environment Ministry is the owner of the Blue Angel label and regularly informs the public about the decisions of the eco-label jury.

The Blue Angel eco-label scheme uses a simplified lifecycle analysis which relies on an assessment of key environmental characteristics for each product and service group. The Blue Angel label is normally licenced for a three year period which, however, can be shortened if the product/service group is deemed to have the potential for more rapid technological progress. Empirical evidence shows that sales figures for small companies in particular have been enhanced by the Blue Angel scheme (UBA, 1998a: 36). However, an OECD report concluded:

> While the Blue Angel is generally considered one of the success stories of eco-labelling in Europe, its environmental effectiveness may lie more in its impact on business and government procurement practices, and on the setting

82   *Environmental governance in Europe*

of environmental standards for certain product groups, than its influence on consumer behaviour (cited in Jordan et al., 2004: 163).

Importantly, the criteria which have been developed by the scheme for eligible product/service groups often act as reference standards even for companies which do not apply for the Blue Angel eco-label (Interview, 2007). The success of the Blue Angel eco-label has been uneven across different product/service groups. For example, there has been a strong uptake of the Blue Angel for low-solvent paints, recycled paper and office equipment, but a relatively low adoption rate for televisions and large household appliances (Jordan et al., 2004: 166).

In a survey in 2008, almost 80 per cent of German consumers stated that they know the Blue Angel while 40 per cent claimed that they look for the eco-label when shopping (UBA, 2008: 2). By 2011 the number of German consumers who knew the Blue Angel scheme had declined moderately to 76 per cent (Blauer Engel, 2011). There are however significant age, gender and educational differences. While a clear majority of German consumers between 40 to 60 years old take into account the Blue Angel when making purchasing decisions the national eco-label is much less widely recognised by younger Germans who pay less attention to it when purchasing products and services. Moreover, women are more aware of the Blue Angel than men. Highly educated Germans also pay more attention to the Blue Angel than poorly educated Germans.

The German government tried to use the 30th anniversary of the Blue Angel in 2008 to raise public awareness for the scheme amongst younger Germans in particular. It incorporated the Blue Angel scheme into its climate change initiative (UBA, 2010b: 1). By late 2010 more than 40 product groups had been agreed for the Blue Angel for products with a reduced impact on the earth's climate; an additional 60 product groups were earmarked for 2011 (UBA, 2010).

Blue Angel labelled products/services will normally have to comply with the best available technology (BAT) principle which fits well the dominant Germany policy style (see Chapter 3). While this arguably constitutes an important underlying reason for its success, the uptake of the Blue Angel eco-label scheme was highly dependent on consumer support (Jordan et al., 2004). The media (especially the specialised and local media) as well as consumer and environment NGOs have been significant in raising the profile of the Blue Angel (Interviews, 2002). Both consumer and environmental groups strongly defended the scheme's transparency and independence from undue business influence while the federal government has spent only moderate amounts of money on promotion campaigns for the Blue Angel eco-label scheme. Another reason for the success of the Blue Angel is arguably the simplicity of its message to consumers although this has also been a source of criticism. The main reason for awarding the Blue Angel for a particular product/ service is listed at the bottom of the logo which states 'environmentally friendly because ...' or, more recently, 'climate friendly because ...'.

Finally market competition can explain some of the success of the Blue Angel scheme. An Environment Agency (UBA, 1998: 14) survey found that 92 per cent of companies awarded the Blue Angel were facing an equivalent product of a competitor which had also gained the eco-label. The survey also suggested that medium and large-sized companies applied for the Blue Angel partly due to concerns about losing their market share to competitors who carry the label. Concern about competition also motivated foreign companies to pursue the eco-label, given the attractiveness of the large German market of more than 80 million people. In 2001, foreign companies formed 16 per cent of the share of eco-labels although this belies the reality where in practice roughly one third of all eco-labelled products have foreign origins (Jordan et al., 2004). The EU eco-label scheme is not widely known in Germany, as it is largely overshadowed by the Blue Angel scheme.

Austria: Early Eco-label Follower

Austria set up its national eco-label scheme *(Das österreichische Umweltzeichen)* in 1990. The Austrian Environmental Minister, Marilies Flemming, proposed it at a time of increased public environmental awareness and rising electoral support for the Green Party (Interviews, 2002; Schwar, 1999). The German Blue Angel served as a model for the Austrian eco-label scheme. At first sight, the adoption of the Austrian eco-label looks like a clear example of policy instrument transfer driven by particular national contextual features (for example, rising public environmental awareness and the emergence of the Green Party as a significant player). However, Austrian policy-makers 'tried not to repeat some of the shortcomings of the Blue Angel' scheme (Interview, 2002). Consequently the Austrian eco-label differs significantly with respect to the German Blue Angel scheme. In the terminology used by Bulmer and Padgett (2005) (see Chapter 2), the transfer of the eco-label to Austria falls between the policy transfer synthesis and influence categories, while being closer to the influence pole.

The organisational arrangements, for example, differ, reflecting the institutional core features of the Austrian political system. The Austrian Environment Ministry awards the eco-label, as opposed to the RAL in Germany. Moreover, a wider number of institutions are included in the

84   *Environmental governance in Europe*

Austrian eco-label scheme: the Economics Ministry, the Association for Consumer Information *(Verein für Konsumenteninformation* – VKI, which is a private technical institute), the Eco-label Committee (or *Beirat Umweltzeichen)* and various working groups providing technical expertise (Jordan et al., 2004: 167). The Austrian eco-label is only awarded for one year (as opposed to three for the German Blue Angel), and it restricts foreign companies from applying unless they have an office in the EU or a European Free Trade Agreement (EFTA) country (Schwar, 1999).

The key actors in governing the Austrian eco-label scheme are the Environment Ministry and the VKI. The Eco-label Committee, which designates the product/service groups and produces general guidelines, consists of different stakeholders although the government remains a crucial actor. The VKI sets up special working groups to develop the award criteria, which are valid for three years. The Austrian eco-label uses a relatively strict life-cycle analysis (BMLFUW, 2000: 2). Its product criteria also require compliance with existing environmental, health and safety regulations, many of which stipulate the BAT (see Chapter 3).

The main aim of the Austrian eco-label scheme is to provide consumers with more reliable information about the environmental impact of products and services (BMLFUW, 2000: 2). Although the symbol on the Austrian eco-label was created by the well-known Austrian artist Friedensreich Hundertwasser, it has remained a label which was not highly recognised among consumers. In order to increase its uptake, several innovations have been adopted including eco-labels for tourism, schools and other educational institutions (Interview, 2011). The Austrian eco-label's applicability for tourism reflects both the importance of this sector for the Austria economy and the vulnerability of the Alpine ecology. The highest number of Austrian eco-labels can be found in the product categories: printing, wood burners, and renewable energy (Interview, 2011). In mid-2011, 1667 products, 219 tourism businesses and 85 schools were allowed to use the Austrian eco-label (Written Communication 9 November 2011).

For Ministry officials, the eco-label 'is not considered as a milestone of Austrian environmental policy', but merely 'a step in the right direction' (Interview, 2001). The Environment Ministry clearly views the Austrian eco-label as an important supplementary, rather than decisive, policy instrument.

The Austrian government tried to boost public recognition of the national eco-label scheme through, for example, awareness raising campaigns and public procurement. The Austrian eco-label has nevertheless had less market impact than the Blue Angel scheme. The relatively small size of the domestic market and Austria's export dependency, have led to a small number of foreign company applications. The importance of the large German market for Austrian companies has triggered limited harmonisation of some product and service criteria between the Austrian eco-label and the German Blue Angel scheme (Interview, 2011). Amongst the Austrian population the EU eco-label scheme has a significantly lower level of recognition then the national eco-label scheme.

European Union: Late Eco-label Follower

The EU eco-label was established a few months after the Austrian eco-label scheme. It was inspired by the German Blue Angel scheme (Wright, 2000: 97). At the same time, there was a wider European dynamic operating beyond mere policy instrument diffusion. There was an (ideational) recognition amongst EU policy actors that moral suasion policy instruments can be useful tools in environmental policy. In particular the Fifth EAP (1992–2002) recognised the need to consider market-based instruments and voluntary instruments which involve stakeholder participation.

Perhaps even more significantly, the Commission perceived a need to harmonise the increasing variety of competing national eco-labels which potentially could distort the Single European Market (Wright, 2000: 98). The EU also responded to increasing concerns that some private (Type II) eco-labels were misleading consumers (Wright, 2000: 98).

The history of the EU eco-label was troubled from the start. The Commission proposed the label in 1991 (CEC, 1991). There was disagreement whether the EU eco-label scheme should be centralised within and coordinated by the Commission. The EP pushed for a wider involvement of stakeholders at all stages of the scheme (Wright, 2000: 98) while defending the co-existence of the EU and national eco-label schemes.

The EU eco-label scheme is a voluntary scheme which promotes products and services that are less damaging to the environment compared to functionally equivalent products/services (CEC, 2004; Eiderström, 1998, Erskine and Lyndhurst, 1996). It is awarded for a period of up to three years, according to criteria based on life-cycle analysis. Applications for the EU eco-label must be submitted to the member state Competent Body before consideration by an Advisory Committee. The Committee consists of officials from the Competent Bodies which are chaired by the Commission. The Advisory Committee determines the product groups and criteria for which (the Competent Bodies in) lead countries undertake much of the preparatory work. There is also a

86 *Environmental governance in Europe*

Consultation Forum for stakeholders although NGOs argue that it is often circumvented by industry groups which directly lobby the Commission (Eiderström, 1998; EEB, 1998).

Between 1992–95, the EU eco-label was awarded to only two companies (OECD, 1997: 36). In 2000, there were merely 41 EU eco-label awards across 15 member states (in contrast to almost 4000 eco-labels awarded under the German Blue Angel scheme). Following a reform in 2000, the number of EU eco-labels rose moderately to 184 by May 2004. However, the Blue Angel and the Nordic Swan schemes still dwarfed these numbers.

Even member states lacking their own national eco-label (such as the UK and Ireland) have shown a very low take up rate for the EU eco-label. In early 2004, the UK had only three EU eco-labels while Ireland had none. In member states with well-established national eco-label schemes there is a widespread public perception that the national scheme is significantly more stringent although this is no longer the case for all products/services that are eligible for the EU eco-label (Interviews, 2001 and 2011). In Germany, research has shown a lack of awareness of the EU eco-label; those who do know it consider it inferior to Blue Angel (IÖW, 1999; UBA, 1996, 1998a). The low consumer recognition makes firms reluctant to apply for the EU eco-label, particularly as they find it costly, unwieldy, and lacking in transparency (IÖW, 1999).

In early 2004, companies from Italy (49), France (35) and Denmark (32) had received by far the highest number of EU eco-labels (see Table 4.1). Norway and Switzerland, members of the European Economic Area but not the EU, also have some EU eco-labels. Interestingly, Australia, South Africa, South Korea and China as well as Hong Kong have also made use of the EU eco-label (Written Communication, Commission Official, 2004).

Large and/or export-oriented companies often express a preference for the EU (or a global) eco-label scheme while small and medium-sized companies tend to prefer national eco-labels (Jordan et al., 2003c: 174). Those companies which apply successfully for product groups for which no EU eco-label has yet been awarded have the difficult task of making the label known to consumers if they want to reap the economic benefits. On the other hand, the presence of the EU eco-label scheme is often used as a benchmark by companies who do not actually apply the label (Interview, UK Official, 2001).

Governing by informational means

Table 4.1   Number of EU eco-label licences 1995–2011

Year	Total number	Leading member states	Product groups	Leading product groups
2011	1152	Italy (359), France (244), Spain (83)	26	Tourist accommodation services (438), all-purpose and sanitary cleaners (160) and indoor and outdoor paints (96)
2002	127	France (27), Italy (27), Denmark (26)	n/a	Textile products (37), indoor paints/varnishes (27); soil improvers (10)
2001	95	France (20), Denmark (19), Italy (14)	n/a	n/a
2000	53	n/a	n/a	n/a
1995	2	n/a	n/a	n/a

Sources: CEC (2004), OECD (1997) and written communications in 2004 and 2011.

Table 4.1 shows that, in 2011, most EU eco-label licences were awarded for tourist accommodation services (438), all-purpose and sanitary cleaners (160) and indoor and outdoor paints (96). In 2011 no licences had yet been awarded in four of the 26 product groups for the EU eco-label. It was extremely difficult to get the white goods sector (in other words, large household appliances such as washing machines and fridges) to apply for the EU eco-label (or national eco-label schemes) although many of its products carry energy efficiency labels. The Commission and – to a lesser degree – member states campaigned hard before one dishwasher and two refrigerator companies were awarded the first EU eco-labels in 2004.

Beyond the competition with extant national (and multi-national) eco-labels, the EU eco-label suffered from inherent problems. Various actors perceived it to have a cumbersome and non-transparent decision-making process (Eiderström, 1998; Erskine and Lyndhurst, 1996; Herrup, 1999; Karl and Owat, 1999; Nadai, 1999). Its fees were relatively high compared to national schemes. There was also opposition from some importers which claimed that the EU eco-label scheme breached WTO rules (Herrup, 1999; Vogel, 1998).

Although the reform of the EU eco-label scheme was scheduled for 1997, its revision was only completed in 2000 because of serious differences between the Commission, Council and EP. The Commission wanted to strengthen the supranational elements of the EU eco-label and favoured the abolition of national eco-label schemes. However, the Council (and especially member states which had in place well-functioning national eco-labels) insisted on the co-existence of EU and member state eco-label schemes. The EP backed the latter position, having initially favoured a single EU eco-label.

The revised EU eco-label scheme established an Eco-labelling Board composed of the national Competent Bodies. It allowed for greater consumer and environmental group involvement and linked the EU eco-label to EMAS by granting a discount to small businesses which had already undergone an environmental audit.

In 2004, the Commission decided to launch an in-depth review of the ailing EU eco-label and EMAS schemes because of 'growing concern ... at a high political level within the Commission that both schemes are losing their way' *(ENDS Europe Daily*, 10 February, 2004). The 2006 report acknowledged problems for both schemes while drawing up the following three scenarios (Consortium (EVER) 2005): (1) maintaining the status quo; (2) a dismantling of both schemes; and (3) their enhancement through a menu of incentives and measures. The 2006 report raised the possibility of merging the EU eco-label and EMAS schemes to increase viability. However, Commission officials never seriously considered this option (Interview, 2006). Instead the Commission concluded that the EU eco-label made an important contribution. Most users thought it improved performance, and non-users treated it as a benchmark (see Consortium (EVER), 2005: 12). Table 4.1 shows that the reforms significantly increased the number of EU eco-label licence takers. In 2001 only 95 EU eco-label licences had been awarded while ten years later the number of licences had shot up to 1152. However, the number of EU eco-label licences awarded to products and services from 27 EU member states and seven non-EU states (namely, the EFTA countries Norway and Switzerland as well as Australia, South Africa, South Korea, China and Hong Kong) are still dwarfed by the number of licences awarded under the Blue Angel scheme (and the Nordic Swan).

The reform of the EU eco-label brought about a more transparent and speedier decision-making process as well as lower fees. Table 4.1 shows how it triggered a significant uptake of EU eco-label licences. The 2011 figures demonstrate that German companies held 71, Austrian 48, Dutch 46 and British 34 EU eco-label licences. This amounted to a moderate increase in the number of licences for our four case countries; however, it showed a differentiated uptake, with the UK making the least use of the EU eco-label despite lacking a national eco-label scheme.

Governing by informational means 89

In terms of product groups, there was a striking increase in the number of EU eco-label licences for tourist accommodation services (to 436) and all-purpose and sanitary cleaners (160) while laptops (2) and personal computers (3) have remained at the bottom of the EU eco-label licences league table (CEU, 2011a).

Table 4.2 EU eco-label licences and leading product groups in 2010

Country	Italy	France	Spain	Germany	Austria	UK	The Netherlands
Eco-label licences	331	203	71	63	45	31	25
Leading product group	Tourist accommo- dation services	Cleaners	Textiles	Paints and varnishes	Soap and shampoo	Tissue paper	TVs
Number of labels	392	126	90	87	29	33	6

Source: Adapted from CEU (2010a).

Table 4.2 lists the number of EU eco-label licences for the three EU eco-label leaders (Italy, France and Spain) as well as Germany, Austria, the Netherlands and the UK. It shows that the leading product group is different in all of these seven member states. The reform of the EU eco-label has therefore not changed national preferences in terms of the product groups for which businesses apply. The Commission's launch of a proposal for an integrated product policy was meant to preserve the embattled EU eco-label (CEC, 2001d). In the late 2000s the Commission conceded that the EU eco-label scheme suffered from: (1) low awareness and uneven geographic uptake; (2) an insufficient number of product categories; (3) cumbersome procedures and organisational structures; (4) a widespread perception that the fees from the label are a barrier; and (5) a lack of perceived public purchasing benefits (CEC, 2007b: 3–4).

The Netherlands: Eco-label Follower

The Dutch only created a national eco-label scheme, or Milieukeur, in 1992. The fact that the Dutch economy is both small and open to international competition, and the strong presence of certain international corporations with their own branding agenda, gave Dutch actors less incentive to create a scheme. The diverging outlooks of the different leaders of the People's Party for Freedom and Democracy (VVD), who were in charge of the Environment Ministry in the 1980s, help to explain both the initial reluctance and the later change of thinking. Although the Environment Minister Winsemius (VVD) decided that no national eco-label was necessary, his ministerial successor, Nijpels (VVD), changed the government's position in 1989 (Zito et al., 2003: 171). In 1989 eco-labels presented the government with a chance to push further in the direction of green instruments. Dutch environmental groups also pushed for the creation of the national eco-label, with its focus on motivating 'the Dutch consumer ... and to create a "green consciousness"' (Interview, VROM Official, 2001). The Dutch Parliament supported this move, pressing for a national eco-label scheme to be included in the 1989 NEPP.

The Dutch eco-label scheme is voluntary and organised under private law. The key policy actors are the Ministry and the foundation created to operate the system, the *Stichting Milieukeur.* The various societal actors all have a place and voting rights in the foundation's committee structure. Initially NGOs and businesses were fully involved in the Board of Experts, but NGO discomfort with having to make product decisions led to an organisational reform. This reform involved a change of thinking leading to these groups shifting participation to the overall controlling Board for the Foundation (Interview, VROM official, 2002). Independent organisations act as the actual certifying organisations (Communication, Stichting Milieukeur Official, 2002).

The late appearance of the Dutch eco-label scheme suggests some policy instrument transfer from Germany and the Nordic countries, but this was only a transfer of the general idea. The Blue Angel and Nordic Swan inspired the adoption of a Dutch eco-label scheme, which, however, did not copy the rules of any other particular national eco-label scheme. The Dutch policy actors clearly did reflect upon the existing criteria found in the EU eco-label and national labels in developing the Dutch label (Interview, VROM Official, 2001; Communication, Stichting Milieukeur Official, 2002). As is the case for the Austrian and to some extent the German eco-label scheme, the Dutch scheme emphasises lifecycle analysis.

The Dutch have provided some innovative steps, such as creating foodstuff criteria in 1995. A survey had found this consumer area to have substantial public interest (Interview, VROM Official, 2002). The interest in foodstuffs also reflects the importance of Dutch food and flower export market (Zito et al., 2003; Communication with Stichting Milieukeur Official, 2002). This policy instrument transfer reflects mainly inspiration with some elements of synthesis, but not emulation.

Certainly when compared to the Blue Angel and even the Austrian scheme, the Dutch eco-label scheme has not witnessed a large take-up rate. Indeed, Dutch firms that export to Germany have applied to the Blue Angel label in order to protect export market access (Jordan et al., 2003c: 171). Larger companies, which play a fundament role in the Dutch export-oriented economy, did not embrace the idea of rival national eco-labels which can create difficulties for developing brand marketing for different markets (Interview, VROM Official, 2002). Only the small and niche firms have had a significant incentive to participate in the Dutch eco-label scheme which explains the relatively small market share, which in turn contributed to and reinforced the lack of awareness among consumers. The absence of a critical mass of labelled products leads to a vicious cycle: companies have poor incentives to act while consumers react by showing little interest in the national eco-label scheme.

Despite these initial problems, the Dutch Environment Ministry continued to support the domestic eco-label as one of a mix of policy instruments. Furthermore, it believed that the eco-label criteria established in the individual product categories also shaped the actions of non-participating firms. Apart from the Environment Ministry, the *Milieukeur* lacked strong backers that could have given the domestic eco-label a much stronger role in Dutch environmental governance.

In 2004, the Netherlands held only five EU eco-label licences; by 2011 the figure had risen to 46 licences (see Table 4.2). However, the Dutch public and corporate interest in eco-labels remained low. The Dutch government's support for the strengthening of the EU eco-label and its commitment to using eco-label schemes in harness with other policy instruments did not bring about any significant uptake in either the domestic or EU eco-label schemes by Dutch companies in the 2010s. The Dutch government has also sought to induce better co-ordination between the EU and national eco-label schemes with the aim to enhance their mutual impact. This was particularly the case when the EU eco-label contained comparatively stringent criteria for certain products (such as light bulbs).

However, in a clear admission of the weakness of the Dutch eco-label (as well as the EU scheme), the *Stichting Milieukeur* agreed on the marketing of products using the Nordic Swan label (with over 600 product types) in the Netherlands (Stichting Milieukeur, 2011; *ENDS Europe Daily*, 2 March 2006). By 2011 some growth, however, had been seen in both the use of the Dutch and EU eco-labels. In 2011 there were 30 certified product groups and 611 businesses operating with the *Milieukeurcertificaat*; this includes four new certification systems known as 'barometers', which operate a colour rating scheme (Stichting Milieukeur, 2011). Policy research reveals that only 4 per cent of Dutch consumers make a conscious decision to buy sustainable products, but since 2009 there has been a certification push by certain types of retailers, particularly in the agribusiness, ENGOs, and the Dutch national and local government's Green Public Procurement initiative (Communication, SMK Official, 2011).

United Kingdom: Eco-label Laggard

The UK does not have a national eco-label scheme and participates instead in the EU eco-label scheme. The Environment Ministry and the Department for Trade and Industry (DTI) published a joint discussion paper on eco-labelling in 1989 (Haigh, 2011). However, while both ministries favoured the establishment of an EU-wide eco-label, the House of Lords recommended a national eco-label in addition to an EU eco-label scheme. Following a consultation exercise, the UK government indicated its willingness at least to consider the setting up of a national scheme based on a life-cycle assessment approach.

These plans for a domestic UK eco-label scheme were quickly overtaken by the development of the EU eco-label scheme which had the strong support of the UK government. While the EU eco-label scheme was being negotiated, 'it was evident that details of the UK's scheme would have to wait until the EC regulation was agreed' (Haigh, 2011: 11.7). No national UK eco-label scheme was ever established, although the Environment Ministry and an advisory group called NAGEL conducted some preparatory work. NAGEL was eventually disbanded and, in 1992, replaced by an Eco-labelling Board, which became the UK's competent body for the EU's eco-label scheme. However, in 2001 the Environment Ministry took over the role of competent body (Haigh, 2011: 11.7).

The UK government remained adamant that no additional benefit would be gained from establishing rival eco-label schemes. It therefore preferred the setting up of the EU eco-label scheme although its interest in eco-labelling declined, after a 1998 review showed that 'people were not taking up the EU eco-label' (Interview, DEFRA Official, 2002). Four years later, the Environment Ministry (DEFRA, 2002) concluded that 'developments since 1992 (when the EU label was established) show that eco-labeling cannot by itself transform the environmental behavior of industry and consumers, or meet their needs, in the way that was hoped when the (EU) scheme was set up.'

Governing by informational means 93

The UK government has continued offering advice to businesses and consumers on green claims and labels (DEFRA, 2002). However, it strongly supported the use of EMAS (see the following) and a much broader, integrated product policy approach to greening production (Zito and Egan, 1998) rather than eco-labels. This stance appears to fit the preferences of the UK's industry well. Many large businesses in Britain have been opposed to government and EU supported eco-labels and instead prefer self-declaratory schemes such as the 'fair trade' and 'red tractor' (farm assurance) labels (Jordan et al., 2003c: 172). Large retailers (for example, Sainsbury's and Tesco) often argue that their brand name is a sufficient guarantor of quality and that competing labels would simply confuse shoppers. Unsurprisingly, UK companies have failed to promote enthusiastically the EU eco-label. Consequently, UK consumers are largely oblivious to the EU eco-label's very existence even though there is no competing national scheme. The 2011 data in Table 4.1 show a mere 34 UK licences under the EU eco-label scheme.

The UK Environment Ministry claims to be keen to encourage the growth of the EU eco-label (DEFRA, 2011). However, its promotion of the EU eco-label has been very low-key despite the creation of a UK eco-label delivery team (in Glasgow) and an eco-label helpline. Rather than strongly promoting the EU eco-label scheme, the UK government has instead primarily adopted an advisory role. The Environment Ministry produced, for example, the Green Claims Guidance which 'provides advice to business for clear, accurate, relevant and substantiated environmental claims on products, services or in marketing and advertising' (DEFRA, 2011).

On the one hand the UK's limited eco-label experience fits with its reactive national environmental regulatory style and preference for 'trial-and-error' driven policy-making. It also reflects the preferences of UK businesses, which have shown little support for the EU eco-label scheme and even less for a national eco-label scheme. Instead they have favoured company level eco-label schemes and self-declaratory schemes. The UK government considered setting up a national eco-label scheme, but abandoned its efforts with the EU eco-label's establishment. The UK tendency has been to support policy instruments with a larger international market focus. Accordingly, the UK government initially supported the EU eco-label scheme but then gave preference to EMAS and integrated product policy as arguably larger scale initiatives.

94   *Environmental governance in Europe*

ENVIRONMENT MANAGEMENT SCHEMES

As mentioned above, eco-label schemes and EMSs share certain common governance features, notably: non-coercive engagement of different societal actors, environmental information as a potential competitive market advantage and emphasis on continuous environmental improvement. Market share is an important (although not the only) factor to indicate success for both. After discussing the pioneering British Standard (BS) 7750, Chapter 4 concentrates on the EU's EMAS and the impact of the similar scheme which the ISO developed, namely ISO 14001.

United Kingdom: Environment Management Scheme Pioneer

EMSs in the UK co-evolved with EU regulation on environmental self-auditing. The EU EMAS scheme was in fact developed in parallel with the British Standard Institute's (BSI) BS 7750 voluntary standard for environmental management schemes. At crucial stages the UK has shaped EMAS.

In March 1992, the BSI published the draft standard BS 7750, which set requirements for the development, implementation and maintenance of EMSs within companies, with the purpose of ensuring compliance with environmental policy objectives (Northern Ireland Environment Agency, 2009). The BSI is the oldest and largest national standards institute and was an important pioneer in management systems: the BS 5750 was the world's first certifiable management system covering internal systems (Kollman and Prakash, 2002: 52). Eventually published in final form in February 1994, BS 7750 was itself an extension of the popular BS 5750 standard.

The impact of the BS 7750, particularly in the UK but also the rest of Europe, can be explained by the intensive marketing effort the BSI makes to promote its technical and management standards. With the support of the Environment Ministry, the BSI was able to carry out an extensive pilot program of BS 7750 in the UK that helped familiarise companies as well as generate strong publicity amongst interested actors (Kollman and Prakash, 2002: 53).

The move to rapidly launch BS 7750 is a striking example of the UK seeking a 'first mover' competitive advantage (Zito and Egan, 1998: 101–2; Héritier, Knill, and Mingers, 1996). The British discussion of BS 7750 occurred just as the EU was developing its own instrument. Both BSI and British firms saw a rise in the prominence of EMSs and hoped to be part of a standard that helped define the Single European Market and international market from the start.

Following the adoption of EMAS I, there was some subsequent development of BS 7750 to align it with the EU's EMS. Both the BSI and the EU wanted to prevent the two schemes from becoming rivals. However in the meantime the ISO became an important player. In 1996, the ISO launched its own 14001 standard, which was based essentially on the BS 7750 although less stringent (Kollman and Prakash, 2002: 52). These instruments, and the British response to them, are discussed in the next section.

The ISO adoption of its 14001 standard reflected the wish to enhance trade at a time of growing environmental awareness, as reflected, for example, in the UN 1992 Rio Earth Summit. The ISO formed a strategic Advisor Group on the Environment in 1991 to explore the potential of EMSs; the recommendations of this group instigated the 1993 creation of the Technical Committee TC 207 on Environmental Management (Quality Network, 1997; Holmes, 1995). This Committee had the role and aim of creating international standards that were as compatible as possible with established national standards (notably BS 7750).

European Union: Environmental Management Scheme Follower

EMAS exemplifies an instrument pushed by member states and international concerns over competitiveness. The Fifth EAP detailed how the Commission was seeking to develop voluntary mechanisms that would bring various societal stakeholders into the environment standard setting process.

Some Commission officials also feared that the Single European Market might be affected by rival national EMSs (Zito and Egan, 1998). By 1993, Ireland (IS 310), Spain and France had established national EMSs in addition to the BS 7750 (Taschner, 1998: 222). The UK acted as a pioneer and leader through the BSI's standards. Accordingly, Wenk (2005: 5) calls the BS 7750 the 'mother of EMAS'. The UK sought to upload at least elements of its domestic EMS to the EU level (Héritier et al., 1996: 253–62). One German official characterised the EMAS I decision-making process in the following way: 'behind every door in Brussels there seemed to be a Brit' (Interview, 2002). The change in the title of the proposal, from eco-audit to eco-management and audit reflects partly the influence of the British-backed approach (Zito and Egan, 1998: 111–2). The German national representatives, fearing the substantial adjustment that such a British-oriented scheme would require of German firms and possessing their own strong national standards traditions (*Deutsche Industrienorm* – DIN), lobbied hard for changes which reflected German preferences.

96   *Environmental governance in Europe*

The reaction of European industrial associations (within a substantial consultation process) was relatively negative, reflecting concerns with some of the stricter elements of the proposed EU eco-audit standards. Although EMAS I reflected many of the core characteristics of the BS 7750, it also incorporated proposals from other member states (such as Germany), which meant that the EU standard became stricter than the British standard which it partly emulated. Compared to BS 7750, EMAS has a stronger requirement to self-audit and continually reduce the environmental impact. It also has a requirement that reviews should trigger a revision of the environmental targets, and the release of a wider range of information about the environmental performance (Wenk, 1995: 6–7).

EU and UK officials largely failed to influence decisively the parallel negotiations and instrument construction in the ISO, which led to the 1996 adoption of the less ambitious ISO 14001. Compared to EMAS I, ISO 14001 was much less stringent in terms of, for example, its requirements for environmental statements and for performance improvements (see Taschner, 1998). The importance of the BS 7750 again figures here; the ISO was following the lead of the pioneering BSI instrument (rather than EMAS I). Significantly, many European and international businesses later opted for the less rigorous international standard.

In 2001, the EU revised EMAS I to: (1) widen its scope to any organisation (including public authorities, schools and NGOs); (2) address significant indirect environmental effects; (3) put greater emphasis on public reporting; and, (4) adopt a new logo (Haigh, 2012). This revised EMAS II reflected the fierce competition which ISO 14001 posed for EMAS I. One aim of the 2001 revision was to make EMAS II more easily compatible with the ISO 14001 without, however, watering down its more stringent requirements.

The 2001 revision became operational in 2004. It made it possible for public organisations (in addition to private companies) to participate in EMAS which now includes all economic sectors. In Germany, the Environment Agency became the first public authority to have successfully registered for EMAS. In 1997, a Commission Decision (97/265/EC) had already formally recognised the ISO's 14001 as fulfilling part of the EMAS requirements for industrial sites. This recognition, together with the 2001 revision, temporarily breathed new life into the EU's EMS. Although the EU implemented these changes, EMAS II continued to decline in terms of uptake in comparison to its international cousin. Although the EU promoted the fact that EMAS I and II were more environmentally sound, ISO 14001 continued to outstrip EMAS even in Europe (see Tables 4.3 and 4.4). Table 4.3 charts the comparative growth of EMAS certifications versus those of 14001 for the four case countries.

Governing by informational means 97

Table 4.3 Organisations registered with EMAS compared to ISO 14001 certifications

	EMAS 1997 No. of org.[1]	ISO 1997 No. of org.	EMAS 2005 No. of org.	EMAS 2005 No. of sites	ISO 2005 No. of org.	EMAS 2010 No. of org.	EMAS 2010 No. of sites	ISO 2007 No. of org.
Austria	37	30	347	n/a	550	250	616	550
Germany	518	100	2049	n/a	4440	1408	1890	5800
The Netherlands	10	n/a	27	n/a	1073	6	6	1132
UK	24	150	63	n/a	6523	61	328	5400
EU total	n/a	n/a	3093	4137	19 998	4347	7429	45 946

Source: Adapted from Jordan, Wurzel and Zito (2007) and http://ec.europa.eu/environment/emas/documents/articles_en.htm (accessed 26.10.2010).

Note: [1] The European Commission started to collect data on EMAS registered sites (in addition to organisations) only from 2004 onwards.

Table 4.4 adds the per capita figures for EMAS uptake by organisations, which lead to a different ranking. The per capita figures underline the leadership of Austrian and German companies in contrast to the relatively low registration in the Netherlands and UK. Ironically Austria and Germany had initially resisted the adoption of EMAS which was strongly pushed by the UK as explained above. Table 4.4 also details the other top ten countries to provide a broader comparative perspective.

European environmental and consumer groups remained highly critical about the revised EMAS II scheme; they demanded instead 'a substantive reform' which should lead either to 'a transformation into an eco-label for companies or a true system of excellence' (ANEC, 2007: 1). European environmental and consumer groups highlighted, in particular, the 'lack of performance requirements and the absence of a mandatory set of comparable performance indicators which would allow for a differentiation between good and bad performers' (ANEC, 2007: 1).

The 2006 review shows that the Commission was committed to improving EMAS rather than scrap the EU's EMS. DG Environment has contemplated various ideas to improve the uptake of EMAS, including linking the scheme with the Integrated Pollution Prevention and Control (IPPC) Directive. In 2007, the Commission started the consultation

98 — Environmental governance in Europe

Table 4.4 — Ranking order EMAS uptake in EU member states

Ranking order for the number of EMAS registered organisations per million inhabitants in 2010	Ranking order for the total number of EMAS registered organisations in 2010
(1) Austria: 30.48	(1) Germany: 1408
(4) Germany: 16.91	(4) Austria: 250
(20) UK: 1.04	(9) UK: 61
(23) The Netherlands: 0.43	(17) The Netherlands: 6
The other leading member states[*]: (2) Spain: 25.1; (3) Denmark: 42.9; (5) Italy: 16.3; (6) Sweden: 8.2; (7) Portugal: 7.9; (8) Cyprus: 6.3; (9) Greece: 6.2; (10) Finland: 4.9	The other leading member states: (2) Spain: 1227; (3) Italy: 1025; (5) Denmark: 91; (6) Portugal: 76; (7) Sweden: 75; (8) Greece: 67; (10) Belgium: 50

Source: Adapted from /ec.europa.eu/environment/emas/documents/articles_en.htm (accessed 26.10.2010).

Note: [*] The figures are rounded.

process for the EMAS II reform. In November 2009 the EP and Council adopted Regulation 1221/2009, enabling EMAS III to enter into force on 11 January 2010. EMAS III requires eco-audited organisations to produce an environmental statement and report against a set of core indicators including energy efficiency, emissions, water, waste and biodiversity; they must also comply with applicable environmental laws. The new regulation brought about one single EMAS logo that can be used by all certified organisations which are, however, precluded from using it on their products and/or their packaging to avoid any possible confusion with the EU eco-label scheme. Importantly ISO 14001 is accepted as partial fulfilment of EMAS III. However, the latter requires compliance with additional requirements including environmental legal compliance, a verification of the environmental management scheme, continuous improvement of environmental performance and public reporting as well as participation.

In 2007 there were 5301 EMAS-registered organisations compared to over 45 000 ISO 14001 certified organisations (see Table 4.3). An increasing number of firms in Germany, Austria, the UK and the Netherlands have shown a preference for ISO 14001 over EMAS, leading the Commission to contemplate means of boosting incentives and allowing non-EU or EU-associated organisations to join. By 2005, the ISO's

14001 certifications substantially outstripped EMAS registrations even in Austria and Germany, which have had the highest number of registrations ever since EMAS I became operational in 1995.

Turning to the national pioneer's specific response to EMAS and ISO 14001, the UK initially supported both the EU's EMAS and ISO's 14001 (unsurprisingly given the BS 7750 influence in both the EMAS and ISO 14001). However, while ISO 14001, which closely resembled the BSI's EMS standards, has achieved a relatively high UK adoption rate, EMAS initially had a very low uptake amongst UK companies. One reason for this was that EMAS requirements significantly exceeded the BSI and/or ISO's demands. UK businesses also appear to prefer the global branding of the less ambitious ISO 14001.

Only 24 UK companies had registered for EMAS I two years after it had come into operation. By 2007, more than 360 UK companies participated in EMAS (see Table 4.4). However, by mid-2011, the number of UK companies registered for EMAS had dropped to 288 (CEU, 2011b). In some practical respects, the UK has been an enthusiastic implementer of EMAS, being the first EU state to extend EMAS to the manufacturing and non-industrial sectors, as well as to local government. The UK Environment Ministry sponsored attempts to encourage SMEs to register for EMAS have not, however, met with great success (Haigh, 2012).

Germany: From Laggard to Enthusiastic Adopter

Germany's initial resistance to EMAS was partly a reflection of the fact that national policy actors had been developing their own EMS vision (Zito and Egan, 1998). With the UK, Germany has one of the strongest standards institutional bodies and networks: the DIN, which develops norms and standards as a service to German industry, the state and society, represents German interests in European and international standards bodies. In keeping with the strong industrial associations found in Germany, there was a strong interest in protecting and promoting German priorities.

Strong initial opposition to EMAS could also be found amongst Environment Ministry and Environment Agency officials; they were concerned that the EU's procedural environmental measures might lead to a watering-down of German BAT-derived substantive standards (interviews, German officials, 2002 and 2010). German officials and firms were initially sceptical about self-regulatory EMSs (Lauber, 1997a, 1997b, 2003). The German government initially opposed the adoption of EMAS I in the Council negotiations (Kollman and Prakash, 2002: 51–2;

100   *Environmental governance in Europe*

Interviews, 2011). German businesses feared that EMAS would result in greater adaptation pressures and costs compared to rival firms in most other European countries, thus losing the competitive advantage. The BDI and German officials insisted that substantive measures of environmental performance had to be written into the EMAS regulation to prevent such a disadvantage. The German negotiators, facing the growing momentum behind the legislation, held out for the principle of economic viable application of best available technology (a somewhat weakened form of BAT), which became part of the ultimate compromise (Taschner, 1998: 220; Kollman and Prakash, 2002: 51–2). German policy-makers and firms were even more critical of the US influence on the international standard being created in the ISO. They saw the resulting ISO 14001 standard as far too lenient (Taschner, 1998: 222; Zito and Egan, 1998).

The implementation of EMAS I caused a heated debate in Germany about who should be responsible for accrediting the third party auditors and the registration of firms. Given the scheme's voluntary nature, industrial associations resisted having the Environment Agency act in both of these roles (Malek et al., 2001: 107–8). After a two year struggle, both sides agreed in 1995 that the regional chambers of commerce *(Industrie- und Handelskammern)* would serve as a registration body; and a private law company, the German Accreditation and Admission Association *(Deutsche Akkreditierungs- und Zulassungsgesellschaft für Umweltgutachter GmbH* – DAU) owned by the industry associations but overseen by a wide mixture of stakeholders (including NGOs, trade unions and government) would accredit the auditors. This compromise enshrined the role of industry associations, deploying the groups, together with their highly organised network of communication and resources, to implement EMAS. The associations also conducted promotional seminars and conferences, which received substantial attention from the trade and some mainstream media (Kollman and Prakash, 2002: 51–2). After the revision of EMAS I in 2001, the German government also spent significant resources to promote EMAS II. Well known German personalities from politics and other walks of life endorsed EMAS on the website of the German EMAS Advisory Board *(Umweltgutachterausschuß* –UGA) (UGA, 2007).

Despite the German government's initially strong resistance during the EMAS I adoption phase, German (and Austrian) companies soon recorded the highest number of EMAS registrations. In 1997, 518 German companies had registered for EMAS; ten years later there were almost 2000 sites in Germany registered with EMAS (see Table 4.4).

However, between 2005 and 2007 there has been a moderate decline of EMAS registered sites in Germany from 2049 to 1979. The decline of EMAS registrations has continued in Germany although at a slower pace. In 2011, 1903 sites were registered for EMAS in Germany. The main reason for the decline of EMAS registrations in Germany is that German firms increasingly found the ISO 14001 scheme more attractive.

Austria: From Laggard to Enthusiastic Adopter

Despite the Austrian government's initial resistance during the adoption phase of EMAS (see above), Austrian firms soon achieved the second highest number of EMAS registrations (see Tables 4.3 and 4.4). In 2005, about 70 per cent of all registered EMAS sites were in Austria and Germany. It was only in the late 2000s when Italy and Spain overtook Austria in terms of national totals for EMAS registration sites. However, Table 4.3 shows how Austria tops the EMAS registration per capita league table (see also BMLFUW, 2010: 5).

Clearly Austria transformed fairly speedily from an EMAS laggard into an enthusiastic follower, making wide use of this EMS. One important reason for this development is the Austrian government's strong support for EMAS once the scheme had been adopted on the EU level (Interviews, 2011). Another important reason was the Austrian companies' view that a voluntary EMS would benefit them given their compliance with a relatively high number of environmental laws (Interviews, 2002). Moreover, EMS seemed to fit well with the deregulation ambitions of many Austrian firms which had lobbied for soft voluntary environmental policy instruments.

As seen in Germany, the Austrian government invested substantial resources in promoting the EMAS instrument. The Austrian Environment Ministry underwent an EMAS in 2000. Despite these measures, EMAS has continued to suffer from low public recognition (Interview, 2011). It is therefore remarkable that Austrian firms have made wide use of EMAS. While in 1997, 37 Austrian companies had registered for EMAS I, there were 451 Austrian companies registered with EMAS II ten years later (see Table 4.3). There has also been a continued rise in EMAS registrations in Austria from 347 to 451 between 2005 and 2007. By mid-2011 EMAS registrations in Austria further rose to 653 sites (and 288 organisations).

Table 4.4 shows that, in 2007, there were only about 100 more ISO 14001 certifications compared to EMAS registrations in Austria. Importantly, Austria was the exception to the rule, with the ISO 14001 certifications stagnating between 2005 and 2007. However, in the late

102 · *Environmental governance in Europe*

2000s ISO 14001 also became more popular amongst Austrian firms. One Austrian Environment Ministry official (Interview, 2011) explained it as follows: 'ISO is well known in Japan. But no one knows EMAS'. While the Austrian Environment Ministry and NGOs have lobbied for ambitious EMAS revisions, Austrian industry lost some of its early enthusiasm for EMAS registration while showing increasing interest in ISO 14001 (Interviews, 2011).

The Netherlands: EMAS Laggard

The desire for a lessening of regulation in the 1980s led Dutch firms to become interested in EMSs, with the Confederation of Netherlands Industry and Employers (known as VNO-NCW) publishing a brochure outlining the methodology for such systems. As both government and industry sought to implement the National Environmental Plan, the focus on self-regulation induced the government to publish a 1989 memorandum on environmental management (Lulofs, 2000). The government also created a programme of finance to stimulate the environmental learning required to generate satisfactory instruments. The government document aimed to have industries adopting EMS by 1995 (van der Woerd, 1998). Given the Dutch economic position with its international firms, the focus has been on integrating the key international systems, namely BS 7750 at the start and then ISO 14001. Dutch firms have largely shunned EMAS as can be seen from their low number of registrations. In mid-2011 only seven sites and seven organisations were EMAS registered. The Netherlands therefore ranked only 17th in the EMAS league table of 27 EU member states (CEU, 2011b).

Dutch policy makers focused their efforts to implement the Council Regulation establishing EMAS I by co-ordinating its interpretation with that of ISO 14001, resulting in the accreditation for EMAS also giving the firm ISO 14001 accreditation. This has led to a more elaborate interpretation of ISO 14001 (Lulofs, 2000). The Dutch government created *Stichting Coordinatie Certificatie Milieuzorgsysteem* (SCCM) to implement and promote the EMAS regulation. In pushing EMAS, the government embedded the instrument with other environmental policy instruments: meeting both regulatory obligations and entering covenants were a minimum requirement of EMAS registration (Lulofs, 2000).

Table 4.3 demonstrates the enormous discrepancy between the uptake of ISO 14001 and EMAS in the Netherlands. Only 0.36 per cent of the over 6000 Dutch companies participated in EMAS in 2000 (Lulofs, 2000). Those few Dutch companies which opted for EMAS seemed to do so because of the profile of the environmental statement and their image with the government and the public. Nevertheless, even these firms note problems with EMAS: its small number of accredited firms, the marketing advantages of ISO 14001 with its greater international orientation, the lack of a substantial margin in improvement through EMAS, the fact that ISO 14001 is sufficient to ensure possible government co-operation and the relative neutrality of the Dutch government concerning EMAS and ISO 14001 (Lulofs, 2000). The Dutch government's neutrality is reflected in the lack of aggressive marketing of EMAS. In addition, many firms had greater familiarity with the ISO standard and its predecessor BS 7750 before EMAS came into practice. The bigger companies have not taken a lead in embracing EMAS, and smaller companies did not see the benefit of the extra work for little substantial visibility (*ENDS Europe Daily*, 24 March 1999).

In 2007, there were 1132 ISO 14001 certifications by Dutch companies which meant that the Netherlands ranked at number 21 in a world-wide survey of about 150 countries (Written Communication, UBA Official, 2007). In 2010, the Netherlands (with merely six EMAS registrations) was only ranked at number 17 out of the 27 member states (see Table 4.4). This put the Netherlands behind 2004 accession states, such as the Czech Republic with 26 registrations per one million inhabitants.

CONCLUSION

The different adoption patterns of eco-label schemes and EMAS in our five case jurisdictions alert us to the dangers of stereotyping particular jurisdictions as environmental leaders and laggards. The Netherlands, traditionally seen as an environmental pioneer, has a relatively poor uptake for its late-established national eco-label scheme. Dutch companies have also made very little use of the EMAS I-III schemes preferring instead the more lenient but global ISO 14001. The UK, partly due to its strong institutional presence in management standards as well as the focus of its corporations, has a very strong role in the defining of the EMS policy instrument in Europe and the global market, but has shown only a low uptake of the EU eco-label scheme while failing to adopt a national (Type I) eco-label scheme.

In contrast we see the pioneering role of the German national eco-label scheme, Blue Angel. Germany initially opposed the adoption of EMAS I but now has the highest number of EMAS registrations in the EU. However, since the 2000s, registrations from German companies for the ISO standard have increased significantly while there has been a moderate decline in registration for EMAS. Austria, which has the highest number of EMAS registrations per capita, is still bucking the trend. Austrian firms have continued to make wide use of EMAS registrations despite their recognition of the advantages of the globally more widely recognised ISO 14001. Although the Austrian and Dutch governments have created their own national eco-labels, these schemes have not achieved significant market presence and/or consumer recognition (in comparison to Germany's Blue Angel). This scenario also holds true for the EU eco-label.

Both IS0 14001 and EMAS (I-III) have a significant presence in European business management. However, the data in Table 4.3 reveal that the EU's reforms have not stemmed the relative decline (and in many cases absolute decline) in EMAS registrations compared to the ISO's 14001 certifications which have risen steeply in all five jurisdictions assessed in this book. By 2005, the ISO's 14001 certifications substantially outstripped EMAS registrations – even in Austria and Germany which have had the highest number of registrations ever since EMAS became operational in 1995. One interpretation is that a pronounced (although by no means uniform) shift is underway in Europe from a soft 'new' instrument (EMAS) to an even softer 'newer' instrument which is used worldwide (ISO 14001).

Nevertheless, such a shift to 'softer governance' does not give a complete picture of the different environmental policy instruments operating the environmental sector and the overall governance picture. Eco-labels play a relatively marginal role in the UK and the Netherlands, and to some extent Austria. Even in Germany there is no issue of them displacing the more traditional government instruments (see also Chapter 8). EMAS (I-III) certification is high in both Germany and Austria although ISO 14001 registrations have increasingly become more popular also in these two EU member states. Dutch firms have more strongly pursued the international EMS in line with their export concerns within the global market; however, as Chapter 5 shows, this has not led to a discarding of other relatively 'soft' instruments (such as the so-called covenants which constitute the Dutch version of voluntary instruments and are widely used in the Netherlands). The issue of the possible hybridisation of policy instruments as well as the overall policy instrument mixes of different jurisdictions will be assessed in more detail in Chapter 8.

Turning to the theoretical arguments, there are examples of policy transfers which explain some of the nature and direction of policy instrument change. The clearest transfer is the EMS instrument: both the EU scheme and the ISO emulated to some degree the pioneering BS 7750, which can be seen as the progenitor in each case. Part of the policy

Governing by informational means 105

instrument transfer dynamic resulted from the nature of global competition with respect to management standards, with both the EU and ISO seeking to take the lead in creating the most attractive EMS. However, EMAS represents a compromise in which the British standard was changed to reflect the concerns of member states which wanted stricter elements. The ISO 14001 represents essentially a lowest common denominator emulation of the basic principles of the BSI standard. Thus neither EMAS nor ISO 14001 are pure examples of emulation, having strong synthetic characteristics reflecting how both the EU and ISO built consensus.

The EU, with fewer states and a higher proportion of environmentally concerned states, created the stricter EMAS (I-III). To some extent, the dynamic reflects an aspect not emphasised in Chapters 2 and 3, namely the nature of firms and the characteristics of the national market. Nevertheless, institutional dynamics do play an important role. The influential role which the UK played in the design phase of EMAS I and ISO 14001 is in keeping with the strong UK tradition of EMS innovation. Equally noteworthy is Germany, with its own strong legacy of relatively ambitious environmental standards derived from the BAT principle. Germany initially opposed the adoption of EMAS I and then fought for an EU EMS scheme which better reflected its own environmental priorities and regulatory traditions. The Dutch took into account the presence of other important instruments, most particularly the regulations in place as well as its national covenants, when using EMSs (see Chapter 5). The EU's EMS reflected the strong decision-making input of member states, particularly the UK and Germany, seeking to shape EMAS in a manner most appropriate for their enterprises.

Policy transfer and lesson drawing also triggered a significant dynamic in the creation of the various eco-label schemes discussed in Chapter 4. However, the dynamic is much closer to being a synthesis reflecting characteristics of national systems. Thus Germany pioneered the world's first successful national eco-label scheme. Austria, the EU and the Netherlands all borrowed the general idea of the eco-label for their own eco-label schemes; however this was very much a synthetic policy transfer in which policy learning played an important role. For example, the Austrian government emulated certain features of the German Blue Angel while it also tried to avoid some of its weaknesses. In other words, lesson drawing from both positive and negative experience in other countries was important during the adoption phase of the Austrian eco-label scheme. The EU eco-label was partly triggered by concerns about the potentially distorting effects on the single European market by competing national eco-label schemes.

The Netherlands is an eco-label and EMS late-comer. In the Netherlands policy transfer and lesson drawing played an important role for the adoption of informational instruments, but the Dutch eco-label very much reflects national concerns about environmental and market priorities that make it very different from the German pioneering eco-label scheme. By contrast, the UK failed to adopt its own national eco-label scheme and instead has relied on the EU eco-label. The UK favoured the use of EMS (and IPPC) to labelling – a labelling at odds with the preferences of large corporations (such as supermarkets) in the UK and their focus on their own corporate branding.

Having examined these two informational policy instruments, Chapter 5 examines one of the other key instruments associated with a 'soft' governance approach, namely voluntary agreements. Together with eco-labelling and EMS, voluntary agreements constitute instruments that the governance literature claims to be on the rise.

5. Governing by voluntary means

INTRODUCTION

Chapter 5 focuses on voluntary agreements (VAs), which constitute one of two sub-types of suasive policy instruments; Chapter 4 assessed the other sub-type, namely, informational instruments (specifically, EMSs and eco-label schemes). The latter give societal actors the choice to join a particular scheme. VAs involve a process of engendering voluntary commitments from societal actors (namely, primarily companies) which can 'opt out' of such agreements. The conventional governance perspective (see Chapters 1 and 2) expects a strong uptake of self-regulatory policy instruments (such as VAs) which rely on non-hierarchical self-steering mechanisms. As this chapter reveals, however, some VAs are adopted in 'the shadow of hierarchy' (Scharpf, 1994); this presupposes a certain degree of coerciveness that governmental actors exert on societal actors.

The next section of Chapter 5 explores definitional issues associated with VAs; it highlights the significance of competing perspectives and their meaning for understanding the governing effect of this particular policy instrument. Chapter 5 then tracks the chronology of VA adoption in our four case countries and the EU, highlighting the 'pioneers' and 'followers'. We start with Germany and the Netherlands, which are the pioneering countries concerning VAs. Then we discuss the followers: Austria, the UK and EU. We also assess whether policy transfer has occurred across the five selected jurisdictions (for example, due to external pressures such as international competition) or whether the uptake of VAs reflects primarily specific domestic contextual dynamics (for example, domestic policy learning).

Germany and the Netherlands, which have adopted by far the largest number of environmental VAs within the EU, started using this instrument in the early 1970s. However, VAs only became more widespread in other EU member states from the early 1990s. Table 5.1 presents the distribution of VAs adopted on the national level in the EU-15 member states, together with the total number of EU-wide VAs for the mid-1990s.

107

108   *Environmental governance in Europe*

Table 5.1   Voluntary agreements in EU member states in the mid-1990s

Member states	Number of VAs according to the EEA	Number of VAs according to the Commission
Austria	20	25
Belgium	6	14
Denmark	16	16
Finland	2	>2
France	8	n/a
Germany	93	c. 80
Greece	7	0
Ireland	1	1
Italy	11	11
Luxembourg	5	5
The Netherlands	107	>100
Portugal	10	10
Spain	6	6
Sweden	11	13
United Kingdom	9	8
Total for EU-15	312	>234
EU-wide VAs*	n/a	12

Sources: Adapted from EEA (1997: 25–36) and CEC (1996: 23–30).

Note: * The data for EU-wide VAs is based on interview information.

The data discrepancies in Table 5.1 between the EEA and the Commission are largely definitional. Both data sets clearly show that Germany and the Netherlands had instigated by far the largest total numbers of domestic VAs in the EU-15 in the mid-1990s. If one draws up a ranking order of VAs based on per capita figures, then Austria leads, with approximately 8.3 VAs per capita followed by the Netherlands (6.5), Germany (1.5) and the UK (0.2). The EEA (1997: 11) defined VAs as 'covering only those commitments undertaken by firms and sector associations, which are the result of *negotiations* with public authorities and/or explicitly recognized by the authorities'. Meanwhile the EU Commission adopted the following slightly wider definition: 'agreements between industry and public authorities on the achievement of environmental objectives' (CEC, 1996: 5). The OECD (1999a: 4; 2003a: 18) also subscribed to a broad VA definition.

Considerable terminological confusion exists about VAs, which have been labelled 'negotiated agreements', 'long-term agreements' and 'self-commitments' (CEC, 1996, 2002b). Faber (2001: 38–9) provides a list of more than 13 different German terms found in the VA literature. The OECD (2003a: 18–9; see also OECD, 1999c: 9–10) has created the following useful fourfold typology which captures most VA variants: (1) unilateral commitments by polluters; (2) negotiated agreements between industry and public authorities; (3) private agreements between polluters and 'pollutees'; and, (4) voluntary programmes developed by public authorities to which individual firms are invited to participate. Although private polluter ('pollutees') agreements and voluntary public programmes are common in the USA, they are rarely used in Europe. Chapter 5 accordingly concentrates only on unilateral commitments and negotiated agreements, both subsumed under the generic term VAs.

GERMANY: A PIONEER RUNNING OUT OF STEAM?

Germany is one of the early VA pioneers; some VAs actually pre-date modern-day German environmental policy (see Chapter 3). Primarily health-related concerns about car emissions particularly in large cities led the Association of the German Automobile Industry *(Verband der deutschen Automobilindustrie* – VDA) to propose a VA to reduce carbon monoxide emissions from automobiles in the early 1960s (Wurzel, 2002).

Over time a wide range of different VAs were developed in Germany. These include ad hoc informal self-declaratory industry statements *(Selbstverpflichtungen)* to informally negotiated agreements between industry and government. Unsurprisingly, this has resulted in the numerous terms used to describe these instruments. The most common German terms for VAs are *Selbstverpflichtungen* (literally translated self-binding commitments), *Vereinbarungen* (voluntary agreements) and *Absprachen* (agreements) (Faber, 2001).

A key characteristic which all German VAs share and that differentiates them from the other European pioneer, the Netherlands, is the fact that they are legally non-binding. German VAs are not enforceable through the courts and do not trigger sanctions if there is a compliance

110   *Environmental governance in Europe*

failure (CEC, 1996; Öko-Institut, 1998; UBA, 1999a). Furthermore, many German VAs do not stipulate monitoring requirements although there are important exceptions. For example, the climate change VAs have been monitored by an independent research institute which publishes an annual report (BDI, 2000; Buttermann and Hillebrand, 2000). Importantly, many VAs have resulted from German industry seeking to pre-empt government legislation. In other words, they have been agreed 'in the shadow of the law' (Scharpf, 1994; Héritier and Lehmkuhl, 2008; Héritier and Rhodes, 2011b; Wurzel et al., 2003a). The non-binding nature of VAs has led German environmental NGOs to criticise this particular policy instrument; they demand more transparency, better monitoring and the use of sanctions to punish non-compliance (for example, Öko-Institut, 1998; Interviews, 2010). Other critics have asserted that VAs can lead to collusion between industry and government, or even regulatory capture. Despite these concerns, Germany saw a surge in VAs in the early 1990s because a centre-right government (composed of the Christian Democratic Union/Christian Social Union – Liberal Party (CDU/CSU – (FDP)) adopted a coalition agreement giving preference to this policy instrument over traditional command-and-control regulation (UBA, 1999: 30). A Red-Green (Social Democratic Party-Green Party – SPD-Greens) coalition government, elected in 1998, showed initially strong scepticism to VAs; nevertheless, it later accepted a relatively diverse range of VAs including the renewal and extension of the climate change VA in 2000 (Interviews, Environment Agency officials, 2001; BDI, 2000).

The interest in VAs extended beyond the federal level: the *Länder* have adopted a substantial number. The Bavarian environmental pact *(Umweltpakt Bayern)* is one of the most notable *Land* VAs. It consists of several VAs which were negotiated by the Bavarian state government and the regional industry umbrella organizations (UBA, 1999). In his unsuccessful 2002 bid to be chancellor of Germany, Edmund Stoiber, the Bavarian Prime Minister, highlighted the Bavarian pact as a model for the rest of Germany (*ENDS Europe Daily*, 29 July, 2002).

German VAs govern mainly products. Normally industry agrees a voluntary reduction or the phasing out of specific pollutants in order to avoid government regulation. The VAs of particular analytical interest can be found in the energy, waste and transport sectors. The VAs in the transport sector, for instance, focus mainly on the early compliance with EU standards (for example, for unleaded and low sulphur petrol ahead of the designated deadline). The most publicly visible VAs concern the reduction of greenhouse gas emissions. The Federal German Industry Association (*Bundesverband für deutsche Industrie* – BDI) and sectoral industry umbrella groups agreed climate change VAs with the federal government in 1995, 1996 and 2000. However, the 1995 VA was perceived as both vague and lacking in ambition. It was therefore supplemented with another more ambitious VA in 1996; this in turn was updated in 2000. These climate change VAs were frequently cited by industry as evidence that these agreements could work even when involving a large number of actors and extremely complex policy problems.

The public visibility of the climate VAs prevented industry from withdrawing from these agreements when the Red-Green coalition government adopted an ecological tax reform (see Chapter 6) in 1998 (Interview, Industry Representative, 2001). Industry generally views VAs as a viable alternative to traditional regulation while Environment Ministry and Environment Agency officials tend to perceive them as supplementary, rather than primary, tools. The German VA story fits very well with the institutional approach explained in Chapter 2. There is a long tradition of state-society agreements which fit under the rubric of 'regulated self-regulation' (Paterson, 1989: 284). The number of VAs adopted in Germany slowed down considerably in the early 2000s. One Environment Agency official (Interview, 2010) even argued that 'something like a roll back of voluntary agreements' had occurred since the late 1990s. However, VAs have not completely gone out of fashion although they clearly played a much less prominent role in German environmental policy at the beginning of the early 21st century (particularly when compared to the early 1990s). Moreover, as one senior German Environment Ministry official explained (Interview, 2008), the nature of VAs changed in Germany in the 2000s. While their adoption rate declined in numerical terms, new German VAs were adopted in particular for large public events such as the World Cup or the bi-annual *Kirchentag* which is a large gathering organised by the Protestant Church. The main aim of these VA types is to 'green such events' (Interview, 2008).

The return of another centre-right (CDU/CSU-FDP) coalition in government in 2009 has not led to a major revival of VA usage in Germany. Industry still favours VAs while environmental NGOs remain opposed. One important reason why the German adoption of VAs has slowed down is because the EU emissions trading scheme (EU ETS), which Chapter 7 discusses, covers most industrial sources for carbon dioxide emissions. The EU ETS and the 1998 domestic ecological tax reform (see Chapter 6), has left little scope for German VAs in the climate change sub-sector, which used to be a particularly dynamic sub-sector for the adoption of this particular policy instrument.

THE NETHERLANDS: PIONEER FOR NEGOTIATED AGREEMENTS

In comparing the Dutch and German VAs, one must note the importance of terminology. This book uses VA as the umbrella term although it does not fully capture the negotiated and binding nature of the Dutch covenants (Glasbergen, 2004: 170–1). The Dutch prefer the term 'negotiated agreement' (for example, Bressers et al., 2011: 189). The agreement is usually agreed in writing by the government (typically the national government) and industrial groups and organisations but also potentially other actors, such as provincial governments (Koeman, 1993: 174).

Environmental covenants occur when at least two parties, usually (but not always) involving a government agency and an industrial sector representative, create an agreement to realise environmental targets (Glasbergen, 1998: 133). Both officials and the targeted groups recognise stricter command-and-control regulation as being the omnipresent alternative necessary to ensure higher environmental standards; negotiated agreements become an attractive alternative that reduces costs and increases societal innovation (Bressers et al., 2011). The negotiated agreements are technically regarded as private law contracts, to which the rules of the Dutch civil code apply (Koeman, 1993: 174). Throughout the Dutch environmental policy system, covenants remain linked to and are effectuated by the licencing system; the covenants serve as guidance for licencing if the groups do not achieve their goals (Börkey and Lévèque, 1998: 13; Bressers et al., 2011: 190).

The longstanding tradition of negotiation between key parties embedded in Dutch institutional culture made the Netherlands fertile ground for this particular VA type. The interest group patterns, involving tightly organised associations and the relatively inclusive, consensus-building policy-making approach, are a core characteristic of the Dutch modern political system (Chapter 3 notes, however, the more recent polarising politics of populist party leaders such as Fortuyn and Wilders). A 1980s evaluation of the performance of the 1970s environmental legislation induced a recognition of a gap between expectations and performance (Bressers and de Bruijn, 2005: 262–3).

Initial efforts to establish VAs in the 1980s resulted largely in 'gentlemen's agreements': the different parties stated their intentions but the very status and details of the agreement were subject to high uncertainty (Bastmeijer, 1994). The Netherlands witnessed the rapid appearance of covenants in the 1980s. At the time, the centre-right

Governing by voluntary means 113

governing coalition, formed by the CDA (Christian Democratic Appeal) and VVD (Liberal party) government, and the Environment Ministry (under the leadership of its then Minister, Pieter Winsemius) promoted self-regulation as being more efficient than traditional command-and-control regulation. Covenants intersected neatly with the 1980s domestic policy philosophy shift towards involving target groups, but also with the long-standing institutional patterns of the Dutch system. Winsemius and the Ministry pushed the notion of target group policy which encapsulates a group of actors with certain characteristics that are targeted by one or more policy instruments (Bressers et al., 2011: 189; Eurofound, 2010). Accordingly Dutch officials developed their approach to engage entire branches of industry in shared responsibility (Bressers and de Bruijn, 2005).

The year 1986 saw the first extensive effort to agree on a covenant between the government and industry. A working group of central and local authority officials engaged with the industry representatives; together they sought to devise a strategy for reducing VOCs from larger industry and small companies and households (van Vliet, 1993: 114–5; van Vliet, 1994: 43–4). The eventually successful discussions were important because the ensuing agreement was viewed as a test case for covenants and because of its comparatively comprehensive sectoral scope. This sectoral vision was atypical at the start of the surge in covenants although important sector-wide covenants did occur (for example, the 1985 and 1987 covenant to stimulate recycling and decrease drinks packaging waste (Lauber and Ingram, 2000: 129).

The 1990s saw a national spurt in covenants and an evolution in the nature of these agreements (Glasbergen, 1998: 134–6; ELNI, 1999). The 1980s covenants were ad hoc gentlemen's agreements, which many stakeholders believed had substantial scope for improvement in terms of defining strategies and responsibilities. Much of this process seems to have been ad hoc and involved a strong symbolic content, with the purpose of encouraging further voluntary reduction efforts by industry (Glasbergen, 1998: 135–6).

The 1990s saw the rise in the number of cross-sector covenants resembling the VOCs covenant of 1986. The Dutch National Environmental Plans provided impetus for covenants to become 'multiple-issue and composite-actor', reflecting the integrative focus and target group strategies found in the national plans (Glasbergen, 1998: 146). This evolution suggests a certain amount of policy learning both by government and business groups. Another significant development has been the increasingly binding nature of the covenants: parties that sign the agreement enter a contract under private law (Öko-Institut, 1998: 36).

114 *Environmental governance in Europe*

These changes suggest both policy learning and an institutional shift in the approach to involving stakeholders. In the 1986–96 period covenants formed an increasingly important part of the overall Dutch policy instrument mix. A major impetus for the target sector development was the 1989–90 *Nationaal Milieubeleidsplan Plus* (National Environmental Policy Plan Plus). This national document followed the first NEPP with a greater focus on policy instruments (Tweede Kamer, 1990). It included a strategy focusing on specific target reductions in environmental emissions while attaining the commitment of the branches of industry (known as policy target groups) to achieve these reductions. The Environment Ministry created the Environment and Industry Target Group Policy to translate national objectives into specific emission reductions by various industrial sectors. These covenants involved the national government negotiating an agreement with industry branches about the group contribution required to achieve its objectives; the resulting agreement is recorded as a covenant (Bressers and de Bruijn, 2005: 264).

Dutch officials achieved covenants with a range of industries between 1990–96, including the graphics industry (1990 and 1993), chemical industry (1993), and paper and cardboard industry (1996) (de Hoog, 1998; VNO-NCW, 1999: 16). A path-breaking but controversial agreement was the VA between the government and food producers to manage genetically modified crops (IFOAM EU, 2004). Of the target group covenants, the 1993 agreement with the chemical industry was perceived as a model for future agreements. The chemical industry covenant set emission targets for 1995, 2000 and 2010 in six environmental themes: climate change, acidification, diffusion of toxic substances, eutrophication, waste disposal and nuisances such as odour (Börkey and Lévèque, 1998: 13; EEA, 1997).

In 1999 the Environment and Economics Ministries as well as the Dutch Provinces negotiated with industry an Energy Efficiency Benchmarking Covenant which committed companies to equal the world best performances in terms of energy efficiency (Energy Efficiency Benchmarking Covenant, 6 July 1999). This covenant later became a long-term agreement (LTA 2) that was extended beyond the energy intensive sectors to commercial providers, health care providers and others (Bertoldi and Rezessy, 2010: 50–2). Benchmarking, which was extended to other sectors, combined the flexibility of implementation with the setting of a standard at the very highest level of technology. A second significant innovation was the VA between VROM, local authorities and businesses to tackle plastic packaging. Beyond the high targets for recycling, the VA was linked to a series of taxes proposed by the government: the first being a packaging tax, and the other a packaging tax which generated the

Governing by voluntary means 115

revenues used to create an annual waste fund (*ENDS Europe Daily*, 15 August 2007).

A recurring theme in these covenants was the significant role of local authorities, which, together with water boards, were essential participants in the management of drinking and waste water (VROM, 2007). Cities are also VA signatories. In 2006 ten significant Dutch cities agreed to set up *milieuzonering* (or 'environmental zones') to restrict lorry pollution in the inner cities (VROM, 2006). This covenant followed directly from an idea for environmental zones developed in Sweden.

During the 2000–10 period, the focus for negotiated agreements shifted. Many of the most important target sectors met the initial targets. Moreover, the EU now has set specific environmental regulations. The Dutch government therefore shifted its efforts to reach climate change VA targets (Written communication, Economics Ministry official, 2011). However, VAs are being extended into other areas not covered by EU environmental legislation, such as agricultural products and flowers. In 2008, the Agricultural, Economics and Environmental Ministries agreed to a four year covenant on organic products and a clean and efficient agricultural covenant with flower producers; the latter included the 2020 climate and energy targets for the agricultural sector (The Government of the Netherlands, 2008: 2; Berkhout and van Bruchem, 2010). In the area of emissions reductions and energy efficiency, the Economics Ministry modified the original 1999 Benchmarking Covenant in light of the 2008 EU climate and energy package and its targets. Consequently LTA3 entered into force in 2008, focusing on a wide range of economic sectors not covered by the EU ETS. In 2009 the Ministry also created the Long-term Agreement on Energy Efficiency for enterprises covered by the ETS (Bertoldi and Rezessy, 2010: 15, 50–2).

Bressers and de Bruijn (2005, 2003; see also Bressers et al., 2007; Bressers et al., 2009; Bressers et al., 2011) have suggested that successful covenants require a number of core elements including: the presence of concrete, quantified targets; the allocation of clear responsibilities; and some form of 'stick' or other imperative to create the right sense of urgency among the participants in the agreement. Moreover, covenants need to be embedded in a package of policy instruments. Institutional context matters: target groups respond to the whole suite of instruments; VAs that do not complement the other elements of the environmental policy system are seen to be less successful than those that do (Bressers and de Bruijn, 2005: 275–8; Bressers et al., 2007).

AUSTRIA: LATECOMER WITH HIGH USE IN SPECIFIC SECTORS

Austria is a latecomer in the adoption of VAs. The 1996 National Environmental Plan termed VAs as being 'new' (Bundesregierung, 1996). Compared to Germany and the Netherlands, Austria has adopted only a moderate total number of VAs (CEC, 1996; EEA, 1997; Lauber, 1997c; Lauber and Ingram, 2000; Mol et al., 2000; Öko-Institut, 1998). However, Austria was ranked third (out of the 15 member states) in terms of VA usage in a 1997 EEA European Environment Agency report (EEA, 1997). As already mentioned, Austria tops the league table for VAs per capita amongst EU member states if one takes into account population size.

The Austrian Business Chamber (*Wirtschaftskammer*) prefers a wide definition of VAs, which incorporates both negotiated agreements between industry and government as well as unilateral industry self-commitments (Wirtschaftskammer, 2002). The biggest surge in Austrian VAs came in the early 1990s, coinciding with a significant increase of this policy instrument in Germany. Although Austria closely follows environmental policy developments in Germany, there is no evidence of policy instrument transfer (Interviews, 2002 and 2011). Instead, domestic and international developments largely drove the Austrian adoption of VAs; these include concerns about the potential negative impact of traditional command-and-control regulation on the competitiveness of Austrian industry.

In particular Conservative ÖVP-led governments were sympathetic to industry demands for less regulation and more VAs. The adoption of VAs surged in Austria when conservative-right wing *(Österreichische Volkpartei* (ÖVP) – *Freiheitlich Partei Österreichs* (FPÖ)) coalition governments strongly pushed for the increased use of non-regulatory policy instruments within a wider deregulation strategy (Interviews, 2002). Since the 1990s the Austrian Business Chamber and Economics Ministry have both campaigned for the increased adoption of VAs and the reduced use of traditional command-and-control regulation within a wider deregulation strategy (Lauber, 1997c; Mol et al., 2000). The government adopted a deregulation strategy in order to reduce command-and-control regulations across all sectors including the environmental sector. ENGOs and the Workers Chamber (*Arbeiterkammer*) have remained highly sceptical about VAs. SPÖ-led Austrian governments have shown a lower preference for the adoption of VAs.

While EU environmental legislation has increased, it also narrowed the scope for the adoption of VAs in Austria. Moreover, a certain degree of disillusion has set in because the targets of some VAs were not reached. In the 2000s there was a significantly lower uptake of VAs compared to the previous decade. The waste sector has remained the sector where VAs are still most widely used in Austria (Interviews, 2011).

Academic scholarship has used institutional factors to explain the relatively moderate total number of VAs in Austria. All Austrian VAs are legally non-binding for constitutional reasons. Mol and colleagues have attributed the moderate use of VAs to the rigid, traditional meso-corporatist features of Austrian (environmental) policy-making and strong emphasis on consensual policy-making (Mol et al., 2000). The social partnership (*Sozialpartnerschaft*) grants unions, which have traditionally opposed the adoption of VAs (Interviews, 2011), an important role in Austrian policy-making.

However, Austrian corporatism and the importance of the social partnership have waned considerably since the 1980s. The Workers Chamber and environmental NGOs have opposed VAs because of the lack of legally binding sanctions as well as concerns about transparency and third-party representation (Interviews, Workers Chamber and NGO representatives, 2011). The Environment Ministry has remained divided about the use of VAs (Interviews, 2001 and 2011). Even parts of industry and the Workers Chamber have raised concerns about the fact that VAs do not provide adequate sanctions against free-riders (Interviews, 2002 and 2011).

The majority of Austrian VAs can be found in the waste sector where they tackle, for example, the recycling of batteries and the phasing out of environmentally damaging substances (EEA, 1997; Lauber and Ingram, 2000; Mol et al., 2000; Wirtschaftskammer, 2002). The 1990 Waste Management Act served to trigger a number of VAs as industry sought to pre-empt legally binding implementation targets (EEA, 1997; Lauber and Ingram, 2000; Mol et al., 2000; Wirtschaftskammer, 2002). By comparison, very few other sectors contain VAs; this contrasts starkly with Germany and the Netherlands.

UNITED KINGDOM: LAGGARD DESPITE VOLUNTARY FEATURES OF THE NATIONAL POLICY STYLE

The relatively voluntary style of traditional national environmental policy would lead one to expect a favourable UK reaction to VAs. However, UK actors were initially suspicious of VAs. For instance, the highly influential House of Lords Select Committee on the European Communities (HOLSCEC, 1980) argued that VAs 'deserve' no more than 'careful discussion as their legal basis is unclear'. The Committee further suggested that, 'although VAs cannot be expected to replace legislation entirely, (they) may... prove useful supplements'. By the mid-1990s, the UK government's own scepticism had softened. Nevertheless government actors remained unconvinced.

Although industry has been broadly committed to the adoption of more voluntary approaches, detailed discussion (about the need for and content of VAs in specific issue areas) revealed often diverging points of view. Some economic sectors have warmly embraced VAs. Others are ambivalent, and some flatly oppose them. UK industry has been more enthusiastic about the negotiated agreements when threatened with alternative instruments, such as a tax or a regulation. There are, however, a number of more generic issues that have caused the Confederation of British Industry (CBI) particular concern. VAs are open to defection (the free-rider problem), impose an unfair burden on the larger firms that are more likely to sign them, and are not a panacea given the absence of coherent trade associations in some sectors (*ENDS, Report*, 224, 1994: 3–4).

The majority of early, indigenous VAs in the UK were little more than informal 'gentleman's agreements' or non-justiciable codes of good conduct. A striking example of this occurred in 1957: the Pesticides Safety Precautions Scheme (PSPS) was probably the first UK VA. Its main aim was to safeguard human health and the environment. The Royal Commission on Environmental Pollution (RCEP) (1979) criticised this non-statutory scheme for not doing enough to limit pesticide use. More forceful critics denounced it as a:

> 'gentleman's agreement' between the agrochemical industry and government ... Under the [scheme] key committees [were] ... bound by the Official Secrets Act. Experts who were invited ... to discuss the impact of a new insecticide ... were muzzled ... the industry was well represented on the PSPS (indeed it was a source of almost all the data) ... whereas workers' organizations were relegated to relatively powerless advisory panels. It was hardly surprising that industry got the benefit of the doubt, and it took longer to restrict or ban a pesticide in the UK than in more openly governed countries (Rose, 1990: 236).

The PSPS remained in force until 1986 when a legal challenge from the European Commission (on the grounds that it breached free trade rules) forced its replacement by a statutory registration scheme.

Another prominent example concerned stratospheric ozone depletion. In 1980, the EU placed a cap on CFC production and called for a reduction in their use in aerosols. The UK government achieved these targets with ease, praising an unwritten VA with CFC users and producers (Jordan, 1998b). In fact, the cap was set well above existing levels of production (thereby leaving ample room for expansion) while aerosol use was already in decline. The 1980s saw consumption skyrocket as new uses were found for CFCs. Binding controls on production were only applied in 1988 after the EU had signed the Montreal Protocol (Jordan, 1998b).

The number of actual modern VA systems is open to question. This ambiguity partly reflects the different VA definitions. In terms of types of agreements, only half are negotiated agreements (see Table 5.2) while the rest are either unilateral commitments or public voluntary schemes (CEC, 1997b). The latter unilateral commitments include: Responsible Care, CFCs and HCFCs, 'Green Fee' scheme for used tyres, Environment Business Forum, and the 1995 Plus Group. These tend to be unofficial, largely self-assessed schemes, with little or no legal force. Many are more akin to industry codes of best practice than what many continental Europeans would classify as VAs (Jordan and Salmons, 2000).

There is little evidence that UK VAs were inspired by developments abroad. Much more significant were domestic developments between UK regulatory bodies and producer groups; these developments took a path dependent form that helped spur on the gentleman's agreements. The first, modern negotiated agreement was the 1997 Energy Efficiency Agreement. This agreement, brokered by the Environment Ministry and the Chemical Industries Association, aimed to reduce the chemical industries' energy consumption. It was a vital part of the UK's national climate change strategy. It was externally verified but never legally binding for either party. Some observers have claimed that the agreement was little more than an empty ploy to resist or at least slow the introduction of a carbon-energy tax (Salmons, 2001).

Some of the other negotiated agreements listed in Table 5.2 have met equally heavy criticism for doing little more than codify 'business as usual'. It is furthermore alleged that the long-term effectiveness of VAs on HFCs and PFCs has never been systematically analysed by the Environment Ministry or any other external body (*ENDS Report*, 346, November 2003: 10–11).

The main driver for negotiated agreements in this HFC/PFC area is not industry's desire for self-governance or corporate governance, but international and especially EU regulation on global warming and ozone depletion. When the European Commission issued proposals to prohibit

120   *Environmental governance in Europe*

Table 5.2   UK negotiated agreements

Name	Date of Commencement	Topic
Pesticides Safety Precautions Scheme	1957	Health and safety
APEs (domestic fabric washing products)	1972	Water pollution
NTA (domestic fabric washing products	1975	Water pollution
BASIS (pesticides handling)	1978	Health and safety
Recycled content of newsprint	1991	Waste management
Farm Films Recovery Scheme (FFSR)	1995	Waste management
APEs (industrial washing products)	1995	Water pollution
HFCs (aerosol industry)	1996	Climate change
HFCs and PFCs (fire industry)	1996	Climate change
HFCs (foams industry)	1996	Climate change
Energy efficiency agreement (chemical industry)	1997	Climate change
Newspaper	2000	Waste management
Climate change levy agreements (42 in total)	2002	Climate change
Direct mailing	2003	Waste management
Chemical substances (nonylphenol, nonylphenol ethoxylates, octylphenol and octylphenol ethoxylates)	2004	Chemicals
Courtauld Commitment 1	2005	Waste management
Magazines	2005	Waste management
Nanotechnology reporting	2006	Health, hazardous substance
Phase out of incandescent light bulbs	2007	Climate change; Energy savings
Carrier bags	2008	Waste management
Transport	2008	Climate change adaption
Courtauld Commitment 2	2010	Waste management

Source: Based on Jordan and Salmons (2000), http://www.defra.gov.uk/environment (2010).

HFC use in new vehicle air conditioning systems, the Environment Ministry responded by announcing its intent to seek new agreements covering HFC use (for example in refrigerant fluid handling and fire fighting) to meet these and other new legislative demands.

The number of negotiated agreements is quite diminutive when compared to the VAs in Germany and the Netherlands. Although most of the UK VAs have some official status (in other words, they have been negotiated in partnership with, or have been deposited with, a government body), very few have a formal (legislative) status. Some of the schemes have been moderately successful but others have failed miserably (for example, the agreement on newsprint). At least one (the FFSR) has completely collapsed, triggering demands for statutory intervention (Salmons, 2000). In other areas (for example, washing products or car tyre disposal), industry associations eventually have requested Government intervention and regulation to address potential free-rider problems.

Despite encountering these difficulties, the Environment Ministry has continued, since 2000, its active exploration of voluntary instruments to address certain types of environmental problems. This occurred particularly in those sectors where industry flatly opposed the introduction of more intrusive instruments such as market-based instruments and regulation. One example was the Environment Ministry's *Voluntary Initiative* involving pesticide producers and users. Launched in April 2001 to find voluntary ways of reducing pesticide use, it has met widespread criticism for not moving far or fast enough.

The Environment Ministry created the *Chemical Stakeholder Forum* in 2000 to promote early voluntary action on especially hazardous chemicals. Four years later, it had only produced a priority list of chemicals and recommended action on a certain class of bioaccumulating substances known as nonylphenols, nonylphenol ethoxylates and their octylphenols (DEFRA, 2004). Although widely used in a whole range of industrial applications, these chemicals face a long-term decline in use. In 2002, the Environment Ministry announced the intent to negotiate a VA with producers and users, ahead of EU legislation. However, these plans had to be rapidly reformulated when the European Commission came forward with legislative proposals much faster than Whitehall expected (DEFRA, 2004: 2).

Perhaps the most noteworthy examples of a formally negotiated agreement are the *Climate Change Levy Agreements* (CCLA), which have superseded the energy efficiency agreement. CCLAs allow firms within certain economic sectors to obtain an 80 per cent reduction on the Climate Change Levy (which will be assessed in Chapter 6). By 2004, the Environment Ministry had signed 43 CCLAs with trade associations representing over 6000 businesses, primarily in the supermarket and farming sectors (de Muizon and Glachant, 2004: 231–2). Each CCLA runs for 10 years and is formally reviewed every second year. The CCLAs proved to be far more difficult to negotiate than the Environment

Ministry had ever expected, as reliable baseline data on energy use simply did not exist at the beginning of the process (Smith, 2004). The administrative input was also enormous for a supposedly 'light touch' instrument. Altogether, the process of simply negotiating them absorbed 17 years of 31 civil servants' time (*House of Commons Written Answers*, 4 February 2002, col. 751–2W). The *ENDS Report* described the CCLAs as 'one of the most intricate pieces of environmental policy ever implemented in the UK' (*ENDS Report*, 339, 2003: 23). However, their long-term effectiveness is still unknown. In terms of the governance question, the CCLAs are important because of their linkage to other policy instruments, notably the energy tax contained in the name of the agreements.

Waste management has been a particularly conducive sector for VAs since the 1990s (DEFRA, 2009a: 64). There are VAs for the recycling rates of direct mail as well as newspaper and magazines. In 2005, the British Retail Consortium, the major supermarket chains, the UK Environment Minister and other stakeholders agreed the 'Courtauld Commitment' aimed at reducing food and packaging waste (Bio Intelligence Service, 2009b). In 2010, the stakeholders and UK government announced a second phase with a new set of targets, focusing particularly on the entire life-cycle of products (Packaging Europe, 2010). In December 2008, seven of the big UK supermarkets – represented by the British Retail Consortium (BRC) – signed a VA with the government to cut by 50 per cent (against 2006 levels) the number of carrier bags distributed by the end of May 2009 (DEFRA, 2010a).

Since the 1990s, Conservative and Labour governments made strong commitments to the principle of voluntary action. At first glance this suggests a paradox: UK environmental policy becomes more formalised while making use of more (informal) VAs. A strong element of this seemingly contradictory dynamic is the Europeanisation of UK environmental policy in the wake of the increased adoption of EU environmental legislation. In an effort to implement EU regulation as well as international treaties, the UK government has looked more closely at non-regulatory policy instruments such as certain NEPIs. This can be seen clearly in the areas of packaging waste and climate change commitments. Other examples include the UK government agreement to phase out incandescent light bulbs, coming on the back of the EU 2008 decision to start this process (Naughton, 2007), and the 2009 voluntary Energy Efficiency Agreement with road transport fuel suppliers in response to the EU Energy Services Directive (Bertoldi and Rezessy, 2010: 54).

However, the use of VAs still does not follow a well-developed strategic plan; it is not a case of systematic learning at an instrument

Governing by voluntary means 123

level, or at an ideational level as postulated by Hall. There is, for example, no equivalent to the Treasury's strategy on green taxation guiding their design and deployment. Very often, the use of VAs seems to be driven by short term political and economic exigencies, as well as EU regulatory initiatives. Most frequently actors use the agreements to plug short term gaps, or as a precursor of other NEPIs. Interestingly, the Environment Ministry has not promoted VAs as a general mechanism for transposing EU Directives into UK law because this would amount to a breach of EU law. The UK case cautions against using too shallow an understanding of national policy styles which would anticipate stronger interest for negotiated agreements in the UK's case.

EUROPEAN UNION: LEGALLY CONSTRAINED FOLLOWER

The analysis of this Chapter so far indicates widely diverging member state approaches to VAs. However, the differences in popularity and implementation on the member state level only partly explain the EU's difficulties in adopting supranational VAs (CEC, 1996, 2002b; EEA, 1997a; Giebel, 2001; Jordan et al., 2003a, 2006; Kaspar, 2001; Krämer, 2001).

The EU actively considered the adoption of VAs only from the late 1980s onwards; by the 1990s the increased demands for deregulation coincided with the debate about the principle of subsidiarity (see Chapter 3). Increased competition due to globalisation added further pressure on EU environmental policy makers to seriously consider the adoption of voluntary measures (Krämer, 2001: 80; Kaspar, 2001). Moreover, the emergence of new policy problems (for example, climate change) and paradigms (for example, sustainable development) that did not lend themselves easily to traditional regulatory solutions also made VAs more attractive (Mol, Lauber and Liefferink, 2000; Jordan, Wurzel and Zito, 2003a, 2006).

The 1995 Molitor Report (CEC 1995) demanded the repatriation of environmental legislation. In 2002, the action plan *Simplifying and Improving the Regulatory Environment* followed, promising less and simpler EU legislation as well as a greater reliance on self-regulation (CEC, 2002a). The action plan stated that 'voluntary agreements constitute one form of self-regulation' (CEC, 2002a: 7). It argued for co-regulation, which restricts the legislator to stipulating the essential aspects of the legislation (such as the objectives and deadlines) whilst leaving private actors to determine how to implement them. The earlier

2001 Commission *White Paper on European Governance* had already posed demands for self-regulation and co-regulation (CEC, 2001b; see also Chapter 3). Many observers therefore expected the Commission to generate ambitious plans for boosting the uptake of EU-wide VAs in its 2002 *Communication on Environmental Agreements at Community Level*, which followed up the Commission's first Communication on VAs in 1996 (CEC 1996).

Early internal DG Environment drafts of the Commission's 2002 communication on VAs raised great expectations because they proposed seven different options for EU-wide VAs. The most far reaching of these options was a proposal for a Treaty amendment to establish a firm legal base for EU-wide VAs. Other options included an EMAS type of approach (see Chapter 5), the adoption of EU-wide guidelines for VAs at the national level and co-regulation through sectoral agreements (Interview, Commission official, 2002).

However, the Commission eventually discarded most of these options either as politically unrealistic (for example, requiring Treaty amendment) or legally unsound (for example, involving the use of binding VAs without Treaty amendment) after consultation with the Commission's Legal Service. The Commission's 2002 Communication on EU-wide VAs (CEC, 2002b) was therefore short on specific proposals and long on general principles. Compared to the 1996 Communication, the 2002 Communication put more emphasis on self-regulation and co-regulation. It thus followed the path set by the 2001 *Action Plan* and White *Paper on European Governance.*

In 1996, the Commission declared a desire to promote 'effective and acceptable' VAs as a means of supplementing traditional regulation (CEC 1996). However, the 2002 Communication merely stated that:

> the European Commission intends to recognise and make use of environmental agreements at Community level on a selective case-by-case basis. Since the instrument will not necessarily be the most appropriate in all circumstances, it is helpful to identify already a limited number of policy areas in which environmental agreements could offer an added value (CEC, 2002b: 13).

The 2002 Communication cautioned that 'not more than four to six [additional] environmental agreements are likely' (CEC, 2002b: 10) before June 2004. It identified four areas (PVC strategy, Green Paper on Integrated Product Policy, waste management and climate change) as early EU-wide VA candidates. Transparency, legitimacy and free rider concerns explain the low VA uptake at the EU level: VAs have to be adopted outside the formal EU decision-making procedures and thus leave the Council and EP sidelined (see Chapter 3). The EP repeatedly criticised the Commission's desire to increase VA usage at the EU level. The only major exception is a report by the EP's Environment Committee on the Commission's Green Paper on PVC; this report, however, was passed only narrowly with 25 to 18 votes (EP, 2001). Environmental groups have questioned the use of VAs (EEB, 2000; Taschner 1998; Krämer, 2001: 82). Crucially, although European industry has rhetorically supported the increase of EU-wide VAs, it has largely failed to pursue the Commission's repeated invitations to negotiate EU-wide VAs (Interviews, Commission official, 2002 and 2007). The few important exceptions are assessed below.

The incompatibility of competing national models (for example, legally binding Dutch covenants and non-binding German and Austrian VAs) and concerns about free-riders (who may gain a competitive advantage within the SEM by failing to implement VAs) have inhibited efforts to increase EU-wide VAs. Free-riders cannot be taken to court for failing to implement legally non-binding VAs. This explains the Commission's desire to adopt legally binding EU-wide VAs which have no legal base in the existing EU Treaties. Another problem is that well-organised and representative European level industry associations do not exist for all sectors. It is not coincidental that the chemical and automobile sectors, involving a relatively low number of big corporate players, have adopted most of the existing EU-wide VAs.

In terms of policy learning, the Commission's attention to the issue of co-regulation does suggest that a substantial rethinking of the calibration and usage of instruments has occurred (Hall's first and second order policy learning, see Chapter 2). The German and Dutch VAs at best seem to have served as low key inspiration for the EU's efforts which faced substantially more complex contextual challenges.

The first four EU-wide VAs were adopted in 1989–90, all focusing on chemicals (Schnabl, 2005: 93, 104). Three of these VAs set voluntary reduction targets for CFCs by European industry associations while the fourth addressed detergents. Krämer (2001: 83) has noted that the VAs on CFCs had already become redundant in 1991 when the EU adopted legally binding reduction targets that were considerably more ambitious.

The adoption of the earliest four EU-wide VAs shows that this NEPI preceded the Fifth EAP (CEC, 1993b) and Sixth EAP (CEC, 2001c), which both raised the importance of non-regulatory tools for EU environmental policy. The early EU-wide VAs also pre-date the early 1990s debates about the principle of subsidiarity and deregulation. Clearly, the Fifth and Sixth EAP, as well as the changes in wider political and economic discourse, did not lead to an immediate and/or significant increase of EU-wide VAs. Only in 1998 were an additional three VAs adopted at the EU level. Two of them dealt with the energy consumption from television sets while the third one covered detergents for household textiles.

In 1999, the association of the European automobile industry (ACEA) and the European Commission agreed a VA on the reduction of carbon dioxide (CO_2) emissions from passenger cars after 'arduous negotiations' (Interview, Commission Officials, 2002; EEB, 2000). The Commission kept the Environmental Council and the EP, which had demanded ambitious targets, informed about the negotiations. These negotiations lasted for almost five years if one takes as a starting point the Commission's announcement in 1993 of a pending proposal to reduce passenger car CO_2 emissions (Krämer, 2001: 83). The Commission and ACEA initially hailed the VA on CO_2 reductions as 'a great success', which would develop into 'something of a showcase' (Interview, Commission officials, 2001). The VA set a CO_2 emission reduction target of 140g/km (which amounted to a reduction of approximately 25 per cent) by 2008. Environmental groups criticised what they regarded as a lenient reduction target (EEB, 2000; Taschner 1998). In 2000, the Japanese and Korean automobile industry associations (JAMA and KAMA respectively) put forward VAs which used the same reduction target by 2009.

The Commission established an ad hoc group, consisting of member state officials and European automobile industry representatives, to consider measures for the reduction of CO_2 emissions, which had been excluded from the so-called Auto-Oil I Programme (see Friedrich, Tappe and Wurzel, 2000). However, initially the ad hoc group considered the adoption of eco-taxes which, at the time, constituted DG Environment's favoured option (although this position was opposed by the DG responsible for indirect taxation). DG Industry then proposed the negotiation of a VA which was accepted only reluctantly by DG Environment. Initially, ACEA as well as JAMA and KAMA seemed to make good progress with their VAs (*ENDS Report*, February 2004: 60). However, in 2002 progress on ACEA's VA 'stalled with the smallest improvement since 1995' (*ENDS Report*, February 2004: 60). New cars sold in the EU had average emissions of 166g/km – an improvement of just 1 g/km in 2001 to 163 g/km in 2002' (*ENDS Report,* February 2004: 60). JAMA and KAMA in particular fell even further behind.

In 2004, some automobile companies (including German producers) started to question the VAs. They lobbied member governments to take into account competitiveness arguments while insisting on more lenient CO_2 emission reduction targets such as in the USA. In 2006, ACEA blamed European consumers for the failure of its CO_2 emissions VA by arguing that they had failed to show sufficient demand preference for more fuel efficient smaller cars *(ENDS Europe Daily,* 23 November 2006).

The Commission expressed dissatisfaction with the automobile manufacturer's lack of progress (reducing CO_2 emissions from new cars by an average of only 1.2 per cent in 2004) and warned that it would replace the VA with binding legislation *(ENDS Europe Daily,* 30 August 2006). In 2007 the Commission concluded that 'the voluntary approach has delivered a solid CO_2 reduction but has not been as successful as hoped. Given the slower than expected progress to date, the 120g CO_2/km target will not be met by 2012 without additional measures' (CEC, 2007a). These additional measures included the proposal for binding EU legislation which the Commission published in December 2007. This 2007 proposal compelled automobile producers to cut their CO_2 emissions from new passenger cars to 120g CO_2/km by 2015 (Council of the European Union, 2009b).

The problems that the automobile industry's VA has faced supported the conclusion drawn by the OECD (2003a) which expressed grave doubts about the effectiveness and efficiency of VAs. In the early 2000s much of European industry seems to have lost its remaining enthusiasm for EU-wide VAs – a support which has never been very strong in practice. This stance stands in marked contrast to the enthusiastic rhetoric with which industry demanded the adoption of voluntary instruments instead of binding EU legislation.

As an illustration, the European white goods (in other words, large household equipment such as fridges) association, CECED, declared in 2007 that binding legislation was preferable over VAs because it established a level playing field against free-riders. The association also declared that it would not renew any VA on energy efficiency it had concluded with the Commission *(ENDS Europe Daily,* 22 March 2007). Between 1998 and 2004, only two EU-wide VAs were adopted in addition to the VA on CO_2 emissions with the automobile industry. One VA addressed pesticides and mercury, in order to implement the Rotterdam Convention on the Prior Informed Consent Procedure, and the other was a VA with biodegradable plastic producers (Schnabl, 2005; *ENDS Europe Daily,* 21 February 2005; CEC, 2008). Additional EU-wide VAs have been discussed. The Commission actors concluded VAs on climate change (for example, electrical engineering sectors), cadmium in batteries, waste and imaging equipment (for example, photocopiers) (Interview, Commission Official, 2001; Krämer, 2001: 85; *ENDS Europe Daily,* 9 November 2009; CEC, 2009a).

128   *Environmental governance in Europe*

VAs have remained a possible EU policy instrument option. However, since the 2000s, most EU policy makers perceive EU-wide VAs primarily as supplementary tools within a wider policy instrument mix. VAs can be seen as one pillar in an EU strategy that also includes eco-label schemes and EMSs (see Chapter 4), which are the 'second pillar', and market-based instruments (see Chapters 6 and 7) that constitute the 'third pillar' for altering societal behaviour (CEC, 2007a).

In November 2007, the EU Industry Commissioner sought to position the EU for the climate change talks by raising the possibility of global agreements for certain industrial sectors to set benchmarks to reduce CO_2 emissions. The steel industry had already proposed such an agreement in October 2007 to become exempted from ETS (see Chapter 7). In 2009 the Commission issued a report calling on the electrical engineering sector to commit to VAs (*ENDS Europe Daily*, 9 November 2009). However, as in the case of the passenger car CO_2 VA, the promises for reductions in CO_2 emissions from other sectors were overtaken by traditional command-and-control regulation and/or the expansion of market-based instruments as outlined in the so-called 20-20 by 2020 climate change and energy package (Jordan et al., 2011; Wurzel and Connelly, 2011a).

Importantly the Commission (2009b) developed a complementing framework directive which helped provide incentives for industrial sectors to consider VAs: the eco-design Directive which stipulates requirements for products that have an impact on energy consumption. Under the eco-design Directive, the Commission can impose requirements unless the industrial sector opts for 'self-regulation' including VAs (CEC, 2009b). For one Austrian Environment Agency official (Interview, 2008), the EU eco-design Directive therefore is likely to lead to 'a roll back of voluntary agreements' in those EU member states which are characterised by a high level of VAs for 'green' products.

By 2011 there were only 14 EU-wide VAs. This compares with hundreds of national VAs within EU member states (albeit the majority adopted by two pioneering states, namely Germany and the Netherlands). The EU's institutional set up has clearly influenced the selection and adoption of EU-wide VAs. VAs lack a clear Treaty basis in the EU. Moreover, some EU institutions (for example, the EP) object to the Commission's attempt to negotiate EU-wide VAs directly with industry outside the formal EU decision-making procedures. Finally, the widely divergent national traditions for the use of VAs in member states have prevented the widespread use of this policy instrument at the EU level.

CONCLUSION

VAs are more popular in some member states than in others although their uptake can change over time. In the 1990s, almost two-thirds of all VAs adopted in then EU-15 could be found in Germany and the Netherlands while seven member states (including the UK) had adopted less than 12. By 2002, Germany (>130) and the Netherlands (>100) further increased their leadership position although VAs temporarily became more popular in most EU member states (CEC, 2002b; de Clerq, 2002; Jordan, Wurzel and Zito, 2003a). However, the enthusiasm for VAs seems to have decreased (especially in Germany) since the early 2000s. Neither the pioneers (Germany and the Netherlands), followers (for example, Austria) nor laggards (for example, the UK) have adopted a large number of VAs since the early 2000s.

There is considerable divergence concerning the intrinsic nature of VAs. Since the mid-1990s, the majority of Dutch VAs are legally binding contracts (so-called covenants) between private actors and public authorities which can at least theoretically be court enforced (Mol, Lauber and Liefferink, 2000; Zito et al., 2003). In Germany and Austria, all VAs have remained non-binding although they are often adopted 'in the shadow of the law' and put forward by industry as a means of pre-empting regulation (Héritier and Lehmkuhl, 2008; Héritier and Rhodes, 2011; Wurzel et al., 2003c).

As a theoretically strong empirical example of the move towards self-steering governance, the use of VAs in practice raises strong doubts about the pure governance hypothesis (see also Jordan et al., 2011). Only in two out of five jurisdictions was there a high uptake of VAs. Austria was a VA follower which exhibited a moderate uptake of this particular policy instrument. The EU and UK adopted only a very low number of VAs. Importantly, in the five jurisdictions assessed in this book, many VAs co-existed together with other policy instruments as part of policy instrument mixes. As Chapter 8 discusses in more detail, VAs do not seem to have supplanted other policy instruments and thus displaced the traditional mode of governing. Empirical evidence suggests that the EU has found it difficult to adopt EU-wide VAs. The replacement of the VA on CO_2 emissions from cars with regulation and the 20-20 by 2020 climate change and energy package (see Chapter 8) constitute important examples. At the same time, negotiated agreements feature more strongly as showcase instruments, certainly in the Dutch and UK cases; these do not represent the pure ideal type notions of 'self-steering'.

VAs cannot be said to be replacing the traditional government mechanisms in Germany and the Netherlands. Indeed the strong regulatory framework found in Germany, Austria and (to a lesser degree) the Netherlands, is essential to understanding the adoption and design of VAs in these member states. In Germany and Austria as well as in the Netherlands, governments have frequently announced their intention to draft regulation as threat inducements towards target groups which have offered VAs to avoid legislation. In Germany and Austria VAs have often been adopted in the 'shadow of hierarchy' while in the Dutch case negotiated agreements actually involved the exchange of legally binding documents. Reflecting the discussion of differing governing modes in Chapter 1, the evidence for VAs suggests a 'hybrid' position for these instruments in the government-governance continuum.

VAs have only some of the core characteristics of the ideal-typical notion of new modes of governance which rely primarily on horizontal self-co-ordination tools and self-steering. This is because they have the scope to be more directive and controlling or binding as can be witnessed in the Dutch covenants. If there has been a shift from traditional tools of government (namely, top-down command-and-control regulation) towards new instruments of governance (in other words, soft policy instruments which encourage horizontal self-co-ordination), then we should have expected to see a more significant increase in the adoption of VAs across all five jurisdictions according to the governance hypothesis. The strong governance hypothesis would expect a replacement process to occur in which self-organising voluntary instruments take on a more important role in the environmental sector. However, this Chapter has detailed significant constraints which prevent the wider adoption of VAs on the EU level in particular.

The institutional context explains differences in approach to VA design and usage, but not always to the uptake of NEPIs in the first place. The more consensus based policy style found both in Germany and the Netherlands partly help to explain the move towards these instruments. In Germany and Austria, constitutional constraints prevented the adoption of legally binding VAs such as the Dutch covenants. Given the dominant national policy style found in the UK, one would expect VAs to provide an attractive alternative to traditional command-and-control regulation. However, empirical evidence suggests that this is not actually the case in practice. To a considerable extent institutional factors are influencing the uptake and use of VAs. The adoption and implementation of UK environmental regulation has traditionally involved informal interactions between the regulators and the regulated. This helps explain why VAs are not seen as attractive alternative tools for traditional regulation in the UK.

Governing by voluntary means 131

In contrast, the EU provides extremely infirm institutional ground upon which to build strong VAs. The lack of a clear constitutional basis and the institutional question of who negotiates VAs in a transparent and legitimate manner all serve to place major constraints on their adoption.

Based on this chapter's empirical evidence, changes in government coalitions can have an important impact on the adoption of VAs. Centre-right coalition governments in Germany, the Netherlands and Austria perceived VAs as attractive tools to respond to the increased competition from the Single European Market and globalisation. Centre-left and centre-left/green coalition governments were less enthusiastic about VAs. Coalitional changes at certain junctures brought about new paradigms of understanding environmental policy and its relation to other policy priorities, and this had considerable impact on the selection of VAs. The UK arguably constitutes the exception to the rule because there was little difference between Conservative and 'New' Labour governments concerning VA adoption. The role of party and government change tends to get little or no attention in the policy instrument literature although there are notable exceptions (for example, Mol, Lauber and Liefferink, 2000). As Chapter 8 explains in more detail, VAs have not replaced traditional tools of government: rather there was a significant layering of VAs (namely, a 'new' policy instrument) on top of traditional regulation (namely, an 'old' policy instrument).

The Netherlands provides the main instances of policy learning in our case countries. Much of the core learning processes occurred at the second level, as well as the first level (several important covenants have been reformulated over time). Dutch policy-makers moved from informal gentlemen's agreements which focused on relatively narrow issues to more transparent sector-wide covenants; both the design and scope of the instrument changed over time. There is some evidence to suggest limited third order learning, particularly with the CDA and VVD coalition of the 1980s. The above mentioned 1986 covenant involving an agreement between government and a sector reflected a shift in Dutch environmental governing, viewing the state-society interaction through the notion of target groups. Nonetheless, the target group thinking accords with Dutch tradition, so this is not a substantial paradigm change.

Chapter 5 does not reveal the same learning processes in the EU, Austria and UK; this reality reflects partly contextual domestic factors. Although the chronology of the adoption of VAs in the five jurisdictions is suggestive of policy instrument transfer, the empirical evidence for such a transfer is relatively weak. German Environment Agency officials (Interviews, 2002) and EU Commission officials (Interviews, 2002) explored the possibility of emulating elements of the Dutch covenants but were prevented from doing so by institutional and constitutional constraints. The high uptake of VAs in Germany and the Netherlands may have inspired Austria, the EU and the UK to consider VAs more seriously. However, in practice little policy instrument emulation seems to have taken place across jurisdictions. The pioneers arguably helped to generate broad interest in VAs. However, there is too much variation between the different designs and usages of VAs between the five jurisdictions to suggest a strong case for policy instrument transfer.

6. Governing by eco-taxes

INTRODUCTION

Market-based instruments draw a lion's share of attention in studies about new forms of environmental governance (see Chapter 2). Some European countries – in particular the Northern European countries – have used eco-taxes since the 1970s although much of the foundational economic thinking can be traced to the theoretical work which Pigou (1920) carried out in the 1920s (Weale, 1992: 158). Environmental economists widely see the main advantage of eco-taxes as providing price signals about the costs of negative environmental externalities (for example, OECD, 1994).

Table 6.1 compares the changes over time for eco-tax revenue as a share of GDP. The Eurostat (2010b) data includes any tax whose base is a physical unit (or proxy) of something that has a proven, specific negative impact on the environment; it includes taxes on transport, energy pollution and resources. Energy taxes remain the largest amount of eco-taxes across Europe (more than 50 per cent of the total revenue) (Eurostat, 2010a). Between 1999–2007 the absolute environmental tax revenue increased for the EU-25 although it actually decreased as a share of total taxes and social contributions, as well as the percentage of GDP (Eurostat, 2010a). For 1999–2007 Austria showed an increase in the total tax and social contributions. In Germany and the Netherlands, eco-tax revenue as a share of total tax and social contribution increased while the share of GDP decreased.

Initially most eco-taxes took the form of a charge on specific pollution, while the revenue would often go to support specific remedial efforts. By the mid-1970s the Nordic countries, Germany, the Netherlands and France had introduced such charges and levies on water and air pollution.

Full scale ecological tax reform, which, as explained below (see also Chapter 2) includes a more systematic approach to the use of eco-taxes, represents a newer development. Ecological tax reforms were carried out in several European countries (including Germany and the Netherlands) only from the 1990s onwards. The main intent behind ecological tax reform is to increase the cost of the consumption of non-renewable

133

134   *Environmental governance in Europe*

Table 6.1   Total eco-tax revenues as a share of GDP and aggregate totals

Member states	1997	2008	2008 tax revenue, in millions of Euros (rounded figures)
Austria	2.38	2.41	6706
Belgium	2.51	1.97	6780
Denmark	4.87	5.72	13 329
Finland	3.34	2.73	5049
France	2.72	2.11	41 058
Germany	2.15	2.22	55 468
Greece	3.07	1.97	4716
Ireland	3.00	2.43	4409
Italy	3.39	2.43	39 193
Luxembourg	2.96	2.51	986
The Netherlands	3.76	3.87	23 049
Portugal	3.32	2.64	4398
Spain	2.12	1.63	17 773
Sweden	2.95	2.72	8939
UK	2.91	2.42	44 034
Bulgaria	-	3.54	1209
Malta	3.52	3.52	201
Norway	4.35	2.66	8241
Total EU-25	2.75	2.39	295 341

Source: Adapted from Eurostat 2010b and 2010c.

resources or polluting activities while using the generated revenue to reduce labour cost, for example, in the form of reductions to national insurance contributions (CEU, 2009b: 56).

The next chapter sections provide an assessment of eco-taxes in the Netherlands, Germany, UK, Austria and the EU which roughly reflects the timing and degree to which these five jurisdictions have innovated

THE NETHERLANDS: EARLY ECO-TAXES PIONEER

The Netherlands was one of the eco-taxes pioneers. The 1969 Surface Water Pollution Act was its first piece of modern environmental legislation which had the aim to bring about the construction of the next generation of sewage plants and to impose a permit system on all discharges of waste water (Andersen, 1994: 151–2). The Act included a system of levies on both households and industry that provided the finance for public sewage treatment. The Dutch water boards, as the bodies composed of the various user groups with the responsibility for managing the water control system, collected the revenues to pay for construction and maintenance of public sewage plants (Bressers, 1993; EEA, 1996: 21–6).

During the late 1970s the Netherlands witnessed a considerable amount of policy learning concerning the impact of such levies. Taking the macro level policy learning first, in the 1970s Dutch researchers conducted several studies which discovered that environmental levies were substantially altering business behaviour and providing incentives for firms to reduce pollution levels. The tax, which had been mainly intended to provide revenues for constructing sewage infrastructure, was having significant unintended environmental benefits. Simultaneously, several policy studies appeared which suggested that command-and-control regulation was facing significant implementation difficulties (Bressers, 1990: 80, 83; Liefferink, 1997; Andersen, 1994).

All of this work began to filter into the Dutch governing approach by the time the Environmental Protection (General Provisions) Act of 1980 came into being. The surface water policy area had unique characteristics that lent themselves to environmental levies (Andersen, 1994: 201–7; Liefferink, 1998: 90–2). The Surface Waters Act levy set a useful precedent for actors attempting to design regulation elsewhere: it was a relatively straightforward tool that the ministries could develop without too much innovation and policy borrowing.

In the 1970s, Dutch economic instruments generally took the form of fixed charge levies to collect revenue to pay for public services. The OECD (1980: 62, 91) identified the Netherlands and France as the European countries with the greatest application of this instrument. In 1972, the government instituted a fuel levy to control sulphur dioxide emissions and raise revenue to finance the costs of the Air Pollution Act, its monitoring and related scientific research, and compensation to affected members of society. The Dutch Noise Nuisance Act of 1979 provided for the introduction of charges on motor vehicle noise. Following the German example (see the following), the Netherlands created waste oil charges in 1979. This was not a case of full scale policy instrument transfer because it took the characteristics of other Dutch charges: namely a charge fixed at a low rate narrowly designed to finance the administrative cost of waste oil regulation and research (OECD, 1980: 75).

The preference for fiscal charges over other forms of environmental taxation continued to dominate the 1980s Dutch environmental policy approach. A notable example was the 1987 Manure Act which specified various strict regulatory prescriptions and imposed a levy in order to finance research and environmental adjustments in individual farms (Dietz and Termeer, 1991: 128–31).

While this predominance continued there was a growing recognition of the costs of co-ordinating so many levies. In 1984 there were seven environmental levies in force, and there was the possibility of the government creating twice that number to raise revenue for the sector-specific acts. Even though industry had a strong preference for charges as taxation instruments, the government imposed an environmental tax on all fuels in 1988 (VROM, 1992: 6–9). The tax aimed to replace the system of individual, programme-specific levies which reflected the incremental evolution of Dutch eco-tax thinking (Interview, VROM Officials, 1993; VROM, 1992: 7–9; Vermeend and van de Vaarten, 1998: 17).

The new fuel tax achieved the goal of integrating fragmented environmental levies by creating an integrated financing system. Policy makers built more transparency (for taxpayers) and simplicity (increasing administrative efficiency) into the mechanism. Several government memoranda issued before 1988 highlighted the need for a simpler system. The last levy of its generation was a charge on industrial noise that was so complicated that its operating costs for both the government and industry exceeded the revenue generated (Vermeend and van de Vaarten, 1998: 17; Snel, 2000).

The government's target for the fuel tax reflected its strategy to influence polluter behaviour in key areas of air pollution and noise nuisance. The Dutch Environment Ministry administered the fuel tax. It was set at a modest rate, with the revenue earmarked for financing particular environment-related government expenditures. Consequently, the fuel levy retained the basic emphasis on fund-raising objectives established in the Dutch tradition of the 1970s. The tax did not lead to the scrapping of all individual charges as the aircraft noise pollution charge remained in force (CEC, 2000a; OECD, 1993).

In the 1990s the interest in eco-taxes increased significantly. The new 1989 coalition between the Christian Democrats (CDA) and the Social Democrats (PvdA) helped trigger this shift. Policy makers articulated in the 1989 National Environmental Policy Plan (NEPP – see Chapter 3 for details) particular concerns about the rise of carbon dioxide emissions.

The coalition of Christian Democrats and Social Democrats emphasised the need to increase environment expenditure in order to achieve better environmental protection. Charges and eco-taxes were levied to finance this increase in spending. Much of the debate surrounding the 1989 NEPP was focused on how to finance its environmental priorities. Several advisory bodies helped build further momentum for the use of eco-taxes (for example, Financial and Economic Instruments, 1992).

The European Commission vetoed the Dutch mechanism of lowering the VAT rate on electricity generated by renewable energy sources (The Green Tax Commission, 1998). This is an instance of the EU acting as an institutional constraint on Dutch policy instrument calibration selection. Member states' inability to adopt an EU-wide carbon dioxide/energy tax indirectly shaped the Dutch eco-taxes discourse about the overburdening of domestic industries and reducing their competitiveness (Snel, 2000). Efforts by the Nordic countries, particularly Denmark, to develop varying types of eco-taxes did give some momentum to domestic eco-tax reforms.

Vermeend and van der Vaart (1998: 4–5) do not view the 1988–98 developments as involving a 'planned, systematic green tax reform'. Facing economic difficulties in the 1980s/early 1990s, the Dutch government developed an interest in using energy tax revenues to lower the tax burden on labour with the aim of boosting employment and protecting the environment. It formulated the potential role of eco-taxes as a 'double-edged sword', or more notably as producing a 'double dividend' (Heineken, 2002).

The Dutch Parliament conducted a substantial discussion which led to several modifications of the 1988 fuel levy (Vermeend and van der Vaart, 1998; 18–20). The Dutch parliament increased the amount of revenue and more importantly placed the tax revenue in the general government coffers – as opposed to earmarking it for environmental purposes (VROM, 1992: 7). This decision changed the fuel tax from a charge/levy to a true environmental tax administered by the Finance Ministry. The tax also became central to the general budget and revenue in the Netherlands, making the tax attractive to those involved in tax collection and

138   *Environmental governance in Europe*

revenue gathering. Given industry's opposition, the government consulted a wide range of actors (including environment NGOs) and adopted compensating factors (such as labour tax cuts) which helped deliver its adoption (Heineken, 2002).

By 1994, the Parliament faced the prospect of increasing revenue by raising the tax, but there was widespread concern that the increase would place an unacceptable burden on large fuel consuming companies. The Parliament shifted to the idea of fair taxation burden sharing and widening the tax base (VROM, 2010: 1). In 1994, Parliament agreed the Environmental Taxes Act which created new taxes on groundwater extraction and landfill waste. The revenue from both was earmarked for the general government budget.

Elections and government changes are noticeable in the history of the Dutch eco-taxes. After the 1994 elections, the VVD (Liberal Party), the Social Democrats and Democrats 66 formed a coalition, pushing the Christian Democrats into opposition. A majority within this centre-left 'Purple Coalition I' backed the idea of a national energy tax if the EU could not develop a more preferable EU-wide version by 1996 (Heineken, 2002). The coalition agreement included a regulatory energy tax on consumption of gas and electricity by small users (Vermeend and van der Vaart, 1998: 23–7). The new tax, which entered into force in 1996, targeted the reduction of carbon dioxide emissions from small users (for instance, households) while protecting the competitive position of large industrial users (whose environmental behaviour was targeted by the fuel tax). The government envisioned the small user tax as a tool for modifying the behaviour of actors that could not be reached through VAs (see Chapter 5). The 1996 eco-tax was significant for the move towards a more full scale ecological tax reform because it was the first Dutch eco-tax to have its revenue used to reduce other taxes (such as income tax).

The Purple Coalition I instituted a Green Tax Commission to examine the future of eco-taxes. The Commission's 1998 report stated that tax rebates for environmentally friendly behaviour were more effective than energy tax increases but that the energy tax rates should be higher than the increases in VAT (The Green Tax Commission, 1998). The Purple Coalition II (1998–02), which was made up of the same political parties as the Purple Coalition I, incorporated the Green Tax Commission's recommendations in its coalition government agreement. It also instigated a Second Green Tax Commission which issued a report that recommended the wider use of emissions trading schemes (see Chapter 7) and new types of eco-taxes (Interviews, VROM officials, 2002).

As Chapter 3 highlighted, from 2002–04 centre-right Dutch governments faced a period of uncertainty and turmoil. This period saw a substantial shift away from environmental spending and a decreased effort to expand the tax base and to target new objectives (Interviews, Ministry Officials, 2002, 2003). In 2004 the Dutch government reverted towards the more traditional approach to eco-taxes while announcing 2005 budget plans which included a substantial increase in energy taxes (*ENDS Europe Daily*, 21 September 2004). The government compensated for these increases with a reduction in employment-related taxation. In addition to harnessing the tax increase as an incentive for investing in new green technologies, it also helped to keep the Dutch budget deficit within the 3 per cent limit set by the EU for member states which wanted to join the Economic and Monetary Union (EMU).

In 2008, the centre-left coalition led by the Christian Democrats and Labour made a concentrated effort at eco-taxes innovation; it introduced a carbon-based packaging tax which covered the packaging of all products marketed domestically (OECD, 2010; Sevenster et al., 2007). The national recycling targets were defined by the need to implement the EU Packaging Directive (Bio Intelligence Service, 2009). Additionally, however, the tax had the objectives of targeting carbon emissions and the 'greening' of the Dutch fiscal system. A second measure to green the national tax system was the 2008 air passenger tax. However, after only one year, the coalition government abolished the tax, in the face of the global economic crisis and reports that Dutch travellers were opting for German and Belgian airports (Gordijn and Kolkman, 2011). Finally the Government proposed a kilometre road charge to replace vehicle registration and circulation taxes (Ministry of Infrastructure and Environment, 2011).

The EU played an important role in shaping Dutch efforts to innovate with eco-taxes on the domestic level. The 1996 energy tax had to conform to the 2003 EU Directive on the Taxation of Energy Products although it did not involve substantial changes. However, the termination of the 1992 fuel tax for all fuels except coal was due to the requirement of the 2003 EU Directive.

The EU questioned certain aspects of the air passenger tax (for example, on differentiating short haul and long haul flights) and the vehicle registration tax (Interview, Ministry of Finance official, 2011). Nevertheless, the biggest change in Dutch eco-tax policy has come with the 2010 government coalition which includes a right wing populist party (see Chapter 3). One of the items in the included coalition agreement was the government abandonment of the 2008 kilometre charge proposal. The government and its Finance Secretary of State Weekers (VVD-Liberal)

140 *Environmental governance in Europe*

decided to abolish a number of taxes, including eco-taxes, in the interest of having 'solid and simple taxes' (Interview, Ministry of Finance official, 2011). Accordingly in 2011 the government announced plans to abolish the waste tax, the ground water and tap water taxes and the packaging waste tax. The energy tax, which generates €4 billion in revenue will substitute for these taxes and contain a surcharge to fund particular green energy and other programmes.

In 2010, the Dutch ranked 11th among the EU-25 in terms of energy taxes, fourth in terms of transportation taxes and second in pollution/resource taxes (CEU, 2010b: 232–4). These rankings and the fact that the Netherlands has one of the highest proportions of revenue derived from eco-taxes, led the Secretary of State to argue that further Dutch eco-tax efforts would have to be made dependent on other European countries increasing their environmental tax efforts and revenue (Interview, Ministry of Finance official, 2011).

GERMANY: EARLY PIONEER THAT RAN OUT OF STEAM TEMPORARLY

The pattern of eco-tax usage in Germany was largely ad hoc up to the 1990s (Andersen and Sprenger, 2000; EEA, 2000; OECD, 1999b; UBA, 1994). The 1976 waste water levy is widely seen as one of the first eco-taxes in modern German environmental policy (Andersen, 1994). It was implemented only in 1981 after it had been watered-down to accommodate industry objections. Other important reasons for the delayed implementation of the 1976 waste water levy included a protracted constitutional dispute about the competences for this tax between the federal government and the states *(Länder)* (Andersen, 1994: 127–8). The waste water levy soon lost its importance because traditional regulatory instruments stipulated the use of the best available technology (BAT).

Eco-tax initiatives were taken at both the federal and state level. For example, the state Baden-Würtemberg introduced a moderate water extraction charge (nicknamed *Wasserpfennig*) in the 1980s. In the 1990s this charge was emulated by a few other German states. Local authorities also introduced some eco-taxes although the scope for local eco-taxes has been highly constrained by the German constitution. In 1995 the Federal Administrative Court banned the city of Kassel from imposing a levy on disposable cutlery (as can be found in fast food restaurants). Constitutional requirements also constrained the federal government in the use of hypothecation (in other words, earmarking) of taxes, including eco-taxes.

As hypothecated taxes must benefit the targeted tax payers, German governments have tended to prefer general eco-taxes over hypothecated eco-taxes (Interview, Finance Ministry, 2001).

In the 1980s Germany adopted a wide range of fiscal incentives. The fiscal incentives to increase the consumption of unleaded petrol and to accelerate the uptake of the so-called three way catalytic converter in petrol driven passenger cars constitute the most prominent examples (see Wurzel, 2002). Such fiscal incentives failed to internalise the pollution cost generated by the consumption of these products unless they were used in combination with tax rises on more heavily polluting products (for example, the purchase of leaded petrol and cars not equipped with catalytic converters) (Holzinger, 1994; Wurzel, 2002). Fiscal incentives for the early market penetration of less polluting products in combination with eco-taxes on more environmentally damaging products have remained an important policy instrument in Germany since the 1980s.

The academic discussion about the merits of a full scale ecological tax reform gathered pace in Germany only in the 1990s although some environmental economists had advocated such a reform already in the 1970s (Binswanger et al., 1979; Hansmeyer, 1976; Siebert, 1976; SRU, 1974, 1978). The eventual 1998 adoption of an ecological tax reform was preceded by three major debates about the merits of eco-taxes (Interviews, 2001 and 2007; Reiche and Krebs, 1999).

The first major debate, largely restricted to academic circles, took place in the 1970s (Binswanger et al., 1979; Hansmeyer, 1976; Siebert, 1976; SRU, 1974). The economics professor and the first chairperson of the German Environmental Expert Council (SRU), Karl-Heinz Hansmeyer, was an early eco-tax advocate. However, the early debate about the merits of eco-taxes had little impact on the German government's use of NEPIs in practice. One important reason why the 1976 waste water levy remained the only significant domestic eco-tax in the 1970s can be found in the difficult global economic situation triggered by the 1973 and 1976 oil crises.

The second major debate about ecological tax reform occurred in the 1980s (Interviews, 2001 and 2007; Reiche and Krebs, 1999; UBA, 1994). During this debate eco-taxes were explicitly linked with job creation: in exchange for the adoption of eco-taxes, a simultaneous lowering of non-wage labour costs was proposed to improve German industry's international competitiveness. As in the Dutch case, ecological tax reform proponents argued that it would generate a 'double dividend', namely better environmental protection for and increased economic competitiveness. In the 1980s, Ernst Ulrich von Weizsäcker popularised the phrase 'prices must tell the ecological truth', which the Swiss economist

Christoph Binswanger coined in the 1970s (Interviews, 2001; Binswanger et al., 1979; Weizsäcker and Jesinghaus, 1992).

Climate change became a highly salient political issue in Germany in the 1990s. However, the centre-right (CDU/CSU and FDP) coalition government under Chancellor Helmut Kohl (CDU) was unwilling to contemplate unilateral ecological tax reform and instead lobbied hard for EU-wide eco-taxes (see the following). The economic recession, the huge cost of German reunification and the debate about Germany as an investment and production location *(the Standort Deutschland* debate) pushed proponents of ecological tax reform onto the defensive (Wurzel et al., 2003a). In the 1990s, the Environment Minister, Klaus Töpfer (CDU), sought to promote ecological tax reform but was vetoed by Chancellor Helmut Kohl on competitiveness grounds.

Both proponents and opponents commissioned scientific studies on the economic impact of an ecological tax reform. For example, Greenpeace commissioned a study by the more left-orientated German Institute for Economic Research (DIW), which contended that an ecological tax reform would generate a double dividend (DIW, 1995). To counter the double dividend argument the Federal Association of Germany Industry *(Bundesverband der Deutschen Industrie* – BDI) financed a study from (the Finance Institute at) the University of Cologne which, however, did not unequivocally reject the economic benefits of domestic ecological tax reform (Reiche and Krebs, 1999).

As in the Netherlands, a change in government provided the decisive impetus for the German adoption of an ecological tax reform. The 1998 elections produced a Red-Green (SPD-Green Party) coalition government. In the run up to the 1998 elections environmental NGOs campaigned for an ecological tax reform which, however, was opposed by industry that favoured instead the use of VAs (see Chapter 5). The demand by one prominent Green politician to raise petrol prices to DM 5 within 10 years raised sharp controversy and was subsequently rejected by the Green party leadership (Interviews, 2001; Raschke, 2001: 217). The SPD leader (and Chancellor candidate), Gerhard Schröder, feared the electoral consequences of large tax hikes and argued for an upper limit of six *Pfennige* for one litre of petrol (Interview, Finance Ministry Official, 2000; Reiche and Krebs, 1999). The adoption of an ecological tax reform was one of the red lines for the Greens in the coalition agreement negotiations with the SPD leadership whose left wing (led by Oskar Lafontaine) supported the Green Party demands.

The Red-Green coalition government (1998–2005) had initially intended to introduce the first stage of the ecological reform in 1998. However, the start of the ecological tax reform had to be postponed until early 1999 because the EU Commission objected to certain exemptions for high energy users and some fiscal incentives for renewable energy (Interviews, 2001). The ecological tax reform introduced five annual increases of eco-taxes on oil and gas. The intention was to send clear long-term price signals for the use of non-renewable energy sources. Accordingly, the first stage saw an increase in electricity prices of €0.01 per kilowatt hour (kWh), in gas of €1.636 per megawatt hour (mWh), and in mineral oil of €0.031 per litre. The following annual increases only raised taxes on fuels for transport (by €0.031 per litre) and for electricity by €0.003 per kWh.

Importantly, the ecological tax reform granted significant exemptions to manufacturing industries and other high energy intensive industries where the energy tax burden exceeded by a factor of 1.2 the simultaneous reduction in social security contributions. The SPD was concerned about alienating the coal-rich Ruhr area, a traditional SPD electoral stronghold. It therefore accepted only very moderate tax increases on the industrial use of coal despite its high carbon content. Simultaneously, government policy moved towards preferential treatment for renewable energy sources and certain less environmentally damaging sources of energy (such as natural gas for motor vehicles) while also supporting the co-generation of electricity and heat.

Despite generous exemptions for high energy users and coal, the ecological tax reform met strong industry opposition (with the exception of some industries such as renewable energy producers). In the wake of massive protests against rising fuel prices in Germany in 2000 (see also the following section on the UK), the main opposition parties – the CDU/CSU and FDP – initiated a law to abolish the ecological tax reform (*Ökosteuerrücknahmegesetz*) (Interview, 2001). This CDU/CSU and FDP initiative failed because of the Red-Green coalition government's parliamentary majority. However, the Red-Green government adopted measures to compensate socially disadvantaged and politically influential groups by, for example, increasing tax allowances for commuters (*Pendlerpauschale*). The revenue from the ecological tax reform peaked in 2003. The Environment Agency has interpreted the subsequent moderate decline as a sign of the ecological tax reform's success apparently triggering a lowering of fuel passenger car consumption (UBA, 2011a).

The Environment Ministry and Environment Agency defended the ecological tax reform by pointing out that other European countries had also adopted significant eco-taxes without negative economic consequences. In the early 1990s, Germany was a driving force within a group of like-minded European countries that tried to facilitate the adoption and coordination of national eco-taxes in absence of an EU-wide carbon

144   *Environmental governance in Europe*

dioxide/energy tax (see the following). However, by the late 1990s, the coordinated eco-taxes initiative of the group of like-minded countries had faltered.

Importantly, the ecological tax reform was not abandoned either by the grand (CDU/CSU – SPD) coalition (2005–09) or the centre-right (CDU/ CSU-FDP) coalition government (since 2009) which followed the Red-Green coalition government. Instead eco-taxes continued to be extended in a very gradual and largely ad hoc fashion. In 2006 a coal tax was adopted which, however, did not enter into force for households until 2010 (UBA, 2011a). In 2010 the vehicles tax for new passenger cars was changed to reflect at least partly their carbon dioxide emissions. In June 2010 the centre-right (CDU/CSU – FDP) coalition government decided to reduce, by about €80 billion, the federal government's budget. These fairly substantive budgetary savings were to be achieved through, amongst others, cuts to environmentally damaging subsidies, the increase of existing eco-taxes and the adoption of new eco-taxes. The German Environment Agency estimated that environmentally damaging subsidies amounted to €48 billion in Germany in 2008 (UBA, 2011b). New eco-taxes levied to bring about approximately €80 billion in savings include taxes on nuclear power (*Atomsteuer*) and flights (*Flugticket-steuer*). The centre-right (CDU/CSU-FDP) coalition government also reduced the number of exemptions from the ecological tax reform and accelerated the reduction of coal subsidies. However, the German Environment Agency's proposal (UBA, 2011) to further transform the ecological tax reform into a full scale fiscal reform (for all public expenditure to take environmental concerns into consideration) has made little progress.

AUSTRIA: ECO-TAXES LATECOMER

Austria was a relative latecomer to the substantial use of eco-taxes. During the 1980s, Austria adopted a wide range of relatively stringent environmental laws and a large number of fiscal incentives to support the early uptake of environmentally less damaging products. Accordingly, the OECD (1995a) argued that there was a compelling case for a wider use of NEPIs including eco-taxes in Austrian environmental policy. Subsidies including environmental subsidies (for companies which manufacture products that have a less environmentally damaging impact) have traditionally played an important role in Austria (Interviews, Environment Ministry, 2011). Some of the earliest Austrian eco-taxes were levied on motor vehicles and fuels although their main purpose was initially to generate revenue for the Finance Ministry. As in most OECD countries, the transport sector accounts for the bulk of the revenue generated from eco-taxes (OECD, 2001). Like Germany, Austria adopted fiscal incentives to promote the use of unleaded petrol and cars equipped with three-way catalytic converters (Wurzel et al., 2003b). In 1989 Austria adopted a waste tax which helped introduce BAT for landfill sites (OECD, 2001). From 1986 to 1993 Austria also adopted a fertilizer tax which achieved a 20 per cent reduction in chemical fertilizer usage (OECD, 1995a: 38). However, the government deemed it incompatible with Single European Market rules and scrapped it shortly before Austria's 1995 EU accession.

The 1990s constituted a high point for eco-tax adoption in Austria. In 1994 and 1995, mineral oil taxes were raised by between 50 and 150 per cent although these tax increases were mainly driven by fiscal rather than environmental considerations. In the late 1990s, Austrian mineral oil taxes were amongst the highest in Western Europe triggering 'petrol tourism' (*Tanktourismus*) by Austrian motorists who used cheaper petrol stations in neighbouring countries (Interviews, Environment and Finance Ministries, 2001). Austria is a relatively small country which shares borders with seven neighbours. Big differences in petrol and diesel prices therefore easily lead to 'petrol tourism'. However, by the late 2000s Austrian fuel taxes had failed to keep pace with larger increases in many neighbouring countries. Consequently there was a reversal in the direction of 'petrol tourism' with foreign registered cars and lorries taking advantage of lower petrol and diesel prices in Austria. While the Finance Ministry has welcomed this form of 'petrol tourism' because of the additional revenue it generates, it has raised serious concerns within the Environment Ministry because it increased Austrian carbon dioxide emissions (Interviews, 2011).

The early debate about an ecological tax reform can be traced to the 1980s. However, only in the late 1990s was a Tax Reform Commission set up to assess a wide range of tax reforms including the possible adoption of a national ecological tax reform. The Tax Reform Commission failed, however, to endorse the adoption of a national ecological tax reform. Environmental NGOs complained that they were not invited to core consultation meetings organised by the Tax Reform Commission (Interviews, 2011). The recommendations of the Tax Reform Commission contrasted with the Austrian Institute for Economic Research's study of national ecological tax reform; the latter concluded that a national ecological tax reform would boost employment and industrial competitiveness (WIFO, 1995, 1998). The Environment Ministry viewed the Tax Reform Commission recommendations negatively while the Economics Ministry broadly welcomed them (Interviews, 2002 and 2011).

The Austrian Chancellor, Victor Klima (SPÖ), and Vice-Chancellor, Wolfgang Schüssel (ÖVP), settled the debate within the grand coalition government (consisting of the Social Democrats (SPÖ) and Austrian People's Party (ÖVP)) by ruling out a national ecological tax reform. The grand coalition government instead expressed its support for the introduction of an EU-wide carbon dioxide/energy tax because it would protect the competitiveness of Austrian industry.

Under two centre-right wing (ÖVP – Freedom Party (FPÖ)) coalition governments (2000–07) the Workers Chamber teamed up with environmental NGOs to draft a proposal for an alternative budget which was entitled 'Ways out of the crises' and suggested the adoption of additional eco-taxes and income taxes (Interviews, 2011). However, the informal coalition on ecological tax reform between environmental NGOs and the Workers Chamber has not been an easy one (Interviews, 2001 and 2011). The environmental NGOs demanded the taxing of 'environmental ills'. The Workers Chamber, which is one of two social partners (*Sozialpartner*) with significant formal influence in Austrian public policy-making (see Chapter 3), emphasised the need for socially just eco-taxes: these should be designed so that they do not negatively affect the poor and are embedded within a wider tax reform that raises income taxes and reintroduces inheritance taxes (Interviews, 2011).

The Labour Chamber Social Democrats only gradually warmed to the ecological tax reform idea. As Chapter 3 pointed out, the SPÖ fully endorsed the ecological modernisation concept, which assumes that ambitious environmental policy measures are beneficial for both the environment and economy, only from the 1990s onwards. It was the Conservative Austrian People's Party (ÖVP) which first pushed the idea of an 'eco-social market economy' that included the use of market-based instruments such as eco-taxes. Even the Freedom Party (FPÖ), which under its populist leader, Jörg Haider, gravitated to the extreme right wing, became supportive of NEPIs (Lauber, 1997b: 613) although it generally preferred VAs over eco-taxes. Importantly, the Green Party, which has traditionally been the staunchest proponent for ecological tax reform amongst Austria's main political parties, did not participate in any government coalition (see Chapter 3).

The Business Chamber *(Wirtschaftskammer)*, which is the second of two social partners *(Sozialpartner)*, and the Federation of Austrian Industries *(Industriellenvereinigung)* continued their vociferous opposition to ecological tax reform. The harsher economic climate of the 1990s increased concerns about the competitiveness of Austrian businesses. Ecological tax reform therefore became essentially a 'taboo subject' for government and ministry officials (Interviews, 2001 and 2011). Unlike

Germany, Austria failed to adopt an ecological tax reform. Like Germany, Austria also made little progress in reducing environmentally damaging subsidies.

The 2000s saw an incremental ad hoc adoption of eco-taxes. This change did not satisfy the OECD, which repeated its admonition to Austria to increase NEPI usage (OECD, 2001). In 2000 Austria changed its motor vehicle tax to reflect the carbon dioxide emission output of the vehicles. The Austrian Environment Ministry concluded that 12 out of 74 measures adopted under the national climate change strategy could be categorised as market-based instruments although only eight per cent of the total tax revenue was linked to environmental objectives (BMUJF, 1997). Successive Austrian governments increased energy taxes in the 2000s. In 2004 the Austrian government adopted an electronic road pricing system for lorries (Interview, 2011). Taxes on the use of energy and fuels were raised in Austria in 2005 (diesel and heating oil), 2007 (petrol, diesel and heating oil) and 2011 (petrol, diesel and heating oil). Excluding VAT, the 2011 increases of fuel taxes amounted to four Cents per litre petrol and five Cents per litre diesel and heating oil (Interview, 2011).

THE UK: ECO-TAXES LATECOMER WITH INNOVATIVE MEASURES

The UK adopted perhaps one of the world's first 'environmental' taxes when, in 1909, Lloyd George introduced a petrol tax (Tindale and Holtham, 1996: 22). Nevertheless, the UK has a patchy history concerning market-based instruments in general and eco-taxes in particular. The way in which eco-taxes have been used since the 1970s has gradually become more sophisticated. At first simple revenue raising levies (or 'implicit' taxes) were deployed, but over time more complex eco-taxes appeared, employing hypothecation to achieve ecological tax reform.

Eco-taxes were discussed in parts of government throughout the 1970s and 1980s, but they had few powerful political champions. During an inquiry on the polluter pays principle in 1982, the House of Lords asked the eminent economist Partha Dasgupta to brief them on environmental charges (HOLSCEC, 1983). The House of Lords subsequently requested the Environment Ministry to investigate their use in other EU states, which the department duly completed (DoE, 1984). However, any government interest that this report generated soon petered out. UK policy elites have traditionally viewed eco-taxes with a mixture of suspicion and hostility. Many had grown up with regulation and were

148   *Environmental governance in Europe*

well versed in the art of using it to 'muddle through' problems as and when they appeared. In 1972, the Royal Commission on Environmental Pollution looked at how innovators such as the USA, France and the Netherlands were using MBIs, and concluded that:

> We are not convinced that a system of charges would be as effective as [legal] consents ... [which] if properly policed, would guarantee a level of [environmental] quality ... The administration of a system of charges would need an expertise ... which we do not believe exists at present ... (RCEP, 1972: 58–67).

A UK Environment Minister once famously claimed that '[I]ndustry in Britain has always opposed the concept of a general charging system whereby charges are imposed' (HL Hansard, 5th Series, Vol. 444, cols. 1110–2, November 1983). Although economists such as David Pearce and Wilfred Beckerman continued to work on the theories underpinning eco-tax usage throughout the 1970s and 1980s, Britain stood aloof and watched while other states began to innovate.

The burst of political interest in environmental issues in the late 1980s helped energise and broaden the eco-tax debate, which previously had not really extended far beyond the narrow ranks of economists and other technical experts. The Government's 1990 White Paper helped to make more widely known environmental taxes but was not, of itself, sufficient to tip the policy-making balance from regulation to NEPIs. Nonetheless, interest within the Environment Ministry remained moderate once this burst of political interest had subsided. In the foreword to a 1992 update of the White Paper, the Environment Minister, Michael Howard, promised 'a new presumption in favour of economic instruments rather than regulation' (HM Government, 1992). The White Paper emphasised that 'new regulations should be limited to cases where economic instruments ... are either not available or require regulatory underpinning' (HM Government, 1992).

However, the eco-taxes that were actually adopted in the early 1990s were produced in an ad hoc manner. They include higher road fuel duties and the ill-fated tax on domestic fuel which were both adopted in 1993. Eventually both generated so much political controversy that they had to be substantially restructured.

Throughout the 1980s, the Environment Ministry developed extensive plans for eco-taxes to control water pollution, sulphur emissions, waste generation, chlorofluorocarbon usage and tyre disposal (DoE, 1993). In spite of all this work, very few of them ever appeared. Helm (1998: 11) suggests that the vast majority of UK eco-taxes in the late 1990s were

Governing by eco-taxes 149

'implicit' economic instruments – for instance, they are primarily designed to raise revenue rather than to protect the environment.

Under the Major government (1990–97), two of the most well-known implicit taxes were the fuel duty escalator (1993–2000) and VAT on domestic fuel. The escalator was an automatic annual increase in road fuel tax primarily to raise revenue (although it had strong concomitant environmental benefits). Subsequent Chancellors increased the escalator, but Gordon Brown suspended it in 2000 to pacify petrol tax protestors which had staged massive protests. In 1993, the Conservatives also raised the VAT rate on domestic fuel from 0 per cent to 8 per cent; a further increase of 17.5 per cent was hastily abandoned in the teeth of widespread protests that it exacerbated 'fuel poverty'. In 2000, Labour announced that VAT on energy saving devices (including solar technology) would be reduced to the EU minimum of 5 per cent.

The other main environmental 'tax' in this period was not actually a tax, but a tax differential in favour of unleaded petrol (1987–2001). By comparison, Austria, Germany and the Netherlands had all introduced lower taxes for unleaded petrol in the early 1980s. The motor fuel differentiation has remained, with categories broadened to include ultra-low sulphur and sulphur free petrol as well as alternative road fuels (Fullerton et al., 2010).

The most significant Conservative government eco-taxes innovation was the 1996 landfill tax, probably the UK's first modern eco-tax. It aimed to increase recycling and waste reduction. Part of the landfill tax is used to offset the cost of labour through a 0.2 per cent reduction in the National Insurance contributions paid by all employers. The 1997–2010 Labour government continued to drive up landfill tax rates to reduce land filling. However, this was partly due to the need to comply with the 1999 EU Directive on landfills. An automatic price escalator was subsequently added in 2003, and increased in both 2005 and 2008 (Fullerton et al., 2010).

The 1997 arrival of a 'new' Labour government with more ambitious environmental goals gave fresh impetus to the discussion and eventual adoption of eco-taxes. In opposition, Labour had markedly shifted its environmental policy to incorporate NEPIs such as eco-taxes. Left of centre think tanks such as the Institute for Public Policy Research and the Fabian Society were influential in re-modelling Labour's stance on eco-taxes. One Institute for Public Policy Research fellow, Stephen Tindale, became secretary to the Labour Party's Policy Commission on the Environment prior to the 1997 election. He reportedly briefed Labour's Treasury team on the merits of eco-tax reform (Smith, 2004). When Labour actually entered power in 1997, the new Environment Minister, Michael Meacher, hired him as a special adviser.

The two most significant eco-taxes adopted by Labour governments (1997–2010) were the 2001 climate change levy (CCL) and the 2002 aggregates tax. The most notable CCL feature is its linkage to several other NEPIs in a complex policy package. Following industry opposition, the Environment Ministry announced an 80 per cent discount for companies in highly energy extensive sectors that signed up to a negotiated VA (see Chapter 5) – the climate change levy agreement (CCLA). The title CCL is somewhat of a misnomer as the instrument is directed at the downstream energy use, rather than the carbon intensity of energy use. Like the landfill tax, some of the revenues are offset against employers' national insurance contributions and are also used to finance energy efficiency schemes. In the 2008–09 tax year the revenue from the CCL was £700 million (Fullerton et al., 2010).

The 2002 aggregates tax was actually first mooted in 1998 as a means for addressing the environmental costs of quarrying. The Quarry Products Association fiercely resisted and proposed a VA as an alternative. The Environment Ministry regarded this alternative as insufficiently ambitious and pressed on regardless. Most of the aggregates tax receipts are recycled to reduce employers' national insurance contributions. However, a portion of its revenue is channelled to a sustainability fund which works to remove some of the barriers to re-using aggregates and to promote local environmental benefits in areas affected by quarrying (Fullerton et al., 2010).

Having launched a number of innovative eco-taxes in its first term (1997–2001), the Labour government lost some of its momentum because of resistance from vested interests. The 2000 road fuel protests marked an important watershed in the government's willingness to court political controversy to achieve environmental policy goals. In spite of growing enthusiasm for eco-taxes (and emissions trading) in the Treasury and Industry Ministry, there remained a strong 'unpolitics' of instrument use in the UK.

Government revenues from eco-taxes declined in the post 2000 period largely due to the scale of the post fuel protest concessions handed out to road users. In 2002, the House of Commons Environmental Audit Committee claimed that the Treasury's interest in eco-taxes was fizzling out (*ENDS Report*, 325, 2002: 36). The Confederation of British Industry (CBI) used the committee's inquiry to call for a moratorium on all new eco-taxes. In 2006, the UK Parliamentary Environmental Audit Committee charged the Treasury with failing to respond adequately to the Stern Report; the latter had demanded decisive action to mitigate the effects of climate change and suggested increasing the level of eco-taxes (*ENDS Daily Europe*, 6 November 2006).

An exemplar high profile casualty was the pesticide tax, first mooted in 1998. Work progressed at one point rapidly, but Prime Minister Tony Blair intervened in 2000 to call a halt. The Environment Ministry responded by raising the possibility of a negotiated VA. By 2006, the VA had met the majority of the targets and was continued on a two year rolling basis (Voluntary Initiative, 2010).

Other eco-taxes proposals have faced substantial opposition. The UK's struggle to implement the EU Nitrates Directive kept the fertilizer tax on the domestic political agenda. The EU Water Framework Directive also forced the UK government to consider new eco-taxes to control emissions of diffuse pollution that causes eutrophication.

The 'push factor' of EU legislation witnessed with the Nitrates and Water Framework Directives created a similar interest in the waste sector. The area of waste management found the UK struggling to comply with tough, new EU regulatory targets. The UK government contemplated several solutions, including a variable charging system for household waste. Plans for lorry road use charging were drawn up, but not put into effect.

Much government effort focused on road pricing and congestion charging to ease pressure on urban roads and reduce air pollution while shifting revenue into more environmentally friendly public transportation schemes. This effort achieved two notable successes at the smaller scale (Durham was the first to introduce the system in 2002) and at the largest (London in 2003). The Labour government created a £2 billion fund to support local charging schemes. Local government councils continued to consider such schemes. However the effort may have faced its Waterloo (at least in the intermediate term) in Manchester, with the public rejecting the proposed road pricing scheme with 79 per cent of the vote (Carter, 2008). This came after defeats in York, Cambridge, Edinburgh, Birmingham and elsewhere (BBC, 2010a, 2010b). In 2011 the Conservative Mayor, Boris Johnson, fulfilled a campaign pledge by scrapping the extension of the London scheme to the West of London (Roberts, 2011).

The Conservative-Liberal coalition government, which came to power in 2010, gave strong priority to cutting the deficit while stimulating private sector growth; this in turn greatly reduced the scope for innovative eco-taxes. In terms of the environmental agenda, the coalition government's flagship proposal for a different kind of instrument, Green Investment Bank, has met difficulties (Jansen, 2010). As Leader of the Opposition and Shadow Chancellor, both Cameron and Osborne had stated their support for market mechanisms to reflect the true environmental cost of externalities (The Environmental Industries Commission, 2010a). The emergency 2010 budget proposed tinkering, but did not

152   *Environmental governance in Europe*

dispense with the three key 'new' Labour ecological innovations (Environmental Industries Commission, 2010b). The emergency budget promised to issue proposals to reform the CCL to provide more certainty concerning the price but would keep the rates in line with inflation. It also announced the increase in the standard rate of the landfill tax and the rate of the aggregates levy (Environmental Industries Commission, 2010b).

This coalition government's response is not a radical departure from the last two decades of UK government policy on eco-taxes. Both Conservative and Labour governments have produced eco-tax innovations, especially the landfill tax, CCL and aggregates levy. However a strong suspicion regarding eco-taxes remains in the British political elite and the general public.

THE EU: ECO-TAXES LAGGARD

Throughout the 1970s and much of 1980s the idea of using eco-tax to supplement or replace traditional environmental regulation was simply absent from the EU agenda. Albert Weale and colleagues have therefore argued that the EU made use of 'illiberal instruments' despite the liberal foundations of the Single European Market (Weale et al., 2000: 458). While some member states adopted a wide range of eco-taxes, traditional regulation remained unchallenged as the main EU environmental policy instrument. Only towards the late 1980s did the Commission, and in particular the Directorate General for Environment (DG Environment), push the idea of an EU-wide carbon dioxide/energy tax. Global warming was becoming important and environmental pioneer states were adopting eco-taxes. Increasing regional and international discourse (for example, within the OECD) developed around the sustainability idea and the need to develop new market-based instruments including eco-taxes (Delbeke, 1991; Opschoor and Vos, 1989).

By the early 1990s DG Environment officials were focusing their efforts on a common carbon dioxide/energy tax (CEC, 1992). The Task Force on the Environment and Internal Market (1990) emphasised the need to use fiscal instruments. The Environment Commissioner, Ripa di Meana, used the impending 1992 UN Rio Earth Summit and increasing climate change concern to highlight the need for this particular NEPI, which had the institutional benefits of increasing the EU's global role and the Commission's scope of influence (Zito, 2000). Although only operating as a strategic guidance document, the Fifth Environmental Action Programme (EAP) emphasised the need to broaden the EU's policy

Governing by eco-taxes 153

instrument mix to include eco-taxes (CEC, 1993b). Commission President, Jacques Delors, backed the White Paper on *Growth, Competitiveness and Employment* (CEC, 1993a) which advocated the adoption of eco-taxes in exchange for a lowering of labour costs to boost economic growth and environmental protection.

The Commission advocates received support for an EU-wide eco-tax from Germany and the Netherlands (as well as other member states). However, the EU institutional context (for instance, the adoption of supranational taxes requires unanimity within the Council) gave opposing member states, motivated for different reasons as seen in the case of the UK (sovereignty fears) and Spain (development fears), the ability to block the proposed tax (Zito, 2000).

Frustrated by the EU's inability to adopt a carbon dioxide/energy tax, a group of like-minded countries initiated a series of meetings between Environmental and Finance Ministry officials and Ministers between 1994 and 1998 (see previous). The main aims of these meeting were to discuss the design and effect of different national eco-taxes, how to avoid eco-taxes damaging economic competitiveness, and how to achieve an EU carbon dioxide/energy tax or at least a minimum harmonisation of national fuel and/or energy taxes (Interview, German official, 2001). Belgium, Denmark, Finland, France, Germany, Italy and Sweden participated in the last meetings (the last in April 1998) of this informal group. These discussions kept the issue of a common carbon dioxide/energy tax on the European agenda despite the fact that it had been vetoed in the Council. Perhaps surprisingly the UK also attended some meetings although it remained opposed to EU-wide taxes.

In 1997, the Commission proposed a directive to harmonise member state taxation on energy products, particularly fossil fuels (CEC, 1997a). This proposal initially also incurred stiff opposition although member states finally agreed on some basic principles – at the cost of keeping the harmonisation levels at the lowest common denominator. The 2002 Danish Presidency managed to get member state agreement on a compromise except for the German government, which feared for the tax rates for domestic road hauliers and opposed the provision for zero taxation of energy intensive businesses (EurActiv, 2002).

In March 2003, the Finance Ministers finally agreed on a framework directive, making heavy use of derogations and transition periods to placate various countries and their economic sectors (*ENDS Europe Daily*, 21 March 2003). The EP (2003) gave its opinion of the Council's position while expressing dissatisfaction and requesting various amendments. At the time, the EP only had limited consultative powers on taxation issues, and the Commission rejected its amendments. On 27

154 *Environmental governance in Europe*

October 2003, the Economic and Finance Minister Council (ECOFIN) formally adopted the Energy Tax Directive (2003/96/EC); it forced national tax measures towards a minimal convergence on the rates for all energy products, specifically minerals, coal, natural gas and electricity (CEC, 2003c). Importantly, the EU Energy Tax Directive 'foresees that under certain conditions taxation can be fully or partially replaced, in particular for energy intensive companies, by some other instrument, including tradable permit schemes' (CEC, 2006a).

Having achieved this modicum of success, the Commission sought to extend some of the principles of the EU Energy Tax Directive. It created a proposal requiring member states to adopt 'greener' national taxes on passenger cars (CEC, 2005). It called on member states to ensure that by 2010 at least 50 per cent of passenger car taxes are based on the vehicles' carbon dioxide emissions. The Commission also debated proposing a carbon dioxide tariff on imports from third party countries which failed to employ adequate greenhouse gas mechanisms and thus had an unfair competitive edge over EU firms (Beunderman, 2008). However, with the exception of France, member states opposed this idea for fear of triggering retaliatory action from non-EU member states.

Two interesting dynamics have evolved in the early 2000s concerning eco-taxes. First, another market-based instrument, namely emissions trading, has become an important NEPI on the EU level (see Chapter 7). In the Commission's internal politics, there was some acknowledgement, not all of it happy, that eco-taxes have given way to emissions trading as the most important NEPI for reducing carbon dioxide from large stationary sources (Interview, Commission Official, 2008).

Nevertheless, the energy tax has shown remarkable staying power on the EU agenda. In 2009, the DG for taxation was planning to revise the 2003 Energy Tax Directive, with the explicit aim of bringing the directive more in line with the EU's climate and energy objectives (*ENDS Europe Daily*, 15 May 2010). The 2010 Swedish EU Presidency articulated its desire to push for an EU-wide eco-tax for carbon dioxide emissions falling outside the scope of the EU ETS (*ENDS Europe Daily*, 22 June 2010). In the first half of 2010, the EU Tax Commissioner, Algirdas Šemeta, renewed the call for the revision of the 2003 Energy Tax Directive to include a minimum levy on the carbon content of fuels for cars, heating or electricity production (*ENDS Europe Daily*, 5 March 2010). The DG For Taxation was supposed to begin work on a draft proposal after the Commissioners debated the revisions in June 2010. Taxation Commissioner Šemeta received the support of the other 26 Commissioners although several raised concerns about the impact of such a tax on certain sectors (*ENDS Europe Daily*, 23 June 2010).

Although the Commission has renewed its focus on the carbon dioxide/energy tax idea, the Council unanimity requirement remains a hurdle which tax proponents have been unable to overcome. In practice there is only one EU-wide eco-tax but it is not particularly innovative. The 2003 Energy Tax Directive constitutes little more than the lowest common denominator agreement due to the reluctance by some member states to surrender sovereignty on taxation and budgetary issues.

CONCLUSION

Over time there has been an increase in the use of eco-taxes (although it has taken place at variable speeds) in the four member states assessed in this book. The UK government created arguably one of the first 'environmental' taxes in 1909 (see above), but it is only in the 1970s that a significant number of eco-taxes have been adopted in Europe (Andersen, 1994: 28). However, the EU failed to adopt significant EU-wide eco-taxes that go beyond lowest common denominator tax harmonisation measures. The adoption of national eco-taxes was initially ad hoc and incremental although more systematic and far reaching ecological tax reforms have been adopted in the Netherlands and Germany. The Austrian and UK political elites merely contemplated the adoption of ecological tax reforms without putting them into practice.

What has ensued is therefore largely to a recalibration of policy instruments (namely, a wider range of eco-taxes – including environmental charges and levies). In Hall's terminology this amounts to first order policy (instrument) learning although there have arguably also been incidents of second order learning in cases where full scale ecological tax reform took place (namely, the Netherlands and Germany). In Austria and the UK second order learning was advocated by important policy actors, however the proposals were not enacted. The EU has been least innovative with eco-taxes because it was unable to overcome the unanimity requirement. Importantly, a fundamental paradigm shift in the form of a radical ecological reform of the entire tax and fiscal system, which would amount to paradigm shift or third level policy (instrument) learning, has not occurred in any of the five political systems assessed in this book.

Between the early 1990s and the early 2000s, the Dutch have arguably been the most systematic in incorporating eco-taxes into their fiscal system. Germany adopted an ecological tax reform in 1998 and a raft of additional eco-taxes in 2010. Austria and the UK adopted more modest eco-taxes in a narrower range of sectors. For the reasons previously explained, the EU has failed to adopt significant EU-wide eco-taxes.

There is wide variation in the type of eco-taxes adopted in the five jurisdictions assessed in this book. The Dutch eco-taxes evolved from environmental charges and levies which were used to support specific regulatory efforts to much more encompassing general eco-taxes, German eco-taxes evolved more gradually and in an ad hoc fashion until the 1998 adoption of the ecological tax reform. Austria established a Tax Reform Commission which discussed ecological tax reform. However, such a comprehensive reform was not adopted in practice. The UK has innovated with hypothecated eco-taxes and a wide range of eco-taxes. Importantly, high energy users which are in direct competition with companies abroad have been granted generous exemptions from eco-taxes in Austria, Germany, the Netherlands and the UK. Moreover, Germany, the Netherlands and the UK innovated with eco-taxes which were explicitly linked to a reduction in labour costs (for example, in the form of reduced national insurance and/or pension contributions). Only Austria failed to adopt such an eco-tax.

The role of institutional context, acting as a constraint through goodness of fit and path dependency dynamics, is clearly prominent in all of the five political systems. It helps to explain the differences in approach to the design and use of eco-taxes although not always to the uptake of this particular policy instrument. The EU provides the clearest affirmation for the path dependency approach. It has been greatly constrained by the fact that eco-taxes are subject to Council unanimity voting. The German case shows an equally strong influence of institutional dynamics: constitutional limitations channelled debates on levies, placing restrictions on ear-marked taxes and pushing the discussion in the direction of more general taxation.

The Dutch case more generally also shows a strong tendency towards path dependency and instrumental learning (second and first order learning) by the institutions involved. Environmental charges, in the language of Streeck and Thelen (2005a), were subject to a displacement dynamic, as they took on a larger concrete and symbolic policy role in altering societal behaviour. This was particularly true of the original water charge, which only after it was seen to significantly alter economic behaviour that triggered a move to a number of charges, which eventually created so much complexity that the Dutch actors were forced to look for more general environmental taxation dimensions. This second order learning developed new ideas about governing strategies as well as the nature of instruments (second level and perhaps partly third level learning).

Nevertheless, the move towards more general taxation and the use of environmental tax revenue to relieve labour costs seen in three out of four national political systems reflects some second order learning dynamic. There is not much empirical evidence for direct policy instrument transfer. All four national governments were operating primarily within a domestic political context, responding to national institutional and interest group input. However, international competitiveness concerns played a major role for the design of particular national eco-taxes. A much more limited impact was discernible from the 'good example' set by eco-taxes pioneers as well as the efforts of like-minded countries which lobbied for the use of a wider range of eco-taxes on both the national and supranational EU level. The OECD's benchmarking efforts were used by national policy actors (such as environmental NGOs) to put pressure on domestic governments to adopt eco-taxes. They were also used by national Environment Ministries (and Environment Agencies) to defend and/or argue in favour of eco-tax proposals.

Electoral politics and changes in governments played an important role for the adoption of full scale ecological tax reforms. Accordingly, it was with the arrival of the Purple coalition government in the Netherlands, the Red-Green coalition government in Germany and the 'New' Labour government in the UK that proposals for full scale ecological tax reforms became actual policy. In Austria, the grand (SPÖ-ÖVP) coalition ultimately held back from ecological tax reform. Green parties and reform-minded Social Democratic parties were most susceptible to the double dividend argument which assumes that eco-taxes increase both the protection of the environment and international competitiveness. Conservative, Christian Democratic, Liberal and Right Wing parties seemed less convinced about the double dividend argument. The analysis of the member state adoption of eco-taxes therefore requires research into the impact of political parties, which has been neglected by most policy instrument studies.

7. Governing by emissions trading

INTRODUCTION

This chapter focuses on emissions trading which is a novel policy instrument, at least in Europe. As Chapter 2 explained, the principle idea behind emissions trading is to create a market for (emission) allowances to reduce emissions in the most cost-efficient manner. The US first innovated with emissions trading schemes (ETSs) in the 1980s, Denmark, the UK and the Netherlands established the first European ETSs in the 1990s. In 2003 the EU adopted the world's first supranational ETS which became operational in 2005.

The next section explains how emissions trading arrived on the political agenda in Europe. It also explains some of the core differences between different types of ETSs. The sections which then follow assess the evolution of emissions trading in the UK, the Netherlands, the EU, Germany and Austria in roughly the order in which these five jurisdictions first innovated with ETSs. The final section offers a concluding analysis.

ORIGINS OF EMISSIONS TRADING

The Canadian economist John Dales (1968) is widely credited as having laid the intellectual foundations for ETSs (see Chapter 2) (Hansjürgens, 2005: 5; Lafeld, 2003: 44; Wurzel, 2008a: 3). Some European environmental economists praised emissions trading from as early as the 1970s (for example, Bonus, 1976; Siebert, 1976). However, European policy makers shunned it until the late 1990s.

The principle idea behind emissions trading is relatively simple and universal to all ETSs. Countries and/or companies are allocated pollution rights in the form of emission allowances which can be traded in the market place. However, the detailed rules applicable to particular ETSs vary considerably. For example, emission allowances can be allocated for free (so-called grandfathering) or sold through auctions. The so-called cap-and-trade ETS sets a cap for the total amount of emissions, which countries and/or companies are allowed to release while leaving it up to the market to determine the price for allowances. Theoretically it is possible to adopt a floor and/or ceiling for the price of emission allowances. In practice, none of the ETSs assessed in Chapter 7 have a floor and/or ceiling for the price of emission allowances. However, in March 2011, the British Secretary of State for the Treasury, George Osborne, announced the introduction of a floor for CO_2 emission allowances from April 2013 onwards (*ENDS Europe*, 24 March 2011).

Over time the cap can be lowered to bring about reductions in the emissions total and thus to achieve environmental objectives. A lowering of the cap normally increases the scarcity of emission allowances and triggers price rises which in turn create incentives for countries and/or companies to reduce emissions. Theoretically ETSs encourage polluters to reduce emissions in the most cost-efficient manner while stimulating innovative emission reduction technologies and/or procedures. However, as is explained below, the politically contested adoption and implementation process of emissions trading in practice does not always follow the theoretical logic of economics textbooks.

Economists have produced excellent studies on the British ETS (for example, National Audit Office, 2004; Smith and Swierzbinski, 2007) and the EU ETS (for example, Ellerman, Convery and de Perthuis, 2010; Ellerman et al., 2007a; Grubb, Betz and Neuhoff, 2007; Hansjürgens, 2005; Lafeld, 2003; Zapfel, 2005, 2007) most of which generally praise emissions trading as the most cost-effective policy instrument although they also acknowledge the flaws in the design of particular ETSs. Environmental lawyers on the other hand tend to be much more critical about emissions trading (for example, Bogojevic, 2009; Winter, 2010). Many public policy studies of national European ETSs and the EU ETS take a middle position (for example, Lawrence, 2007; Meckling, 2011; Rudolph, 2005; Skjærseth and Wettestad, 2008; van Asselt, 2010; Wettestad, 2005; Wurzel, 2008a) although there are also some highly critical assessments (for example, Lauber, 2007). However, very few studies on emissions trading in Europe take a cross-jurisdictional comparative perspective and pay attention to: (a) the existing policy instrument repertoire within which a particular ETS operates; and (b) the wider institutional and political context variables within a particular jurisdiction.

EARLY AMERICAN EMISSIONS TRADING EXPERIENCE

The analysis starts with the US for the following two main reasons. First, the early American emissions trading experience became an important

160   *Environmental governance in Europe*

reference point for European emission trading advocates (Interviews, 2005–11; Ellerman, Convery and de Perthuis, 2010; Rudolph, 2005; Wurzel, 2008a; Zapfel and Vainio, 2002). DG Environment officials conducted several visits to the US EPA to improve their understanding of the American emissions trading experience (Interview, US EPA Official, 2011). The US gained practical experience with sulphur dioxide (SO_2) and nitrogen oxide (NO_x) ETSs already in the 1980s. Second, the US insisted on the inclusion of emissions trading in the 1997 Kyoto Protocol (Grubb, Vrolijk and Brack, 1999; Jordan et al., 2011; Wurzel, 2008a; Wurzel and Connelly, 2011a). The EU and its member states, which initially strongly opposed the inclusion of emissions trading in the 1997 Kyoto Protocol, eventually gave in to American political pressure (for example, Ellerman, Convery and de Perthuis, 2010; Damro and Méndez, 2003; Grubb, Vrolijk and Brack, 1999; Wettestad, 2005). The EU therefore became 'a reluctant emissions trading pioneer' (Wurzel, 2008a, 2008b) when it adopted the world's first supranational ETS in 2003. Ironically two years earlier US President George W. Bush announced that the US no longer intended to ratify the Kyoto Protocol that his predecessor, Bill Clinton, had signed.

Damro and Méndez (2003: 74) have argued that 'the introduction of an emissions trading system in EU environmental policy stems from a process of policy transfer, derived from the negotiations between the US and the EU at the Kyoto summit'. The UK ETS has also been perceived as the result of policy transfer from the 1997 Kyoto Protocol (Lawrence, 2007). These arguments are in line with studies that explain the increased worldwide use of NEPIs as a result of policy transfer from 'first mover' countries through a global diffusion process (Jörgens, 2003; Kern, Jörgens and Jänicke, 2000).

Using Dolowitz and Marsh's (1996) terminology (see Chapter 3), it is arguable that the US encouraged both 'voluntary' policy instrument transfer (that is, the emulation of its early ETSs) and imposed 'coercive' policy transfer (that is, the insertion of emissions trading into the 1997 Kyoto Protocol against the opposition of the EU, and Germany in particular). The US tried to offer a model for others by providing the first practical emissions trading experience; it acted as a political hegemon by imposing its preference for emissions trading upon the 1997 Kyoto protocol signatories. American officials attempted to soften up European opposition to emissions trading by praising the positive early American experience of this instrument (Interview, Commission official, 2002; Interview, US EPA official, 2011; Rudolph, 2005; Wurzel, 2008a). One EU Commission official (Interview, 2005) pointed out that around the time of the Kyoto Protocol negotiations, American interest groups:

which strongly favoured emissions trading, kept on attending important international conferences in Europe in order to praise the benefits of emissions trading ... For example, the Environment Defense Fund[1] sent people over to Europe ... Later on the Americans stayed away.

However, as is explained in the following, the specific rules of the European ETSs differed substantially from the American ETSs. If anything, it was the principal idea rather than specific emissions trading rules which were transferred from America to Europe via the 1997 Kyoto protocol (Jordan, Wurzel and Zito, 2005; Wurzel, 2008a).

THE UK: AN EMISSIONS TRADING PIONEER

In 2002 the UK established the world's first ETS for six main greenhouse gases (DEFRA, 2003b). Denmark had adopted a domestic ETS already in 1999; it, however, covered only CO_2 emissions from power stations. The UK Environment Ministry's interest in emissions trading dates back to the late 1980s. Plans for large power stations to engage in sulphur trading were developed by the early 1990s, but had to be dropped when they conflicted with EU regulation (for example, the EU Large Combustion Directive) and the traditional policy style employed by technical agencies (Sorrell, 1999; see also Chapter 3). The UK government also initiated studies on the effectiveness of emissions trading in the water sector while the Environment Agency for England and Wales consulted on a water abstraction rights trading scheme. The Environment Ministry mooted the use of ETSs for waste as a means of achieving targets set by the EU Landfill Directive but planning proceeded extremely slowly. Proposals for ETSs covering certain agricultural pollutants (such as fertilizers and pesticides) were also advanced.

The UK's emissions trading pioneer status is surprising when considering its belated uptake of eco-taxes (see Chapter 6). The UK Treasury-commissioned 1998 Marshall Report strongly advocated eco-taxes while reviewing less positively emissions trading (Marshall Report, 1998; see Chapters 3 and 6). Initial signs indicated that the New Labour government of 1997 would prefer eco-taxes over emissions trading (Lawrence, 2007). However, British industry and in particular BP lobbied hard for a national ETS as a means of escaping eco-taxes (Ellerman, Convery and de Perthuis, 2010; Meckling, 2011; Wurzel, 2008a). The Confederation of British Industry (CBI) feared that the newly adopted climate change levy (CCL) would 'negatively affect the competitiveness of the UK's industry' (Interview, CBI representative, 2007). In 1999, the CBI and the

162 *Environmental governance in Europe*

Advisory Committee on Business and the Environment therefore established the Emissions Trading Group (ETG). One of the ETG's main aims was to persuade the Labour government to introduce a domestic ETS prior to an EU ETS adoption (Interview, 2007). The ETG developed into an influential lobby organisation (Lawrence, 2007; Meckling, 2011); it published a proposal, which became the blueprint for the UK ETS, in March 2000.

BP, which had already created an in-house ETS, took a leading role within the ETG (Interview, 2007). BP's conversion from climate change villain – which supported the so-called Global Climate Coalition that denounced as unfounded scientific findings about anthropogenic causes for climate change – to emissions trading pioneer occurred with remarkable speed (Lawrence, 2007: 122). BP's desire to gain a first mover advantage vis-à-vis its competitors and the British government was a major factor in its conversion. Moreover, acting as a 'good corporate citizen' by adopting a company-internal ETS helped improve BP's public image, which its support for the Global Climate Coalition had damaged (Interview, 2007).

The Labour government abandoned its initial reluctance to establish a national ETS scheme for the following four main reasons (Interviews, 2006–07; DEFRA, 2003a). First, it recognised the importance of gaining practical emissions trading experience ahead of EU-wide emissions trading (and a possible global ETS); second, it was keen to be able to offer a model for the EU; third, it wanted to achieve significant greenhouse gas emissions reductions at a reasonable cost; and, fourth, it wanted to help the City of London to establish itself as a global centre for emissions trading.

British environmental NGOs, which had initially opposed emissions trading on ethical grounds, began to reconsider their positions after the Kyoto Protocol's 1997 signing. In particular the WWF and the Green Alliance started supporting emissions trading although only under strict rules and with ambitious targets. Friends of the Earth (FoE) and Greenpeace were slower in accepting emissions trading as a policy instrument to bring about greenhouse gas reductions (Interviews, 2006–07; Wurzel, 2008a: 11). Greenpeace and FoE also became critical again about emissions trading in the early 2010s (Interviews, 2011).

In 2001 the CCL came into effect (see Chapter 6). It formed part of a complex policy instrument mix under the UK's Climate Change Programme that also included voluntary Climate Change Agreements (CCAs) and the UK ETS. Importantly, emissions trading (namely, the UK ETS), eco-taxes (namely, the CCL) and voluntary agreements (namely, the CCAs) became interlinked. These policy instruments formed part of a mixed approach as recommended in the 1998 Marshall Report. Companies which participated in CCAs received an 80 per cent reduction from the CCL while becoming so-called indirect participants in the UK ETS (Smith and Swierzbinski, 2007).

Because industry fiercely opposed mandatory emissions trading, the UK ETS became a voluntary scheme. This necessitated creating incentives for participating companies (Interview, former Environment Ministry Official, 2007). One British environmental NGO representative (Interview, 2007) argued: 'If you have a voluntary scheme then it is self-selecting. The people who take on absolute caps are the people who think that they meet them easily. The businesses who think that their emissions are rising will not take on absolute reduction targets voluntarily'.

The UK government therefore made available £215 million in financial incentives over five years (DEFRA, 2003a). Two chemical companies, Ineos Fluor and DuPont, were granted more than £13.8 million in fiscal incentives (Wurzel, 2008a). The *ENDS Report* (2002, 335 and 327: 3–5) claimed that these two companies merely fitted abatement equipment which existing legislation had already required. It accused the UK government of encouraging the trade with 'hot air' to achieve wide voluntary participation although British government officials strongly denied this accusation (Interviews, 2007). A National Audit Office report (2004: 3) concluded that 'for some Direct Participants [of the UK ETS], their targets to reduce emissions had been achieved even *before* the Scheme came into operation [Italics added]'. The National Audit Office nevertheless decided that the Environment Ministry 'successfully set up a novel and functioning emissions trading scheme, which has the potential to benefit the UK economy' although it also warned that the 'wider benefits to the UK and participants in the UK Scheme may be less than hoped for' (National Audit Office, 2004: 2).

Pressured to reduce the direct participants' huge windfall profits, the Environment Ministry issued an August 2004 consultation document aimed at persuading companies to undertake significant additional emission reductions (Smith and Swierzbinski, 2007: 143; Wurzel, 2008a). In late 2004, six direct participants (Ineos Fluor, Rhodia, DuPont, BP, British Airways and Lafarge Cement) agreed to make additional emissions reductions although these reductions fell short (by about 6 million tonnes CO_2-equivalent) of the consultation document target (Smith and Swierzbinski, 2007: 143).

Whether the UK ETS actually achieved any significant greenhouse gas emission reductions has remained contested. However, there is widespread agreement that the government's 'doing by learning approach'

164   *Environmental governance in Europe*

(Interviews, 2007) allowed Britain to gain valuable practical experience before the 2005 start of the EU ETS. The UK ETS also helped to establish the City of London as the global emissions trading capital. Whether it also helped the UK to influence the EU ETS will be discussed below.

THE NETHERLANDS: EARLY SUPPORTER OF EMISSIONS TRADING

The Netherlands has been a notable European emissions trading pioneer. International influences shaped the Dutch emissions trading learning process. Already in 1983, a Dutch government and industry delegation visited the US to examine its ETSs. It returned with the idea of creating 'plant bubbles' for sulphur dioxide and nitrous oxide emissions from combustion plants (Dekkers, 1999: 109–10). Dutch officials viewed the US experimentation with ETSs to limit SO_2 and NO_x emissions as a success worth investigating. They also monitored closely UK and German developments (Interviews, Economics Ministry officials, 2000, 2002). Dutch policy-makers therefore had an interest in emissions trading already well before signing the Kyoto Protocol. Nevertheless, the Kyoto Protocol was significant in leading the Dutch government to accept greenhouse gas emissions reduction targets that would be difficult to achieve without emissions trading: other policy instruments were seen as endangering the competitiveness of Dutch export industries (Interview, VROM official, 2002). Climate change raised further the Dutch interest in emissions trading (Interviews, 2000).

Separately, Dutch agricultural policy actors experimented extensively with emissions trading in four sectors (Interview, 2002). Domestic market schemes for milk and the manure quotas were developed already in the 1980s (Interview, Finance Ministry official, 2001, 2002). The 1987 Manure Act established 'free production rights' covering cattle, swine and poultry, and was extended in 1992 to other farm animals. Each farm was 'grandfathered' a certain amount of allocations for manure on the basis of actual production; farmers that produced manure beyond the regulatory limit required additional production rights (Wossinck, 2003). These rights became widely tradable in 1994 (Dietz and Termeer, 1991: 140–2; EEA, 2006b: 22). However, these early ETSs encountered various problems, especially concerning legal rights and administrative complexity. The early agricultural emissions trading experience provided some negative lessons for environmental policy actors (Interview, VROM official, 2002). Given this context, the larger international environment seems to have had a significant role in explaining the Dutch enthusiasm for greenhouse gas emissions trading.

In 1990, the national government, together with the provinces and municipalities, agreed a covenant with the Electricity Board (see Chapter 5). This covenant allowed existing plants to be covered in a cost optimisation scheme which resembles features of ETSs. In 1995, the Environment Ministry decided to re-examine the means for restricting nitrous oxide and sulphur dioxide emissions. Government representatives explored various possibilities with industry, including emission trading. Indeed it was industry (and in particular the chemical industry) which pushed the idea of a nitrous oxide ETS. By 1996 the chemical industry had become concerned that it could not meet the nitrous oxide reduction targets set in the national covenants. It therefore was willing to contemplate the idea of creating an ETS (Interview, Industry Representative, 2002). The discussion moved on to include other major industries to avoid imposing costs only on the chemical industry. This partly reflected the fear that the government would impose more strict regulatory systems.

The industry discussions generated a 1997 study which concluded that an ETS could offer major reductions in NO_x emissions (Dekkers, 1999: 112–9). Environment Ministry officials thought that emissions trading was a good idea because it would enable Dutch policy actors to gain practical experience of operating an ETS for environment purposes and acidification objectives (Interviews, 2002). The policy actors created the basic design in 2000. Environment and Economics Ministry officials then worked out the details with industry, particularly led by the VNO-NCW (the Confederation of Netherlands Industry and Employers). Dutch policy makers and industry paid close attention to US and UK emissions trading developments, but the actual design indicates that domestic thinking was decisive.

The proposal for a NO_x ETS was not an isolated Dutch effort to explore emission trading. Concerns about global warming and relatively ambitious Dutch CO_2 emission reduction targets under the 1997 Kyoto Protocol led the Economics and Environment Ministers in the Purple Coalition II (1998–2002), to create a CO_2 Trading Commission to study the problem of reducing emissions and devising options for a domestic ETS (Kuik, Mulder and Verbruggen, 2002). This commission, which published its findings in February 2002, was composed of various stakeholders including industry and NGO representatives. Environment Ministry officials, who pushed the idea of a Dutch CO_2 ETS, initially met resistance from the Economics and Finance Ministries (Interviews, VROM, Finance Ministry and Economics Ministry officials, 2002). The

166   *Environmental governance in Europe*

Economics Ministry were persuaded of the economic benefits of a cap-and-trade system which differentiated between industries 'exposed' and 'sheltered' from international economic competition with a relative cap (based on emissions per production unit rather than an absolute limit) provided for the former. In light of the above mentioned agricultural ETS experience, the Finance Ministry raised concerns about the complexity of the proposed ETS compared to the more easily designed eco-tax systems that generated significant revenue.

Although the CO_2 Trading Commission was quite successful in furthering Dutch emission trading thinking, EU developments overtook Dutch recommendations (*ENDS Daily*, 5 February 2002). Despite preferring the Dutch solutions, the government decided that the Netherlands would gain more in participating in an EU-wide ETS than creating a national ETS (Interviews, Economics Ministry and VROM Officials, 2002). The Economics Ministry's own policy institute, the Central Planning Bureau, supported this view, arguing that a national system was less efficient than an international system (Interview, Economics Ministry Officials, 2002). Dutch officials communicated their views during the EU-level negotiation process that created the EU ETS, but did not expect to convert the European Commission to the Dutch perspective. Prior to the 2002 election, Dutch policy actors had also considered an ETS for landfill, but shelved this initiative due to concerns about complexity and a lack of supporting societal actors.

With the Commission's EU ETS proposal, the Dutch government started to plan the implementation of the resulting directive (see the following). In October 2004, the Dutch government decided to launch a NO_x ETS alongside the EU ETS which focused only on CO_2 emissions (*ENDS Europe Daily*, 10 November 2004). The Dutch scheme applied to all industrial facilities with a total thermal capacity surpassing 20MWh, which in 2005 involved roughly 250 facilities (Kingdom of the Netherlands, 2005; EEA, 2006b: 21).

The Dutch government's ambition was to match as closely as possible the starting dates for the Dutch NO_x ETS and the EU CO_2 ETS, so that domestic industries could link their trading efforts (VROM, 2004). This multi-track approach recognised that the two ETSs largely affected the same industries. It was institutionalised by the creation of the Netherlands Emissions Authority (NEA) within the Environment Ministry (VROM, 2005a). Changing from a temporary to a permanent agency in 2008, the NEA's main task is to provide supervision and ensure compliance with the legal requirements of the Dutch NO_x and EU CO_2 schemes (Algemene Rekenkamer, 2007: fn 8). The Dutch NO_x ETS came into effect in June 2005, with smaller sized businesses able to apply for an opt-out in the initial years (VROM, 2005). The Dutch implementation of the EU ETS is assessed in a following section.

THE EU: A RELUCTANT EMISSIONS TRADING PIONEER

Adoption of the EU ETS

As Chapter 6 explained, the Commission's 1992 proposal for an EU-wide carbon dioxide/energy tax failed to achieve the required unanimous endorsement in the Environmental Council. Frustrated by the lack of progress of its carbon dioxide/energy tax proposal and spurred on by the desire to adopt more cost-efficient market-based instruments, the Commission used the policy window created by the 1997 Kyoto Protocol to propose EU-wide emissions trading (Ellerman, Convery and de Perthuis, 2010; Wettestad, 2005; Wurzel, 2008a). A group of DG Environment officials, consisting largely of economists and led by (the Dutch national) Jos Delbeke, pushed emissions trading as the Commission's newly preferred policy instrument for tackling climate change (see Ellerman, Convery and de Perthuis, 2010: fn9; Delbeke, 2006). Prior to the 1997 Kyoto Protocol, the Commission had commissioned emissions trading studies (Interviews, 2002). It also initiated the Concerted Action on Market-Based Instruments Programme (1996–98); the Concerted Action on Tradable Emission Permits followed this after the EU signed the Kyoto Protocol in 1997 (Ellerman, Convery and de Perthuis, 2010: 14).

In 2000 the Commission published a *Green Paper on Greenhouse Gas Emission Trading within the European Union* (CEC, 2000b). Following consultations with the main stakeholders and all member governments in September 2001, the Commission published an EU ETS proposal in late 2001 (CEC, 2001c). The Environment Council and the EP adopted the proposal for an EU ETS Directive after arduous but speedy negotiations in 2003 (CEC, 2003a; Skjærseth and Wettestad, 2008; Wettestad, 2005). In the first reading, the EP tabled more than 60 amendments which all aimed to make 'the scheme hit harder, faster and wider' *(ENDS Daily* 30.4.2003). The EP demanded, for example, mandatory auctioning and more centralised control through the Commission (Ellerman, Convery and de Perthuis, 2010: 24). In the second reading the EP upheld only 14 of its first reading amendments.

The EP and Environmental Council negotiations focused primarily 'on the overarching architecture of the scheme and not on details' (Zapfel, 2007: 34). The adoption of the detailed rules (for example, on new entrants, transfer rules, closure rules and *ex-post* adjustments) were left to member states which had to draw up so-called national allocation plans (NAPs). The EU ETS therefore became a highly decentralised scheme; the Commission issued several guidance notes, which many member states chose to ignore. The strongly decentralised structure of the EU ETS helps explain why the Commission's proposal was adopted with relatively few amendments in 'an ultra quick process' (Wettestad, 2005). The perceived need for a functioning EU ETS by the time the Kyoto Protocol entered into force in 2005 made the EP and Environmental Council willing to accept a compromise deal (Wettestad, 2005; Wurzel, 2008a: 17).

In 2003 the Commission proposed a so-called linking directive; it linked the EU ETS with the project-based mechanisms in the Kyoto Protocol, namely the clean development mechanism (CDM) and joint implementation (JI). The CDM grants developed countries so-called emission reduction units (ERUs), which can be traded within the EU ETS, for sponsoring certified greenhouse gas emission reduction projects in developing countries. JI allows developed countries (listed in Kyoto Protocol) jointly to implement greenhouse gas emissions reduction projects.

In the drafting phase of its EU ETS proposal, the Commission showed an interest in the US as well as the British, Danish and, to a lesser degree, the Dutch, practical emissions trading experience. In the proposal's drafting stage, the UK government seconded national officials with emissions trading expertise to the Commission. However, the EU ETS emerged as quite different from the UK ETS (Smith and Swierzbinski, 2007: 152; Wurzel, 2008a). For example, the UK ETS was a voluntary scheme which covered six greenhouse gases from a wide range of sectors excluding the electricity sector. The EU ETS became a mandatory scheme which covered CO_2 emissions from a wide range of sectors including the electricity sector. Clearly the UK did not upload its domestic ETS rules to the EU level. It nevertheless benefited from its 'learning-by-doing' experience with its national ETS. As one British official (Interview, 2007) explained, '[i]t was not so much the specifics but more an understanding of how an emissions trading scheme works. We were able to approach the EU scheme with considerable practical experience'.

Germany and Austria had failed to adopt national ETSs ahead of the EU ETS and were therefore unable to offer the Commission advice on how emissions trading works in practice (see also the following). The German Chancellor, Gerhard Schröder, initially even threatened to torpedo the EU ETS (Interviews, German and Commission officials, 2007;

Governing by emissions trading 169

Wurzel, 2008a). However, once Germany had accepted the inevitability of the EU ETS, the German government and stakeholders quickly organised a damage limitation lobbying exercise which led to last minute demands for changes to the EU ETS rules.

The EU ETS, which (like the Kyoto Protocol) became applicable in 2005, covered more than '10 000 installations in the energy and industrial sectors which are collectively responsible for close to half of Europe's emissions of CO_2' (CEC, 2006b: 1). The EU ETS initially distinguished between the following two trading phases: the first phase from 2005–07 and second phase from 2008–12. A third trading phase (2013–20) was added during the revision of the EU ETS.

Implementation of the EU ETS: First Trading Phase

The main EU ETS institutional structures were established during the first trading phase (2005–07), which was widely seen as a pilot phase (Ellerman, Convery and de Perthuis, 2010; Ellerman and Buchner, 2007a; Grubb, Betz and Neunhoff, 2007; Zapfel and Vainio, 2002). The second phase (2008–12), which coincided with the first global trading phase under the Kyoto Protocol, brought about the fine tuning of the implementation rules.

Because Germany is the EU's largest CO_2 emitter, it has by far the largest number of installations covered by the EU ETS. The EU ETS in the first trading phase covered almost 60 per cent of CO_2 emissions released in Germany. About half of Germany's CO_2 emission allowances were allocated to its four biggest energy producers (E.ON, RWE, Vattenfall and EnBW).

The UK is the second largest CO_2 emitter in the EU and therefore has the second largest number of installations under the EU ETS, which covered approximately 46 per cent of its CO_2 emissions in 2003 (Harrison and Radow, 2007: 46). By far the largest number of emission allocations in the UK went to power companies which are the biggest domestic CO_2 emitters.

Power companies in Austria and the Netherlands have also been allocated the highest number of national emissions allowances. Table 7.1 shows the allocation of CO_2 allowances in the first trading phase for Austria, Germany, the Netherlands and the UK as well as the total for the (then) EU-25.

For the first and second trading period member states were obliged to draw up so-called National Allocation Plans (NAPs) which set caps (in other words, national totals for CO_2 emissions) that must be in line with a member state's Kyoto Protocol reduction target. The EU's so-called

170 *Environmental governance in Europe*

Table 7.1   Installations and allowances in the first trading phase (2005–2007)

Member state	Number of installations	Allowances in million	Allowances in percentage points
Austria	205	99.0	1.5%
Germany	1849	1497.0	22.8%
The Netherlands	333	285.9	4.3%
UK	1078	736.0	11.2%
Total EU-25	11 428	6572.0	100%

Source: Adapted from Zapfel (2007: 26).

burden sharing agreement set the targets, allocating differentiated national reduction targets for Austria (-13), Germany (-21), the Netherlands (-6) and the UK (-12.5) and all of the other EU member states on the basis of the EU's collective eight per cent Kyoto Protocol reduction target.

According to one Commission official (Zapfel, 2007: 30) '[i]n late 2003, before the first draft allocation plans were released for public consultation, there was a reluctance across member state capitals to be the first to announce a cap figure'. In January 2004 the UK was first in submitting a relatively ambitious NAP in the first trading phase (NAP-I) after it had been urged by the Commission 'to set a good example for other member states' (Interview, former British official, 2007). Austria, the Netherlands and Germany submitted on time their NAP-Is which, however, were all fairly unambitious (Wurzel et al., 2003a, 2003c; Zito et al., 2003). According to British officials (Interviews, 2005–07), the UK government had informed the Commission that the NAP-I which it submitted in January 2004 was merely a draft NAP. In November 2004 the UK government tried to submit a less ambitious revised NAP-I which increased the total number of allowances by 20 million (Zapfel, 2007: 26). However, the Commission refused to accept the revised NAP-I. The UK government subsequently took the Commission to the ECJ but later 'abandoned its court action and settled for a compromise in order not to create uncertainty for British businesses and possibly damage the fledgling EU emissions trading scheme which the British government strongly supported in principle' (Interview, British official, 2007).

In the UK, the Environment Ministry became the lead department for the implementation of the EU ETS, with the Industry Ministry also taking on an important role. The Environment Agency for England and Wales became the competent authority with responsibility for reporting, verification and issuing allowances. Due to the UK's devolved government, separate agencies were put in charge in Scotland and Northern Ireland with the Environment Agency holding overall coordinating responsibility. Drawing up the NAP-I took the British authorities more than two years. Up to 15 Environment Ministry and between ten and 15 Environment Agency officials were involved in drawing up and implementing the NAP-I (Interviews, 2007). These figures do not include officials responsible for the implementation of the EU ETS in Scotland and Northern Ireland.

Initially the UK (greenhouse gases) ETS continued to operate in parallel with the EU (CO_2) ETS. However, UK companies that participated in the UK ETS were eligible to apply for an opt-out from the EU ETS. The power sector, which was not covered by the UK ETS, was allocated fewer allowances than it needed under business-as-usual predictions because of its ability to pass on to customers the cost of participating in the EU ETS. The British Labour government rejected as unsubstantiated claims that the EU ETS led to an average seven per cent rise in electricity bills for British customers while generating huge windfall profits for power companies (BBC, 2007).

With the EU ETS going ahead, the Dutch government and industry prepared for its implementation. As was mentioned above, NEA was allocated some implementation responsibilities (VROM, 2005; de Gelder, 2005). In 2010 NEA moved to the Infrastructure and Environment Ministry which has primary responsibility for implementing the Dutch NO_x and EU CO_2 ETS. Because the 2012 allocation of allowances is based on EU rules, the authority for implementation shifted to the NEA (Written communication, Economics Ministry official, 2011). Its main task is to provide supervision and ensure compliance with the legal requirements of the EU CO_2 ETS and Dutch NO_x ETS. Nine out of 43 NEA staff work on the implementation of the EU ETS (NEA, 2011), with six people working in the Ministry of Environment and two people in the Economics Ministry (Communication, Environment Ministry Official, 2011).

The NEA authorises company monitoring protocols and approves annual emission monitoring reports (Communication, NEA official, 2011). It has the authority to levy sanctions on companies that fail to meet their obligations (de Gelder, 2005: 26; Dekkers, 2003; VROM, 2004). The NEA issued 195 CO_2 allowances covering 95 per cent of

172   *Environmental governance in Europe*

Dutch industries (registering the participants for the EU ETS) between October 2004 and January 2005, before the emissions trade register came into effect in February 2005.

In the Netherlands, the implementation of the EU ETS, which has not been without difficulties, has been the shared responsibility of the Environment and Economics Ministries. Two Economics Ministry and about four or five Environment Ministry staff dealt with EU ETS issues in the first and second trading phase. The Ministry of Finance also had competences on auctioning and the use of the revenue generated by it.

The German NAP-I was adopted by the government in April 2004 and approved by the EU Commission in July 2004 (Matthes and Schafhausen, 2007: 75). In line with the juridification of German politics (see Chapter 3), several companies started legal action against the German government; they aimed to torpedo the EU ETS and/or secure more generous emissions allowances. However, the courts largely backed the German government's position.

The German NAP-I was extremely complex – it stipulated 58 different allocation options – for four main reasons (Wurzel, 2008a). First, Germany had by far the largest number of installations and the most complex industrial sectors covered by the EU ETS; second, industry lobbying for special rules was successful; third, Germany was seeking 'technically very ambitious standards' (Interview, Environment Ministry Official, 2005); fourth, 'embedding of emissions trading in the policy mix of energy and environmental policy played an important role' (Matthes and Schafhausen, 2007: 98). The German NAP-I took into account existing laws and environmental policy instruments including the ecological tax reform (1999), the renewable energy law (2000), the decision to phase out nuclear power (2000) and voluntary agreements by industry on the reduction of carbon dioxide emissions (see Chapters 5 and 6).

In Germany the NAP-I adoption process reopened rifts between the Environment and Economics Ministries with the former demanding an ambitious NAP-I and the latter defending what it perceived as the German industry's interests. In 2004 conflicts about the German NAP-I threatened even the survival of the SPD-Green coalition government *(Süddeutsche Zeitung* 31.3.2004; *Die Zeit*, 1 April 2004). On 30 March 2004, Chancellor Schröder (SPD), Economics Minister Clement (SPD), Environment Minister Trittin (Greens), Foreign Minister and Vice-Chancellor Fischer (Greens) and Chancellery Minister Steinmeier (SPD) held an arduous five-hour meeting on the German NAP-I; they agreed to the German cap setting at 503 million tonnes (Wurzel, 2008a). The meeting also agreed upon favourable allowance allocation rules for the carbon intensive coal industry which was given fuel-specific benchmarks (*Süddeutsche Zeitung*, 31 March 2004).

As explained in the following, the Environment Agency (*Umwelt-bundesamt* – UBA) became the competent authority in Austria. Approximately four or five staff deal with the implementation of the EU ETS in the Agency which, however, has contracted out the emissions register to a private organisation. In the Austrian Environment Ministry (BMLFUW) about four staff deal with EU ETS and other climate change related issues (Interview, 2011).

The price for emissions allowances was low during much of the first trading phase. When data about actual CO_2 emissions was released in early 2006, it showed that member states had allocated significantly more allowances than needed by companies. Subsequently, a steep fall in the price for CO_2 allowances occurred from about €30 to around €11 per ton CO_2 *(ENDS Europe Daily,* 5 May 2007). In early May 2007, the price for allowances plummeted to a mere €0.15 per ton. Even a price of €30 was 'much less than the price that modeling exercises indicate as needed to affect a major reduction of greenhouse gas emissions' (Ellerman, Convery and de Perthuis, 2010: 292).

According to the Commission the first trading phase 'proved to be a valuable learning period not only as a basis for Member States' national allocation plans for the second trading period 2008 to 2013, but also to inform the review of the scheme' (CEC, 2006a: 10).

Implementation of the EU ETS: Second Trading Phase

While the first EU ETS trading phase (2005–07) has been widely regarded as a pilot or 'learning by doing' phase, the second trading phase (2008–12) constituted the start of EU emissions trading in earnest. Germany and the UK, which had both insisted on grandfathering when the EU ETS was negotiated, allowed for the auctioning of seven and 8.8 per cent of their national carbon dioxide emission allowances respectively in the second trading phase. The allocation of 8.8 per cent of allowances in the German NAP-II, which was adopted by the German parliament in June 2007, constituted a policy u-turn. Following elections in 2005, the Christian Democratic Union (*Christlich Demokratische Union* – CDU), Christian Social Union (*Christlich Soziale Union* – CSU) and the SPD formed a so-called grand coalition. Under the grand coalition government (2005–09) the conflict between the Environment and Economics Ministries about emissions trading eased; the new Economics Minister was from the Bavarian CSU which does not stand for elections in North Rhine-Westphalia, the location of the bulk of

174 *Environmental governance in Europe*

Germany's chemical and coal industries which both opposed emissions trading (Wurzel, 2008a). Moreover, after Chancellor Schröder and Economics Minister Clement's departure, the SPD gradually warmed to the idea. In 2007, a majority of Social Democratic MPs demanded the full use of the ten per cent auctioning option allowed for under the EU ETS second trading period. However, the CDU MPs favoured a lower auctioning limit. A compromise was therefore reached at 8.8 per cent. Green opposition MPs voted against the grand coalitions' 8.8 per cent auctioning limit because they supported the auctioning of the full ten per cent of allowances. The only party represented in parliament which opposed emissions trading was the left-wing Left Party *(Die Linke)*.

The Commission accepted, largely unchanged, the UK's NAP-II in October 2006. It set a cap that was about three per cent lower compared to the NAP-I allocations. It introduced an eight per cent limit for the use of JI and CDM. Compared to Germany, the UK adopted a more ambitious cap for its NAP-II. However, one German official argued that Britain's 12.5 per cent Kyoto Protocol target was considerably less ambitious than Germany's 20 per cent target (Interview, 2005).

The German NAP-II set the cap at 482 million tonnes for CO_2 emissions. However, in late 2006 the Commission rejected the cap as inconsistent with Germany's Kyoto Protocol target, reducing it to 465 million tonnes. The German Economics Ministry demanded legal action against the Commission. However, Chancellor Merkel decided to accept the Commission's decision for two main reasons (Interviews, 2007). First, in 2007 Germany simultaneously held the EU and G8 Presidencies for which it made climate change a major political priority in both roles. Taking the Commission to the ECJ for lowering Germany NAP-II cap could therefore have damaged Germany's reputation as an environmental leader and pro-integrationist EU member state. Second, a legal challenge would have created uncertainty for German industry.

The Netherlands also had difficulties in implementing correctly the EU ETS. The Dutch NAP-II reduced windfall profits for electricity producers (Algemene Rekenkamer, 2007: 8). The Netherlands independent Court of Audit concluded that the total amount of emissions allowances that the Dutch government was planning to set aside in NAP-II imposed little restriction on CO_2 growth (thereby endangering national Kyoto targets – a claim the government rejected) and was crafted to protect Dutch industrial competitiveness (Algemene Rekenkamer, 2007: 11–12). The EU Commission warned the Netherlands to adopt a more ambitious NAP-II cap *(ENDS Europe Daily*, 29 September 2006). It took a tough stance with the Netherlands, Austria, Germany and seven other member states when it 'called for an average cut in emissions of seven per cent' for the first NAP-IIs that had been submitted (*ENDS Europe Daily*, 29 November 2006).

The EEA (2006a) found significant member state differences during the implementation of the EU ETS. It therefore demanded an increased harmonisation of the EU ETS and made 'suggestions for reducing the administrative burden imposed by the Emission Trading Directive' (EEA, 2006a: 9).

Extension and Review of the EU ETS

In 2008 the Council and EP adopted a Directive (2008/101/EC) which extended the EU ETS to the aviation sector. The Commission also started work on plans to include the shipping industry in the EU ETS. A group of American airlines subsequently challenged the aviation Directive, which affects all flights from and to EU member states, before the ECJ on the grounds that it constituted a violation of international aviation agreements and sovereignty. However, the ECJ rejected as unfounded the legal challenge in its December 2011 ruling that the aviation Directive was compatible with EU law (BBC, 21 December 2011; *Der Spiegel*, 21 December 2011; *Frankfurter Allgemeine Zeitung*, 21 December 2011). The fact that the US and China have threatened retaliatory measures, which could lead to a trade war between those two countries and the EU, suggests the potential coercive nature of the EU ETS (BBC, 21 December; Pop, 2011).

The EU ETS review, which adopts a third trading phase for 2013–20, attempted to repair some of the main weaknesses of the rules for the first and second trading phase (Skjærseth and Wettestad, 2010). Austria, the Netherlands, Germany and the UK gradually accepted the need for increased centralisation and harmonisation of the highly decentralised EU ETS which allowed for widely differentiated national interpretations of the implementation rules and procedures. However, although these four member states generally favoured more harmonisation and better monitoring, they were concerned also that greater harmonisation increases the EU's powers and the Commission's powers in particular (Interviews, 2005–07).

The most important changes introduced by the review for the third trading period (2013–20) include: first, the adoption of a single EU-wide cap which makes NAPs obsolete; second, auctioning will become the main allocation method for allowances although grandfathering will continue for energy intensive installations threatened by global competition; third, benchmarking for industrial sectors will be introduced; fourth, a solidarity clause for less affluent member states which stipulates

176   *Environmental governance in Europe*

that more affluent member states will make available to them ten per cent of the revenue accrued through auctioning emission allowances; and, fifth, the rules for CDM and JI will be included in the revised EU ETS directive (see also Skjærseth and Wettestad, 2010). The review overall amounted to a significant centralisation of the EU ETS and a harmonisation of its rules.

Ellerman and colleagues (2007a: 4) have argued that the EU ETS has 'not only [created] the world's largest environmental market ... but it is the embryo from which a future global regime may emerge'. Leading Austrian, British, Dutch and German politicians have advocated linking the EU ETS with other ETSs (such as the Californian ETS). However, concerns have been raised about the possible participation of authoritarian and corrupt regimes in a global ETS (Nordhaus, 2007; Wurzel, 2008a).

Corruption and fraud are substantial issues as the EU ETS has fallen victim to fraudsters and several attacks by criminal hackers in 2009–11. In 2009 criminal gangs, which operated in several EU member states over an 18 month period, defrauded national tax authorities by more than €5 million in VAT (*Frankfurter Allgemeine Zeitung*, 20 January 2011). In late 2011 six Deutsche Bank traders were tried because they defrauded the tax authorities of more than €230 million in turn over taxes (*Financial Times Deutschland*, 12 December 2011). In early 2011 the Commission suspended for several weeks spot trading of emissions allowances because criminal hackers had illegally accessed six national electronic registers and carried out fraudulent transactions potentially worth millions of Euros (*ENDS Europe Daily*, 4 February 2010; *Frankfurter Allgemeine Zeitung*, 20 January 2011; *Süddeutsche Zeitung*, 20 January 2011). Hackers managed to gain access to the national electronic register in six member states including Austria (*Der Standard*, 19 April 2011). Transparency International's (2011) *Global Corruption Report: Climate Change* details further evidence for fraud and corruption in global greenhouse gas emission reduction schemes including CDM and JI schemes. In order to ensure the functioning of the market-based EU ETS, state authorities had to crack down on fraudsters.

According to one Austrian Environment official (Interview, 2011) incidents of serious fraud did not lead to emissions trading being questioned per se (Interview, 2011). Commission officials have also downplayed the criminal activities, stating that the EU ETS is still a relatively young scheme with teething problems (*Frankfurter Allgemeine Zeitung*, 20 January 2011). The Commission has, however, used the security lapses to call for a central register and a single trading platform.

GERMANY: FROM EMISSIONS TRADING LAGGARD TO RELUCTANT FOLLOWER

The theoretical debate about emissions trading amongst German economists can be traced to the 1970s (Lafeld 2003; Wurzel 2008a). Most environmental economists and the German Environment Expert Council *(Sacherständigenrat für Umweltfragen – SRU)* initially favoured eco-taxes over emissions trading (for example, Lübbe-Wolff, 2001). Large parts of German industry also opposed emissions trading although there were important exceptions (for example, the banking sector). Parts of the chemical industry even claimed that a cap-and-trade ETS would lead to a 'planned economy' because the cap sets an absolute limit (Interviews, 2005–07). Industry representatives argued that this untested additional environmental policy instrument was unnecessary because German industry had already adopted VAs to reduce CO_2 emissions (see Chapter 5) and been burdened by an ecological tax reform (see Chapter 6). Up to the late 1990s, German environmental NGOs fiercely opposed emissions trading (Interviews, 2007; Wurzel, 2008a).

Environment Ministry officials were largely sceptical while opposition to emissions trading was even more pronounced in the Economics Ministry (Interviews, 2007). In the early 1990s, the Environment Ministry made three half-hearted and ultimately unsuccessful attempts to establish a domestic emissions trading pilot scheme (Schafhausen, 1999: 35). In the late 1990s, the state *(Land)* Hesse, where Germany's largest banks have their headquarters, initiated an emissions trading simulation game (Interviews, 2007).

The German government used the threat of an imposed EU ETS – the Commission's proposal for an EU ETS fell under qualified majority voting rules – to create an emissions trading working group *(Arbeitsgemeinschaft Emissionshandel – AGE)* in late 2000 (Interviews, 2005–07). The AGE was modelled on the British ETG (Interviews, 2002; Lafeld, 2003; Rudolf, 2005). The Environment and Economics Ministries founded it jointly. BP seconded a company representative to the AGE's secretariat where he worked for free (Interview, 2007).

The AGE acted as an important information and discussion forum for stakeholders (for example, industry and environmental NGO representatives), government officials, MPs and representatives from the German states *(Länder)*. Importantly it also provided a negotiating forum which helped the Environment and Economics Ministries to arrive at the German national position for the EU negotiations. There were, however, deep splits within the AGE. The chemical, coal and energy intensive

178 *Environmental governance in Europe*

industries all fiercely opposed emissions trading. The rapidly growing renewable energy industry initially also campaigned against emissions trading (Eurosolar, 2001; Lafeld, 2003: 184). Industries favouring emissions trading (such as oil companies and the banking sector) were in a minority within the AGE. Disagreements between stakeholders within the AGE came to a head when the chemical industry stayed away from meetings in late 2001 (Interviews, 2007). Because the Association for the Chemical Industry *(Verband der chemischen Industry* – VCI) is an influential member of the BDI (which makes decisions by common consent), the chemicals industry was able to prevent constructive discussions about the EU ETS between the association and the German government (Interviews, 2007).

The chemical industry relied on its traditionally close contacts to the German Chancellor in a determined but ultimately unsuccessful effort to prevent the EU ETS (Interviews, 2005–07). At first sight, the chemical industry's reliance on Chancellor Schröder seems a flawed lobbying strategy because, theoretically, Germany could have been outvoted on the EU level as the Commission's proposal for an EU ETS fell under QMV rules. However, in practice, there is a 'prevalence [of] unanimity as *de facto* mode of decision even where QMV is available under treaty rules' (Padgett, 2003: 242). It is unlikely that Germany, which is both the EU's largest economy and CO_2 emitter, would have been outvoted had Chancellor Schröder continued to object to the EU ETS on the grounds of vital national interest.

The Mining, Chemical and Energy Industrial Union (*Industriegewerkschaft Bergbau, Chemie, Energie* – IGBCE), which has close links with the SPD, also opposed the adoption of the EU ETS. It lobbied Chancellor Schröder and Economics Minister Clement because the chemical and coal industries provide many jobs, particularly in North Rhine Westphalia (traditionally the SPD's political heartland). One Environment Ministry official (Interview, 2005) argued that '[e]missions trading is such a complex and technical instrument that most top politicians, who are under great time pressure, will look at it primarily through the spectacles of their most trusted lobby organisation'.

In the 2002 German election campaign, Chancellor Schröder (SPD) attacked the Commission for allegedly neglecting German industrial interests while mentioning the EU ETS (Wurzel, 2008a). However, in the same election campaign Environment Minister Trittin (Greens) supported the EU ETS. The Greens, which had initially opposed emissions trading, changed their position during the EU ETS adoption phase. German environmental NGOs, the WWF, Germanwatch and BUND/Friends of the Earth Germany, which all attended AGE meetings, underwent a similar conversion (Interviews, 2005–7; Lafeld, 2003; Rudolf, 2005; Wurzel, 2008a). In the 2002 *Bundestag* elections the Greens gained eight additional seats while the SPD lost 47 seats. This increased the Greens' bargaining power during the negotiations of the new SPD-Greens coalition government treaty, which endorsed the EU ETS (SPD-Grüne, 2002: 29–30).

In October 2003, a High Level Group of senior Environment Ministry and Economics Ministry officials was founded to meet regularly with industry representatives and find a NAP-I compromise; other stakeholders represented in the AGE were not invited (Matthes and Schafhausen, 2007). However, in January 2004, the Economics Ministry (and industry) abandoned the High Level Group (Interview, 2007). As mentioned above, the deep-seated disagreement between the Environment and Economics Ministries about the German NAP-I had to be resolved in a meeting chaired by Chancellor Schröder in early 2004.

In 2004, the German Emissions Trading Authority (*Deutsche Emissionshandelsstelle* – DEHSt) was set up within the Federal Environment Agency (see DEHSt, 2012). The DEHSt is responsible for the allocation of allowances and the register. It also has monitoring and control functions. The Federal Environment Agency fought hard to be allocated the political responsibility for the DEHSt which has a staff of about 100 (Interviews, 2007).

AUSTRIA: AN EMISSIONS TRADING LATECOMER

Like Germany, Austria initially gave preference to other environmental policy instruments such as regulation, environmental subsidies and, although to a lesser degree, VAs. Austria had no significant domestic emissions trading experience prior to the EU ETS. The Austrian Clean Air Act allowed for so-called bubble solutions, which exhibited some core features of ETSs, although their use remained limited (Glatz, 1995: 5). Emissions trading was listed as a possible environmental policy instrument in the 1996 National Environmental Plan (*Nationaler Umweltplan*) which was modelled on the Dutch National Environmental Policy Plan (Interviews, 2002; Bundesregierung, 1996: 22). Austria subsequently adopted an eco-point system for heavy goods vehicles (for noise and air emissions as well as for the weight of lorries) on certain Alpine roads; this, however, did not constitute an ETS.

In 1998 the Economics Ministry created a Working Group on Economic Instruments (*Arbeitsgruppe ökonomische Instrumente*) which met

180   *Environmental governance in Europe*

about every two to three weeks (Interviews, 2002). Members included the Economics Ministry, the Environment Ministry and Finance Ministry officials, representatives from the states *(Länder)* and the social partners (namely, the Business Chamber and the Workers Chamber); environmental NGOs were not represented (Interviews, 2011). However, the working group focused primarily on a possible ecological tax reform (see Chapter 6) rather than a domestic ETS. Arguably the closest Austria came to a domestic ETS before the EU ETS was the revised 2001 Electricity Management Act. It liberalised the domestic electricity market, allowing for an emissions trading quota system for small hydropower stations (BMLFUW, 2001).

In the late 1990s the Environment Ministry commissioned a first feasibility study for a national ETS from the Austrian Institute for Economic Research (*Österreichisches Institut für Wirtschaftsforschung* –WIFO) which was published in 2000 (WIFO, 2000). However, the Environment Ministry pushed harder for an ecological tax reform than for emissions trading (Interviews, 2002 and 2011). The Economics Ministry was initially highly sceptical about emissions trading (Interviews, 2001). Austrian environmental NGOs and most businesses as well as the Workers Chamber and the Business Chamber also opposed emissions trading. Environmental NGOs and the Workers Chamber demanded an ecological tax reform while most businesses and the Business Chamber pleaded for the adoption of VAs and environmental subsidies (Interviews, 2002 and 2011).

In the early 2000s emissions trading nevertheless gradually became an acceptable policy instrument in Austria for the following two main reasons. First, under the EU burden sharing agreement, Austria was committed to a 13 per cent carbon dioxide emissions reduction target by 2012. As the 2012 deadline drew closer, Austrian policy makers increasingly realised that this target could only be achieved either with costly additional reduction efforts or less expensive purchases of emissions allowances under the EU ETS. The Conservative-Right Wing (ÖVP-FPÖ) coalition government (2000–07) ruled out an ecological tax reform and additional regulatory measures on the grounds that they would negatively affect Austria's economic competitiveness. Second, after the Commission's 2001 proposal for an EU ETS, opposition against emissions trading waned in Austria. In 2011 the Environment Ministry estimated that Austria would need allowances for about 36 million tonnes of CO_2 to close the gap between its 13 per cent burden sharing agreement target and actual emissions (Interview, 2011).

Since 2006 a High Level group has met to discuss EU ETS issues. It has consisted of officials from the Environment, Economics and Finance

Ministries as well as the Chancellery, the social partners, the Federation of Austrian Industries (*Industriellenvereinigung*) and Energy Austria. Amongst Austrian policy makers and stakeholders marked differences emerged about the best ETS design. The Environment Ministry and Labour Chamber favoured a mandatory scheme and the auctioning of allowances. The Economics Ministry and the Business Chamber preferred voluntary participation and the free allocation of allowances (Interviews, 2002 and 2011).

Austria's unions and businesses found it difficult to generate a united position on emissions trading within their respective umbrella organisations. Austria's largest companies are organised in the Federation of Austrian Industries which was generally favourably disposed towards the EU ETS early on. However, individual company directors remained opposed to emissions trading. The most prominent example is the outspoken director of steel producer Voestalpine AG which held approximately one fifth of Austria's EU ETS emission allowances in 2011. The Business Chamber, which represents mainly small and medium sized companies, found it difficult to convince its members of the merits of emissions trading. The Workers Chamber only reluctantly accepted emissions trading as an inevitable environmental policy instrument which needed to be designed to benefit both the environment and Austrian workers.

Austrian environmental NGOs initially strongly opposed emissions trading. Only when it became clear that the EU ETS would be adopted anyway, most of them start to lobby for stringent caps, full auctioning, extensive monitoring and severe penalties in cases of non-compliance. However, in the early 2010s, some of Austria's environmental NGOs became again highly sceptical about the merits of emission trading in general and the EU ETS in particular (Interviews, 2011).

Already in 2000, the Economics Ministry created a working group on CDM and JI. Austria's historically close political and economic links with, and geographic proximity to, Central and Eastern European states made JI an attractive CO_2 reduction option. One Economics Ministry official (Interview, 2002) stated bluntly: 'Emissions trading is very important for Austria. Because the US has not ratified the Kyoto Protocol cheap allowances will be available from the Russian Federation'.

The reasons for Austria's failure to develop a domestic ETS are multifaceted. National preferences for different policy instruments are one important reason. There was initially also a lack of knowledge amongst small and medium sized Austrian companies about the highly complex emissions trading instrument. The Economics Ministry and Business Chamber offered emissions trading seminars and simulation

182   *Environmental governance in Europe*

exercises for businesses which were affected by the EU ETS. However, some company directors and managers had an aversion to emissions trading which a better understanding of emissions trading did not ameliorate. According to one Economics Ministry official (Interview, 2002),
Austria's market was also too small for a viable domestic ETS. However, the small size of its market did not prevent Denmark from becoming an emissions trading pioneer.

CONCLUSION

Emissions trading has only been used as a policy instrument in Europe since the 1990s. Only a small number of European countries (including the UK and the Netherlands) innovated with emissions trading before the EU ETS became operational in 2005. The earlier American emissions trading experience became an important reference point for European emissions trading proponents. At the US insistence and against the resistance of the EU and its member states, the 1997 Kyoto Protocol listed emissions trading as a possible policy instrument to reduce greenhouse gas emissions. The EU and some of its member states therefore became somewhat reluctant emissions trading entrepreneurs.

It has been argued that the adoption of emissions trading in Europe amounted to a process of policy transfer (Damro and Méndez, 2003; Lawrence, 2007). This argument fits the explanation that the adoption of NEPIs generally follows a pattern of policy transfer according to which 'first mover' countries export their innovative policy instruments through a global diffusion process (Jörgens, 2003; Kern, Jörgens and Jänicke, 2000). Following Dolowitz and Marsh's (1996) differentiation between voluntary and coercive policy transfer, it could be argued that the US encouraged both voluntary policy instrument transfer (namely, the emulation of its early domestic emissions trading experience) and imposed coercive policy instrument transfer (namely, the insertion of emissions trading into the Kyoto protocol). Clearly without America providing a model and insisting on emissions trading in the 1997 Kyoto Protocol it is unlikely that emissions trading would have arrived in Europe as quickly.

However, the specific rules of the ETSs in the UK, the Netherlands and the EU differed significantly from the early American schemes. It was therefore the principal idea rather than specific rules which were transferred from America to Europe via the 1997 Kyoto protocol (Jordan, Wurzel and Zito, 2005; Wurzel, 2008a). The main reasons for the

Governing by emissions trading 183

differences in the American and European ETSs (as well as the differences between the British, Dutch and EU ETSs) are due to different institutional contexts.

Preferences for different environmental policy instruments, opposition from important societal actors and a lack of expertise amongst policy makers constituted important barriers for the early adoption of emissions trading in Europe (for example, Holzinger, 1987; Jordan, Wurzel and Zito, 2003c: 206; Sandhövel, 1994). Up to the late 1990s, all major European environmental NGOs strongly opposed emissions trading on ethical grounds (Interviews, 2007 and 2011). Many European businesses were initially also opposed to emissions trading. However, European oil companies (and in particular BP), some energy producers and the banking sector supported the use of emissions trading early on (Skjærseth and Wettestad, 2008; Wettestad, 2005; Wurzel, 2008a).

In 2002 the UK acted as a European emission trading pioneer when it adopted the world's first national ETS for six greenhouse gases (after Denmark adopted a national ETS for CO_2 from power stations in 1999). While the environmental benefits of the UK ETS have remained contested there is widespread agreement that Britain gained valuable 'learning by doing' emissions trading experience. The early adoption of a domestic ETS also helped to establish the City of London as the global centre for emissions trading. Importantly, BP, which had already set up an in-house emissions trading scheme, played a central role in setting up the ETG which convinced the British Labour government of the merits of emissions trading. BP later also offered its expertise to the German government which set up the AGE, which was modelled on the UK's ETG. Although the UK played an influential role in the EU ETS adoption process, it was not able to 'upload' all of its core national preferences to the EU level. The rules of the EU ETS turned out to be different from the UK ETS.

The Netherlands had already experimented with American inspired 'bubble policy' concepts (for combustion plants) in the 1980s. The Dutch have also innovated with tradable allowances in the agricultural policy sector since the 1980s. However, the early domestic ETSs were bureaucratic and plagued with legal difficulties. If anything they provided negative lessons for Dutch policy makers. In the late 1990s, Dutch policy makers started to design a more successful ETSs for reducing NO_x emissions which became operational in the same year as the EU ETS. The Netherlands played a very constructive role in the adoption phase of the EU ETS although it later encountered difficulties with its implementation phase when the Commission criticised the Dutch NAP-I and NAP-II as being too lenient.

The EU ETS was adopted at surprising speed in 2003 and became operational in 2005. It was initially a highly decentralised ETS for CO_2 emissions from stationary sources. The EU ETS initially distinguished a first trading phase from 2005–07 and a second trading phase from 2008–12. A third trading phase (2013–20) was added during the revision of the EU ETS which greatly centralised the rules of the scheme. The Commission acted as an emissions trading policy instrument entrepreneur. Frustrated by the lack of progress of its carbon dioxide/energy tax proposal and concerned about competing national ETSs, the Commission used the policy window created by the 1997 Kyoto Protocol to propose EU-wide emissions trading. It was strongly supported in its efforts by the majority of member states (including the UK and the Netherlands) and the EP. The German government remained opposed to emissions trading until well into the adoption phase of the EU ETS. It was only after the 2002 national elections in which the Greens gained a significant number of seats in parliament that the German government started to support the adoption of the EU ETS.

Austria and Germany initially acted as emissions trading laggards. The German Chancellor Schröder (SPD) almost torpedoed the adoption of the EU ETS. However, Austria and Germany (as well as the Netherlands and the UK) have since supported the tightening and centralisation of the rules of the EU ETS. In the second trading phase Germany has made wide use of auctioning. Austria realised that the EU ETS can help it to comply with its 13 per cent Kyoto Protocol greenhouse gases reduction target.

Using Hall's analytical classification (see Chapter 2), it could be argued that emissions trading constitutes not only a change in the use of existing instruments (first level change) and the adoption of new policy instruments (second level change) but also a paradigm change (third level change). Third level changes involve changes in overarching policy goals that are driven by a core set of ideas or paradigm (Hall, 1993: 279). The EU ETS, which became the world's first supranational ETS, has been called a 'bold public policy experiment' (Ellerman, Convery and de Perthuis, 2010: 288) that 'lifted the environment from the boiler room to the boardroom, from ministries of environment to ministries of finance, from councils to Cabinet tables' (Ellerman, Convery and de Perthuis, 2010: 1).

However, although the EU ETS is a market-based instrument, it cannot rely solely on (new modes of) governance but also needs (traditional tools of) government. This became particularly apparent during the setting up phase of the EU ETS which necessitated the adoption of EU and member state laws and institutional structures with a significant number of ministry, agency and Commission officials who dealt with the adoption, implementation and revision of this novel policy instrument. One British official (Interview, 2007) warned that '[i]t is an astonishingly common misperception that market-based instruments will lead to significantly less bureaucracy and legislation. They can work only because of regulatory back up. The market needs government protection'. Top-down state authority intervention has also been necessary to protect the EU ETS from fraud and corruption. The expansion of top-down government authority is perhaps further established by the extension of the EU ETS scheme to the aviation sector including third country airlines with destinations in EU member states.

As Chapter 8 will explain in more detail, what stands out in the adoption process of the EU ETS and the various national ETSs is the important role which corporations (and especially BP) have played. Moreover, increased electoral support for the Green Party has been an important factor in bringing about a change in the attitude of the German government towards emissions trading. Finally, because emissions trading is a highly complex, novel policy instrument, all five jurisdictions undertook reasonably wide stakeholder consultations and/or set up emissions trading advisory committees/working groups in which stakeholders discussed the advantages of emission trading and different ETS designs. Whether the EU ETS has indeed brought about 'a radical innovation in governance', as Voß (2007: 330) has claimed, will be assessed in Chapters 8 and 9.

NOTE

1. The Environmental Defense Fund is an US environmental NGO which has long campaigned for the use of market-based policy instruments in general and emissions trading in particular (see http://www.edf.org/home.cfm).

PART IV

Emerging patterns of governing

8. Changing patterns of environmental policy instrument use

INTRODUCTION

This chapter examines how NEPIs have developed over time and assesses whether they have supplanted or merely supplemented traditional tools of environmental regulation. Having analysed NEPI usage in Chapters 4–7, it is necessary to briefly assess the main changes in the use of traditional command-and-control regulations before we can definitively evaluate the changing patterns in the use of all policy instruments. First, as Chapter 3 already suggested, traditional regulation has been a fundamental instrument for governing environmental policy since the early 1970s. The interaction between 'old' and 'new' policy instruments is therefore vital. Second, traditional command-and-control regulation has undergone transformations which change the nature of how society is steered by regulation.

This chapter starts with a brief analysis of the adoption and usage patterns of traditional command-and-control environmental regulations in the five contexts. Like the previous NEPI chapters, Chapter 8 starts with the pioneers which first innovated with a significant number of modern-day environmental regulations. It then shifts to a macro-level analysis of the general patterns in NEPIs usage while identifying innovators, followers and laggards. Having assessed the role of regulation, the third section explores the overarching pattern of NEPI usage in the member states and the EU. The fourth section examines the pattern of instrument adoption to see if there are any general sequential patterns in the usage of different types of environmental policy instruments in different jurisdictions. Finally, Chapter 8 examines the degree to which policy (instrument) learning and diffusion affect the adoption and usage patterns of 'old' and 'new' policy instruments.

TRADITIONAL REGULATIONS: CHANGING PATTERNS IN USE

Gunningham, Grabosky and Sinclair (1998: 38) have argued that '[t]he dominant government response [to the arrival of environmental issues on the political agenda], ... has been the application of "direct" or "command and control" regulation designed to prohibit or restrict environmentally harmful activities'. This is certainly true for the EU and its member states, where traditional command-and-control regulation quickly became 'the standard instrument of environmental policy' (Jordan, Wurzel and Zito, 2013). At first sight, the differences in national and EU policy styles (see Chapter 3) have had little impact on the environmental policy instrument choices, as policy-makers in all five jurisdictions have relied heavily on traditional regulations. However a closer look at the environmental regulations adopted in the five different European jurisdictions reveals important differences.

There has been an upsurge in environmental regulations in highly industrialised liberal democracies since the early 1970s (for example, Faure and Ruegg, 1994; Gunningham, Grabosky and Sinclair, 1998; Jordan, Wurzel and Zito, 2003a, 2007, 2013; Jordan et al., 2012a; Weale, 1992a). However, three factors hinder the collation of precise figures on the environmental regulations adopted over the last four decades. First, because environmental policy is typically cross-cutting (see Chapter 1), it is difficult to delineate environmental regulations from, for example, certain health and transport regulations. Over time, the demarcation between 'environmental' and 'non-environmental' regulation became increasingly more difficult because environmental policy progressively intruded into non-environmental policy fields. Second, while most of the early environmental regulations focused narrowly on particular pollutants (for example, lead in petrol) or the use of parts of the environment (for example, drinking water), some of the more recent environmental regulations are framework laws (for example, the EU water framework directive). By adopting framework laws, governments and the EU have tried to reduce the number of detailed command-and-control regulations. However, in practice framework laws are often implemented through detailed technical instructions and/or administrative laws although the latter are frequently not listed in statistics on environmental regulations (see the following).

Third, environmental regulations are adopted not only at the national level but also at the supranational and subnational levels. Subnational level environmental regulations play an important role especially in federal states such as Austria and Germany. In the quasi-federal EU political system (see Chapter 3), it is impossible to assess member state environmental regulations in isolation from supranational ones (Jordan, 2002). Rather than compile very imprecise data on the number of environmental regulations, Chapter 8 assesses the trends in the adoption and usage patterns of environmental regulation in the five jurisdictions.

Germany: The Dominance of the Best Available Technology

The state of law (*Rechtsstaat*) tradition helps to explain the high degree of juridification of policy sectors in Germany (see Chapter 3; Dyson, 1992). Héritier, Knill and Mingers (1996) have characterised Germany as a 'high regulatory state' because of its strong reliance on traditional command-and-control environmental regulations (see also Kloepfer, 2004; Weale, 1992b; Wurzel, 2002, 2008c; Wurzel et al., 2003b). Müller-Brandeck-Bocquet (1996: 138) estimated that Germany had about 35 000 technical instructions in place in the mid-1990s. Reiche and Krebs (1999: 63) have quoted government data for the late 1990s which identified 800 laws, 2700 ordinances and 4690 technical instructions in the environmental policy field. Sprenger (2000: 14) has cited similar figures – 800 acts, 2800 ordinances and 4700 technical instructions. However, one German Environment Agency official (Interview, 2001) dismissed such high estimates as:

> futile number games [which] arrive at grossly inflated figures by taking into account also the environmental laws of the *Länder* of which there are now 16. In essence, we [in Germany] have about eight or nine major environmental acts which are then specified by ordinances and technical instructions.

Because of the adoption of a large number of relatively ambitious environmental regulations, Edda Müller (1986) categorised the period from 1969–74 as an 'offensive phase' for German environmental policy. Examples of early environmental regulations include the 1971 law on noise emissions from aviation, 1971 lead in petrol law and the 1974 Federal Air Quality Control Act (*Bundes-Immissionsschutzgesetz* – BImSchG) (Müller, 1986: 75; Hartkopf and Bohne, 1983). While the 1974 Federal Air Quality Control Act has been called the Magna Carta of German air pollution control (Genscher, 1980: 120), most of the other environmental regulations adopted in the offensive phase were much narrower in scope. The Federal Air Quality Control Act was implemented through a more detailed administrative law called Technical Instructions on Air Quality Control (*Technische Anleitung (TA) Luft*). Importantly, the 1974 TA Luft, which was revised in 1983, 1988 and 2002, allows (under certain circumstances) for so-called compensation solutions (*Kompensationslösungen*) which permit companies to adopt higher emission reductions for some plants in order to compensate for the failure to achieve the required reductions in other plants. Compensation solutions therefore allow companies to opt for more cost-efficient solutions than

192 *Environmental governance in Europe*

would be possible through rigid uniform emission limits. German environmental policy makers borrowed the basic idea for compensation solutions from the American bubble policy concept (Interviews, 2000 and 2002). However, there was no full scale policy instrument transfer from America to Germany because the compensation solutions under the TA Luft did not constitute a market-based instrument, which is how bubble policy was used in the USA. Instead, the compensation solutions stipulated in the TA Luft are deeply embedded in detailed administrative law derived from the BAT principle. The introduction of compensation solutions in the TA Luft reveal that some early German environmental regulations were more flexible and innovative than many critics of regulations would acknowledge.

Following the 1973 oil crisis, German environmental policy went through a 'defensive phase' from 1974–78. However, there was no roll back of existing environmental regulations although the adoption rate of new environmental regulations slowed (Müller, 1986). It increased again in the 1980s, when Germany adopted the role of an environmental leader which pushed for ambitious EU environmental laws and progressive international environmental treaties (Weale, 1992a; Wurzel, 2003, 2008c). However, following unification in 1990, Germany became more cost-conscious about the economic competitiveness impact of environmental regulations. A centre-right (CDU/CSU-FDP) coalition government (1982–98) adopted a coalition agreement in 1991 which formally gave preference to VAs over environmental regulations (Wurzel et al., 2003a). However, although the number of VAs increased significantly (see Chapter 5), regulations remained dominant in German environmental policy although this was partly due also to the requirement to transpose and implement EU environmental laws (see the following). Moreover, most German VAs were adopted in the 'shadow of the law' (see Chapter 5).

In the late 1990s, a SPD-Greens Party coalition government launched a first unsuccessful attempt to get adopted an Environmental Code (*Umweltgesetzbuch*); this code would have rationalised and modernised German environmental laws while also making it easier to implement EU laws. A second attempt to adopt the Environmental Code, which was undertaken by a grand coalition (CDU/CSU-SPD) government in the late 2000s, also failed due to opposition from the *Länder* which feared a loss of environmental competences (Wurzel, 2010).

In Hall's terminology (see Chapter 2), the adoption of the Environmental Code constituted level two learning because it aimed at more than the mere recalibration of existing environmental policy instruments (namely, level one learning). Instead the Environmental Code would have signified a new, innovative macro-level policy instrument.

The German environmental policy instrument learning process has been largely confined to level one and two learning. Level three learning, essentially a paradigm shift that involves major changes in policy goals, took place in German environmental policy primarily at the beginning of the 1970s offensive phase, which saw the adoption of a large number of novel environmental regulations. It also occurred some thirty years later when German governments decided to phase out nuclear power which clearly amounts to a paradigm shift that will require significant gains in energy efficiency and renewable energy production. Importantly, the phasing out of nuclear power was enshrined in the Atomic Law (*Atomgesetz*), that is, in regulation which was supplemented by a range of additional policy instruments (including NEPIs) aimed at boosting renewable energy.

Media-centred environmental regulations for air, water and soil which stipulate emission limits derived from the BAT principle have remained the dominant German policy instrument (for example, Wurzel et al., 2003a; Wurzel, 2008c). They have often been justified with reference to the precautionary principle (*Vorsorgeprinzip*) that was adopted in the 1971 Environmental Programme which, however, also stipulates the polluter pays principle and cooperation principle (*Kooperationsprinzip*) used to justify the use of flexible NEPIs (see Chapter 3).

Media-centred BAT-derived environmental regulations were highly successful in combating mass pollutants (such as sulphur dioxide) from point sources (such as exhaust pipes). They fitted well with the concept of ecological modernisation (see Chapter 3): Germany's successful pollution abatement industry is sometimes used to justify the continued reliance on ambitious command-and-control environmental regulations. For example, Jänicke (2011: 138–9) identified a booming "climate protection industry"' which created a significant number of German jobs.

However, media-centred BAT derived emission limits, which encouraged the development of end-of-pipe technology, were less successful in reducing pollution from diffuse sources. Moreover, they are only of limited use in implementing the sustainable development concept, which became an important macro level action guiding principle at the EU and international level from the 1990s onwards.

Héritier, Knill and Mingers (1996) have argued that, up to the 1990s, Germany was very successful in uploading to the EU level its domestic environmental standards and regulatory philosophy. However, since the early 1990s, Germany increasingly had to download EU environmental regulations which created considerable domestic adaptation pressures. The EU adopted a range of procedural environmental regulations (such as environmental impact assessment), regulations which stipulated EQOs

194   *Environmental governance in Europe*

and framework laws that supplemented the existing traditional German media-centred BAT-derived emissions limits (Héritier, Knill and Mingers, 1996; Wurzel, 2003, 2004).

The Netherlands: Proactive Regulatory Making

According to Liefferink (1996: 73) '[t]the first broad environmental law in the Netherlands was the Nuisance Act' which was first enacted in 1875. The main Dutch impetus for centralised environmental regulations came in the 1970s with the rise in environmental concerns and the creation of the Ministry of Public Health and Environmental Hygiene (see Chapter 3; Liefferink, 1996: 74). In order to deal effectively with environmental problems and to avoid the poor implementation witnessed in the local authority implementation of the Nuisance Act, the Dutch government pushed through a number of central regulations which focused on discrete sectors (Liefferink and Wiering, 2007). The authority over this legislation varied according to the Act. Municipalities were responsible for authorising strict command-and-control licences to the many small polluters, but provincial governments had competency concerning the larger industrial installations (Liefferink and Wiering, 2007; van der Woerd, 1998).

The Dutch government took a relatively interventionist approach to 1970s environmental policy, relying heavily on command-and-control regulations. In order to monitor the effectiveness of environmental regulations, the Dutch government has used periodic indicative multi-year programmes since the 1970s (Liefferink, 1996: 74). Assessments indicate that traditional regulation has remained an important environmental policy instrument (for example, OECD, 2003c; Liefferink and Wiering, 2007). The OECD (1995c: 200) has praised the Dutch approach to environmental planning as 'indicative, comprehensive, action-oriented and based on some of the most innovative and sophisticated analytical work in the world. There is much to learn from it for other countries'. The National Environmental Policy Plans (NEPPs), which were emulated by Austria (see the following), played an important role in the improved planning and monitoring of traditional environmental regulations.

Broadly speaking, the top-down command-and-control control character of the early Dutch environmental legislation was gradually supplanted with more flexible and cost-effective environmental regulations; the government developed the latter only after extensive stakeholder consultations. However, the greatly increased flexibility of, for example, certain climate change policy measures has led some observers to view the post-2000 Dutch role as little more than 'cost free leadership' in climate change politics (Liefferink and Birkel, 2011).

Environmental regulation in the Netherlands is driven by both domestic initiatives and efforts to implement EU environmental regulations and international environmental treaties. In some cases the EU actually became an important driver for the sustained use of traditional regulation and a barrier to NEPIs. As Smith and Ingram (2002: 593) have pointed out '[w]hen the Netherlands implemented a European environmental policy directive through a covenant, Brussels thus reacted negatively'. The ECJ has consistently taken the view that EU Directives have to be transposed into legally binding national legislation rather than covenants or administrative acts (see the following).

The Netherlands, which has often tried to be a mediator in EU environmental policy-making, can be placed somewhere between the law-based BAT-derived environmental standards approach which dominate German and Austrian environmental policy and the more flexible discretionary approach UK governments have traditionally preferred (see the following). The best practicable means (BPM) and best technical means (BTM) are two key action guiding principles that have traditionally guided Dutch environmental regulations (Weale et al., 2000: 171–2).

There is a pattern of obligations created in covenants (see Chapter 5) which can be enshrined into formal legislations or individual licences (Liefferink and Wiering, 2007; Enevoldsen, 2000). The cost-effectiveness of Dutch legislation:

> was consolidated and simplified by the passing of the Environmental Management Act in 1993. The central, provincial and local authorities have become more active in the late 1980s and early 1990s in making sure the activities of enterprises conform to the law and in monitoring the enforcement of *laws* and *regulations* (OECD, 1995c: 205).

The 1993 Environmental Management Act aimed to simplify the complicated licencing system which had developed in the Netherlands since the early 1970s. It also further developed the BPM and BTM principles by introducing the As Low As Reasonably Achievable (ALARA) principle (see Chapter 3).

Since the 1990s considerable government efforts have been made to simplify the environmental licencing process. In April 2005, the Environment Ministry's State Secretary, Pieter van Geel, announced a programme to simplify and update domestic environmental permitting procedures (*ENDS Europe Daily*, 5 April 2005). Its aim was to avoid imposing permits on the majority of companies that have a low environmental

196   *Environmental governance in Europe*

impact. Instead a general regulation would be in place for all but the most significant polluting businesses. These new regulations aimed to improve implementation and enforcement, merging the current general regulations for non-agricultural companies into one decree to help simplify the process and reduce administrative expenses (VROM, 2005b).

To implement this approach, the Dutch government revised the overarching Environmental Management Act in 2008. For many operations that do not impose a significant environmental impact (for instance, service industries as opposed to power stations, large scale production facilities), operators no longer require a licence but instead can follow standard procedures to notify the authorities as to the nature and scope of the pollution source (OECD, 2009: 140).

'Framework licences' have also been developed. They specify only general targets and leave the means for achieving them to the firms in question. In order to qualify for a framework licence, the company must fulfil certain requirements including having either ISO 14001 or EMAS certified operations (Liefferink and Wiering, 2007). The target group approach (see Chapter 3) also tried to bring about better implementation by simplifying regulations in combination with the principle of internalisation.

The 2008 Environmental Management Act also has the benefit of taking an integrated approach to environmental issues, highlighting their interrelationships. Its chapters cover sectors such as waste and water. These policy sectors provide useful examples of the transformation of 1970s legislation over time. The 2008 Act incorporated the principles of a hierarchy of waste management solutions into the approach (Eionet, 2009). This regulatory provision is shaped by an ongoing national Waste Management Plan (the first covering 2002–12, and the second 2009–21). This plan guides national, provincial and municipal authorities in terms of setting the rules for the management of specific waste streams (Eionet, 2009: section 2). Similarly, the Water Act of 2009 acts as framework legislation that is further implemented by secondary legislation, specifically governmental decrees and ministerial regulations. It takes an integrated water management approach to address all the relationships within the water systems (Rijkswaterstaat, 2011: 75–6). The National Water Plan reviews the national policy instruments and overarching management over the course of its planning cycle.

These developments demonstrate two critical aspects of Dutch innovation in environmental regulations. First, policy learning and innovation is not restricted simply to the adoption of NEPIs; traditional regulations have also been evolving while reflecting policy (instrument) learning (first and second levels of policy change). Second, the innovations in traditional regulation (for example, greater consultation, flexibility and cost-effectiveness) and NEPIs are increasingly interacting and being made dependent on each other. This led the OECD's (2009: 2) review of Dutch environmental policy to conclude that the 'characteristic policy mix of regulation/licencing plus economic instruments plus environmental agreements continues to be productive'.

Austria: A Belated Preference for the Best Available Technology

Austria has been labelled 'an extremely legalistic state' in which 'most relevant government decisions must have the form of law' (Müller, 1992: 103; see also Chapter 3). Therefore, unsurprisingly, Austria has relied heavily on environmental command-and-control regulations (Interviews, 2002 and 2011; Lauber, 1997b, 2000; OECD, 2003b; Pesendorfer, 2007; Wurzel et al., 2003b). Lauber (1997a: 96) has argued that Austria has one of 'Europe's highest ratios of law graduates among its civil servants; this goes hand-in-hand with the practice that relies strongly on command-and-control measures and is averse to economic instruments'. According to the OECD (2003b: 16), Austrian environmental policy has relied 'on detailed environmental regulations, targeted investment support, use of best available technology and solid federal and provincial environmental administrations'.

In the 1970s most Austrian environmental regulations focused narrowly on particular pollutants such as lubricants and detergents (Lauber, 1997a: 84). Many of the early Austrian environmental regulations were not very ambitious – at least compared to similar policy measures found in European environmental leader states (Lauber, 1997a, 1997b; Pesendorfer, 2007). Austria's reluctance to adopt more stringent environmental regulations in the 1970s has been attributed to the Austrian notion of corporatism: a close tripartite relationship between the government, employers and union that excluded environmental interest groups. The highly institutionalised social partnership between the Business Chamber and Workers Chamber initially gave priority to economic growth and high employment over the adoption of ambitious environmental regulations (see Chapter 3; Mol, Lauber and Liefferink, 2000).

In the 1980s Austria transformed from an environmental latecomer into an environmental pioneer when it adopted a wide range of relatively ambitious environmental regulations (Lauber, 1997a). The 1980 Steam Boiler Emissions Law (*Dampf-Kessel-Emissionsgesetz*) is widely seen as a 'milestone in Austrian environmental policy' (Pesendorfer, 2007: 108). It stipulated BAT-derived regulatory standards that were more stringent than those in force in the EU and many of its member states (Lauber,

198   *Environmental governance in Europe*

1997a: 82; Pesendorfer, 2007; Pesendorfer and Lauber, 2006). New, ambitious environmental regulations which soon followed the Steam Boiler Emissions Law included the Hazardous Waste Law (1983) and Detergent Law (1984).

A break-through (*Durchbruch*) was achieved for more ambitious environmental regulations between 1985 and 1992 (Pesendorfer, 2007: 103; see also Lauber, 1997b). The adoption of a wide range of relatively stringent environmental regulations transformed Austria from an environmental latecomer into an 'internationally recognised pioneer' (Pesendorfer, 2007: 103). Many of these regulations were derived from the BAT and precautionary principles, which were also guiding environmental policy principles in neighbouring Germany (see above) – Austria's largest export market. However, Austrian environmental policy makers studied closely not only the environmental laws in Germany but also those in the Netherlands and the Scandinavian countries. These countries were perceived as environmental leader states by Austrian policy-makers, who aspired to attain this status for Austria in the late 1980s and early 1990s (Interviews, 2002). For example, the 1994 Austrian Environmental Plan was modelled on the Dutch NEPP (Interview, 2002; see also Chapter 3).

In the mid-1990s, the OECD (1995a: 158) concluded that 'Austria has been *very successful* in dealing with all major environmental issues of the late 1970s. Its achievements concerning conventional pollutants such as SO_x (a reduction of 81 per cent between 1980 and 1992) put it among the top in the OECD in this regard'. However, Austria was less successful in reducing pollution from diffuse sources because they are difficult to target with media-centred BAT-derived regulations which constituted the main type of Austrian environmental regulation.

When Austria joined the EU in 1995, it was allowed to keep temporarily – initially for a period of five years – some of its domestic regulations which stipulated environmental standards that were more stringent than those enshrined in EU legislation. Under the so-called review process the EU subsequently ratcheted upwards its supranational environmental laws to the more stringent Austrian standards.

However, Austria's environmental pioneer status was relatively short-lived. Largely due to economic difficulties and changes in government, Austria's enthusiasm for the adoption of stringent environmental regulations waned again in the late 1990s and remained relatively low for much of the 2000s (Interviews, 2002 and 2011). Austria lost its environmental pioneer status when a centre-right (ÖVP-FPÖ) coalition government (2000–07), which subscribed to 'neoliberal minimalism' (Lauber, 1997c; Pesendorfer, 2007: 189), downgraded the importance of environmental policy in relation to economic issues. Pesendorfer (2007: 673)

Changing patterns of environmental policy instrument use 199

maintains that this resulted in a 'break in environmental policy' during which the EU became the most important driver for Austrian environmental policy. Pesendorfer's argument helps to explain why environmental regulations remained the dominant Austrian environmental policy instrument in the 2000s despite the centre-right coalition government formally giving preference to VAs over environmental regulations. Under the centre-right coalition government Austrian civil servants were instructed to refrain from 'gold plating' EU laws including environmental laws (Interviews, 2002 and 2011; see Chapter 3). In other words, Austrian officials were asked to ensure that Austria would not adopt national measures which exceeded the letter of EU environmental regulations.

The adoption of ambitious environmental regulations increased only moderately again under the grand (SPÖ-ÖVP) coalition government which came to power in 2007. It also gave priority to rectifying Austria's economic difficulties over the adoption of ambitious domestic environmental regulations. One Austrian Environment Ministry official (Interview, 2011) therefore stressed '[w]e are now glad about Austria's EU membership because the EU is currently the main driver of Austrian environmental policy'.

Austria has shown a clear preference for media-centred (uniform) emissions limits which were derived from the BAT principle (Lauber, 1997a; Pesendorfer, 2007: 109; Wurzel et al., 2003b). When acting as an environmental pioneer, Austria made heavy use of the precautionary principle to justify stringent environmental regulations. Due to the above mentioned domestic break in environmental policy (Pesendorfer, 2007: 673), Austria found itself under less intensive adaptation pressures (compared to Germany) when the EU adopted procedural measures, framework directives and regulations which stipulated EQOs that were alien to Austria's traditionally preferred type of environmental regulations. Tensions between the EU and Austria increased however over Austrian measures to limit trans-Alpine road traffic; these involved a mix of traditional regulations and economic instruments including eco-points for lorries (see Chapter 6).

The OECD (1995a, 2003b) has repeatedly acknowledged the effectiveness of Austrian environmental regulations although it criticised the low cost-effectiveness of such measures. In the mid-1990s the OECD (1995a: 161) concluded that:

> [i]t is reasonable to state that the achievements … while effective, have not
> been reached at the lowest cost. Current approaches, largely based on

200 *Environmental governance in Europe*

regulations and best technology, may have to be streamlined and supplemented by efforts to integrate environmental and economic decisions.

Austrian business representatives are often highly critical about Austria's heavy reliance on traditional environmental regulations, preferring VAs and environmental subsidies. However, many business representatives hesitate to endorse the greater use of market-based instruments (Interviews, 2000, 2002 and 2011) as propagated by the OECD (1995a; 2003b). For competitiveness reasons Austrian businesses are particularly wary of eco-taxes which are, however, strongly endorsed by environmental groups that continue also to support ambitious traditional environmental regulations (Interviews, 2002 and 2011).

The wide use of traditional environmental regulations in combination with environmental subsidies has failed to meet Austria's relatively ambitious Kyoto Protocol greenhouse gas emission reduction target (−13 per cent). In 2003 the OECD (2003b: 163–4) therefore warned that, in Austria, '[i]t will ... be necessary to develop aggressive, cost-effective programmes and to implement them with determination'. Austrian environmental policy makers have recognised this need by making much greater use of purchasing emission allowances under the EU emissions trading scheme and CDM and JI participation (Interviews, 2011; see also Chapter 7).

The EU: An Environmental Regulatory State

When assessing the EU's use of command-and-control regulations, it is important to clarify the status of its legislation and how it is implemented (see also Chapter 3). Primary legislation consists of the EU Treaties while secondary legislation comprises of Regulations, Directives and Decisions.

The overwhelming majority of secondary EU environmental legislation consists of Directives which are binding member states 'as to the result to be achieved' but leave open the exact form of implementation. The EU's Treaties also specify so-called Recommendations and Opinions which are legally non-binding soft policy instruments, but these have played no significant role in EU environmental policy.

Majone (1996) has characterised the EU as a 'regulatory state' because it relies heavily on traditional regulation. In 2002, the Commission stated that 'the body of Community law runs to over 80 000 pages' (CEC, 2002a: 13). Traditional regulation has long been the dominant EU environmental policy instrument for two main reasons. First, environmental policy was initially perceived as an inherently regulatory policy.

Second, the EU can make use only of a very limited number of redistributive policy instruments (for example, the structural funds) while their use remains highly circumscribed (for example, structural funds being earmarked for infrastructure measures such as sewerage facilities). The EU's budget remains miniscule at approximately 1 per cent of GDP.

The authoritative *Manual on Environmental Policy* suggests that the EU had adopted well over 1000 items of environmental laws by the early 2000s (Haigh, 2011). Importantly, despite some fluctuations in the annual adoption rates there has been a significant overall increase in the number of EU environmental laws adopted between 1972–2001. The annual adoption rate of EU environmental legislation declined significantly between 2002 and 2007 although the number of EU environmental laws adopted between 2007–09 increased again (see Figure 8.1) (Haigh, 2011). However, in the early 2010s, the adoption rate of EU environmental laws declined again. In fact, in 2012, the EP's Environment Committee 'expressed concerns over a drop in the number of legislative proposals put forward by the EU executive, which is reducing the committee's activity' *(ENDS Europe Daily*, 27 May 2012).

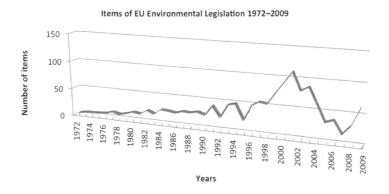

Source: Haigh (2011).

Figure 8.1 Items of EU environmental legislation 1972–2009

The principle of subsidiarity, which was adopted in 1992 in the wake of the first Danish Maastricht Treaty referendum (see Chapter 3), and increasing global competitiveness pressures made EU policy makers

202   *Environmental governance in Europe*

more reluctant to adopt new environmental regulations. However, Figure 8.1 indicates that there was no sustained decline in the adoption rate of EU environmental legislation in the 1990s. A 'hit list', which the French and British governments drew up in the 1990s, earmarked for repatriation more than 100 (including 24 environmental) EU laws (Jordan, 2002; Wurzel, 2002). Importantly, none of the listed EU environmental laws were later scrapped. A 'roll back' of traditional EU environmental regulation did not occur (Hey, 2005; Bauer et al., 2012). However, there was a more subtle change in EU environmental regulations.

In the early 1990s, the Commission shifted its preference for BAT-derived emission limits towards cost-effective EQOs, procedural measures (such as environmental impact assessment) and framework directives (Héritier, Knill and Mingers, 1996; Wurzel, 2008b). The Commission's White Paper on *European Governance* (CEC, 2001b) stated that regulation ought to be only a last resort while preference should be given to non-regulatory EU instruments. Given the Commission's new preference for non-regulatory instruments, the decline in the adoption rate of EU environmental regulations (see Figure 8.1) has been relatively modest. However, the data from Haigh's manual, on which Figure 8.1 is based, requires cautious interpretation because it includes minor technical amendments to existing EU environmental legislation. Some scholars have argued that the EU's environmental regulatory output slowed down significantly already in the early 1990s (for example, Krämer, 1997; Macrory and Purdy, 1997). Whether this is indeed the case is open to interpretation for the reasons explained above. What is undisputed in the EU environmental policy literature is that traditional command-and-control regulations have remained the dominant EU environmental policy instrument (for example, Halpern, 2010; Holzinger, Knill and Schäfer, 2003, 2006; Jordan, Wurzel and Zito, 2006, 2007, 2012; Jordan et al., 2012a).

Although regulations have remained the most important EU environmental policy instrument, their content and form has changed over time. Typical EU environmental laws in the 1970s included Directives on chemical substances (76/769/EEC) and bathing water (76/160). Since the late 1980s procedural laws (such as the Directive on environmental impact assessment (85/337)) supplemented the emission limits and EQOs stipulated in the earlier EU environmental laws.

Importantly EU environmental regulations often resemble a patchwork which reflects different member state preferences and regulatory philosophies (Héritier, 1996; Héritier, Knill and Mingers, 1996). Especially in the 1970s there was a dispute between the island states (UK and Ireland),

Changing patterns of environmental policy instrument use 203

which insisted on EQOs, and continental states (led by Germany) which demanded the adoption of (uniform) emission limits (Wurzel, 2002). In order to overcome serious Anglo-German differences, some of the early EU environmental regulations stipulated both EQOs and (uniform) emission limits rather than expressing a clear preference (Wurzel, 2002: 25). A similar compromise was adopted concerning EU environmental laws which specified the BATNEEC principle. In some EU environmental regulations it was defined as the best available *technique* not entailing excessive costs (resembling the British BATNEEC principle). However, other EU environmental laws referred to it as the best available *technology* not exceeding excessive costs (close to the German BAT principle). For example, the directive for air pollution from industrial plants stipulated both the BATNEEC and BAT principles and made use of both EQOs and emission limits (Wurzel, 2002).

Broad framework laws which specify only the most important environmental objectives (leaving it up to so-called daughter directives to fill in the regulatory details) have become more popular since the early 2000s. The EU water framework directive (2000/60) constitutes a good example. Since the mid-1990s all Commission environmental proposals have to contain a cost-effectiveness statement. Over time EU environmental command-and-control regulations therefore took into account more strongly cost-effectiveness considerations and became more flexible.

A good example is the EU Large Combustion Plant Directive (88/609/EEC), which was adopted in 1988 after long and arduous negotiations. It was modelled on the German Large Combustion Plant Ordinance (*Großfeuerungsanlagenverordnung*) and stipulated emission limits derived from the BAT principle (Boehmer-Christiansen and Skea, 1991; Weale, O'Riordan and Kramme, 1991). The 2001 revision of the Large Combustion Plant Directive (2001/80/EC) allowed for more flexibility for old plants unable to comply with the BAT. Compliance with the revised 2001 Large Combustion Plant Directive can be achieved either through the installation of end-of-pipe emission abatement equipment (for instance, flue gas desulphurisation) or by 'opting out' of the directive which requires case plant operations to be restricted after 2007 and the plants closed by the end of 2015.

The 2007 creation of the High Level Group of Independent Stakeholders on Administrative Burdens (HLG) has reinforced this EU regulatory trajectory. Chaired by Edmund Stoiber (former prime minister of Bavaria), this 15 member body advises the Commission on implementing the Action Programme for Reducing Administrative Burdens in the EU (HLG, 2011). The 2011 HLG report explicitly extols the virtues of

204 *Environmental governance in Europe*

incorporating smart regulation ('the least burdensome regulation necessary to achieve the desired policy objectives') into the EU legislation (HLG, 2011: 22). The HLG highlights improved stakeholder and end-user involvement, examining perceived burdens, risk-based approaches, digital solutions and so forth (HLG, 2011: 8).

The UK: Advocating Flexible and Cost-Effective Regulatory Tools

The UK has traditionally been reluctant to set legally binding long-term environmental policy objectives, especially if their achievement could not be guaranteed through the adoption of cost-effective measures (see Chapter 3). The UK's preference was instead for environmental targets to be negotiated incrementally between industry and technical agencies (Jordan, 1998a, 2002; Weale, 1997). The adoption of EQOs, which defined the desired quality of certain parts of the natural environment (such as a river), allowed the regulator and regulated actors a considerable degree of flexibility when agreeing on emissions limits from point sources in a negotiation process. The main action guiding principle for UK environmental policy was initially the best practicable means (BPM) principle. The principles of the best practicable environmental option (BPEO) and best available technique not entailing excessive costs (BATNEEC) superseded it. Where long-term goals were set in UK environmental policy, they tended to be associated with distinct geographical areas as opposed to (uniform) emission limits favoured by Germany particularly and many other continental European states. The BAT principle, which strongly influenced Austrian and German environmental regulations, never took root in the UK.

However, over time EU environmental legislation greatly influenced UK environmental policy. Jordan (2002: 211) has argued that '[t]he need for change first arose in 1974, when the Commission proposed to regulate the emission of dangerous substances to water'. Serious disputes between the UK and continental member states (and especially Germany) about the best approach to EU environmental policy continued throughout the 1970s and much of the 1980s. Hotly disputed EU environmental regulations include the 1976 Dangerous Substances Directive, 1983 Large Combustion Plant Directive and most of the car emissions Directives adopted in the 1980s (Jordan, 2002; Weale, O'Riordan and Kramme, 1991; Wurzel, 2002).

Regulation is widely seen as a hierarchical (or vertical tool) although Smith and Ingram (2002: 591) have pointed out that 'it can be used in strongly horizontal ways by giving certain actors rights and possibilities instead of prescribing their behaviour'. The UK pioneered innovative procedural regulatory instruments such as environmental impact assessment and integrated pollution prevention and control (IPPC). In the 1970s and 1980s the UK had often acted as a 'policy taker' in EU environmental policy. In the early 1990s the UK transformed into a 'policy shaper' by trying to upload innovative domestic environmental regulations to the EU level (Jordan and Liefferink, 2004).

In the late 1990s the RCEP estimated that around 80 per cent of UK environmental policy originated in, or was negotiated with, the EU (RCEP, 1998: 1.24). Since most EU environmental policy was regulatory in nature, UK environmental policy remained heavily reliant on regulation. In fact, the steady Europeanisation of national policy has, if anything, made UK legislation much more formally regulatory, by inserting numerical standards and compliance deadlines where administrative rules of thumb and unwritten 'gentleman's agreements' used to be the norm (Jordan, 1998a, 2002a). So, somewhat paradoxically, in the early 2010s UK environmental policy was considerably *more* regulatory in nature and style than it had been some 40 years ago, although there are now also many more NEPIs. The EU is not, of course, the only force at work here. The Environment Ministry stressed that regulation is often required to implement and enforce NEPIs (for example, establishing the rules of the system and compliance mechanisms) (DoE, 1993: 24).

Interestingly, the UK debate about how to develop 'policy packages' that combine different instrument types started relatively early (DoE, 1993: 26). Another dynamic is the concerted opposition often provoked by plans to deregulate sectors, such as water, that have a long history of regulation. When asked to consider NEPIs, government, industry and (of course) environmental NGOs began to quantify the administrative work and financial costs associated with adopting new tools. Industry in particular abhors uncertainty, which plans for deregulation followed by an intense period of innovation with NEPIs, would almost certainly increase. Simultaneously, the worsening post-2008 economic conditions have reinforced governing philosophies seeking to reduce and simplify environmental regulation. In 2010 the new Conservative/Liberal Democratic coalition government adopted an on-going plan to target regulatory burdens on industry. For example, it has sought to simplify the requirements of the Environmental Impact System and the Environmental Permitting framework (HM Government, 2012).

From Command-and-Control to More Innovative Regulations?

All five jurisdictions have relied heavily on regulations in environmental policy. However, the specifications of the environmental regulations in different jurisdictions have varied notably. Austria and Germany, which accumulated the densest national bodies of environmental regulations, have overall shown a clear preference for media-centred, BAT-derived regulations that stipulate emission limits (although some Austrian and German environmental regulations have specified EQOs). The Netherlands has also relied heavily on relatively ambitious environmental regulations. However, the term 'command-and-control' became somewhat of a misnomer for Dutch environmental regulations when considering the introduction of extensive stakeholder consultation processes since at least the early 1990s.

Moreover, environmental regulation does not necessarily have to take the form of hierarchical, top-down interventionism. The UK pioneered innovative procedural regulatory instruments such as environmental impact assessment and IPPC, and the EU has adopted an Access to Environmental Information Directive. All of these examples have a primarily horizontal effect. The UK was initially hesitant to adopt environmental regulations that stipulate legally binding emission limits. Instead it relied heavily on EQOs and non-statutory environmental standards which granted considerable flexibility to regulators on the ground. As was mentioned above, it was the EU's heavy reliance on environmental regulations (together with other factors) that drove the increased use of regulations in UK environmental policy.

A cross-jurisdictional trend towards greater flexibility in environmental regulations is discernible across all five jurisdictions where traditional environmental regulations have become less rigid and more flexible. For example, rudimentary 'bubble policy' concepts that were embedded into traditional command-and-control regulations can be found even in high regulatory states such as Austria and Germany (see previous). Since the early 1990s, the Commission has included cost-effectiveness statements in all of its legislative proposals. Around the same time the EU started to use framework laws. Clearly, EU and member state environmental regulations have become more flexible and innovative. In other words, European environmental regulations have become smarter (Gunningham, Grabosky and Sinclair, 1998).

The decision-making processes leading to the adoption of traditional environmental regulations have become less top-down. The wide consultation of stakeholders prior to the adoption of environmental regulations has had a long tradition in the Netherlands in particular. It has also frequently been used in the UK. Since the 1990s, wide stakeholder consultation and increased transparency have gained in importance also for the Commission as well as, though to a lesser degree, Austria and Germany.

Changing patterns of environmental policy instrument use 207

Gunningham, Grabosky and Sinclair's (1998) term 'smart regulation' successfully captures the above mentioned innovations in environmental regulations in our five systems. However, Gunningham, Grabosky and Sinclair (1998) have subsumed NEPIs (such as eco-labels, EMSs, VAs, eco-taxes and ETSs) under the term smart regulation. Importantly, this book makes a conceptual distinction between environmental regulations and NEPIs. This is not to deny the emergence of hybrid forms of 'old' and 'new' policy instruments consisting of elements of both traditional regulation and NEPIs (see the following). As Chapters 4–7 show, regulations are often necessary to adopt and/or implement NEPIs (see also Jordan, Wurzel and Zito, 2007: 490). However, before discussing the hybridisation of 'old' instruments (namely, regulations) and 'new' tools (namely, NEPIs), it is necessary first to analyse the changing NEPI usage patterns.

CHANGING PATTERNS IN INSTRUMENT USE

Salamon (2002c: 609) has argued that the 'last fifty years have witnessed a remarkable revolution … in the tools or instruments used to address public problems.' The empirical evidence in Chapters 4 to 7 broadly supports his claim. However, as discussed above, environmental regulation remains dominant even in jurisdictions which have made heavy use of NEPIs such as the Netherlands and Germany. Moreover, although the overall use of NEPIs has risen significantly, different jurisdictions have adopted distinctive policy instrument mixes. Importantly, no jurisdiction has been a leader in all NEPI types. Conversely, no jurisdiction has been a laggard in all NEPI types.

Table 8.1 summarises the patterns for the five jurisdictions. Importantly the analytical descriptors – innovator, follower and laggard – used in Table 8.1 (and Table 8.2) offer a relative assessment between the above mentioned five jurisdictions, rather than an absolute ranking. NEPI innovators as defined in Table 8.1 are jurisdictions which have first made significant use of a particular NEPI type. Followers eventually also adopt the NEPI first used by the innovator(s). Laggards either fail to adopt a particular NEPI or utilise it only in an insignificant manner.

Importantly, followers may eventually overtake the innovator(s) in using a particular NEPI type: for example, Austria and Germany, which initially had opposed EMAS, later became the highest users of this NEPI (see Chapter 4). In order to achieve a better domestic fit and/or to improve its effectiveness, followers often modify a particular NEPI which they have emulated or transferred from another jurisdiction. For example, Germany acted as an early innovator for eco-label schemes when it set up

208 *Environmental governance in Europe*

Table 8.1 Innovators, followers and laggards for different NEPI types

	Innovator	Follower	Laggard
Eco-label	Germany	Austria, EU, the Netherlands	UK
EMS/EMAS	UK, EU	Germany, Austria	The Netherlands
Voluntary Agreements	Germany, the Netherlands	Austria, UK	EU
Eco-taxes	The Netherlands, Germany	Austria, UK	EU
EU emissions trading	UK, EU, the Netherlands	Austria, Germany	–

its domestic Blue Angel scheme in 1978. Austria (1990), the Netherlands (1992) and the EU (1992) followed the German example after a considerable time lag. However, the followers did not simply copy the German Blue Angel scheme. Instead they adopted domestic eco-label schemes which exhibited some novel features that reflected both domestic priorities (for example, tourism and food production) and the desire to achieve a good domestic fit and increased effectiveness. For example, the successful Austrian eco-label scheme included the economically vital tourism services. The Dutch and EU eco-label schemes have both suffered from a low uptake and poor public recognition. As Chapter 4 explained, British companies have shown very little interest in the EU eco-label despite the UK's failure to adopt a national eco-label scheme. Clearly the eco-label scheme has been diffused across jurisdictions. However, it was primarily the general idea behind this NEPI type which was transferred rather than the specific rules of the first (German) eco-label scheme.

These empirical findings support the view taken by contingentists and constitutivists who argue that the 'goodness of fit' and institutional context respectively play an important role for the adoption and use of policy instruments in particular jurisdictions (see Chapter 2). They also justify Bulmer and Padgett's (2005) more finely-grained categorisation of policy transfer, reflecting in most instances influence rather than the other stronger forms of transfer.

The UK set the pace for EMSs with its innovative BS 7750 voluntary standard which strongly influenced the EU's EMAS (see Chapter 5). Germany and Austria initially opposed EMAS. However, once the EU had adopted EMAS, the followers Germany and Austria quickly became

Changing patterns of environmental policy instrument use   209

by far the highest EMAS users leaving well behind the UK in EMAS registrations. Germany and Austria lobbied hard both to make EMAS more ambitious and to extend its scope from private companies to public institutions (such as government ministries and agencies). The Netherlands never developed a national EMS and has made only little use of EMAS. Dutch firms preferred the ISO 14001 standard instead, which is environmentally less ambitious but has a global reach.

Considering the influence of BS 7750 on the original EMAS (namely, EMAS-I), it could be argued that the EU acted as a 'transfer platform' (Radaelli, 2000: 6), which allowed Britain to upload its domestic EMS to the EU. Because EMAS is a voluntary scheme, the resulting policy instrument transfer has been voluntary (rather than a coercive). However, in the case of EMAS, a 'negotiated transfer' (Bulmer and Padgett, 2005: 105–6) took place which involved governance ideas and/or instruments originating in one or more member states being incorporated into an EU instrument (see Chapter 2). Importantly, only some core features of the BS 7750 found their way into EMAS which also stipulated novel requirements, which suggests a moderate 'synthetic transfer' (Bulmer and Padgett, 2005). Moreover EMAS-I was later revised (namely, EMAS-II and EMAS-III) which further increased the differences between the EU's and UK's EMSs.

The Netherlands and Germany have been early innovators and heavy users of VAs. However, as Chapter 5 explained, the core features of Dutch and German VAs differ significantly. The Netherlands makes wide use of sector-wide covenants which are legally binding (although in practice they have rarely been enforced through the courts) and monitored by independent institutions. German VAs are non-binding agreements (most of which are *Selbstverpflichtungen*, that is, self-binding agreements) usually put forward by companies with the aim of pre-empting government regulation. Only a small number of German VAs have been monitored by an independent verifier. Austria became a VA follower in the 1980s when it partly emulated the non-binding German VAs (rather than the Dutch covenants). However, after extensive usage in the 1990s there was a steep decline in VA usage in Austrian and German environmental policy in the 2000s. Constitutional reasons have prevented Austria and Germany from adopting legally binding VAs such as the Dutch covenants, which Austrian and German environmental policy makers closely examined (Interviews, 2010 and 2011). The UK has adopted only a moderate number of VAs whose use is insignificant at the EU level (see Chapter 5). The lack of a clear Treaty base for VAs prevented EU Commission officials from trying to emulate the Dutch covenants (Interviews, 2001 and 2004).

Overall, there is only weak empirical evidence for the transfer of VAs across the five jurisdictions assessed in this book. Austria adopted VAs which resembled some of the core features of German VAs. However, Austrian VAs also included distinctive novel features. Moreover, the main target sectors for VAs differ in Austria (waste) and Germany (energy/ climate change).

Importantly, although the early innovators (the Netherlands and Germany) have remained the largest users of VAs within the EU, their popularity declined even in the two innovator states in the 2000s (see Table 8.2). Moreover, as was explained in Chapter 5, in the 2000s, German VAs were adopted primarily for large public events such as the 2008 World Cup or bi-annual *Kirchentage* (that is, large gatherings organised by the church) with the aim of staging 'green events'. One important explanation for the declining popularity in VA usage is that they have been supplanted by other NEPIs and/or traditional environmental regulations. For example, the adoption of the EU ETS rendered obsolete some Dutch, German and Austrian VAs aimed at reducing greenhouse gas emissions while legislation has overwritten the EU-wide CO_2 emissions VA by the European car industry (see Chapter 5).

The Netherlands was an early eco-taxes innovator which has consistently made use of a wide range of eco-taxes. Germany was also an early eco-taxes pioneer when it adopted the 1976 waste water levy (Andersen, 1994). However, although Germany strongly supported the adoption of an EU-wide carbon dioxide/energy tax, its domestic use of eco-taxes remained moderate until the adoption of an ecological tax reform in 1998. Austria and the UK were followers which made use of eco-taxes only belatedly when compared to the Netherlands and Germany. However, the UK adopted some innovative eco-taxes (for example, the fuel escalator) which influenced the eco-tax thinking of environmental policy makers in Austria, Germany and the Netherlands (Interviews, 2002 and 2011).

The EU is clearly an eco-taxes laggard because it failed to adopt a supranational eco-tax. The Commission's failed 1992 proposal for an EU-wide carbon dioxide/energy tax constitutes an example of an 'aborted policy instrument transfer' (Padgett, 2003). Because the EU could not be used as a transfer platform for the diffusion of eco-taxes, a group of like-minded European countries met between 1994 and 1998 to discuss the design and impact of different national eco-taxes (see Chapter 6). At first sight, these meetings seem to provide empirical evidence for the instrumentalist perspective (see Chapter 2) which argues that some policy instruments are championed because of their inherent characteristics (for example, eco-taxes put a price on environmental ills and generate

Changing patterns of environmental policy instrument use 211

revenue). However, a closer look at the different eco-tax types adopted in Austria, Germany, the Netherlands and the UK reveals significant national differences as regards their stringency (including exemptions), scope and targets.

The UK became an emissions trading innovator when it set up Europe's first domestic ETS for greenhouse gases in 2002. Up to the early 2000s, the Netherlands experimented only with rudimentary small-scale domestic ETSs (for example, for manure). In 2003 the EU adopted the world's first supranational ETS for CO_2 emissions. Austria and Germany initially acted as reluctant ETS followers, with Germany threatening to block the adoption of the EU ETS (Wurzel, 2008a). However, over time, Austria and Germany became supportive of a relatively ambitious EU ETS.

Importantly, emissions trading constitutes the only NEPI type assessed in this book for which the EU has acted as a genuine innovator. However, the EU was only a reluctant emissions trading pioneer (Wurzel, 2008a, 2008b). It is highly unlikely that the EU ETS and UK ETS 'could have been adopted as quickly as they were without America setting a domestic example and insisting on emissions trading in the 1997 Kyoto Protocol' (Wurzel, 2008a: 5). The adoption process of the EU ETS suggests a certain degree of coerciveness if one accepts that the USA not only provided a domestic model (in the form of regional level NO_x emissions trading) for others to follow but also acted as a political hegemon insisting on the inclusion of emissions trading in the Kyoto Protocol (Gupta and Grubb, 2000; Jordan et al., 2011; Wurzel, 2008a, 2008b; Wurzel and Connelly, 2011b). Following Dolowitz and Marsh's (1996) differentiation between voluntary and coercive policy transfer, it can be argued that the USA encouraged both voluntary policy transfer (namely, the emulation of its early emissions trading experience) and imposed coercive policy transfer (by insisting on emissions trading in the Kyoto protocol). However, the specific rules of both the EU (CO_2) ETS and UK (GHGE) ETS turned out to be significantly different from the American (NO_x) ETSs. It was therefore 'the principal idea rather than specific emissions trading rules which were transferred from America to Europe via the 1997 Kyoto protocol' (Wurzel, 2008b: 5). For Voß (2007: 330) the EU ETS constitutes 'a radical innovation in governance'.

To sum up the overall patterns assessed in this book, Germany (eco-labels, VAs and, although to a lesser degree, eco-taxes) and the Netherlands (VAs, eco-taxes and, although to a lesser degree, emissions trading) have both acted as innovators for three types of NEPIs, the UK (EMS and emissions trading) for two types of NEPIs and the EU (emissions trading) for only one NEPI type. Austria is the only jurisdiction which failed to act as

212 *Environmental governance in Europe*

an early innovator for any of the five NEPIs assessed in this book. Nevertheless, Austria always followed the NEPIs innovator thus avoiding the status of NEPIs laggard. Similarly Germany always acted as a follower in those cases where it did not act as a NEPIs innovator. The UK (eco-labels) and EU (VAs and eco-taxes) acted as laggards for one and two NEPI types respectively. The EU had adopted only about a dozen EU-wide VAs by the late 2000s; this clearly amounts to an insignificant use of VAs when compared to the large number of VAs adopted by the Netherlands, Germany and Austria. The Netherlands can be classified as an EMS laggard because it made only insignificant use of EMAS and failed to adopt a domestic EMS. However, Dutch firms have made relatively wide use of the ISO 14001 (see Chapter 5).

The analytical classification of innovator, follower and laggard can mask significant changes in the use of a particular type of NEPI that may take place in a certain jurisdiction over time. Table 8.2 illustrates the temporal usage patterns for the different types of NEPIs in each of the five jurisdictions. It shows that once a certain type of NEPI has been adopted by a particular jurisdiction its usage tends to change only gradually. This finding is in line with historical institutionalist explanations which, however, are less well able to explain the adoption of novel policy instruments (see Chapter 2). The usage of VAs seems to have peaked in the Netherlands, Germany and Austria in the 1990s. Similarly the drive for eco-taxes lost momentum in the 2000s. The EU ETS, which became operational in 2005, is the only NEPI whose usage expanded significantly in the 2000s (and early 2010s).

Policy Instrument Sequencing

The chronological breakdown of NEPIs usage in Table 8.2 enables us to assess patterns of sequencing. Much of the policy instrument literature prescribes a pattern of sequencing which starts with soft instruments and proceeds to harder ones (for example, Gunningham, Grabosky and Sinclair, 1998; Salamon, 2002a; Vedung, 1997). While drawing on Doern and Wilson (1974), Vedung (1997: 40) has argued that 'the least coercive instruments are introduced first in order to gradually weaken the resistance of certain groups of individuals and adjust them to government intervention in the area. After some time, the authorities feel entitled to regulate the matters definitely by employing their most powerful instrument'. Similarly, Gunningham, Grabosky and Sinclair (1998: 123) have argued for the sequencing of environmental policy instruments: it enables 'escalation from the preferred least interventionist option, if it fails, to increasingly more interventionist alternatives'.

Table 8.2   The use of different NEPIs and environmental regulations since the 1970s

Instrument type	Jurisdiction	1970s	1980s	1990s	2000s
Eco-label scheme	Austrian scheme (*1990)	–	–	Medium	Medium
	German scheme (*1978)	Medium	High	High	High/medium
	Dutch scheme (*1992)	–	–	Low	Low
	UK scheme	–	–	–	–
	EU scheme average usage (*1992)	–	–	Low	Low
EU EMAS (*1993)	Austrian usage	–	–	High	High/medium
	German usage	–	–	High	High/medium
	Dutch usage	–	–	Low	Low
	UK usage	–	–	Low	Low
	EU average usage	–	–	Low	Low
Voluntary agreements	Austria	Low	Low	Medium/high	Medium/low
	Germany	Low	High	High	Medium/low
	The Netherlands	Low	High	High	Medium
	UK	Low	Low/medium	Low/medium	Low
	EU-wide VAs average usage	–	–	Low	Low

Table 8.2   continued

Instrument type	Jurisdiction	1970s	1980s	1990s	2000s
Eco-taxes	Austria	Low	Medium	Medium	Low
	Germany	Low	Medium	High	Medium
	The Netherlands	Medium	High	High	Medium
	UK	Low	Low	Medium	Medium
	EU-wide eco-taxes	–	–	–	–
ETS	Austrian ETS	–	–	–	–
	German ETS	–	–	–	–
	Dutch ETS	–	–	Low	Low
	UK ETS (*2002)	–	–	–	Medium
	EU ETS (*2005)	–	–	–	High
Environmental regulation	Austria	Low	Medium	High	Medium
	Germany	High	High	High	High
	The Netherlands	High	High	High/Medium	Medium
	UK	Low	Medium	Medium	Medium
	EU	High	High	High	Medium

The gradual ratcheting upwards of policy instruments according to their degree of coerciveness – starting with soft policy instruments (namely, horizontal self-governance) and ending with hard policy instruments (namely, coercive top-down government) – is principally also in line with liberal/neoliberal economic thinking. This perspective argues that government intervention should be avoided and, if this is not possible, then it should be restricted to the least interventionist policy instrument.

However, the empirical evidence put forward in this book shows a very different pattern (see also Jordan et al., 2012b). Germany, the Netherlands and the EU all relied almost exclusively on traditional regulations in their environmental policies in 1970s. Austrian and UK environmental policy initially used less heavily environmental regulations. However, by the 1980s, environmental regulations were also the dominant Austrian policy instrument. Importantly, with the exception of the UK, none of the five jurisdictions assessed in this book first adopted soft policy instruments (for example, eco-labels and VAs) before adding hard policy instruments (namely, regulation). On the contrary, in four out of five jurisdictions traditional environmental regulations were adopted first and then supplemented by softer environmental policy instruments. One German Environment Ministry official (Interview, 2001) explained Germany's heavy reliance on traditional environmental regulation in the early 1970s by arguing that NEPIs were 'deemed inappropriate for the defence against dangers *(Gefahrenabwehr)* to the environment and human health. You need regulations for such a task'. By contrast, the UK was initially reluctant to adopt clearly defined statutory environmental standards (see Chapter 3). However, the UK had to implement a rapidly increasing number of EU environmental regulations from the mid-1970s onwards. Clearly particular policy instruments are considered more appropriate and legitimate in certain jurisdictions regardless of their theoretical advantages, for example, in terms of efficiency (for example, Howlett, 1991; Salamon, 2002b: 24).

Table 8.2 highlights another important empirical finding which emerged in Chapters 4 to 7. Since the 1970s, there has been a significant expansion in the range of the different policy instruments used in all five jurisdictions. In the 1970s, environmental policy makers in Austria, Germany, the Netherlands and the UK as well as the EU used little besides regulations as governing tools. By the late 2000s, the environmental policy instrument repertoires of all five jurisdictions included a wide range of different tools allowing for much more sophisticated and differentiated environmental policy approaches.

The total number and diversity of NEPIs used in the five jurisdictions has grown, in some cases spectacularly. However, no single NEPI type is

216 *Environmental governance in Europe*

overwhelmingly popular across all five jurisdictions. In some jurisdictions, the adoption of NEPIs has been stunningly fast (for example, the Netherlands and Germany), whereas in others they have been adopted only more slowly (for example, the EU). Moreover, just as there were enduring national differences in the way that traditional environmental regulation was applied in the past (for example, Vogel, 1986) there appear to be important differences in the implementation of NEPIs today.

Salomon (2002b: 18) has pointed out that '[f]ar from simplifying the task of public policy solving, the proliferation of tools has importantly complicated it even while enlarging the range of options and the pool of resources potentially brought to bear'. Questions have therefore been raised about what constitutes the most appropriate or 'best' environmental policy instrument mix (for example, Jordan, Wurzel and Zito, 2007). The empirical findings and theoretical considerations put forward in this book suggest that what constitutes the most appropriate policy instrument mix is likely to vary from jurisdiction to jurisdiction. Moreover, it may change over time. The different organisational structures, policy styles and policy goals help explain why in some cases the same type of NEPI was used in dissimilar ways in different jurisdictions; a tendency which has important implications for policy innovation at EU level (Jordan et al., 2012b).

What has further complicated the picture of how environmental policy is governed is the hybridisation of policy instruments. We explain its implications for the debate about (hierarchical top-down) government and (horizontal self-steering) governance in the concluding Chapter 9. At this point it is sufficient to state that, as the number of available environmental policy instruments increased over time, the environmental policy instrument mixes became more complex.

CONCLUSION

This chapter has sought to identify the main usage patterns for environmental regulations and NEPIs in five European jurisdictions. The cross-comparative findings are essential for drawing robust conclusions about the alleged shift from government to governance.

The first essential finding that emerges is that regulation has remained the dominant environmental policy instrument in all five jurisdictions. This picture reinforces the argument of Bell and Hindmoor (2009) about the continued importance of the state. In the EU case, the constraints of operating as a regulatory state have led EU decision-makers to rely on environmental regulations. In four out of five jurisdictions assessed in this book, regulations formed the initial core response to environmental problems and have continued to do so. This development has occurred across states that diverge in terms of organisational structures, policy style and policy goals and strategies (see Chapter 3). The core operating principles and specification of regulatory standards reveal some divergence in approach, particularly between Austria and Germany, which have relied heavily on BAT-derived emission limits, and the UK which has made wide use of BATNEEC-derived EQOs. However, the overarching trend has been one of smarter regulations and more complex policy instrument mixes including the hybridisation of different types of environmental policy instruments.

This finding cautions us against the assumption that innovation in environmental governing takes place only when a shift occurs from traditional tools of government towards new modes of governance. Much of the evolution of European environmental policy has occurred in the most traditional instrument in the policy instrument repertoire. This has involved the addition of greater stakeholder consultation in extant legislation as well as the clear tendency towards more flexible regulatory design when adopting new regulations and/or revising old regulations.

Having established the role of regulation to conceptualise the usage of NEPIs, this chapter then turned to overall analytical patterns in the use of 'old' and 'new' policy instruments. Out of our five jurisdictions all but Austria have acted as innovators for at least one NEPI. However, three out of four innovators have also acted as laggards for at least one environmental policy instrument. Austria constituted the only jurisdiction which acted as a follower for all NEPI types assessed in this book. The UK acted as an innovator for EMSs and emissions trading while for eco-label schemes it has consistently remained a laggard. As Chapter 8 explained, the formal and informal institutional context that governs a particular jurisdiction is an important explanatory variable for the adoption of particular environmental policy instruments.

A second pattern which emerges from our analysis is that, once established within a particular jurisdiction, policy instruments tended to retain their relative role in the prevailing basket of environmental policy instrument for the EU and its member states for a considerable period of time, albeit with some examples of displacement and drift (Streeck and Thelen, 2005). Regulatory instruments were supplemented by an increasingly wide range of different NEPIs within the member states and the EU, a core theme explored in Chapter 9. The evolution of regulations and the accretion of NEPIs bear out the argument of Smith and Ingram (2002: 598): 'the tool box is not constant. It changes over time as a result of the invention of new tools, national and international developments, and the interactions of the supranational institutions'.

The stickiness of the institutional context goes a considerable distance towards explaining the relatively weak evidence for policy instrument transfer across different jurisdictions. There is evidence of weak voluntary transfer in some of the cases, most notably eco-labels, voluntary agreements and EMS. Nevertheless, in all of these cases policy-makers seemed to have examined the original policy idea (for example, the German Blue Angel eco-label scheme, Dutch negotiated agreements and the UK's BS 7750), but the emerging policy instrument strongly reflected domestic legal and political limitations. The EU did not play a particularly strong transfer platform role for NEPIs although its environmental laws had a decisive impact on member state environmental policy. The EU did create EMAS and the EU eco-label, but again these reflected negotiated processes that moved the instruments beyond the original models. The strongest evidence of policy transfer comes with the successful US effort to incorporate emissions trading into the Kyoto Protocol, but again the EU adopted and modified the instrument, learning as much about things they wished to avoid concerning the US systems. Although institutional dynamics clearly play a strong role in defining and limiting NEPI usage, some noticeable policy learning did occur. It is discussed in greater detail in Chapter 9.

The overarching dynamic articulated in the empirical Chapters 5 to 7 is one of relative institutional continuity. Regulations, the major policy response the 1970s, remain the dominant policy instrument in the early 2010s. Chapter 9 addresses the implications of this and the other findings for the much wider debate about governing.

9. Out with the 'old' and in with the 'new'? Governing with policy instruments

INTRODUCTION

We began Chapter 1 by arguing that, while there has been a huge upsurge in governance studies, most have remained 'over-theorised' and 'under-empiricised'. In contrast, much of the policy instrument literature that has emerged since the 1970s has tended to be 'under-theorised' and 'over-empiricised'. In this book we have tried to fit these two literatures together in ways that seek to directly inform and benefit both. Throughout, we have used policy instruments as empirical touchstones for scrutinising the claim, which has been widely made in the governance literature (for example, Rhodes, 1996), that top-down hierarchical *government* has increasingly given way to self-steering horizontal *governance*. In the policy instruments literature, the associated debate concerns the extent to which 'new' instruments have replaced the 'old' instrument of regulation.

We have sought to inform both debates by critically assessing the adoption and subsequent use of *both* 'old' and 'new' environmental policy instruments in five European jurisdictions – Austria, Germany, the Netherlands and the UK as well as the EU – from the early 1970s to the early 2010s. Adhering to Sabatier's (1999) recommendation to study public policy over a long time period (in our case over four decades) has enabled us both to analyse how particular instruments have evolved over time, and also how the overall mix of instruments has changed. It has permitted us to draw cross-jurisdictional, cross-sectoral and cross-temporal comparisons of the adoption and use of policy instruments in Europe that were absent from the existing literatures (see in particular Chapter 8). In particular, the previous chapters have provided us with a sufficiently strong empirical base for assessing the alleged shift from (the 'old' instruments of) government towards (the 'new' modes and instruments of) governance within an analytical framework which is considerably more systematic and fine-grained than most existing approaches in the 'new' governance literature.

The first section of this final chapter returns to the question of whether changes in European environmental policy instrument selection and usage reflect a much deeper underlying transformation from government to more society-led governance. The second section interrogates the degree to which the selection and adaption of 'old' and 'new' environmental policy instruments reflects path dependencies inherent in the environmental policy systems of the four member states and the EU. The third section assesses the evidence for policy learning and transfer in the selection and usage of new and more innovative (that is, compared to the pre-existing mix of) policy instruments. The final section considers the possible directions that future research on these important and highly topical matters could take.

PATTERNS OF USE: HAS GOVERNANCE ECLIPSED GOVERNMENT?

Empirical Trends

Chapters 4–7 clearly showed that there has been a significant increase in the adoption and use of NEPIs. In the early 2010s, all five jurisdictions had in place a wider range and larger number of NEPIs compared to the early 1970s. For example, Germany acted as an instrument innovator in the 1970s when it became the first country in the world to adopt an *eco-label* scheme. Austria, the Netherlands and the EU became eco-label scheme followers in the 1990s while the UK remains a laggard. *Emissions trading* schemes were not used in Europe before the late 1990s. Out of our case countries, it was only the UK and the Netherlands which had experimented with national schemes before the EU ETS became applicable across the EU in 2005. However, Chapter 8 has shown that there has been no linear increase in the adoption of all types of NEPI in our five jurisdictions since the early 1970s. For example, the adoption of *voluntary agreements* seems to have peaked in Austria and Germany in the 1990s, and never really took off at the EU level.

During the last four decades there has, therefore, been a significant increase in the uptake of NEPIs in all five jurisdictions. However, the Austrian, British, Dutch, German and EU environmental policy instrument repertoires were and have remained substantively different. There is therefore little evidence of significant and enduring convergence in relation to policy instruments. These empirical patterns support a constitutive perspective which argues that what is or is not 'new' is very much context and time specific. For example, *voluntary agreements* became relatively popular in Germany and the Netherlands in the 1970s while they were only used – albeit initially only sparingly – in Austria and the UK from the 1980s onwards.

If one accepts the argument that policy instruments constitute good empirical touchstones for measuring the relative increase in 'new' governance, does it mean that governance has decisively eclipsed government? Judging from our detailed empirical findings presented in Chapters 4–8, the answer has to be no. First, although there has been an increase in NEPIs, regulation has not disappeared. In fact, despite some cross-jurisdictional (and cross-sectoral) variations and temporal fluctuations, regulation has remained a key policy instrument in all five jurisdictions. Traditional forms of regulation of course remain, but in general regulation has only been able to preserve its dominant status by changing and becoming 'smarter' and/or more innovative over time (see Chapter 8).

Second, environmental regulation has gradually taken on an important supporting role for the adoption of many NEPIs. This is particularly the case for more market-based policy instruments such as eco-taxes and emissions trading, which simply could not function without it (see Chapters 6 and 7). Gunningham, Grabosky and Sinclair (1998: 391) have pointed out that '[s]ome economic instruments, such as taxes and charges, are high on coercion and low on prescription'. It is therefore debatable whether market-based instruments are indeed less coercive or 'softer' than regulation. Importantly, many VAs in Germany and Austria would never have been promoted by corporate actors had it not been for the long 'shadow of the law'. The Dutch covenants, which are negotiated between corporate actors and the government, constitute quasi-legal agreements that can, at least theoretically, be enforced through the courts. Many 'new' policy instruments therefore rely on regulation to support the specific NEPI in question. As Héritier and Rhodes (2011b: 163) have helpfully argued, 'the shadow of hierarchy ... looms large over ... new modes of governance'.

Third, in all five jurisdictions complex policy instrument mixes have emerged which blend the 'old' and the 'new' in puzzlingly different ways. In some cases this has led to the co-existence or competition between 'old' and 'new' policy instruments. In other cases it has triggered complex hybrid policy instruments which are the result of a fusion or layering process of particular types of NEPIs with traditional forms of regulation. A good example are the climate change levy agreements in the UK which initially combined traditional regulation with eco-taxes and VAs before they became linked also to the UK's domestic ETS and later the EU ETS (see Chapter 7). Elsewhere the use of some NEPIs has triggered substantial institutional reconfigurations in domestic administrative and/or implementation measures. The EU ETS is a classic example. It led, for example, to the creation of the German Emissions Trading Authority with a permanent staff of more than 100 officials (see Chapter 7). Austria, the Netherlands, the UK and the EU either created new administrative units and/or sub-units of existing institutions for officials who deal with emissions trading issues. So, far from heralding a decline in the role of government, some NEPIs have directly required the creation of *new* state capacities.

In summary, we have been unable to detect that much empirical evidence to substantiate the claim that NEPIs have supplanted traditional regulation. In the language of the (new modes of) governance literature what we seem to be witnessing is best described as 'governance-cum-government' (Héritier and Rhodes, 2011b: 169). Moreover (and contrary to perceived wisdom), some NEPIs have themselves been supplanted by other NEPIs. For example, the EU ETS has replaced many climate change related VAs in Austria and Germany as well as, though to a lesser degree, in the Netherlands and the UK. Moreover, the EU ETS has also replaced some eco-taxes. Even within one and the same type of NEPI there have been displacement pressures. This can be seen, for example, in the decreasing popularity of the EU's more ambitious EMAS amongst corporate actors, in favour of the less stringent but globally recognised ISO 14001 standard (see Chapter 4). Crucially, it was only by carefully mapping the empirical patterns of use across time and space that we were able to establish what was really happening with respect to the governing of environmental problems via policy instruments. The next section begins to explore in more detail the patterns of continuity and change that were revealed by our analysis.

Policy Instrument Innovation

This book has identified evidence of both continuity and change. Many 'hybrid' policy instruments exist which contain elements of 'old' *government* tools and 'new' modes of *governance*. However, before we conclude that government has not been greatly affected by the uptake of NEPIs and may even have been strengthened by it, we should consider two possibilities. The first is that our empirical observations remain time-bound and that substantial governance transformations might still be occurring (in other words, the 'new' governance transformation may not yet be complete). This suggests that such transformations are over a very long time period, and that current analysis can only be preliminary.

The second possibility focuses on the potential for 'incremental change with transformative results' (Streeck and Thelen, 2005b: 9). In other words, the move towards governance is happening in such an incremental, time-bound fashion that makes it difficult to detect with snapshot assessments of 'new' instruments (which come and go out of fashion relatively quickly). The incremental overall impact of temporary, small changes in policy instrument use may be more fundamental (or transformative) than a snapshot of a particular type of instrument in a particular jurisdiction over a relatively short time period is able to show. However, by adopting a cross-comparative perspective of the use of four different types of NEPIs (and traditional) regulation in five jurisdictions over a period of more than four decades, we are in a strong position to discount both possibilities.

So we are left with a puzzling mixture of continuity and change. As detailed in Chapter 2, Streeck and Thelen (2005a) offer five analytical categories to make sense of this pattern of change – displacement, layering, drift, conversion and exhaustion – that are, we shall argue, also applicable to the analysis of (environmental) policy instruments. Recall that our findings broadly reveal that NEPIs have supplemented rather than supplanted traditional regulation, which itself has become smarter. This finding suggests that regulation has not been significantly *displaced*. Meanwhile there have been no major cases of environmental policy instrument *drift* in the five jurisdictions, although the use of VAs has declined significantly in Austria and Germany since the 1990s (see Chapters 5 and 8). Significantly, the only major case of *displacement* has occurred between different types of NEPIs, rather than between NEPIs and regulation. As was shown in Chapter 4, despite repeated attempts by the European Commission and some member governments to arrest its decline, the EU's EMAS has been gradually displaced by the ISO 14001. To a much lesser extent, *conversion* (namely, the redeployment of 'old' policy instruments to new purposes) also figures. For instance, as was pointed out in Chapter 4, the focus of VAs in Germany and the Netherlands has shifted from major economic sectors and their pollution reduction priorities to a more experimental use in newer areas such as the 'greening' of public events (including the 2008 World Cup and bi-annual *Kirchentage*) in Germany or climate targets for flower production (in the Netherlands. Similarly, command-and-control regulation has increasingly morphed into smarter types of regulation; Chapter 8 mentioned the Dutch example of the 2008 Environmental Management Act, which incorporates a role for EMSs as well as new understandings of environmental protection, such as waste hierarchies and integration of media approaches. Another example is the compensation solutions (*Kompensationslösungen*) in the Technical Instructions on Air Quality Control (*Technische Anleitung (TA) Luft*) in Germany. The reformed *TA Luft* permits companies to adopt higher emission reductions for some plants in order to compensate for the failure to achieve the required reductions in other plants.

Finally, policy instrument *exhaustion* also has affected some instruments, but interestingly, *not* regulation. Examples of this include the Dutch decision to move from a system of tailored charges to broader tax instruments because the complexity of the original system proved too burdensome to implement. Where policy instrument exhaustion threatened to set in, major reform efforts were made (think back to the steps made to revise the EU's eco-label and the German Blue Angel eco-label as well as EMAS).

The empirical findings presented in this book therefore suggest that the *layering* of existing policy instrument (namely, new elements being grafted onto existing policy instrument repertoires to produce new 'mixes') is the most likely form of policy instrument change. Importantly (and very much in harmony with our broader point about the specificity of instruments), there is no one optimal policy instrument mix for all jurisdictions, just as there is no instrument that is simultaneously 'new' in all jurisdictions. As was shown in Chapters 4–8, different institutional contexts have produced different policy instrument mixes. In some cases the same instrument type has been used very differently in neighbouring jurisdictions (for example, VAs in the Netherlands are very different to those in Germany). Exactly how and why different policy instruments interact with each other in these ways is still a relatively under-researched subject, although at least our analyses have put the literature on a much firmer empirical footing. The existing literature cautions however that policy makers need to be careful not to fall 'into the trap of simply adding a new instrument to their arsenal of weapons without giving sufficient thought to how this will impact on their overall regulatory strategy' (Gunningham, Grabosky and Sinclair, 1998: 13–4). Indeed the biggest challenge confronting environmental policy makers today is not so much which instrument to select next (in theory, the choice between the main types and sub-types is infinitely large), but how to adopt policy instrument mixes which simultaneously alleviate existing problems without disrupting the efficacy and efficiency of the prevailing instrument mix (Rengeling and Hof, 2001). In order to understand this important but under-researched aspect more fully, in the next section we employ a slightly different analytical approach.

Policy Instrument Mixes

As noted in Chapter 1, Eberlein and Kerwer (2004) have developed the following fourfold categorisation of policy instrument change on the EU level. Government and governance instruments: (1) complement each other (*co-existence*); (2) merge with each other (*fusion*); (3) compete with each other (*competition*); and, (4) one form (namely, government or governance) supplants the other and thus replaces it (*replacement*). We have applied Eberlein and Kerwer's fourfold policy instrument categorisation to the use of NEPIs in earlier work (see Jordan, Wurzel and Zito, 2007). In this section we concentrate in particular on Eberlein and Kerwer's second category – 'fusion' – because this appears to be the dominant pattern of change: when 'new' instruments are added to a policy field (such as the environment), which is already populated with 'old' instruments.

Table 9.1 illustrates the 'governance-cum-government' argument put forward in the previous section. It shows that there is a considerable degree of blurring between different types of 'new' instruments which are supposed to resemble 'strong governance' and 'old' tools (namely, regulations) which are perceived as a 'strong government' in much of the governance literature. Broadly speaking, 'strong government' lodges in the top left hand cell of Table 9.1 and, the further one moves towards the bottom right hand cell, the more important societal 'self-steering' (in other words, 'strong governance') becomes. However, on closer inspection, aspects of government can be found in all four cells. Thus neither eco-taxes nor emissions trading are devoid of government involvement; on the contrary, national governments and/or EU institutions are very much involved in initiating, designing and monitoring these types of NEPI. Concerning VAs, only unilateral commitments are instruments of 'self-organising' governance because they offer corporate actors a voluntary tool of communicating with their customers, public authorities and the general public. Voluntary agreements that are formally negotiated (such as, the Dutch covenants) normally involve so much government activity that they actually sit closer to the government end of the governance-government continuum. Similarly, most EMSs involve regulation; only a few do not. Eco-label schemes are widely regarded as soft policy instruments, but only self-declaratory company eco-labels normally constitute 'self-organising' governance tools which are designed, adopted and implemented without the involvement of public authorities. In short, government has some role to play in all NEPI types assessed in this book.

226   *Environmental governance in Europe*

Table 9.1   A simple governance-cum-government typology

	Government determines the goals	Societal actors determine the goals
Government selects the policy instruments	STRONG GOVERMENT (hierarchical top-down steering): *Traditional 'command-and-control' regulation*	HYBRID: *Regulatory standards which stipulate relatively flexible standards and processes (such as BATNEEC), eco-taxes and emissions trading; some smart regulations (which stipulate, for example, compensation rules)*
Societal actors select the policy tools	HYBRID: *Some VAs (e.g. Dutch covenants); some market-based instruments (e.g. choice between VAs and eco-taxes or between eco-taxes and emissions trading); EMAS*	STRONG Governance (self-organising society): *some VAs (i.e. unilateral commitments); some eco-labels; ISO 14001*

Source: Based on Jordan, Wurzel and Zito (2007) with updates and amendments.

Reflecting back on the data presented in Chapters 4–8 (see Table 8.2 for a pictorial synopsis), we can identify examples in all five political systems that fit in all four cells of Table 9.1. Starting with the two top cells, all four member states and the EU continue to adopt environmental regulation. Moreover, much of it has taken the traditional form (corresponding to top-down hierarchical government) over the last four decades, particularly in Austria and Germany but also the Netherlands and the EU, although smarter environmental regulations have become more popular in recent years. The UK's traditional approach to regulation has focused much more on structured negotiation and flexibility: that is, negotiating with regulatees. However, as Chapter 8 demonstrated, in the 1970s and 1980s, UK environmental regulation became much more prescriptive under the influence of the EU. In the early 1990s, a drive towards more flexible regulation took place in the Netherlands and the EU. It also occurred, although to a lesser degree, in Austria and Germany. Efforts to combat climate change have led the EU to embrace emissions trading, informed by experiments in the UK and the Netherlands as well as the US (see Chapter 7). Indeed the EU ETS is very much the epitome of a hybrid instrument. Its adoption and use was dependent on EU legislation and demanded the creation of new state capacities. These movements suggest a shift of focus from the top left hand cell to the one in the top right.

If one briefly excludes the striking but unrepresentative exception of ISO 14001 (which has outstripped the usage of EMAS in particular in the Netherlands but increasingly also in the UK, Germany and Austria), the five political systems exhibit a much less prominent use of self-organising instruments (the bottom right hand cell). By comparison, more hybrid instruments that allow societal actors to select the goals while governmental actors select the tools (the top right hand cell and vice versa the bottom left hand cell) are becoming more prominent in member states such as the Netherlands.

Voß (2007: 329) has argued that '[t]he development and adaptation of policy instruments can be interpreted as innovation processes in governance'. However, the linkage between the adoption of policy instruments and innovation is even more complex than he seems to imply. One of the main reasons for this complexity is that there is a 'far richer tapestry of [pre-existing] policy instruments then is commonly realized' (Gunningham, Grabosky and Sinclair, 1998: 88). The increase in the range of NEPIs has complicated the task of selecting policy instrument mixes which work with the grain of pre-existing institutional contexts, and are effective and efficient. It is to this important task that we now turn.

EXPLAINING POLICY INSTRUMENTATION: THE IMPORTANCE OF CONTEXT

Chapter 2 pointed out that constitutivists emphasise the importance of the pre-existing context in which an 'old' or 'new' policy instrument is adopted and subsequently used in practice (adapted from Linder and Peters, 1998). In order to be able to encapsulate policy instrument change over time, this book has made use of an institutional theoretical framework which incorporated actor-centred dynamics into the more static path-dependency perspective of traditional institutional approaches (such as historical institutionalism). This allowed us to analyse both incremental and revolutionary policy instrument change – the latter of which amounts to a paradigm change or, in Hall's (1993) terminology, third level learning. The next section focuses on the evidence for learning; it assesses the role of policy instrument change and stability, and its implications for the wider governance debate.

If we accept the self-organising hypothesis found in much of the new governance literature, then we should expect environmental policy to

228 *Environmental governance in Europe*

exhibit a substantial change in the direction of softer, less hierarchical instruments. From a governance perspective, we should certainly expect a move in all five jurisdictions towards the softer VAs that, at least in theory, should come closest to the self-organising dynamics (see also Chapter 1). However, as should now be clear, our empirical findings suggest a much more differentiated picture. The fact that the initial innovator for EMS was the UK (see Chapter 4) generally fits well the constitutivist/institutionalist argument about achieving a fit between instrument and context. However, Austria and Germany, which initially opposed the adoption of EMAS, quickly became by far the greatest users. From a constitutivist/institutionalist perspective, this is a surprising finding because, in the environmental policy literature, these two member states are usually characterised as high regulatory states which rely heavily on the use of BAT-derived emissions standards (see Chapter 3). In theory therefore EMAS should have produced a relatively poor institutional fit in the Austrian and German policy systems; something which explains the initial frictions and delays, but not the subsequently smooth uptake.

The Netherlands and Germany followed by Austria have adopted the largest number of VAs. However, the exact types of VAs which were adopted in these three contexts differed quite significantly. In Germany and Austria all VAs are (for constitutional reasons) legally non-binding while the Dutch covenants have a quasi-legal status (with the civil code incorporating private law agreements). One and the same policy instrument has therefore been used very differently in five institutional contexts, a finding that only becomes apparent when – as we have done – the use of instruments is carefully tracked over time and space.

Importantly, Chapter 5 has also shown that at least in Austria, Germany and the Netherlands, Christian Democratic and Liberal parties have exhibited a significantly stronger preference for VAs compared to Social Democratic and Green parties. Broadly speaking, the reverse is the case for the adoption and use of eco-taxes, although there are some exceptions: a right wing Conservative government in the UK adopted the so-called fuel escalator which automatically raised taxes on petrol and diesel on an annual basis (see Chapter 6). The neglect of politics in general and political parties in particular constitutes a major deficiency in instrumentalist and proceduralist policy instrument approaches. Peters (2002: 560) has pointed out that:

> ideas in the form of political ideologies also may have some influence over the selection of more or less direct policy tools. Varone (1999) has argued that parties of the left are more likely to adopt direct policy instruments, whereas

Governing with policy instruments 229

those on the political right tend to opt for more indirect tools. This is so because indirect tools tend to disguise government involvement and leave a wider arena for individual choice, both of which are attractive to the political right.

We return to the theme of 'bringing party politics back' into the study of policy instruments in the final section.

The constitutivist/institutionalist approach does, however, explain the relatively low number of VAs at the EU level. The fact that the EU has adopted only about a dozen VAs highlights the crucial constraints imposed by the EU treaties, the fear of corporate actors about free-riders and the concerns of the EP about being side-lined as VAs are adopted outside the formal EU decision-making procedures (see Chapter 5). However, it is less able to explain why VAs are also used relatively little in the UK, which has a tradition of flexible instrument use (see Chapter 3). In this context, British economic actors arguably had relatively few incentives to move towards VAs. In fact, British efforts to adopt negotiated agreements sometimes resulted from the need to implement EU directives (in other words, regulation).

The broader point we wish to make is that, in decoding the patterns of instrument selection and use, one must also understand the interaction between different *levels* of governance. Indeed this book has shown that with the possible exception of emissions trading, the main supranational actor, the EU, has not had a broad ranging impact on member states' policy instrument choices (namely, between the main categories of instrument – these choices tend to reside at Member State level). However, as will be explained in the following, it has influenced the specific designs of particular NEPIs which were adopted by member states. For example, in 1999, the German government had to delay its ecological tax reform by several months in light of concerns raised by the Commission about the generosity of tax exemptions for industrial high energy users. Meanwhile, Austria scrapped its fertilizer tax shortly before joining the EU in 1995. The 2003 EU Directive on Taxation of Energy Products directly led to the termination of the 1992 Dutch fuel tax and the reconsideration of the 1996 Dutch energy tax.

To summarise, the supranational institutional and quasi-constitutional context has been critically important for the limited range of policy instruments which the EU was able to select and, which are then downloaded onto the member states. At the same time, the EU has constrained the design of particular domestic policy instruments in our four case countries. This does raise the question, however, as to whether the EU process leads to a convergence in policy instrument choices and

230 *Environmental governance in Europe*

usage. This question is tackled in the discussion of policy transfer and learning in the next section.

POLICY INSTRUMENTATION: THE ROLE OF LEARNING AND TRANSFER

Although the importance of institutional context in shaping both the overall policy instrument mix and the design of particular policy instruments is our general finding, there is substantial evidence of policy instrument change and innovation in all five jurisdictions that cannot be fully accounted for by constitutive-institutional theories. Chapter 2 drew on Hall's schema (with its combination of ideational and institutional elements) together with the policy transfer literature to provide a theoretical framework to explain the puzzling co-existence of both continuity and change.

Policy Transfer

Starting with the policy transfer argument first, our findings suggest only a limited, even marginal, role for this factor. In using Bulmer and Padgett's (2005) fourfold policy transfer classification – emulation, synthesis, influence and abortive transfer (see Chapter 2) – our book has found empirical evidence primarily for *influence*. Starting first of all with eco-labels, the transfer of the eco-label scheme from the innovator (Germany) to the followers (Austria, the Netherlands and the EU) looks suspiciously like a clear case of *emulation*. However, on closer inspection the Austrian, Dutch and EU schemes contain features which are significantly different from the German Blue Angel scheme. Clearly, domestic considerations (for example, tourism in the case of Austria and foodstuffs in the Dutch case) informed the actions of the followers who did not simply copy the German Blue Angel. EMAS on the other hand arguably constitutes a limited form of *synthetic* transfer from the BS 7750 which initially acted as the 'mother of EMAS' (see Chapter 4). However, two major reviews introduced new rules which made EMAS II and III quite different from EMAS I.

As regards emissions trading, although the European innovators (the UK, the Netherlands and the EU) studied the early US experience, very little direct transfer took place with regard to the specific design of the various European ETSs. The fact that the US insisted upon inserting emissions trading into the Kyoto Protocol can be described as exerting an indirect influence (to use Bulmer and Padgett's (2005) terminology) or as coercive policy instrument transfer (to use Dolowitz and Marsh's (2000) classification) (see Chapter 7). However, it was the general emissions trading *idea* which was transferred rather than the detailed rules governing trading in the UK, the Netherlands and the EU. These rules had to work with the prevailing institutional context of these three jurisdictions.

To summarise, there is surprisingly little empirical evidence of conscious transfer by emulation, even between member states that have strong market ties, relatively similar environmental policy styles and broadly comparable environmental administrations. The differences between German and Austrian eco-label schemes, VAs and eco-taxes clearly illustrate this broad point. The absence of strong emulation is surprising because the EU is often thought of as a 'massive transfer platform' (Radaelli, 2000: 6) and thus a case 'most likely' to exhibit examples of instrument transfer. This is in no small part due to the fact that its relatively open and competitive policy-making process involves 28 member states and several EU institutions (Jordan et al., 2006). There was of course evidence of innovator states seeking to 'upload' their own particular domestic NEPI onto the EU level with consequent adjustment or 'download' implications for other member states. The EU eco-label, EMAS and the EU ETS as well as the aborted supranational carbon dioxide/energy tax constitute important examples. But the complexity of the EU's decision-making procedures and the multitude of potential veto players that normally obtain at EU level have led to the emergence of policy instruments that share only a limited resemblance to those promoted by the original innovator. For example, Commission officials studied key policy instrument types in the Netherlands (including eco-taxes and covenants), Germany (eco-label) and UK (emissions trading), but no direct transfer (in the form of emulation) occurred. The compromises that actors are forced to make in such complex, multi-levelled settings, make straightforward copying highly unlikely.

Policy Learning

So, if instrument innovation was not driven primarily by policy transfer, what triggered it? In contrast, a policy learning approach, with its more encompassing empirical focus, resonates more strongly with our empirical findings. As Hall would expect, there was substantial first and second level learning (namely, the recalibration of existing policy instruments and the adoption of new instruments respectively). However, paradigm shifts or third level learning involving a fundamental reconceptualisation of the policy problem and the adoption of 'revolutionary' policy instruments were rare; emissions trading schemes with ambitious caps and the

232 *Environmental governance in Europe*

full auctioning of emissions allowances as well as ecological tax reforms that radically shift taxation burdens away to protect the environment are possible examples. However, none of the ETSs and domestic ecological tax reforms adopted in our five jurisdictions amounted to a 'revolutionary' policy instrument, although the introduction of the EU ETS probably comes closest. The design and use of these 'new' instruments in practice diverged considerably from the significantly more radical policy instrument solutions advocated in some of the economic textbooks. Clearly there was also no significant ideational shift amongst European policy makers and societal actors either towards radical free market environmentalism or a deep green environmentalism.

Taking each instrument in turn, our research suggests that the presence of second level learning about *eco-labels* started with the German Blue Angel in 1978. At the institutional level, however, this did not represent displacement of regulation, but rather it supplemented the existing environmental legislation by adding market incentives and consumer choice dynamics on top of the command-and-control regulation. Its supplementary status is indeed the story for all of the informational instruments assessed in this book. The only possible exception is EMAS, which allowed participating corporate actors in Austria and Germany a slightly lighter touch regulatory regime (see Chapter 4). For Austria, the Netherlands and the EU, there was an element of exogenous second level learning about eco-labels which, however, was combined with endogenous learning about NEPIs. For example, Austrian policy-makers did not seek merely to emulate the German Blue Angel scheme. Instead they tried to design an improved eco-label scheme (for example, by adopting a full life-cycle analysis) which also took into consideration the domestic institutional context and the interests of important Austrian policy actors (such as the tourism industry). Rising public environmental awareness and party political competition provided the triggers for the adoption of the Austrian eco-label scheme. The adoption of eco-labels at the EU level was also influenced by endogenous learning (for example, life cycle analysis) although here exogenous dynamics included a stronger imperative to respond to the potential threat posed to the Single European Market by member states adopting their own schemes.

The evolution of *EMSs* in the European context also provides evidence for the importance of second level learning. As was mentioned above, of particular importance was the UK's innovative scheme which was developed to influence similar but separate schemes promoted by the EU and the ISO. This pattern suggests an endogenous learning development (which continued with the parallel development of EMAS and ISO 14001). However, the attraction of gaining a competitive advantage in the

Governing with policy instruments 233

global market place was an important driver for the eco-audit and environmental management standards innovators.

Turning to *VAs*, the rise of the Dutch covenants since the 1980s suggests the presence of a successive second level learning bordering possibly on third level learning. Here we see the importance of the change in government with the rise in the 1980s of a centre-right coalition government (see Chapter 3). This contextual change suggests at least a partial ideational shift in the nature of how environmental protection should be governed with policy instruments, giving greater scope to the role of target groups. Endogenous learning in the Netherlands about policy instruments stimulated the increased use of VAs between the Dutch government and the principal domestic societal groups. The subsequent time period showed a considerable evolution in the design of the Dutch covenant.

Turning more specifically to the role of learning in *eco-taxes*, our case studies provide substantial evidence for first and second order learning. All five jurisdictions assessed in this book recalibrated existing taxes to take account of environmental objectives. For the reasons explained in Chapters 3 and 6, the EU was restricted to recalibrating a few existing taxes (for example, the harmonisation of excise fuel duties) and unable to adopt new eco-taxes. The Dutch, German and Austrian eco-taxes all reveal incremental endogenous second order learning about the importance of tax incentives for the uptake of environmentally less damaging products. The Dutch and German ecological tax reforms were the closest to third level learning, but still stopped some way short of it. The UK and Austria also exhibited considerable second level learning while adopting new eco-taxes which, however, did not amount to a full scale ecological tax reform.

The history of *emission trading* provides evidence for a linkage between endogenous policy learning and exogenous political pressure pursued by the US through the Kyoto Protocol (see Chapter 7). There can be no doubt that policy-makers in the UK, the Netherlands and the EU Commission had to undertake a substantial amount of second level learning in order to design ETSs which fitted their particular institutional contexts. The EU ETS and to a much lesser degree the UK ETS provided the only cases which could be said to involve third level learning. The EU ETS constituted an innovative NEPI which triggered a paradigm change by establishing a market for carbon dioxide emissions from large industrial sources in the EU's member states. However, its use in practice was much less 'revolutionary' compared to the ETS proposals which had been advocated by some environmental economists and individual European Commission officials.

234   *Environmental governance in Europe*

To summarise, (endogenous and exogenous) policy learning has played an important role in the recalibration of 'old' instruments (to smarter forms) and the adoption of 'new' ones. By contrast, our research has uncovered surprisingly little evidence for strong policy instrument transfer beyond the level of political influence – a dynamic which reflects a substantial degree of second level policy learning by policy-makers who usually seek to ensure that NEPIs fit their pre-existing domestic institutional context. Nevertheless, policy learning only explains partly why certain policy instrument mixes are selected and not others.

Institutionalists would, of course, not see this finding at all surprising, yet it jars with broad swathes of the existing literature on policy instruments. As was pointed out in Chapter 8, much of the policy instrument literature actively prescribes a pattern of sequencing which starts with soft instruments and proceeds to harder ones (for example, Salamon, 2002a; Vedung, 1997). For example, Gunningham, Grabosky and Sinclair (1998: 24, 123) favour the 'pragmatic' sequencing of environmental policy instruments which enables 'escalation from the preferred least interventionist option, if it fails, to increasingly more interventionist alternatives'. The gradual ratcheting upwards of policy instruments according to their degree of coerciveness – starting with soft policy instruments (namely, horizontal self-governance) and ending with hard policy instruments (namely, coercive top-down government) – is also in line with neoliberal economic thinking which argues that government intervention should be avoided and, if this is not possible, then it should be restricted to the least interventionist policy instrument. Policy makers should, in other words, slowly ascend a dynamic instrument pyramid, one level at a time, if necessary ending in regulation at the very peak.

However, the empirical evidence assembled in this book reveals that governments are not following this advice. Governments in Germany, the Netherlands and the EU have relied very heavily on traditional regulations in their environmental policies since the 1970s. Austria and the UK made wide use of environmental regulations only from the 1980s onwards. Importantly, in all five jurisdictions a significant number of NEPIs was added only after environmental regulation had been adopted.

Although Gunningham, Grabosky and Sinclair (1998: 402–4) accept that an integrated escalation up the regulatory pyramid does not occur in each and every case, they still over-emphasise the importance of agency over the constraining effect of institutional structures. Using an analytical framework which combines policy instrument learning with the understanding of the specific institutional context within which particular instruments are used helps us to explain better the peculiar but changing policy instrument mixes which have emerged in different jurisdictions over time. It helps us to explain why the empirical evidence put forward in our book neither supports the 'rational' sequencing of policy instruments from soft to hard instruments as suggested in parts of the policy instrument literature nor a 'random' adoption of instruments as one would expect when using garbage can models to explain the adoption of instruments in public policy (for example, Kingdon, 1984).

Why is there such a striking discrepancy between normative appeals for either more 'new' instruments and/or a rational mixing of the 'old' and the 'new', and what we have empirically observed to be the case in practice? It is important to remember that a good deal of the early environmental policy instrument literature was written by economists; most of these scholars argued strongly in favour of market-based instruments on the basis of their superior cost-effectiveness – at least when compared to traditional 'command-and-control' (see Chapter 2). However, they tended to compare market-based instruments as they were meant to function according to textbooks with 'command-and-control' regulation as they were implemented in practice (see also Jordan et al., 2011) Many of the early policy instrument studies by environmental economists pointedly did not mention some of the everyday problems that are now known to afflict NEPIs in practice. One example is corruption, which, as was pointed out in Chapter 7, affected the EU ETS. Moreover, the incomplete and/or incorrect implementation of traditional regulation due to the actions of powerful (domestic and/or EU) veto actors has often been described as 'normal' or inherent characteristic of regulation while the problems that have afflicted the EU ETS have been played down ('teething problems') (for example, Ellerman, Buchner and Carroro, 2007).

NEW DIRECTIONS

Having offered a uniquely comprehensive study of 'new' and 'old' environmental policy instruments in four member states and the EU covering a period of more than four decades, which directions could future studies take? We offer the following five suggestions.

First, there is still a need for more systematic, detailed and comparative research on specific types of instruments. Much of the early literature on environmental instruments tended to focus on one or two types, often in one or at best just a few countries. But this is no longer sufficient, a point made by other researchers (Ward and Cao, 2012). More research, perhaps of the larger 'n' variety, is needed to understand some of the macro influences that shape the (environmental) policy instrument adoption and usage patterns revealed in this book. Regarding potential independent variables, our research strongly suggests the importance of political and/or party ideology for the selection of policy instruments. This is not a new idea: back in 1970, Burnham (1970) argued (in a US context) that critical elections can transform clusters of policies (Brady, 1970). Hall (1993: 283–4) explicitly noted the importance of the 1979 election of Thatcher in reshaping British macro-economic policy, with all of the resulting implications for policy instruments. As was mentioned above, Peters (2002) has also flagged up the significance of party politics for the adoption of certain policy instruments (such as eco-taxes). Nevertheless, on the whole, the environmental policy instrument literature has tended either to overlook or downplay political factors in general and partisan/ ideological shifts in particular.

The evidence presented in this book suggests that government (coalitions) may have an important but under-explored impact on the adoption of instruments. For example, in the early 1990s a centre-right (CDU/ CSU-FDP) coalition government in Germany and in the 2000s a conservative-right wing (ÖVP-FPÖ) coalition government in Austria both preferred VAs over regulation. In all three cases, the conservative coalition governments viewed VAs as attractive instruments to respond to increased market competition and globalisation pressures. Similarly, the entry into power of the Purple I coalition in the Netherlands in 1994, the 'New' Labour government in the UK in 1997 and the Red-Green coalition government in Germany in 1998, all triggered second level learning that revealed itself in the adoption of ecological tax reforms. Yet this learning was refracted through and bounded by domestic institutional factors.

The failed adoption of full scale ecological tax reform in Austria is illustrative in this regard. In the 1990s (and 2000s) Austrian coalition governments were either grand coalitions, which included the two main parties (Social Democrats and Conservatives) or a conservative-right wing government – neither of which generated the political momentum necessary to implement the eco-taxes recommendations of leading research institutes in Austria (for example, WIFO) and Austria's long-standing Tax Commission. Although it can only be a matter of speculation, there is nevertheless considerable evidence (for example, from party manifestos and statements from leading SPÖ and Green Party politicians) to suggest that, if there had been a Red-Green coalition government in Austria, it would have been likely to adopt ecological tax reform. Our analysis therefore provides strong empirical grounds for bringing party politics back into the study of policy instruments (at least within a

European context), especially at a time when the neoliberal drive towards radical deregulation wave seems to have ebbed in the wake of the financial crisis.

A second priority is to secure a more systematic comparison of environmental policy with other policy sectors. Studies by Bähr (2010), Capano et al. (2012), Héritier and Rhodes (2011a) and Kassim and Le Galès (2010), have all made an extremely useful start in this regard. However, more systematic comparisons are needed to understand whether the trends that we have described in this book are unique to the environment sector or whether they mirror the patterns in other policy sectors. In other words, to what extent does policy type or sector 'matter'? Scholars have traditionally viewed environmental policy as an inherently regulatory policy sector, dominated by command-and-control regulations (for example, Weale, 1992a). Do we also see similar patterns in other regulatory areas where, perhaps, technological change and scientific uncertainty are less significant? If we consider the other basic types of policy in Lowi's seminal typology, do distributive and redistributive policies (for example, welfare, agricultural policies) reveal different patterns of policy instrument adoption and governance (Lowi, 1972), and to what extent do these exert an influence on policy impacts and outcomes (Bauer et al., 2012)? Bähr (2010) has directly tackled this latter question in his comparison of EU environmental and social policies (regulation being the dominant mode in both EU sectors). His comparison controls for the potential difference that the particular policy context and/or the array of policy actors may have on instrument selection and the governance mode. He concludes that the hierarchical, regulatory mode remains the key option in both policy sectors, but that the EU has made substantive progress in experimenting with new policy instruments (in environmental and social policies).

Looking across sectors may also tell us if there is something distinctive about policy instruments (and perhaps governing more generally) which leads politicians to make inflated claims about their adoption which do not match their usage and performance in practice. The limited evidence that we have of the non-use of 'detector' (as opposed to 'effector') instruments (Hood and Margetts, 2007) in the formulation (as opposed to the implementation) of policy goals, such as computer models, cost benefit analysis and scenarios, suggests that there might well be (Nilsson et al., 2008).

This takes us to a third priority: to understand better spatial variations in the (non) use of certain policy instruments. Comparing different types of jurisdictions (such as federal and unitary states and supranational organisations (for example, the EU) and international organisations (for

238 *Environmental governance in Europe*

example, the UN) could generate many new insights into what facilitates and what hinders adoption. As the sections above have detailed, there has been a substantial literature investigating the role of 'context', but with some exceptions (for example, Rietbergen-McCracken and Abaza, 2000) the tendency has been for comparative researchers to focus on similar political systems within an OECD, and particularly a European or North American context. However, Breton et al. (2007) have offered a hugely ambitious survey of environmental governance patterns, including instrument usage, for a range of non-OECD countries. The aim of their volume was to understand the role of federal structures in shaping environmental governance, and a specific analysis on instruments was not the focal point. Current shifts in economic power towards the BRIC countries (Brazil, Russia, India and China) in particular make it more urgent to research instrument patterns in rapidly and less rapidly developing countries. Will leaps in economic development in these areas be matched by an increasing use of innovative environmental regulation and new modes of (environmental) governance? How far does the influence of the diffusion of ideas about NEPIs extend to these countries? And how much difference do regional and international organisations make to the adoption and implementation of NEPIs? We are still awaiting answers to these hugely important questions.

Fourth, there is a need for more work on the evaluation of instruments, both singly and in combination (Taylor et al., 2012), and especially in areas of society-led steering (Prakash and Gugerty, 2010; Bulkeley and Jordan, 2012). Put very simply, in some contexts NEPIs do seem to work, but in many others their performance has fallen well short of expectations (Niles and Lubell, 2012: 43). Indeed, our empirical findings suggest that incomplete and/or incorrect implementation may be at least as 'normal' for NEPIs as it is for environmental regulation.

Instead of adopting a rather static perspective which simply describes the presence and/or absence of particular instruments of governing, future work could usefully explore the causal relationship between policy instruments and outcomes 'on the ground' (for good examples, see Enevoldsen (2005) and Skou Andersen and Ekins (2010)). If, to paraphrase Rhodes (1997:53), 'the mix between the modes is what really matters', it is surely important to know more about what forms of governing lead to what sorts of outcomes, whilst ensuring that they all remain legitimate and publicly accountable. The problem here is that evaluation is very much the poor relation of environmental policy analysis (Huitema et al., 2011). Some pioneering attempts have been made to identify salient evaluation criteria (Mickwitz, 2003); the challenge now is to employ them to explore the 'twist' that different

Governing with policy instruments 239

instruments impart on the operation of policy programmes (Salamon, 2002b: 2). There is certainly ample scope to relate these questions to work on policy feedback (Bauer et al., 2012) – that is how policies, once enacted, restructure subsequent policies and politics (Pierson, 1993). In the wider public policy literature, analysts are beginning to investigate what design features (the scope of calibration of instruments for example) are more likely to ensure the *political* (as opposed to environmental) sustainability of different policy interventions (Patashnik, 2008: 3). Work specifically on policy instruments stands to inform and be greatly informed by such work.

Finally, there is a need for more theoretical work to guide research on instruments. It is unlikely that there will ever be a single 'theory of policy instruments'. However, this does not mean that we do not need better policy instrument theories. Indeed elsewhere we have argued that the policy instruments literature has often side-stepped debates about explanation in favour of definition and classification (Jordan et al., 2012a). Yet arguably core aspects of the policy instrument selection process still remain poorly explored (Peters, 2002). Works such as Pedersen (2007) and Daugbjerg and Svendsen (2001) are suggestive of new and fruitful lines of inquiry, in asking whether the vital motivator is in fact symbolic (giving the impression to core constituencies that something is being done), rather than policy problem-solving. Related to that, we know relatively little about the reform and possible dismantling of existing instruments after they have been adopted. The failure to investigate the 'neglected butt' (Behn, 1978: 413) of the policy instrument process has become more apparent since the world economy fell into a deep recession in 2008. Our broader point, though, is that it is probably more productive in the short-term to build a policy instruments perspective into existing and well tested theories of the policy process, than to continue to develop an entirely separate theory and practice of policy instruments (Jordan et al., 2012a).

To conclude, all five of the outlined research trajectories powerfully re-confirm the importance of actively studying policy instruments. Policy instruments represent a critical focus to debate broader questions of governing including the actual impact of steering on societal actors at different levels of governance. There is an urgent policy need for the renewed study of policy instruments; after all, policy makers are increasingly being called upon to address an increasing number of 'super wicked' problems, such as climate change, that combine complex and changing policy demands (Levin et al., 2012). If we turn to the regulation of financial markets and economic management, the conventional wisdom prior to 2008 was that government intervention and regulation

240   *Environmental governance in Europe*

should be minimised where possible (Baker, 2010). The global financial and economic crisis is yet one more example, albeit a highly contentious and serious one (van Appeldorn et al., 2012), of the need to assess the interaction of *both* the wider policy philosophy and the concrete policy instruments that steer societal behaviour and/or allow for societal self-steering.

At the same time, analyses of policy instruments can also shed new light on politics more generally. We have shown, for example, how and why instruments have become positive (and negative) focal points for political contention in Europe. Our empirical findings support Smith and Ingram's (2002: 597) striking reference to policy instruments as being 'political weapons and marching banner alike'. The massive protests by both the US and Chinese governments in 2011–12 against the application of the EU ETS to non-EU registered aircraft carriers (see Chapter 7) clearly illustrate that environmental policy instruments are not politically neutral (see Chapter 3). Another pertinent example was the large scale protests made by fuel tanker drivers in 2000 against the rise of fuel prices in the UK; this forced the government to perform a significant and long lasting policy U-turn (see Chapter 6). One way or another, we remain confident that the choice and application of different policy instruments will always repay close analysis because they constitute the very essence of governing (Hood, 2007: 142–3); that most extensively debated and discussed topic in the social sciences.

Bibliography

Aguilar Fernández, S. (1994), 'Convergence in environmental policy?' *Journal of Public Policy*, **14** (1), 39–56.

Algemene Bestuursdienst (2010), 'Benoemingen ministerie van Infrastructuur en Milieu', http://www.algemenebestuursdienst.nl/abd_algemeen/index.cfm?fuseaction=nieuwsdetail&artikelen_id=110660A5-AFDB-237D-5ACA065D0C34E1BA&trefwoord=&datumvan=&datumtot=&StartRow=1 (accessed 10.11.2010).

Algemene Rekenkamer (2007), *The European Emissions Trading Scheme and Its Implementation in the Netherlands*, The Hague: Algemene Rekenkamer.

Andersen, M.S. (1994), *Governance by Green Taxes: Making Pollution Prevention Pay*, Manchester: Manchester University Press.

Andersen, M.S. and Ekins, P. (eds) (2010), *Carbon-energy Taxation: Lessons from Europe*, Oxford: Oxford University Press.

Andersen, M.S. and Liefferink, D. (1997), 'Introduction: the impact of the pioneers on EU environmental policy', in M. Andersen and D. Liefferink (eds), *European Environmental Policy. The Pioneers*, Manchester: Manchester University Press, 1–39.

Andersen, M.S. and Sprenger, R.-U. (eds) (2000), *Market-based Instruments for Environmental Management: Politics and Institutions*, Cheltenham: Edward Elgar.

Anderson, C. (1971), 'Comparative policy analysis: the design of measures', *Comparative Politics*, **4** (1), 117–31.

ANEC (2007), 'Joint ANEC / ECOS comments on the ISO 14000 series review', ANEC-ENV-2007-G-030final, October 2007.

Ashby, E. and Anderson, M. (1981), *The Politics of Clean Air*, Oxford: Clarendon Press.

Aspinwall, M. and Schneider, G. (2001), 'Institutional research on the European Union: mapping the field', in G. Schneider and M. Aspinwall (eds), *The Rules of Integration: Institutionalist Approaches to the Study of Europe*, Manchester: Manchester University Press, 1–18.

Bache, I. and Flinders, M. (eds) (2006), *Multi-level Governance*, Oxford: Oxford University Press.

Bähr, H. (2010), *The Politics of Means and Ends*, Farnham: Ashgate.

Bailey, I. (2003), *New Environmental Policy Instruments in the European Union*, Aldershot: Ashgate.

Baker, A. (2010), 'Restraining regulatory capture? Anglo-America, crisis politics and trajectories of change in global financial governance', *International Affairs*, **86** (3), 647–63.

242 *Environmental governance in Europe*

Bartolini, S. (2011), 'New modes of European governance: an introduction', in A. Héritier and M. Rhodes (eds), *New Modes of Governance in Europe: Governing in the Shadow of Hierarchy*, London: Routledge, 1–18.

Bastmeijer, C. (1994), 'The covenant as an instrument of environmental policy in The Netherlands', VROM, http://greenplans.rri.org/resources/greenplanning archives/netherlands/nethlerlands_94 (accessed 8.9.2007).

Bauer, M., Jordan, A., Green-Pedersen, C. and Héritier, A. (eds) (2012), *Dismantling Public Policy: Preferences, Strategies and Effects*, Oxford: Oxford University Press.

Baumol, W.J. and Oates, W.E. (1988), *The Theory of Environmental Policy*, Cambridge: Cambridge University Press (second edition).

BBC (British Broadcasting Corporation) (2007), 'Carbon Trade Scheme "is failing"', *File on Four*, 5.6.2007, London: British Broadcasting Corporation. http://news.bbc.co.uk/1/hi/programmes/file_on_4/default.stm (accessed 10.6.2007).

BBC News (2010a), 'Congestion charge plans on hold', http://news.bbc.co.uk/1/hi/england/cambridgeshire/8547010.stm (accessed 3.3.2010).

BBC News (2010b), 'York residents reject congestion charge plan', http://news.bbc.co.uk/1/hi/england/north_yorkshire/8671090.stm (accessed 9.5.2010).

BDI (2000), *Vereinbarung zwischen der Regierung der Bundesrepublik Deutschland und der deutschen Wirtschaft zur Klimavorsorge*, Berlin: Bundesverband der Deutschen Industrie.

Behn, R. (1978), 'How to terminate a public policy: a dozen hints for the would-be terminator', *Policy Analysis*, **4** (3), 393–414.

Bell, S. and Hindmoor, A. (2009), *Rethinking Governance: The Centrality of the State in Modern Society*, Cambridge: Cambridge University Press.

Bellamy, R. and Palumbo, A. (eds) (2010), *From Government to Regulation*, Farnham: Ashgate.

Bemelmans-Videc, M., Rist, R. and Vedung, E. (1997), *Carrots, Sticks and Sermons: Policy Instruments and Their Evaluation*, London: Transaction Publishers.

Bemelmans-Videc, M.-L. and Vedung, E. (1997), 'Conclusions: instrument types, packages, choices, and evaluation', in M.L. Bemelmans-Videc, R.C. Rist and E. Vedung (eds), *Carrots, Sticks and Sermons: Policy Instruments and Their Evaluation*, New Brunswick and London: Transaction Publishers, 249–76.

Bennett, C. (1988), 'Regulating the computer: comparing policy instruments in Europe and the US', *European Journal of Political Science*, **16** (5), 437–66.

Bennett, C. (1991), 'What is policy convergence and what causes it?', *British Journal of Political Science*, **21** (2), 215–33.

Benson, D. and Jordan, A. (2011), 'What have we learned from policy transfer research? Dolowitz and March revisited', *Political Studies Review*, **9** (3), 366–78.

Benson, D. and Jordan, A. (2012), 'Policy transfer research: still evolving, not yet through?', *Political Studies Review*, **10** (3), 333–8.

Benz, A., Lütz, S., Schimank, U. and Simonis, G. (eds) (2007), *Handbuch Governance: Theoretische Grundlagen und empirische Anwendungsfelder*, Opladen: Verlag für Sozialwissenschaften.

Berkhout, P. and Van Bruchem, C. (eds) (2010), *Agricultural Economic Report 2010 of the Netherlands: Summary*, The Hague: Agricultural Economics Research Institute.

Bertoldi, P. and Rezessy, S. (2010), *Voluntary Agreements in the Field of Energy Efficiency and Emission Reduction: Review and Analysis of the Experience in Member States of the European Union*, Brussels: European Commission of the EU).

Beunderman, M. (2008), 'Brussels considering climate tax on imports', *EUobserver*, http://euobserver.com (accessed 7.1.2008).

Binswanger, H., Geussberger, C. and Ginsburg, T. (1979), *Wege aus der Wohlstandsfalle. Der NAWU-Report. Strategien gegen Arbeitslosigkeit und Umweltzerstörung*, Frankfurt.

Bio Intelligence Service (2009a), 'Carbon tax on packaging (Netherlands)', *Waste Prevention Best Practice Factsheets*, June.

Bio Intelligence Service (2009b), 'Courtauld Commitment (United Kingdom)', *Waste Prevention Best Practice Factsheets*, June.

Blauer Engel (2010), http://www.blauer-engel.de/ (accessed 15.11.2010).

Blauer Engel (2011), http://www.blauer-engel.de/ (accessed 15.15.2011).

BMLFUW (2000), *Das Österreichische Umweltzeichen*, Vienna: Bundesministerium für Land- und Forstwirtschaft, Umwelt und Wasserwirtschaft.

BMLFUW (2001), *Third National Climate Report of the Austrian Federal Government*, Vienna: Bundesministerium für Land- und Forstwirtschaft, Umwelt und Wasserwirtschaft.

BMLFUW (2010), *IV. Bericht an den Nationalrat über die Anwendung der EMAS-Verordnung und die Vollziehung des Umweltmanagementgesetzes*, Vienna: Bundesministerium für Land- und Forstwirtschaft, Umwelt und Wasserwirtschaft.

BMUJF (1997), *Überblick über die bestehenden umweltökonomischen Instrumente in Österreich. Stand Jänner 1997*, Vienna: Bundesministerium für Umwelt, Jugend und Familie.

Boehmer-Christiansen, S. and Skea, J. (1991), *Acid Politics: Environmental Politics – Environmental and Energy Policies in Britain and Germany*, London, Belhaven Press.

Bogojević, S. (2009), 'Ending the honeymoon: deconstructing emissions trading discourses', *Journal of Environmental Law*, **21** (3), 443–68.

Bomberg, E. and Peterson, J. (2000), 'Policy transfer and Europeanization: passing the Heineken test?', IES Queen's University of Belfast: Queen's Papers on Europeanisation.

Bonus, H. (1976), 'Möglichkeiten der Internalisierung externer Effekte als Instrument der Koordination von Unternehmenszielen und gesellschaftlichen Zielen', in H. Albach and D. Sadowski (eds), *Die Bedeutung gesellschaftlicher Veränderungen für die Willensbildung in Unternehmen*, Berlin: Duncker und Humblot.

Börkey, P. and Lévèque, F. (1998), *Voluntary Approaches for Environmental Protection in the EU*, ENV/EPOC/GEEI (98) 29/final. Paris: OECD.

Börzel, T. (2000), 'Why there is no Southern problem: on environmental leaders and laggards in the European Union', *Journal of European Public Policy*, **7** (1), 141–62.

244 *Environmental governance in Europe*

Börzel, T. (2007), 'European governance – negotiation and competition in the shadow of hierarchy', paper prepared for the European Studies Association meeting. Montreal, May 17–20, 2007, http://www.polsoz.fu-berlin.de/polwiss/forschung/international/europa/team/mitarbeiter/boerzel/Was_ist_Governance.pdf.

Börzel, T. (2010), 'European governance: negotiation and competition in the shadow of hierarchy', *Journal of Common Market Studies*, **48** (2), 191–219.

Brady, D. (1978), 'Critical elections, congressional parties and clusters of policy changes', *British Journal of Political Science*, **8** (1), 79–99.

Bressers, H. (1990), 'Environmental policy instruments in Dutch practice', in European Parliament DG for Research (ed.), *Economic and Fiscal Incentives as a Means of Achieving Environmental Policy Objectives*, No. 16. Luxembourg: EP: 79–96.

Bressers, H. (1993), 'A comparison of the effectiveness of incentives and directives: the case of Dutch water quality policy', paper presented at the International Comparison of Achievements in Environmental Protection Conference, Berlin, 8–10 January.

Bressers, H. and de Bruijn, T. (2005), 'Environmental voluntary agreements in the Dutch context', in Edoardo Croci (ed.), *The Handbook of Environmental Voluntary Agreements: Design, Implementation and Evaluation Issues*, Dordrecht: Springer, 261–81.

Bressers, H., de Bruijn, T., and Dinica, V. (2007), 'Integration and communication as central issues in Dutch negotiated agreements on industrial energy efficiency', *European Environment*, **17**, 215–30.

Bressers, H., de Bruijn, T., and Lulofs, K. (2009), 'Environmental negotiated agreements in the Netherlands', *Environmental Politics*, **18** (1), 58–77.

Bressers, H., de Bruijn, T., Lulofs, K. and O'Toole (Jr), L. (2011), 'Negotiation-based policy instruments and performance: Dutch covenants and environmental policy outcomes', *Journal of Public Policy*, **31** (2), 187–208.

Bressers, H. and Plettenburg, L. (1997), 'The Netherlands', in M. Jänicke and H. Weidner (eds), *National Environmental Policies: A Comparative Study of Capacity-building*, Berlin: Springer: 109–31.

Breton, A., Brosio, G., Dalmazzone, S. and Garrone, G. (eds) (2007), *Environmental Governance and Decentralisation*, Cheltenham: Edward Elgar.

Bulkeley, H. and Jordan, A. (2012), 'Transnational environmental governance: new findings and emerging research agendas', *Environment and Planning C*, **30** (4), 556–70.

Bulmer, S. and Padgett, S. (2005), 'Policy transfer in the European Union: an institutionalist perspective', *British Journal of Political Science*, **35** (1), 103–26.

Bundesregierung (1996), *Nationaler Umweltplan*, Vienna: Österreichische Bundesregierung.

Burnham, W. (1970), *Critical Elections and the Mainsprings of American Politics*, New York: W.W. Norton.

Busch, P.-O. and Jörgens, H. (2005), 'The international sources of policy convergence: explaining the spread of environmental policy innovations', *Journal of European Public Policy*, **12** (5), 860–84.

Bibliography 245

Buttermann, H. and Hillebrand, B. (2000), 'Third monitoring report: CO_2 Emissions in German industry 1997–1998', RWI paper 70.

Capano, G., Rayner, J. and Zito, A. (2012), 'Governance from the bottom up: complexity and divergence in comparative perspective', *Public Administration*, **90** (1), 56–73.

Carter, H. (2008), 'Road pricing blow as Manchester rejects congestion charge', *The Guardian*, 13 December, 18.

CEC [Commission of the European Communities] (1991), *Proposal for a Regulation on a Community Award Scheme for an Eco-Label*, Brussels: Commission of the European Communities.

CEC (1992), *Proposal for a Council Directive Introducing a Tax on Carbon Dioxide Emissions and Energy, COM(92) 226 final*, Brussels: Commission of the European Communities.

CEC (1993a), 'Growth, competitiveness and employment: the challenges and ways forward in the twenty first century', *EC Bulletin*, Supplement 93–6, Brussels: Commission of the European Communities.

CEC (1993b), 'Towards sustainability: A European Community Programme of policy and action in relation to the environment and sustainable development', *Official Journal C* 138 of 17 May, 5–98, Brussels: Commission of the European Communities.

CEC (1995), *Report of the Group of Independent Experts on Legislative and Administrative Simplification*, COM(95)288 final, 21 June, Brussels: Commission of the European Communities.

CEC (1996), *Communication from the Commission to the Council of the European Parliament on Environmental Agreements*, COM(96) 561 final, Brussels: CEC.

CEC (1997a), *Environmental Taxes and Charges in the Single Market*, COM(97) 9 final, Brussels: CEC.

CEC (1997b), *Study on Voluntary Agreements Concluded Between Industry and Public Authorities in the Field of the Environment*, Brussels: DG III.

CEC (2000a), *Database on Environmental Taxes in the EU Member States*, Brussels: CEC.

CEC (2000b), *Green Paper on Greenhouse Gas Emission Trading within the European Union*, COM(2000) 87 final, Brussels: Commission of the European Communities.

CEC (2001a), 'Commission recommendation of 7 September 2001 on guidance for the implementation of Regulation (EC) No 761/2001 of the European Parliament and of the Council allowing voluntary participation by organisations in a Community eco-management and audit scheme', *Official Journal of the European Communities L 247*, **44**, 17 September 2001, 1–23.

CEC (2001b), *European Governance: a White Paper*, COM(2001) 428 final, Brussels: CEC.

CEC (2001c), *Proposal for a Directive Establishing a Scheme for Greenhouse Gas Emission Allowance Trading*. COM(2001)581, Brussels: Commission of the European Communities.

CEC (2001d), *Green Paper on Integrated Product Policy*, COM(2001) 68 final, 7.2.2011, Brussels: Commission of the European Communities.

246 *Environmental governance in Europe*

CEC (2002a), *Communication from the Commission. Action Plan 'Simplifying and Improving the Regulatory Environment*, COM(2002)278 final of 05.06.2002, Brussels: Commission of the European Communities.

CEC (2002b), *Communication from the Commission. Environmental Agreements at Community Level*, COM(2002)0412 final, Brussels: Commission of the European Communities.

CEC (2003a), *Directive 2003/87/EC establishing a scheme for greenhouse gas emission allowance trading*, Brussels: Commission of the European Communities.

CEC (2003b), 'Council Directive 2003/96/EC of 27 October 2003 restructuring the Community Framework for the Taxation of Energy Products and Electricity', *Official Journal L* 283/51.

CEC (2005), *Proposal for a Council Directive on Passenger Car Related Taxes*, COM(2005) 261 final, Brussels: Commission of the European Communities.

CEC (2006), *Building a Global Carbon Market – Report Pursuant to Article 30 of Directive 2003/87/EC, COM(2006)676 final. Communication from the Commission*, Brussels: Commission of the European Communities.

CEC (2007a), *Questions and Answers on the EU Strategy to Reduce CO2 Emissions from Cars*, Memo/07/46, 07 February, http://europa.eu/rapid/pressReleasesAction.do?reference=MEMO/07/46 (accessed 1.11.2010).

CEC (2007b), *Report on the Public Consultation Revision of the EU Ecolabel Regulation (EC) No. 1980/2000*, Brussels: Commission of the European Communities.

CEC (2008), 'Environment: Commission welcomes voluntary agreement on safe storage of mercury', IP/08/2047, 22 December 2008, Brussels: Commission of the European Communities.

CEC (2009) *2008 Environment Policy Review*, Luxembourg: Office of the European Communities.

CEU [Commission of the European Union] (2010a), 'Ecolabel. Facts and figures', http://ec.europa.eu/environment/ecolabel/about_ecolabel/facts_and_figures_en.htm#distribution, Commission of the European Union (accessed 18.11.2010).

CEU (2010b), *Taxation Trends in the European Union: Data for the EU Member States, Iceland and Norway*, Luxembourg: Commission of the European Union, Office of Official Publications.

CEU (2011a), 'EU Ecolabel. Facts and figures', http://ec.europa.eu/environment/ecolabel/index_en.htm, Commission of the European Union (accessed 20.12.2011).

CEU (2011b), *EMAS Statistics*, http://ec.europa.eu/environment/emas/documents/articles_en.htm, Commission of the European Union (accessed 20.12.2011).

Cohen, M. (2000), 'Ecological modernisation, environmental knowledge and national character: a preliminary analysis of the Netherlands', *Environmental Politics*, **9** (1), 77–106.

Common, M. (1988), *Environmental and Resource Economics. An Introduction*, London: Longman.

Consortium (EVER) (2005), *EVER: Evaluation of EMAS and Ecolabel for their Revision*, Brussels: Commission of the European Communities.

Bibliography   247

Council of the European Communities (1992), 'Council Regulation (EEC) No 880/92 of 23 March 1992 on a Community eco-label award scheme', *Official Journal of the European Communities L 99*, 11.4.1992, 1–7.

Council of the European Communities (1993), 'Council Regulation (EEC) No 1836/93 of 29 June 1993 allowing voluntary participation by companies in the industrial sector in a Community eco-management and audit scheme', *Official Journal of the European Communities L 168*, 10.7.1993, 1–18.

Council of the European Union (2009), 'Regulation (EC) No 443/2009 of the European Parliament and of the Council of 23 April 2009 setting emission performance standards for new passenger cars as part of the Community's integrated approach to reduce CO2 emissions from light-duty vehicles', *Official Journal of the European Union L 140*, 5.6.2009, 1–15.

Crepaz, M. (1995), 'An institutional dinosaur: Austrian corporatism in the post-industrial age', *West European Politics*, **18** (4), 64–88.

Croci, E. (2005), 'Preface', in E. Croci (ed.), *The Handbook of Environmental Voluntary Agreements*, Dordrecht: Springer, ix–xiv.

Dachs, H. *et al.* (eds) (1997), *Handbuch des politischen Systems Österreichs: Die zweite Republik*, Vienna: Manzsche Verlags- und Universitätsbuchhandlung (3rd edition).

Dales, J. (1968), *Pollution, Property and Prices*, Toronto: University of Toronto.

Damro, C. and Méndez, P. (2003), 'Emissions trading at Kyoto: from EU resistance to Union innovation', *Environmental Politics*, **12** (2), 71–94.

Daugbjerg, C. and Sønderskov, K.M. (2012), 'Environmental policy performance revisited: designing effective policies for green markets', *Political Studies*, **60** (2), 399–418.

Daugbjerg, C. and Svendsen, G. (2001), *Green Taxation in Question*, Basingstoke: Palgrave.

Davies, J. (2011), *Challenging Governance Theory: from Networks to Hegemony*, Bristol: Policy Press.

De Bruijn, H. and Hufen, H. (1998), 'The traditional approach to policy instruments', in B.G. Peters and F. van Nispen (eds), *Public Policy Instruments: Evaluating the Tools of Public Administration*, Cheltenham: Edward Elgar, 11–32.

De Búrca, G., and Scott, J. (eds) (2006), *Law and New Governance in the EU and the US*, Oxford: Hart Publishing.

De Clerq, M. (ed.) (2002), *Negotiating Environmental Agreements in Europe: Critical Factors for Success*, Cheltenham: Edward Elgar.

De Gelder, T. (2005), 'Strategies for supervision of carbon dioxide and nitrogen oxides emissions trading', summary of paper presented at the 7th International Compliance and Enforcement Conference, 9–15 April, Marrakech, Morocco.

De Hoog, M. (1998), 'Environmental agreements in the Netherlands: sharing the responsibility for sustainable industrial development', *UNEP Industry and Environment*, January–June: 27–30.

De Muizon, G. and Glachant, M. (2004), 'The UK Climate Change Levy Agreements: combined negotiated agreements with tax and emission trading', in A. Baranzini and P. Thalmann (eds), *Voluntary Approaches in Climate Policy*, Cheltenham: Edward Elgar, 231–48.

248   *Environmental governance in Europe*

DEFRA [Department for Environment, Food and Rural Affairs] (2002), *Finding out about the Ecolabel and Other Environmental Labels, UK-Ecolabel Guidance Note 3*, London: Department for Environment, Food and Rural Affairs.

DEFRA (2003a), *UK Emission Trading Scheme*, London: Department for Environment, Food and Rural Affairs http://www.defra.gov.uk/environment/climatechange/trading/reia.htm (accessed 5.5.2008).

DEFRA (2003b), *UK Emissions Trading Scheme. Auction Analysis and Progress Report*, London: Department for Environment, Food and Rural Affairs, http://www.defra.gov.uk/environment/climatechange/trading/pdf/trading-progress.pdf (accessed 5.5.2008).

DEFRA (2004), 'Voluntary agreement for the reduction in risk from nonylphenol, nonylphenol ethoxylates, octylphenol and octylphenol ethoxylates', http://archive.defra.gov.uk/environment/quality/...va/voluntary-ag.pdf (accessed 21.12.11).

DEFRA (2009a), *Commercial and Industrial Waste in England: Statement of Aims and Actions 2009*, London: Department for Environment, Food and Rural Affairs.

DEFRA (2009b), *Making the Most of Packaging: A Strategy for a Low-carbon Economy*, London: www.defra.gov.uk.

DEFRA (2010a), 'Carrier bag waste', http://www.defra.gov.uk/environment/quality/local/litter/bags (accessed 14.12.10).

DEFRA (2010b), 'Direct mail and the waste strategy', http://www.defra.gov.uk/environment/waste/strategy/factsheets/directmail.htm (accessed 14.12.10).

DEFRA (2011), 'Green claims and labels', http://www.defra.gov.uk/environment/economy/products-consumers/green-claims-labels/ (accessed 20.12.2011).

DEHSt [Deutsche Emissionshandelsstelle] (2012), 'German Emissions Trading Authority – Deutsche Emissionshandelsstelle (DEHSt)', http://www.dehst.de/EN/Home/home_node.html (accessed 25.7.2012).

Dekkers, C. (1999), 'Trading emissions and other economic instruments to reduce NOx in the Netherlands', in S. Sorrell and S. Skea (eds), *Pollution for Sale: Emissions Trading and Joint Implementation*, Cheltenham: Edward Elgar: 109–23.

Delbeke, J. (1991), 'The prospects for the use of economic instruments in EC environmental policy', Paper presented at the CEPS Seminar Setting New Priorities in EC Environmental Legislation, Brussels, 11 April 1991.

Delbeke, J. (2006), 'The Emissions Trading Scheme (ETS): the cornerstone of the EU's implementation of the Kyoto Protocol', in J. Delbeke (ed.) *EU Energy Law, Vol. IV of EU Environmental Law: The EU Greenhouse Gas Emissions Scheme Trading Scheme*, 1–13.

Dietz, F. and K. Termeer (1991), 'Dutch manure policy: the lack of economic instruments', in D. Kraan, and R. in'tVeld, (eds), *Environmental Protection: Public or Private Choice*, Dordrecht: Kluwer, 123–47.

DiMaggio, P. and Powell, W. (1983), 'The Iron Cage revisited: institutional isomorphism and collective rationality in organizational fields', *American Journal of Sociology*, **48** (2), 147–60.

DIW [Deutsches Institut für Wirtschaftsforschung] (1995), *Wirtschaftliche Auswirkungen einer ökologischen Steuerreform*, Berlin: Deutsches Institut für Wirtschaftsforschung.

DoE [Department of the Environment] (1978), *Environmental Standards in Britain: How They Work*, HMSO: London.

DoE (1984), *Pollution Control Subsidies for Industry in Europe*, DoE Statistics and Economics Division, DoE, London.

DoE (1993), *Making Markets Work for the Environment*, London: HMSO.

Doern, G. and Wilson, V. (eds) (1974), *Issues in Canadian Public Policy*, Toronto: Macmillan of Canada.

Dolowitz, D. and Marsh, D. (1996), 'Who learns from whom?', *Political Studies*, **44** (2), 343–57.

Dolowitz, D. and Marsh, D. (2000), 'Learning from abroad: the role of policy transfer in contemporary policy-making', *Governance*, **13** (1), 5–23.

Dyson, K. (1982), 'West Germany: the search for a rationalist consensus', in J. Richardson (ed.), *Policy Styles in Western Europe*, London: George Allen and Unwin, 17–46.

Dyson, K. (ed.) (1992), *The Politics of German Regulation*, Aldershot: Dartmouth.

Dyson, K. and Goetz, K. (eds) (2003), *Germany and Europe: A Europeanized Germany?*, London: British Academy.

Dyson, K. and Padgett, S. (2005), 'Introduction: global, Rhineland or hybrid capitalism', *German Politics*, **14** (2), 115–24.

Eberlein, B. and Kerwer, D. (2004), 'New governance in the EU: a theoretical perspective', *Journal of Common Market Studies*, **42** (1), 121–42.

EEA [European Environment Agency] (1996), *Environmental Taxes: Implementation and Environmental Effectiveness*, Luxembourg: EEA.

EEA (1997), *Environmental Agreements*, Copenhagen: EEA.

EEA (2006a), *Market-based Instruments for Environmental Policy in Europe*, Copenhagen: EEA.

EEA (2006b), *Using the Market for Cost-effective Environmental Policy: Market-based Instruments in Europe*, Copenhagen: EEA.

EEB [European Environmental Bureau] (1998), *EEB's Contribution to the EU Eco-label Scheme*, Brussels: European Environmental Bureau.

EEB (2000), *A Critical Analysis of the Voluntary Fuel Economy Agreement*, Brussels: European Environmental Bureau.

Eberg, J. (1997), *Waste Policy and Learning*, Delft: Eburon.

Eiderström, E. (1998), 'Ecolabels in EU environmental policy', in J. Golub (ed.), *New Instruments for Environmental Policy in the EU*, London: Routledge, 190–214.

Eionet (2009), 'Factsheet for Netherlands', Copenhagen: EEA.

Ekins, P. (1999), 'European environmental taxes and charges: recent experience, issues and trends', *Ecological Economics*, **31** (1), 39–62.

Ellerman, D., Buchner, B. and Carroro, C. (eds) (2007), *Allocation in the European Emissions Trading Scheme*, Cambridge: Cambridge University Press.

Ellerman, D. and Buchner, B. (2007), 'The European Union Emissions Trading Scheme: origins, allocation, and early results', *Review of Environmental Economics and Policy*, **1** (1), 66–87.

250   *Environmental governance in Europe*

Ellerman, A.D., Convery, F.J. and de Perthuis, C. (2010), *Pricing Carbon: The European Emissions Trading Scheme*, Cambridge: Cambridge University Press.

ELNI [Environmental Law Network International] (1999), *Environmental Agreements: the Role and Effect of Environmental Agreements in Environmental Policies*, London: Cameron May.

ENDS Europe Daily (various years), E-mail service, London: Environmental Data Services.

ENDS Report (various years), Environmental Data Services, accessed at http://www.endsreport.com/.

Endres, A. (2000), *Umweltökonomie,* Stuttgart: Kohlhammer (2nd edition).

Enevoldsen, M. (2000), 'Industrial energy efficiency', in A. Mol, V. Lauber and D. Liefferink (eds), *The Voluntary Approach to Environmental Policy*, Oxford: Oxford University Press, 62–103.

Enevoldsen, M. (2005), *The Theory of Environmental Agreements and Taxes*, Cheltenham: Edward Elgar.

Environmental Industries Commission (2010a), 'Coalition government misses first opportunity to boost green industries', press release, www.eic-uk.co.uk.

Environmental Industries Commission (2010b), 'Emergency budget – June 2010', www.eic-uk.co.uk.

EP [European Parliament] (2001), *Report on the Commission Green Paper on Environmental Issues of PVC. Committee on the Environment, Public Health and Consumer Protection A5-0092/2001 of 21 March 2001*, Luxembourg: General Directorate of the European Parliament.

Erskine, C. and Lyndhurst, C. (1996), 'Eco-labelling in the EU: a comparative study of the pulp and paper industry in the UK and Sweden', *European Environment*, **6** (2), 40–7.

EurActiv (2002), 'Germany blocks energy deal', 4 December, http://www.euractiv/com/Article?tcmuri=tcm:29-112130-16&type=News.

Eurofound (2010), 'Doelgroepenbeleid (target-group policy)', www.eurofound.europa.eu/emire/.../TARGETGROUPPOLICY-NL.htm (accessed 10.11.2010).

Eurosolar (2001), *Unsere Luft ist keine Ware. Erneuerbare Energien statt fossilen Emissionshandel*, advertisment in *Die Zeit*, 12 July 2001.

Eurostat (2010a), 'Environmental taxes – statistics explained', http://epp.eurostat.ec.europa.eu/statistics_explained/index.php/Environmental_taxes (accessed 2.9.2010)

Eurostat (2010b), 'Total environmental tax revenues as a share of GDP', http://epp.eurostat.ec.europa.eu/ (accessed 5.1.11).

Eurostat (2010c), 'Environmental tax revenue', http://epp.eurostat.ec.europa.eu/ (accessed 5.1.11).

Faber, A. (2001), *Gesellschaftliche Selbstregulierung im Umweltrecht – unter besonderer Berücksichtigung der Selbstverpflichtungen*, Cologne: Kohlhammer.

Falkner, G. and Müller, M. (eds) (1998), *Österreich im europäischen Mehrebenesystem. Konsequenzen der EU-Mitgliedschaft für Politknetzwerke und Entscheidungsprozess*, Vienna: Signum Verlag.

Faure, M. and Ruegg, M. (1994), 'Environmental standard setting through general principles of environmental law', in M. Faure, J. Vervaele, and A.

Weale (eds), *Environmental Standards in the European Union in an Inter-disciplinary Framework*, Antwerp: Maklu, 39–60.

Financial and Economic Instruments in Dutch Environmental Policy (1992), AVT 92, Final Report.

Finer, S. (1970), *Comparative Government*, Harmondsworth: Penguin.

Frances, J., Levačić, R., Mitchell, J. and Thompson, G. (1991), 'Introduction', in G. Thompson, J. Frances, R. Levačić, and J. Mitchell (eds), *Markets, Hierarchies & Networks: the Coordination of Social Life*, London and Newbury Park: Sage Publications, 1–19.

Friedrich, A., Tappe, M. and Wurzel, R.K.W. (2000), 'A new approach to EU environmental policy-making? The Auto-Oil Programme', *Journal of European Public Policy*, **7** (4), 593–612.

Fullerton, D., Leicester, A. and Smith, S. (2010), 'Environmental taxes: appendix', Prepared for the Report of a Commission on Reforming the Tax System for the 21st Century, Chaired by Sir James Mirrlees, London: Institute for Fiscal Studies.

Gehrlich, P. (1992), 'A farewell to corporatism', *West European Politics*, **15** (1), 132–46.

Genschel, P. and Zangl, B. (2007), 'Die Zerfaserung von Staatlickkeit und die Zentralisierung des Staates', *Aus Politik und Zeitgeschichte*, **20–1**, 10–6.

Genscher, H.-D. (1980), 'Umweltpolitik und Verfassung', in J. Jekewitz, M. Melzer and W. Zeh (eds), *Politik als gelebte Verfassung: aktuelle Probleme des modernen Verfassungsstaates*, Opladen: Westdeutscher Verlag, 113–28.

Giebel, C. (2001), *Vereinbarungen als Instrument des Umweltschutzes. Eine vergleichende Untersuchung des französischen, deutschen und europäischen Rechts*, Baden-Baden: Nomos.

Giswijt, A. (1987),'The Kingdom of the Netherlands', in G. Enyedi, A. Gijswijt and B. Rhode (eds), *Environmental Policies in East and West*, London: Taylor Graham, 267–89.

Glasbergen, P. (1998), 'Partnership as a learning process. Environmental covenants in the Netherlands', in P. Glasbergen (ed.), *Co-operative Environmental Governance*, Dordrecht: Kluwer Academic, 133–56.

Glasbergen, P. (2004), 'The architecture and functioning of Dutch negotiated agreements', in A. Baranzini and Philippe Thalmann (eds), *Voluntary Approaches in Climate Policy*, Cheltenham: Edward Elgar, 170–88.

Glatz, H. (1995), *Österreichische Umweltpolitik. Eine kritische Einschätzung der Instrumente*, Vienna: Bunderskammer für Arbeiter und Angestellte.

Golub, J. (ed.) (1998), *New Instruments of Environmental Policy*, London: Routledge.

Gordijn, H. and Kolkman, J. (2011), *Effects of the Air Passenger Tax: Behavioural Responses of Passengers, Airlines and Airports*, The Hague: KiM Netherlands Institute for Transport Policy Analysis.

Government of The Netherlands (2008), 'Convenant: Schone en Zuinige Agro-sectoren (version 1.10)', http://www.government/nl/.

Government of The Netherlands (2010), 'Coalition agreement', http://www.government/nl/Government/Coalition_agreement.

Green Tax Commission (1998), *A Summary of Its Three Reports 1995–1997*, The Hague.

252 *Environmental governance in Europe*

Greenwood, J. and Cram, L. (1996), 'European level business collective action: the study agenda ahead', *Journal of Common Market Studies*, **34** (3), 449–63.

Greenwood, J., Grote, J. and Ronit, K. (1992), 'Conclusions: evolving patterns of organizing interests in the European Community', in J. Greenwood, J. Grote and K. Ronit (eds), *Organized Interests in the European Community*, London: Sage, 238–52.

Grubb, M., Betz, R. and Neuhoff, K. (2007), *National Allocation Plans in hte EU Emissions Trading Scheme. Lessons and Implications for Phase II*, London: Routledge.

Grubb, M., Vrolijk, C. and Brack, D. (1999), *The Kyoto Protocol*, London: Earthscan.

Gunningham, N. (2011), 'Enforcing Envrionmental Regulation', *Journal of Environmental Law*, **23** (2), 169–201.

Gunningham, N., Grabosky, P. and Sinclair, D. (1998), *Smart Regulation: Designing Environmental Policy*, Oxford: Clarendon Press.

Gunningham, N. and Sinclair, D. (2002), *Leaders and Laggards. Next-Generation Environmental Regulation*, London: Greenleaf Publishing.

Gupta, J. and Grubb, M. (ed.) (2000), *Climate Change and European Leadership: A Sustainable Role for Europe?* Dordrecht: Kluwer Academic Publishers.

Haigh, N. (1984), *EEC Environmental Policy and Britain*, London: Environmental Data Services Ltd (ENDS).

Haigh, N. (ed.) (2011), *Manual of Environmental Policy: The EC and Britain*, Harlow: Cartermill Publishing.

Hajer, M. (1995), *The Politics of Environmental Discourse*, Oxford: Oxford University Press.

Hall, P. (1993), 'Policy paradigms, social learning and the state', *Comparative Politics*, **25** (3), 275–96.

Hall, P. and Taylor, R. (1996), 'Political science and the three 'new' Institutionalisms', *Political Studies*, **44** (4), 936–57.

Halpern, C. (2010), 'Governing despite its instruments? Instrumentation in EU Environmental Policy', *West European Politics*, **33** (1), 39–57.

Hanf, K. and van de Gronden, E. (1998), The Netherlands: joint regulation and sustainable development', in K. Hanf and A. Jansen (eds), *Governance and Environment in Western Europe: Politics, Policy and Administration*, Harlow: Longman, 152–80.

Hansjürgens, B. (ed.) (2005), *Emissions Trading for Climate Policy*, Cambridge: Cambridge University Press.

Hansmeyer, K.-H. (1976), 'Die Abwasserabgabe als Versuch einer Anwendung des Verursacherprinzips', in O. Issing (ed.), *Ökonomische Probleme der Umweltschutzpolitik*, Berlin: Springer, 75–91.

Harrison, D. and Radow, D. (2007), 'United Kingdom', in A. Ellerman, B. Buchner and C. Carraro (eds), *Allocation in the European Emissions Trading Scheme*, Cambridge: Cambridge University Press, 41–71.

Hartkopf, G. and Bohne, E. (1983), *Umwelt 1. Grundlagen, Analysen und Perspektiven*, Opladen: Westdeutscher Verlag.

Hayward, J. (1996), 'Conclusion: has European unification by stealth a future?', in J. Hayward (ed.), *Elitism, Populism, and European Politics*, Oxford: Clarendon Press Oxford, 252–8.

Heclo, H. (1974), *Modern Social Politics in Britain and Sweden*, New Haven: Yale University Press.

Heineken, K. (2002), 'The history of the Dutch Regulatory Energy Tax: how the Dutch introduced and expanded a tax on small-scale energy use', in J. Milne, K. Deketelaere, L. Kreiser and H. Ashiabor (eds), *Critical Issues in Environmental Taxation, Volume I: International and Comparative Perspectives*, Oxford: Oxford University Press, 189–209.

Heinelt, H., Malek, T., Smith, R. and Töller, A. (eds) (2001), *European Union Environmental Policy and New Forms of Governance*, Aldershot: Ashgate.

Heinelt, H. and Töller, A. (2001), 'Comparing EIA and EMAS in Germany, Britain and Greece', in H. Heinelt, T. Malek, R. Smith, and A. Töller (eds), *European Union Environmental Policy and New Forms of Governance*, Aldershot: Ashgate, 350–89.

Helm, D. (1998), 'The assessment: environment policy', *Oxford Review of Economic Policy*, **14** (4), 1–19.

Héritier, A. (1996), 'The accommodation of diversity in European policy-making and its outcomes: regulatory policy as a patchwork', *Journal of European Public Policy*, **3** (2), 149–67.

Héritier, A., Knill, C. and Mingers, S. (1996), *Ringing the Changes in Europe. Regulatory Competition and the Redefinition of the State. Britain, France and Germany*, Berlin: de Gruyter.

Héritier, A. and Lehmkuhl, U. (2008), 'The shadow of hierarchy and new modes of governance: sectoral governance and democratic government', *Journal of Public Policy*, **28** (1), 1–17.

Héritier, A. and Rhodes, M. (eds) (2011a), *New Modes of Governance in Europe. Governing in the Shadow of Hierarchy*, London: Routledge.

Héritier, A. and Rhodes, M. (2011b), 'Conclusion. New modes of governance: emergence, execution, evolution and evaluation', in A. Héritier and M. Rhodes (eds), *New Modes of Governance in Europe. Governing in the Shadow of Hierarchy*, London: Routledge, 163–74.

Herrup, A. (1999), 'Eco-label: benefits uncertain, impacts unclear', *European Environmental Law Review*, **8** (5), 144–53.

Hey, C. (2005), 'EU environmental policies: a short history of the policy strategies', in S. Scheuer (ed.), *EU Environmental Policy Handbook* (Brussels: European Environmental Policy), 18–31.

Hey, C., Jacob, A. and Volkery, A. (2008), 'REACH als Beispiel für hybride Formen von Steuerung und Governance', *Politische Vierteljahreschrift*, special issue, 430–51.

HLG (2011) *Europe Can Do Better. Report On Best Practice in Member States to Implement EU Legislation in the Least Burdensome Way. High Level Group of Independent Stakeholders on Administrative Burdens*, http://ec.europa.eu/dgs/secretariat_general/admin_burden/best_practice_report/docs/bp_report_signature_en.pdf (accessed 15.3.2012).

HM Government (1992), *This Common Inheritance. Britain's Environmental Strategy*, Cmnd 2068, London: HMSO.

HM Government (2012), *One-in, One-out: Third statement of New Regulation*, London: HMSO.

254   *Environmental governance in Europe*

Holman, O. (2006), 'Trans-national governance without supra-national government: the case of the European Employment Strategy', *Perspectives on European Politics and Society*, **7** (1), 91–107.

Holmes, R. (1995), 'Environmental management: the systems available to improve the environmental performance of industrial operations', paper presented at the Seminar Emerging Environmental Management Standards, 25 April 1995, University of Pittsburgh, Pennsylvania.

HOLSCEC [House of Lords Select Committee on the European Communities] (1980), *EEC Environment Policy, Fifth Report, House of Lords Select Committee on the European Communities, Session 1980–1*, London: HMSO.

HOLSCEC (1983), *The Polluter Pays Principle, Tenth Report, House of Lords Select Committee on the European Communities, Session 1982–3*, London: HMSO.

Holzinger, K. (1987), *Umweltpolitische Instrumente aus der Sicht der staatlichen Bürokratie – Versuch einer Anwendung der Ökonomischen Theorie der Bürokratie*, Munich: Ifo Instut.

Holzinger, K. (1994), *Politik des kleinsten gemeinsamen Nenners? Umweltpolitische Entscheidungsprozesse in der EG am Beispiel der Einführung des Katalysators*, Berlin: Edition Sigma.

Holzinger, K., Knill, C. and Lenschow, A. (2009), 'Governance in EU environmental policy', in I. Tömmel and A. Verdun (eds), *Innovative Governance in the European Union*, Boulder: Lynne Rienner, 45–62.

Holzinger, K., Knill, C. and Schäfer, A. (2003), 'Steuerungswandel in der europäischen Umweltpolitik', in K. Holzinger, C. Knill and D. Lehmkuhl (eds), *Politische Steuerung im Wandel: Der Einfluss on Ideen und Problemstrukturen*, Opladen: Leske + Budrich, 103–29.

Holzinger, K., Knill, C. and Schäfer, A. (2006), 'Rhetoric or reality? "New Governance" in EU environmental policy', *European Law Journal*, **12** (3), 403–20.

Hood, C. (1983), *The Tools of Government*, London: Macmillan.

Hood, C. (2007), 'Intellectual obsolescence and intellectual makeovers: reflections on the tools of government after two decades', *Governance*, **20** (1), 127–44.

Hood, C. and Margetts, H. (2007), *The Tools of Government in the Digital Age*, London: Palgrave Macmillan.

Hooghe, L. and Marks, G. (2003), 'Unravelling the central state, but how? Types of multi-level governance', *American Political Science Review*, **97** (2), 233–43.

Howlett, M. (1991), 'Policy instruments, policy styles and policy implementation: national approaches to theories of instrument choice', *Policy Studies Journal*, **19** (2), 1–21.

Howlett, M. (2011), *Designing Public Policies: Principles and Instruments*, Abingdon, Oxford and New York: Taylor and Francis.

Howlett, M. and Ramesh, M. (1993), 'Patterns of policy instrument choice', *Policy Studies Review*, **12** (1/2) 3–24.

Howlett, M., Rayner, J. and Tollefson, C. (2009), 'From government to governance in forest planning? Lessons from the case of the British Columbia Great Bear Rainforest initiative', *Forest Policy and Economics*, **11** (5–6), 383–391.

Huitema, D., Jordan, A., Massey, E., Rayner, T., van Asselt, H., Haug, C., Hildingsson, R., Monni, S. and Stripple, J. (2011), 'The evaluation of climate policy: theory and emerging practice in Europe', *Policy Sciences*, **44** (2), 179–198.

IFOAM EU – [EU Group of the International Federation of Organic Agriculture Movements] (2004), 'IFOAM EU Group criticizes Dutch GM Coexistence Agreement for making non-GM food producers pay for GM contamination damage', 2 November, Brussels: IFOAM.

IÖW [Institut für ökologische Wirtschaftsforschung] (1999), *The European Eco-label in Germany: Development of Recommendations for Action to Increase Acceptance,* Wuppertal: Institut für ökologische Wirtschaftsforschung.

Jachtenfuchs, M. (2001), 'The governance approach to European integration', *Journal of Common Market Studies*, **39** (2), 245–64.

James, O. and Lodge, M. (2003), 'The limitations of "Policy Transfer" and "Lesson Drawing" for Public Policy Research', *Political Studies Review*, **1** (2), 179–193.

Jänicke, M. (2011), 'German Climate Change Policy. Political and economic leadership', in R.K.W. Wurzel and J. Connelly (eds), *The European Union as a Leader in International Climate Change Politics*, London: Routledge, 129–46.

Jänicke, M. and Jörgens, H. (2004), 'Neue Steuerungskonzepte in der Umweltpolitik', *Zeitschrift für Umweltpolitik und Umweltrecht*, **27** (3), 297–348.

Jänicke, M. and Weidner, H. (1997), 'Germany', in M. Jänicke and H. Weidner (eds), *National Environmental Policies: a Comparative Study of Capacity Building*, Berlin: Springer, 133–56.

Jansen, M. (2010), 'Green Investment Bank faces critical test over funding shortfall', *The Ecologist*, http://www.theecologist.org/investigations/politics_ and_economics/691428/green_investment_bank_faces_critical_test_over_ funding_shortfall.html (accessed 8.12.2010).

Jessop, B. and Sum, N.-L. (2006), *Beyond the Regulationalist Approach*, Cheltenham: Edward Elgar.

Jordan, A. (1998a), 'The impact on UK environmental administration', in P. Lowe and S. Ward (eds), *British Environmental Policy and Europe*, London: Routledge, 173–94.

Jordan, A. (1998b), 'The ozone endgame: the implementation of the Montreal Protocol in the UK', *Environmental Politics*, **7** (4), 23–52.

Jordan, A. (1999), 'The implementation of EU environmental policy: a policy problem without a political solution?' *Environment and Planning C: Government and Policy*, **17** (1), 1–17.

Jordan, A. (2002), *The Europeanization of British Environmental Policy*, London: Palgrave.

Jordan, A. (2004), 'The United Kingdom: from policy "taking" to policy "shaping"', in A. Jordan and D. Liefferink (eds), *Environmental policy in Europe: The Europeanisation of National Environmental Policy*, London: Routledge, 205–23.

Jordan, A. (2008), 'The governance of sustainable development: taking stock and looking forwards', *Environment and Planning C: Government and Policy*, **26**, 17–33.

256   *Environmental governance in Europe*

Jordan, A, Benson, D., Wurzel, R. and Zito, A. (2011), 'Climate policy instruments in practice', in J. S. Dryzek, R. B. Norgaard, and D. Schlosberg (eds), *Oxford Handbook of Climate Change and Society*, Oxford: Oxford University Press, 536–49.

Jordan, A.J., Benson, D., Wurzel, R. and Zito, A. (2012a), 'Environmental policy: governing by multiple policy instruments?', in J. Richardson (ed.) *Constructing a Policy State? Policy Dynamics in the EU*, Oxford University Press: Oxford, 104–24.

Jordan, A. and Lenschow, A. (eds) (2008), *Innovation in Environmental Policy? Integrating the Environment for Sustainability*, Cheltenham: Edward Elgar.

Jordan, A. and Liefferink, D. (eds) (2004), *Environmental Policy in Europe: The Europeanisation of National Environmental Policy*, London: Routledge.

Jordan, A. and Salmons, R. (2000), *The Use of Voluntary Agreements in the UK*, CSERGE mimeo, Norwich and London: CSERGE, UCL and UEA.

Jordan, A. and Schout, A. (2006), *The Coordination of the European Union. Exploring the Capacities of Network Governance*, Oxford: Oxford University Press.

Jordan, A., van Asselt, H., Berkhout, F., Huitema, D. and Rayner, T. (2012b), 'Understanding the paradoxes of multi-level governing: climate change policy in the European Union', *Global Environmental Politics*, **12** (2), 41–64.

Jordan, A., Wurzel, R. and Zito, A. (eds) (2003a), *New Instruments of Environmental Governance*, Frank Cass: London.

Jordan, A., Wurzel, R. and Zito, A. (2003b), '"New" instruments of environmental governance: patterns and pathways of change', *Environmental Politics*, **12** (1), 3–24.

Jordan, A., Wurzel, R. and Zito, A. (2003c), '"New" Environmental Policy Instruments: An Evolution or a Revolution in Environmental Policy?', *Environmental Politics*, **12** (1), 201–24.

Jordan, A., Wurzel, R. and Zito, A. (2005), 'The rise of "new" policy instruments in comparative perspective: has governance eclipsed government?' *Political Studies*, **53** (3), 477–96.

Jordan, A., Wurzel, R. and Zito, A. (2006), 'Policy instruments in the European Union: a realistic model for international environmental governance?' in G. Winter (ed.), *Multilevel Governance of Global Environmental Change*, Cambridge: Cambridge University Press, 470–92.

Jordan, A., Wurzel, R. and Zito, A. (2007), 'New modes of environmental governance: are "new" environmental policy instruments (NEPIs) supplanting or supplementing traditional tools of government?' *Politische Vierteljahresschrift*, **39** (special issue), 283–98.

Jordan, A., Wurzel, R. and Zito, A. (2013), 'Still the century of "new" environmental policy instruments? Taking stock and exploring the future', *Environmental Politics*, **21**, special issue **22** (1), 155–73.

Jordan, A., Wurzel, R., Zito, A. and Brückner, L. (2004), 'Consumer responsibility-taking and national eco-labelling schemes in Europe', in M. Micheletti, A. Follesdal and D. Stolle (eds), *Politics, Products and Markets: Exploring Political Consumerism, Past and Present*, New Brunswick: Transaction Publishers, 161–80.

Jörgens, H. (2003), *Governance by Diffusion – Implementing Global Norms Through Cross-National Imitation and Learning, FFU-Report 07–2003*, Berlin: Environmental Policy Research Unit, Free University of Berlin.

Karl, H. and Orwat, C. (1999), 'Environmental labelling in Europe: European and national tasks', *European Environment*, **9** (5), 212–20.

Kaspar, M. (2001), *Deregulierung durch Umweltvereinbarungen in der Europäischen Gemeinschaft*, Frankfurt: Peter Lang.

Kassim, H. and Le Galés, P. (2010), 'Exploring governance in a multi-level polity: a policy instrument approach', *West European Politics*, **33** (1), 1–21.

Keohane, N., Revez, R. and Stavins, R. (1998), 'The choice of regulatory instruments in environmental policy', *Harvard Environmental Law Review*, **22** (2), 313–67.

Kern, K., Jörgens, H. and Jänicke, M. (2000), 'Die Diffusion umweltpolitischer Innovationen. Ein Beitrag zur Globalisierung von Umweltpolitik', *Zeitschrift für Umweltpolitik*, **23**, 507–46.

Kern, K., Jörgens, H. and Jänicke, M. (2001), 'The diffusion of environmental policy innovations: a contribution to the globalisation of environmental policy', Discussion Paper FS II 01 – 302, Berlin: Wissenschaftszentrum Berlin für Sozialforschung.

Kingdom of the Netherlands (2005), 'Act of 28 April 2005 Amending the Environment Management Act and the Economic Offences Act for the purpose of establishing a scheme for emission allowance trading with a view to reducing nitrogen oxide emissions', *Bulletin of Acts and Decrees of the Kingdom of the Netherlands*, The Hague: Kingdom of the Netherlands.

Kingdon, W. (1984), *Agendas, Alternatives and Public Policies*, New York: Harper Collins.

Kitschelt, H. (1986), 'Political opportunity structures and political protest: anti-nuclear movements in four democracies', *British Journal of Political Science*, **16** (1), 57–85.

Kitschelt, H. (1991), 'Industrial governance structures, innovation strategies and the case of Japan. Sectoral or cross-national comparative analysis', *International Organization*, **45** (4), 453–93.

Kitschelt, H. and Streeck, W. (eds) (2003), *Germany Beyond the Stable State*, London: Frank Cass.

Kloepfer, M. (2004), *Umweltrecht*, Munich: Verlag C.H. Beck (3rd edition).

Knill, C. (1998), 'European policies: the impact of national administrative systems', *Journal of Public Policy*, **18** (1), 1–28.

Knill, C. (2001), *The Europeanisation of National Administrations: Patterns of Institutional Change and Persistence*, Cambridge: Cambridge University Press.

Knill, C. (2005), 'Introduction: cross-national policy convergence: concepts, approaches and explanatory factors', *Journal of European Public Policy*, **12** (5), 764–74.

Knill, C. and Lenschow, A. (eds) (2000), *Implementing EU Environmental Policy*, Manchester: Manchester University Press.

Koeman, N. (1993), 'Bilateral agreements between government and industry in Dutch environmental law', *European Environmental Law Review*, **2** (6), 174, 183–4.

Kollman, K. and Prakash, A. (2002), 'EMS-based environmental regimes as club goods: examining variations in firm-level adoption of ISO 14001 and EMAS in U.K., U.S. and Germany', *Policy Sciences*, **35** (1), 43–67.

Kooiman, J., (ed.) (1993a), *Modern Governance: New Government-Societal Interactions*, London: Sage.

Kooiman, J. (1993b), 'Social-political governance: introduction', in J. Kooiman (ed.), *Modern Governance. New Government-Societal Interactions*, London: Sage, 1–6.

Kooiman, J. (2003), *Governing as Governance*, London: Sage.

Krämer, L. (1997), 'Recent developments in EC environmental law', in J. Holder (ed.), *The Impact of EC Environmental Law in the UK*, Chichester: John Wiley & Sons, 9–26.

Krämer, L. (2001), 'Umweltvereinbarungen im Gemeinschaftsrecht', in H. Rengeling and H. Hof (eds), *Instrumente des Umweltschutzes im Wirkungsverband*, Baden-Baden: Nomos, 80–94.

Kuik, O., Mulder, M., and Verbruggen, H. (2002), 'CO_2 emissions trading in the Netherlands: an assessment of the proposal of the Dutch CO_2 Trading Commission', paper presented at the 2nd CATEP Workshop on the Design and Integration of National Tradable Permit Schemes for Environmental Protection, UCL, London, 25–26 March.

Lafeld, S. (2003), *Emissionshandel in Deutschland im Zeitalter der Global Governance. Inaugural-Dissertation*, Münster: Westfälische Wilhelms-Universität Münster.

Lascoumes, P. and P. Le Galés (2007), 'Introduction: understanding public policy through its instruments – from the nature of instruments to the sociology of public policy instrumentation', *Governance*, **20** (1), 1–22.

Lauber, V. (1997a), 'Austria: a latecomer which became a pioneer', in M. Andersen and D. Liefferink (eds), *European Environmental Policy: the Pioneers*, Manchester: Manchester University Press, 81–118.

Lauber, V. (1997b), 'Umweltpolitik', in H. Dachs *et al.* (eds), *Handbuch des politischen Systems Österreichs: Die zweite Republik*, Vienna: Manzsche Verlags- und Universitätsbuchhandlung (third edition), 608–27.

Lauber, V. (1997c), 'Freiwillige Umweltvereinbarungen in der Europäischen Union und in Österreich: Bestandsaufnahme und Perspektiven', *Recht der Umwelt*, 107–11.

Lauber, V. (2000), 'The political and institutional setting', in A. Mol, V. Lauber and D. Liefferink (eds), *The Voluntary Approach to Environmental Policy. Joint Environmental Approach to Environmental Policy-making in Europe*, Oxford: Oxford University Press, 32–61.

Lauber, V. (2001), 'Geschichte der Politik zur Umwelt in der Zweiten 'Republik. Vom Nachzügler zum Vorreiter – und zurück?', in S. Hahn and R. Reith (eds), *Umweltgeschichte. Arbeitsfelder – Forschungsansätze – Perspektiven*, Vienna, 181–203.

Lauber, V. (2004), 'The Europeanisation of Austrian environmental policy', in A. Jordan and D. Liefferink (eds), *Environmental Policy in Europe: The Europeanisation of National Environmental Policy*, London: Routledge, 47–63.

Lauber, V. (2007), 'Neo-liberal cap-and-trade schemes: hypotheses on origin and impact', paper at the Energy and Climate Change Policy conference, Salzburg, 24–28 September 2007.

Lauber, V. and Ingram, V. (2000), 'Packaging waste', in A. Mol, V. Lauber and D. Liefferink (eds), *The Voluntary Approach to Environmental Policy*, Oxford: Oxford University Press, 104–55.

Lawrence, A. (2007), 'The Kyoto Protocol and emissions trading in the United Kingdom, 1997–1999: a study of policy transfer', unpublished PhD thesis, Keele University.

Levin, K., Cashore, B., Bernstein, S. and Auld, G. (2012), 'Overcoming the tragedy of super wicked problems: constraining our future selves to ameliorate global climate change', *Policy Sciences*, **45** (2), 123–52.

Liefferink, D. (1996), *Environment and the Nation State: The Netherlands, the European Union and Acid Rain*, Manchester: Manchester University Press.

Liefferink, D. (1997), 'The Netherlands: a net exporter of environmental policy concepts,' in M.K. Andersen and D. Liefferink (eds), *European Environmental Policy: the Pioneers*, Manchester: Manchester University Press, 210–50.

Liefferink, D. (1998), 'New environmental policy instruments in the Netherlands', in J. Golub (ed.), *New Instruments for Environmental Policy in the EU*, London: Routledge, 86–106.

Liefferink, D. (1999), 'The Dutch National Plan for sustainable society', in N. Vig and R. Axelrod (eds), *The Global Environment: Institutions, Law, and Policy*, London: Earthscan, 256–78.

Liefferink, D. and Birkel, K. (2010), 'The Netherlands: a case of "cost-free leadership"', in R.K.W. Wurzel and J. Connelly (eds), *The European Union as a Leader in International Climate Change Politics*, London: Routledge, 147–162.

Liefferink, D. and van der Zouwen, M. (2004), 'The Netherlands: the advantages of being "Mr. Average"', in A. Jordan and D. Liefferink (eds), *Environmental Policy in Europe: The Europeanization of National Environmental Policy*, London: Routledge, 136–53.

Liefferink, D. and Wiering, M. (2007), 'The Netherlands: an integrated participatory approach to environmental policymaking', in A. Breton, G. Brosio, S. Dalmazzone and G. Garrone (eds), *Environmental Governance and Decentralisation*, Cambridge: Cambridge University Press, 558–83.

Linder, S. and Peters, B.G. (1989), 'Instruments of government: perceptions and contexts', *Journal of Public Policy*, **9** (1), 35–58.

Linder, S. and Peters, B.G. (1998), 'The study of policy instruments: four schools of thought', in D.G. Peters and F. van Nispen (eds), *Public Policy Instruments: Evaluating the Tools of Public Administration*, Cheltenham: Edward Elgar, 33–45.

Lowe, P. and Flynn, A. (1989), 'Environmental policy and politics in the 1980s', in J. Mohan (ed.), *The Political Geography of Contemporary Britain*, Macmillan: Basingstoke, 255–79.

Lowe, P. and Ward, S. (eds) (1998), *British Environmental Policy and Europe*, Routledge: London.

Lowi, T. (1972), 'Four systems of politics, policy and choice', *Public Administration Review*, **32** (4), 298–310.

260 *Environmental governance in Europe*

Lübbe-Wolff, G. (2001), 'Der britische Emissionshandel – Vorbild für Deutschland?', *Energiewirtschaftliche Fragen*, **51** (6), 342–5.

Luhmann, N. (1982), *The Differentiation of Society*, New York: Columbia University Press.

Luhmann, N. (1984), *Soziale Systeme. Grundriß einer allgemeinen Theorie*, Frankfurt: Surhkamp Verlag.

Lulofs, K. (2000), 'Implementation of EMAS in the Netherlands: a case study on national implementation, environmental effectiveness, allocative efficiency, productive efficiency and administrative costs', Research Paper 2000-b-5, Paris: CERNA.

Luther, K. and Müller, W. (1992a), 'Consociationalism and the Austrian political system', *West European Politics*, **15** (1), 1–15.

Luther, K. and Müller, W. (1992b), 'Austrian consociationalism: victim of its own success', *West European Politics*, **15** (1), 201–23.

Macrory, R. (1991), 'Environmental law: shifting discretions and the new formalism, in O. Lomas (ed.), *Frontiers of Environmental Law*, London: Chancery Law, 8–23.

Macrory, R. and Purdy, R. (1997), 'The enforcement of EC environmental law against member states', J. Holder (ed.), *The Impact of EC Environmental Law in the UK*, Chichester: John Wiley & Sons, 27–50.

Maier, H. (1980), *Die ältere Staats- und Verwaltungslehre*, Munich: Beck (2nd edition).

Majone, G. (1976), 'Choice among policy instruments for pollution control', *Policy Analysis*, **2**, 589–613.

Majone, G. (1991), 'Cross-national sources of regulatory policy making in the Europe and the US', *Journal of Public Policy* **11** (1), 79–106.

Majone, G. (1994), 'The rise of the regulatory state', *West European Politics*, **17** (3), 77–101.

Majone, G. (1996), *Regulating Europe*, London: Routledge.

Malek, T. and Töller, A. (2001), 'The Eco-management and Audit Scheme (EMAS) Regulation', in H. Heinelt, T. Malek, R. Smith and A. Töller (eds), *European Union Environmental Policy and New Forms of Governance*, Aldershot: Ashgate, 43–60.

Marinetto, M. (2003), 'Governing beyond the centre', *Political Studies*, **51** (3), 592–608.

March, J. and Olsen, J. (1989), *Rediscovering Institutions*, Free Press: New York.

March, J. and Olsen, J. (1998), 'The institutional dynamics of international political orders', *International Organisation*, **52** (4), 943–69.

Marks, G., Hooghe, L. and Blank, K. (1996), 'European integration from the 1980s', *Journal of Common Market Studies*, **34** (3), 341–78.

Marshall Report (1998), *Economic Instruments and the Business Use of Energy*, London: HM Treasury, http://www.hm-treasury.gov.uk/media//C4314/marshall.pdf.

Matthes, F.C. and Schafhausen, F. (2007), 'Germany', in D. Ellerman, B. Buchner and C. Carraro (eds), *Allocation in the European Emissions Trading Scheme*, Cambridge: Cambridge University Press, 72–105.

Mayntz, R. (1993), 'Governing failures and the problem of governability: some comments on a theoretical paradigm', in J. Kooiman (ed.), *Modern Governance*, London: Sage, 9–20.

Mayntz, R. (2008), 'Von der Steuerungstheorie zu Global Governance', *Politische Vierteljahreschrift*, **41** (special issue), 43–60.

Mayntz, R. and Scharpf, F. (1995), 'Steuerung und Selbstorganisation in staatsnahen Sektoren', in R. Mayntz and F. Scharpf (eds), *Gesellschaftliche Selbstregulierung und politische Steuerung*, Frankfurt: Campus Verlag, 9–38.

Mazey, S. and Richardson, J. (1993a), 'Conclusion: a European policy style?', in S. Mazey and J. Richardson (eds.), *Lobbying in the European Community*, Oxford: Oxford University Press, 246–58.

Mazey, S. and Richardson, J. (1993b), 'EC policy making: an emerging European policy style?' in D. Liefferink, P. Lowe and A. Mol (eds), *European Integration and Environmental Policy*, London: Belhaven, 114–25.

Mazey, S. and Richardson, J. (1996a), 'EU policy-making: a garbage can or an anticipatory and consensual policy style?', in Y. Mény, P. Muller and J.-L. Quermonne (eds), *Adjusting to Europe, the Impact of the European Union on National Institutions and Policies*, London: Routledge, 41–58.

Mazey, S. and Richardson, J. (1996b), 'The logic of organisation: interest groups', in J. Richardson (ed.), *European Union: Power and Policy-Making*, London: Routledge, 200–215.

McCormick, J. (2001), *Environmental Policy in the European Union*, Houndmills, Basingstoke: Palgrave.

Meckling, J. (2011), *Carbon Coalitions: Business, Climate Politics, and the Rise of Emissions Trading*, Cambridge, Mass.: MIT Press.

Micheletti, M, Follesdal, A. and Stolle, D. (eds) (2004), *Politics, Products and Markets. Exploring Political Consumerism Past and Present*, New Brunswick and London: Transaction Publisher.

Mickwitz, P. (2003), 'A framework for evaluating environmental policy instruments', *Evaluation*, **9** (4), 415–36.

Middendorp, C. (1991), *Ideology in Dutch Politics: the Democratic System Reconsidered, 1970–1985*, Assen and Maastricht: Van Gorcum.

Mingers, J. (1998), *Self-producing Systems: Implications and Applications of Autopoiesis*, London: Plenum Press.

Ministry of Infrastructure and Environment (2009), 'Kilometre charge: most people will end up paying less', *Nieuwsbericht*, 14 November 2009, http://www.ministryofinfrastructureandtheenvironment.nl/news/newsitems/kilometre charge.

Mol, A., Lauber, V. and Liefferink, D. (eds) (2000), *The Voluntary Approach to Environmental Policy. Joint Environmental Approach to Environmental Policymaking in Europe*, Oxford: Oxford University Press.

Müller, E. (1986), *Innenpolitik der Umweltpolitik. Soziale-liberale Umweltpolitik – (Ohn)Macht durch Organisation?*, Opladen: Westdeutscher Verlag.

Müller, W. (1992), 'Austrian governmental institutions: do they matter?', *West European Politics*, **15** (special issue), 92–131.

Müller-Brandeck-Bocquet, G. (1996), *Die institutionelle Dimension der Umweltpolitik*, Baden-Baden: Nomos.

Nadai, A. (1999), 'Conditions for the development of a product ecolabel', *European Environment*, **9** (5), 202–11.

National Audit Office (2004), *The UK Emission Trading Scheme*, London: National Audit Office.

Naughton, P. (2007), 'UK to phase out traditional light bulb by 2011', *Times Online*, 27 September.

NEA (2011), 'Netherlands Emissions Authority', http://english.verkeerenwater staat.nl/english/topics/organization/organization_of_the_ministry/organization_ elements/netherlands_emissions_authority/ (accessed 5.11.2011).

Niles, M. and Lubell, M. (2012), 'Integrative frontiers in environmental policy', *Policy Studies Journal*, 40 (S1), 41–64.

Nilsson, M., Jordan, A., Turnpenny, J., Hertin, J., Nykvist, B. and Russel, D. (2008), 'The use and non-use of policy appraisal tools in public policy making: an analysis of three European countries and the European Union', *Policy Sciences*, **41** (4), 335–55.

Nordhaus, W. (2007), 'To tax or not to tax: alternative approaches to slowing global warming', *Review of Environmental Economics and Policy*, **1** (1), 26–44.

North, D. (1990), *Institutions, Institutional Change and Economic Performance*, Cambridge: Cambridge University Press.

Northern Ireland Environment Agency (2009), *Measuring the effectiveness of Environmental Management Systems*, Belfast: Northern Ireland Environment Agency.

OECD [Organisation for Economic Co-operation and Development] (1980), *Pollution Charges in Practice*, Paris: OECD.

OECD (1991), *Environmental Labelling in OECD Countries*, Paris: OECD.

OECD (1993), *Taxation and the Environment: Complementary Policies*, Paris: OECD.

OECD (1994), *Managing the Environment: The Role of Economic Instruments*, Paris: OECD.

OECD (1995a), *Environmental Performance Reviews: Austria*, Paris: OECD.

OECD (1995b), *Environmental Taxes in the OECD Countries*, Paris: OECD.

OECD (1995c), *OECD Environmental Performance Reviews: Netherlands*, Paris: OECD.

OECD (1997), *Eco-labelling: Actual Effects of Selected Programmes*, Paris: OECD.

OECD (1999a), *Economic Instruments for Pollution Control and Natural Resources Management in OECD Countries: A Survey*, Paris: OECD.

OECD (1999b), *Environmental Taxes and Green Reform*, Paris: OECD.

OECD (1999c), *Voluntary Approaches for Environmental Policy*, Paris: OECD.

OECD (2001), *Environmentally Related Taxes in OECD Countries. Issues and Strategies*, Paris: OECD.

OECD (2003a), *Voluntary Approaches for Environmental Policy*, Paris: OECD.

OECD (2003b), *OECD Environmental Performance Review: Austria*, Paris: OECD.

OECD (2003c), *OECD Environmental Performance Review: Netherlands*, Paris: OECD.

Bibliography   263

OECD (2009), *Ensuring Environmental Compliance; Trends and Good Practices*, Paris: OECD.

OECD (2010), *OECD/EEA Database on Instruments Used for Environmental Policy and Natural Resources Management*, http://www2.oecd.org/ecoinst/queries/index.htm (accessed 5.1.11).

Öko-Institut e.V. (1998), *New Instruments for Sustainability- the New Contribution of Voluntary Agreements to Environmental Policy*, Freiburg: Öko-Institut e.V.

Opschoor, J. and Vos, H. (1989), *Economic Instruments for Environmental Protection*, Paris: OECD.

Packaging Europe (2010), 'Courtauld Commitment 2 targets and signatories unveiled', http://www.packagingeurope.com/PrintFriendly.aspx?nNewsID=34826 (accessed 1.6.2010).

Padgett, S. (2003), 'Between synthesis and emulation: EU policy transfer in the power sector', *Journal of European Public Policy*, **10** (2), 227–45.

Palumbo, A. (2010), 'Introduction. Governance: meanings, themes, narratives and questions', in R. Bellamy and A. Palumbo (eds), *From Government to Regulation*, Farnham: Ashgate, xi–xxx.

Patashnik, P. (2008), *Reforms at Risk*, Princeton: Princeton University Press.

Pearce, D. *et al.* (2000), *Market-based Instruments in the UK*, Report for the UK Round Table on Sustainable Development, London and Norwich: EFTEC/CSERGE, http://www.uea.ac.uk/env/cserge/research/fut_governance/papers.htm.

Pedersen, L. (2006), 'Transfer and transformation in processes of Europeanization', *European Journal of Political Research*, **45** (6), 985–1021.

Peglau, R. (2007), 'Peglau-Liste: anzahl der gemäss ISO 14001 zertifizierten und/oder nach EMAS registrierten', http://www.14001news.de/ISO___EMAS/Peglau-Liste/body_peglau-liste.html (accessed 07.2007).

Pehle, H. (1998), *Das Bundesministerium für Umwelt, Naturschutz und Reaktorsicherheit: Ausgegrenzt statt integriert?* Wiesbaden: Deutscher Universitätsverlag.

Pesendorfer, D. (2007), *Paradigmenwechsel in der Umweltpolitik. Von den Anfängen der Umwelt- zu einer Nachhaltigkeitspolitik: Modellfall Österreich*, Wiesbaden: VS Verlag für Sozialwissenschaften.

Pesendorfer, D. and Lauber, V. (2006), 'Umweltpolitik', in Dachs, H. et al. (eds), *Handbuch Politik in Österreich*, Vienna: Manz Verlag, 663–74.

Peters, B.G. (2002), 'The politics of tool choice', in L. Salamon (ed.), *The Tools of Government. A Guide to the New Governance*, Oxford: Oxford University Press, 552–64.

Pierre, J. and Peters, B.G. (2000), *Governance, Politics and the State*, Basingstoke: Macmillan.

Pierson, P. (1993), 'When effect becomes cause: policy feedback and political change', *World Politics*, **45** (4), 595–628.

Pierson, P. (2000), 'Increasing returns, path dependence, and the study of politics', *American Political Science Review*, **94** (2), 251–68.

Pigou, A. (1920), *The Economics of Welfare*, London: Macmillan.

Pop, V. (2011), 'China joins legal battle against EU aviation tax', *EUobserver.com*, http://euobserver.com/884/114700 (accessed 21.12.2011).

264   *Environmental governance in Europe*

Powell, W. (1991), 'Neither market nor hierarchy: network forms of organization', in G. Thompson, J. Frances, R. Levačić, and J. Mitchell (eds), *Markets, Hierarchies & Networks: the Coordination of Social Life*, London and Newbury Park: Sage Publications, 265–76.

Prakash, A. and Gugerty, M. (2010), 'Trust but verify? Voluntary regulation in the non-profit sector', *Regulation and Governance*, **4** (1), 22–47.

Quality Network (2012), 'ISO14000 – introduction', http://www.quality.co.uk/iso14000.htm#intro (accessed 9.1.2012).

Radaelli, C. (2000), 'Policy transfer in the European Union: institutional isomorphism as a source of legitimacy', Governance, **13** (1), 25–43.

Raschke, J. (2001) *Die Zukunft der Grünen."So kann man nicht regieren"*, Frankfurt/New York: Campus Verlag.

RCEP [Royal Commission on Environmental Pollution] (1972), *Pollution in Some British Estuaries and Coastal Waters*, Cmnd 5054, London: HMSO.

RCEP (1979), *Agriculture and Pollution*, Cmnd 7644, London: HMSO.

RCEP (1984), *Tackling Pollution*, Cmnd 9149, London: HMSO.

RCEP (1998), *Setting Environmental Standards, Cmnd 4053*, London: HMSO.

Reiche, D. and Krebs, C. (1999), *Der Einstieg in die ökologische Steuerreform*, Frankfurt: Peter Lang.

Rengeling, H. and Hof, H. (eds) (2001), *Instrumente des Umweltschutzes im Wirkungsverband*, Baden-Baden: Nomos.

Rhodes, R. (1996), 'The new governance: governing without governance', *Political Studies*, **44** (4), 652–67.

Rhodes, R. (1997), *Understanding Governance: Policy Networks, Governance, Reflexivity and Accountability*, Milton Keynes: Open University Press.

Richards, D. and Smith, M. (2002), *Governance and Public Policy*, Oxford: Oxford University Press.

Richardson, J., Gustafsson, G. and Jordan, G. (1982), 'The concept of policy style', in J. Richardson (ed.), *Policy Styles in Western Europe*, London: George Allen & Unwin, 1–16.

Richardson, J. and Watts, N. (1985), *National Policy Styles and the Environment: Britain and West Germany Compared*, Berlin: Wissenschaftzentrum Berlin für Sozialforschung.

Rijkswaterstaat (2011), *Water Management in The Netherlands*, Den Haag: Rijkswaterstaat.

Rietbergen-McCracken, J. and Abaza, H. (eds) (2000), *Economic Instruments for Environmental Management*, London: UNEP and Earthscan.

Risse, T. and Lehmkuhl, U. (2007), 'Governance in Räumen begrenzter Staatlichkeit', *Aus Politik und Zeitgeschichte*, 20–21, 3–9.

RIVM [Rijksinstituut voor Volksgtezondheit en Milieu or National Institute for Public Health and the Environment] (2004), *Natuurbalans 2004*, Bilthoven: RIVM.

Roberts, G. (2011), 'West London freed from congestion charging', *The Independent*, 4 January 2011.

Rose, C. (1990), *The Dirty Man of Europe*, London: Simon and Schuster.

Rose, R. (1991), 'Lesson drawing across nations', *Journal of Public Policy*, **11** (1), 3–30.

Rose, R. (1993), *Lesson Drawing In Public Policy*, Chatham House: New York.

Bibliography 265

Rosenau, J. and Czempiel, E.-O. (eds) (1992), *Governance without Government*, Cambridge: Cambridge University Press.

Rudolph, S. (2005), *Handelbare Emissionslizenzen*, Marburg: Metropolis.

Sabatier, P. (1999), 'The need for better theories', in P. Sabatier (ed.), *Theories of the Policy Process*, Boulder: Westview Press, 3–17.

Salamon, L. (ed.) (2002a), *The Tools of Government: A Guide to the New Governance*, Oxford: Oxford University Press.

Salamon, L. (2002b), 'The' new governance and the tools of public action: an introduction', in L.M. Salomon (ed.), *The Tools of Government: A Guide to the New Governance*, Oxford: Oxford University Press, 1–47.

Salamon, L. (2002c), 'The tools approach and the new governance: conclusion and implications', in L. Salamon (ed.), *The Tools of Government: A Guide to the New Governance*, Oxford: Oxford University Press, 600–10.

Salmons, R. (2000), *Case Studies of Negotiated Environmental Agreements: The UK: Agreement with the Farm Films Producers Group*, London: CSERGE.

Salmons, R. (2001), *Case Studies of Negotiated Environmental Agreements: The Agreement on Energy Efficiency Improvement*, London: CSERGE.

Sandhövel, A. (1994), *Marktorientierte Instrumente in der Umweltpolitik*, Opladen: Westdeutscher Verlag.

Sartori, G. (1970), 'Concept misformation in comparative politics', *American Political Science Review*, **64** (4), 1033–53.

Schaffrin, A. (2011), 'Political and economic capacities in national climate policies – a comparative analysis of 25 EU member states', paper presented at the 6th ECPR General Conference 2011, Reykavik.

Schafhausen, F. (1999), 'Zertifikatslösugen – Konzeptionelle Schwierigkeiten, instrumetelles Leistungsvermögen, erforderliche Rahmenbedingungen', *Arbeitsgemeinschaft für Umweltfragen*, 25 November 1999, Bonn: AGU.

Scharpf, F. (1994), 'Games real actors could play. positive and negative coordination in embedded negotiations', *Journal of Theoretical Politics*, **6** (1), 27–53.

Scharpf. F. (1996), 'Negative and positive integration in the political economy of European welfare states', in G. Marks, F. Scharpf, P. Schmitter and W. Streeck (eds), *Governance in the European Union*, London: Sage, 15–39.

Scharpf, F. (1997), *Games Real Actors Play: Actor-Centred Institutionalism in Policy Research*, Boulder: Westview Press.

Schnabl, G. (2005), 'The evolution of environmental agreements at the level of the European Union', in E. Croci (ed.), *The Handbook of Environmental Voluntary Agreements: Design, Implementation and Evaluation Issues*, Dordrecht: Springer, 93–106.

Schneider, V. (2004), 'State theory, governance and the logic of regulation and administrative control', in A. Warntjen and A. Wonka (eds), *Governance in Europe*, Baden-Baden: Nomos Verlagsgesellschaft, 25–41.

Schuppert, G.F. (2008), 'Governance – auf der Suche nach Konturen eines "anerkannt uneindeutigen Begriffs"', *Politische Vierteljahreschrift*, **41**, special issue, 13–40.

Schuppert, G.F. and Zürn, M. (eds) (2008), 'Governance in einer sich wandelnden Welt', *Politische Vierteljahreschrift*, **41**, special issue, 1–600.

Schwar, B. (1999), *Umweltzeichen und betrieblicher Umweltschutz*, Vienna: Verlag Österreich.

266   *Environmental governance in Europe*

Scruggs, L. (1999), 'Institutions and environmental performance in seventeen western democracies', *British Journal of Political Science*, **29** (1), 1–31.

Scruggs, L. (2001), 'Is there really a link between neo-corporatism and environmental performance? Updated evidence and new data for the 1980s and 1990s', *British Journal of Political Science*, **31** (4), 686–92.

Sevenster, M., Wielders, L., Bergsma, G. and Vroohof, J. (2007), 'Environmental indices for the Dutch packaging tax', Report, Delft: CE Delft.

Siebert, H. (1976), *Analyse der Instrumente der Umweltpolitik*, Göttingen: Schwartz.

Skjærseth, J. and Wettestad, J. (2008), *EU Emissions Trading: Initiation, Decision-making and Implementation*, Aldershot: Ashgate.

Skjærseth, J. and Wettestad, J. (2010), 'Fixing the EU Emissions trading system? understanding the post-2012 changes', *Global Environmental Politics*, **10** (4), 101–23.

Smith, A. (2004), 'Policy transfer in the development of UK climate policy', *Policy and Politics*, **32** (1), 79–93.

Smith, S. and Ingram, H. (2002), 'Policy tools and democracy', in L. Salamon (ed.), *The Tools of Government. A Guide to the New Governance*, Oxford: Oxford University Press, 565–84.

Smith, S. and Swierzbinski, J. (2007), 'Assessing the performance of the UK Emissions Trading Scheme', *Springer Online*, **37**, 131–58, http://www.springerlink.com/content/0331110775841480/?p=e2ec0371e279476d8262cb3 de1c4dbbe&pi=8.

Snel, M. (2000), 'Green tax reforms: the Dutch experience, paper presented at the Symposium on "Green Fiscal Reforms in Europe"', Paris, 10–11 October.

Sorrell, S. (1999), 'Why sulphur trading failed in the UK', in S. Sorrell and J. Skea (eds), *Pollution For Sale*, Cheltenham: Edward Elgar, 354–79.

Spitalsky, H. (1994), 'Eco-labelling: österreichisch – europaweit' in C. Mittendorfer (ed.), *Umweltzeichen und Öko-Audit. Was können die sanften Instrument?*, Vienna: Bundesarbeiterkammer, 4–11.

Sprenger, R.-U. (2000), 'Market-based instruments in environmental policies: the lessons of experience', in M.S. Andersen and R.-U. Sprenger (eds), *Market-based Instruments for Environmental Management. Politics and Institutions*, Cheltenham: Edward Elgar, 3–26.

SPD-Grüne (2002), *Erneuerung – Gerechtigkeit – Nachhaltigkeit*, Berlin: Sozial Demokratische Partei Deutschlands – Die Grünen.

SRU [Rat von Sachverständigen für Umweltfragen] (1974), *Die Abwasserabgabe – Wassergütewirtschaftliche und gesamtökologische Wirkungen. 2. Sondergutachten*, Wiesbaden: Rat von Sacherverständigen für Umweltfragen.

SRU (1978), *Umweltgutachten 1978*, Bundestags-Drucksache 8/1938.

SRU (2002), *Umweltgutachten 2002, Für eine neue Vorreiterrolle*, Berlin: Rat von Sachverständigen für Umweltfragen.

Stavins, R. and Whitehead, B. (1992), 'Dealing with pollution', *Environment*, **34** (7), 7–42.

Stichting Milieukeur (2011), 'Milieukeur. Een duurzame keuze', http://www.smk.nl/nl/s357/SMK/Programma-s/Milieukeur/c324-Milieukeur (accessed 3.12.2011).

Stoker, G. (1998), 'Governance as theory', *International Social Science Journal*, **155**, 17–28.

Stone, D. (2004), 'Transfer agents and global networks in the "transnationalization" of policy', *Journal of European Public Policy*, **11** (3), 546–66.

Stoppford, J. and Strange, S. (1991), *Rival States, Rival Firms. Competition for World Market Shares*, Cambridge: Cambridge University Press.

Streeck, W. and Schmitter, P. (1991), 'From national corporatism to transnational pluralism: organized interests in the Single European Market', *Politics and Society*, **19** (2), 133–64.

Streeck, W. and Thelen, K. (eds) (2005a), *Beyond Continuity: Institutional Change in Advanced Political Economies*, Oxford: Oxford University Press.

Streeck, W. and Thelen, K. (2005b), 'Introduction: institutional change in advanced political economies', in W. Streeck and K. Thelen (eds.), *Beyond Continuity: Institutional Change in Advanced Political Economies*, Oxford: Oxford University Press, 1–39.

Taschner, T. (1998), 'Environmental management systems: the European regulation', in J. Golub (ed.), *New Instruments for Environmental Policy in the EU*, London: Routledge, 215–41.

Task Force Environment and the Internal Market (1990), *'1992' The Environmental Dimension: Task Force Report on the Environment and the Internal Market*, Bonn: Economica Verlag GmbH.

Taylor, C., Pollard, S., Rocks, S. and Angus, A. (2012), 'Selecting policy instruments for better environmental regulation', *Environmental Policy and Governance*, **22** (4), 268–92.

Ten Brink, P. and Medhurst, J. (1999), 'Environmental agreements', *Greener Management International*, **26**, Summer 1999, 33–56.

Tews, K. (2002), *Der Diffusionsansatz für die vergleichende Policy-Analyse. Wurzeln und Potentiale eines Konzepts. Eine Literaturstudie, FFU-Report 02-2002,* Berlin: Environmental Policy Research Unit, Free University of Berlin.

Tews, K., Busch, P. and Jörgens, H. (2003), 'The diffusion of new environmental policy instruments', *European Journal of Political Research*, **42** (4), 569–600.

Thelen, K. (2004), *How Institutions Evolve: the Political Economy of Skills in Germany, Britain, the United States and Japan*, Cambridge: Cambridge University Press.

Tindale, S. and Holtham, G. (1996), *Green Tax Reform*, London: IPPR.

Toke, D. and Lauber, V. (2006), 'Anglo-Saxon and German approaches to neoliberalism and environmental policy: the case of financing renewable energy', *Geoforum*, **38** (4), 677–87.

Tollefson, C., Gale, F. and Haley, D. (2008), *Setting the Standard: Certification, Governance and the Forest Stewardship Council*, Vancouver: UBC Press.

Tömmel, I. (2009), 'Modes of governance and the institutional structure of the European Union', in I. Tömmel and A. Verdun (eds), *Innovative Governance in the European Union. The Politics of Multilevel Policymaking*, Boulder: Lynne Rienner Publishers, 9–26.

Tömmel, I. and Verdun, A. (eds) (2009a), *Innovative Governance in the European Union. The Politics of Multilevel Policymaking*, Boulder: Lynne Rienner Publishers.

268 *Environmental governance in Europe*

Tömmel, I. and Verdun, A. (2009b), 'Innovative governance in the European Union', in I. Tömmel and A. Verdun (eds), *Innovative Governance in the European Union. The Politics of Multilevel Policymaking*, Boulder: Lynne Rienner Publishers, 1–8.

Töpfer, K. (1989), 'Ecological modernisation of the industrialised state: a federal perspective', in T. Ellwein *et al.* (eds), *Yearbook on Government and Public Administration*, Baden-Baden: Nomos, 489–520.

Transparency International (2011), *Global Corruption Report*, London: Earthscan.

Tribe, K. (1984), 'Cameralism and the science of government', *Journal of Modern History*, **56** (2), 263–84.

Trubek, D., Cottrell, P. and Nance, M. (2006), 'Soft law, hard law and European integration: towards a theory of hybridity', in G. de Búrca and J. Scott (eds), *Law and New Governance in the EU and the US*, Oxford: Hart Publishing, 65–94.

Trubek, D. and Trubek, L. (2007), 'New governance and legal regulation: complementarity, rivalry or transformation', *Columbia Journal of European Law*, **13**, 542.

True, J., Jones, B. and Baumgartner, F. (1999), 'Punctuated-equilibrium theory: explaining stability and change in American policymaking', in P. Sabatier (ed.), *Theories of the Policy Process*, Boulder: Westview Press, 97–115.

Tweede Kamer der Staten-Generaal (1990), *National Environmental Policy Plan Plus'*, 21 137, no. 20–21, The Hague: Tweede Kamer.

UBA [Umweltbundesamt] (1994), *Umweltabgaben in der Praxis,* Berlin: Umweltbundesamt.

UBA (1996), *Das Europäische Umweltzeichen: Wege zum produktbezogenen Umweltschutz in Europa*, Berlin: Umweltbundesamt.

UBA (1998a), *Erfolgskontrolle Umweltzeichen für Produkte und Dienstleistungen,* Berlin: Umweltbundesamt.

UBA (1998b), *Logo? Ökologisch ausgerichtete Kennzeichen für Produkte und Dienstleistungen*, Berlin: Umweltbundesamt.

UBA (1999), *Selbstverpflichtungen und normersetzende Umweltverträge als Instrumente des Umweltschutzes*, Berlin: Umweltbundesamt.

UBA (2008), '30 years of the Blue Angel: start-up festivals for the big anniversary', *Newsletter*, **21**, March 2008, Dessau: Umweltbundesamt, http://www.blauer-engel.de/en/blauer_engel/press/newsletter/newsletter_detail.php?we_objectID=166 (accessed 15.11.2010).

UBA (2010a), 'Umweltzeichen und Markenentwicklung', http://www.blauer-engel.de/de/blauer_engel/index.php (accessed 15.11.2010).

UBA (2010b), 'Deutschlands Umweltzeichen in der Offensive', *Pressemitteilung*, No.49/2010, Dessau: Umweltbundesamt.

UBA (2011a), *Umweltbezogen Steuern und Gebühren, Ökologische Steuerreform, Ökologische Finanzreform,* Dessau: Umweltbundesamt, http://www.umweltbundesamt-daten-zur-umwelt.de/umweltdaten/public/theme.do?nodeIdent=2621 (accessed 11.10.2011).

UBA (2011b), *Umweltschädliche Subventionen,* Dessau: Umweltbundesamt, http://www.umweltbundesamt-daten-zur-umwelt.de/umweltdaten/public/theme.do?nodeIdent=5897 (accessed 11.10.2011).

UGA [Umweltgutachterausschuss] (2007), 'Umweltgutachterausschuss beim Bundesministerium für Umwelt, Naturschutz und Reaktorsicherheit', http://www.uga.de/ (accessed 20.12. 2007).

Van Apeldoorn, B., de Graaff, N. and Overbeek, H. (2012), 'The rebound of the capitalist state: the rearticulation of the state–capital nexus in the global crisis', *Globalizations*, **9** (4), 467–70.

Van Asselt, H. (2010), 'Emissions trading: the enthusiastic adoption of an "alien" instrument', in A. Jordan, D. Huitema, H. van Asselt, T. Rayner and F. Berkhout (eds), *Climate Change Policy in the European Union*, Cambridge: Cambridge University Press, 125–44.

Van den Bos, J. (1991), *Dutch EC Policy Making: A Model Guided Approach to Coordination and Negotiation*, Amsterdam: Thesis Publishers.

Van der Woerd, F. (1998), 'Environmental management systems in the Netherlands: towards the third generation of environmental licensing?', in U. Collier (ed.), *Deregulation in the European Union: Environmental Perspectives*, Routledge: London, 198–211.

Van Kersbergen, K. and van Waarden, F. (2004), '"Governance" as a bridge between disciplines', *European Journal of Political Research*, **43** (2), 143–171.

Van Tatenhove, J. (1993), *Beleidsvoeringsprocessen in het Nederlandse Milieubeleid in de Periode 1970–1990*, Wageningen: Agricultural University.

Van Tatenhove, J., Mak, J. and Liefferink, D. (2006), 'The Inter-play between formal and informal practices', *Perspectives on European Politics and Society*, **7** (1), 8–24.

Van Vliet, M. (1993) 'Environmental regulation of business: options and constraints for communicative governance', in J. Kooiman (ed.), *Modern Governance*, London: Sage, 105–18.

Van Vliet, M. (1994), 'Controlling VOCs by government – industry consensus', *Greener Management International*, 6 April, 41–8.

Van Waarden, F. (1995), 'Persistence of national policy styles: a study of their institutional foundations', in B. Ungerer and F. van Waarden (eds), *Convergence or Diversity? Internationalization and Economic Policy Response*, Aldershot: Avebury, 333–72.

Varone, F. (1999), *Le choix des instruments des politiques publiques*, Bern: Verlag Paul Haupt.

Vedung, E. (1997), 'Policy instruments: typologies and theories', in M.L. Bemelmans-Videc, R.C. Rist and E. Vedung (eds), *Carrots, Sticks & Sermons. Policy Instruments & Their Evaluation*, New Brunswick and London: Transaction Publishers, 21–58.

Vermeend, W. and van der Vaart, J. (1998), *Greening Taxes: the Dutch Model*, Deventer: Kluwer.

Vogel, D. (1986), *National Styles of Regulation: Environmental Policy in Great Britain and the United States*, Ithaca: Cornell University Press.

Vogel, D. (1998), 'EU environmental policy and the GATT/WTO', in J. Golub (ed.), *Global Competition and EU Environmental Policy*, London: Routledge, 142–60.

Voluntary Initiative (2010), 'Origins', Voluntary Initiative home page, http://www.voluntaryinitiative.org.uk/content/About.aspx (accessed 4.1.2011).

270 *Environmental governance in Europe*

Voß, J.-P. (2007) 'Innovation processes in governance: the development of "emission trading" as a new policy instrument', *Science and Public Policy*, **34** (5), 329–43.

VNO-NCW [The Confederation of Netherlands Industry and Employers] (1999), *Environmental Agreements in the Netherlands*, The Hague: VNO-NCW.

VROM (1992), *The Netherlands' Environmental Tax on Fuels: Questions and Answers*, The Hague: VROM.

VROM (2004), *Decision on Trade in NOx Emissions Rights Submitted to Council of State*, VROM: The Hague, http://www2.vrom.nl/pagina.html?id=9186 (accessed 5.11.2011).

VROM (2005), *Unique Trading System of NOx Emission Rights to Start in June*, 31 May 2005, http://international.vrom.nl/pagina.html?id=9411.

VROM (2006), 'Van Geel sluit convenant schone vrachtauto's in binnensteden', http://www.vrom.nl/pagina.html?id=23058&term=Convenant (accessed 6.11.2007).

VROM (2007), 'Onderlinge samenwerking vatsgelegd in bestuursakkoord waterketen', 5 July, http://www.vrom.nl/pagina.html?id=32072 (accessed 8.9.2007).

VROM (2010), 'Environmental tax on waste', accessed 3 October 2010, http://international.vrom.nl/pagina.html?id=37636.

Waldegrave, W. (1985), 'The British approach', *Environmental Policy and Law*, **15** (3–4), 106–15.

Wallace, W. (1983), 'Less than a federation, more than a regime', in H. Wallace, W. Wallace and C. Webb (eds), *Policy Making in the European Community*, John Wiley: London (second edition), 403–36.

Waltman, J. (1987), 'The strength of policy inheritance', in J. Waltman and D. Studlar (eds), *Political Economy: Public Policies in the United States and Britain*, Jackson, Mississippi and London: University of Mississippi, 259–69.

Ward, H. and Cao, X. (2012), 'Domestic and international influences on green taxation', *Comparative Political Studies*, **45** (9), 1075–103.

Weale, A. (1992a), *The New Politics of Pollution Control*, Manchester: Manchester University Press.

Weale, A. (1992b),'Vorsprung durch Technik? The Politics of German Environmental Regulation', in K. Dyson (ed.), *The Politics of German Regulation*, Aldershot: Dartmouth, 159–83.

Weale, A. (1996), 'Environmental rules and rule-making in the European Union', *Journal of European Public Policy*, **3** (4), 594–611.

Weale, A. (1997), 'The United Kingdom', in M. Jänicke and H. Weidner (eds), *National Environmental Policies*, Berlin: Springer Verlag, 89–108.

Weale, A., O'Riordan, T. and Kramme, L. (1991), *Controlling Pollution in the Round. Change and Choice in Environmental Regulation in Britain and West Germany*, London: Anglo-German Foundation.

Weale, A., Pridham, G., Cini, M., Konstadakopulos, D., Porter, M. and Flynn, B. (2000), *Environmental Governance in Europe*, Oxford: Oxford University Press.

Weizsäcker, E. U. von and Jesinghaus, J. (1992), *Ecological Tax Reform*, London: Zed Books.

Wenk, M. (2005), *The European Union's Eco-Management and Audit Scheme (EMAS)*, Dordrecht: Springer.

Wettestad, J. (2005), 'The making of the 2003 EU Emissions Trading Directive: an ultra quick process due to entrepreneurial proficiency?', *Global Environmental Politics*, **5** (1), 1–23.

Wicke, L. (1987), *Umweltökonomie*, Munich: Franz Wahlen (2nd edition).

WIFO (1995), *Makroökonomische und sektorale Auswirkungen einer umweltorientierten Energiebesteuerung in Österreich*, Vienna: Österreichisches Institut für Wirtschaftsforschung.

WIFO (1998), *Energieverbrauch, CO_2-Emissionen und Energiebesteuerung. Simulation mir dem Energiemodell Daedalus*, Vienna: Österreichisches Institut für Wirtschaftsforschung.

WIFO (2000), *Ein Erstansatz für ein nationales CO_2-Emissions-Trading System*, Vienna: Österreichisches Institut für Wirtschaftsforschung.

Winter, G. (2010), 'The climate is no commodity: taking stock of the Emissions Trading System', *Journal of Environmental Law*, **22** (1), 1–25.

Wirtschaftskammer (2002), 'Freiwillige Vereinbarungen', Vienna Wirtschaftskammer Österreich (unpublished memo).

Wossink, A. (2003), 'The Dutch Nutrient Quota System: past experience and lessons for the future', paper prepared for the OECD workshop on the Ex-Post Evaluation of Tradeable Permit Regimes, 21–22 January, Paris.

Wright, R. (2000), 'Implementing voluntary policy instruments: the experience of the EU Ecolabel Award Scheme', in C. Knill and A. Lenschow (eds), *Implementing EU Environmental Policy: New Directions and Old Problems*, Manchester: Manchester University Press, 87–115.

Wurzel, R. (2000), 'Flying into unexpected turbulence: the German EU Presidency in the environmental field', *German Politics*, **9** (3), 23–43.

Wurzel, R. (2002), *Environmental Policy-making in Britain, Germany and the European Union*, Manchester: Manchester University Press.

Wurzel, R. (2003), 'The Europeanization of environmental policy: an environmental leader state under pressure?', in K. Dyson and K. Goetz (eds), *Germany and Europe: A Europeanized Germany?*, London: British Academy, 289–308.

Wurzel, R. (2004), 'Germany: from environmental leadership to partial mismatch' in A. Jordan and D. Liefferink (eds), *Environmental Policy in Europe. The Europeanization of National Environmental Policy*, London: Routledge, 99–117.

Wurzel, R. (2008a), *The Politics of Emissions Trading in Britain and Germany*, London: Anglo-German Foundation.

Wurzel, R. (2008b), 'Environmental policy: EU actors, leader and laggard states', in J. Hayward (ed.), *Leaderless Europe*, Oxford: Oxford University Press, 66–88.

Wurzel, R. (2008c), 'Germany', in A. Jordan and A. Lenschow (eds), *Innovation in Environmental Policy? Integrating the Environment for Sustainability*, Cheltenham: Edward Elgar, 180–201.

Wurzel, R. (2010), 'Environmental, climate and energy policies: path-dependent incrementalism or quantum leap?', *German Politics*, **19** (3/4), 460–78.

Wurzel, R., Jordan, A., Zito, A. and Brückner, L. (2003a), 'From high regulatory state to social and ecological market economy? "New" environmental policy instruments in Germany', in A. Jordan, R. Wurzel and A. Zito (eds), *'New'*

Instruments of Environmental Governance? National Experiences and Prospects, London: Frank Cass, 115–36.

Wurzel, R., Brückner, L., Jordan, A., and Zito, A. (2003b), 'Struggling to leave behind a highly regulatory past? "New" environmental policy instruments in Austria', in A. Jordan, R. Wurzel and A. Zito (eds), *'New' Instruments of Environmental Governance? National Experiences and Prospects*, London: Frank Cass, 51–72.

Wurzel, R., Varma, A., Jordan, A. and Zito, A. (2003c), 'Das britische Emissionshandelssystem. Design und erste Unternehmenserfahrungen', *Umweltwirtschaftsforum*, **3**, 9–14.

Wurzel, R. and Connelly, J. (eds) (2011a), *The European Union as a Leader in International Climate Change Politics*, London: Routledge.

Wurzel, R. and Connelly, J. (2011b), 'Environmental NGOs: taking a lead?', in R.K.W. Wurzel and J. Connelly (eds), *The European Union as Leader in International Climate Change Politics*, London, Routledge, 214–31.

Yeager, P. (1991), *The Limits of Law: The Public Regulation of Private Pollution*, Cambridge: Cambridge University Press.

Zapfel, P. (2005), 'Greenhouse gas emissions trading in the EU: building the world's largest cap-and-trade scheme', in B. Hansjürgens (ed.), *Emissions Trading for Climate Policy: US and European Perspectives*, Cambridge: Cambridge University Press, 162–76.

Zapfel, P. (2007), 'A brief but lively chapter in EU Climate Policy: the Commission's perspective', in D. Ellerman, B. Buchner and C. Carraro (eds), *Allocation in the European Emissions Trading Scheme*, Cambridge: Cambridge University Press, 13–38.

Zapfel, P. and Vainio, M. (2002), 'Pathways to European greenhouse gas emission trading: history and misconceptions', Milan: Fondazione Eni Enrico Mattei.

Zito, A. (2000), *Creating Environmental Policy in the European Union*, Basingstoke: Palgrave.

Zito, A., Brückner, L., Jordan, A., and Wurzel, R. (2003), 'Instrument innovation in an environmental lead state: "new" environmental policy instruments in The Netherlands', *Environmental Politics*, **12** (1), 157–78.

Zito, A. and Egan, M. (1998), 'Environmental management standards, corporate strategies and policy networks', *Environmental Politics*, **7** (3), 94–117.

Zürn, M. (2008), 'Governance in einer sich wandelnden Welt – eine Zwischenbilanz', *Politische Vierteljahresschrift*, **41**, special issue, 553–80.

Index

ACEA (European Automobile
   Manufacturers Association) 126
AGE (emissions trading working group)
   see Germany
America *see* USA
Association of the German Automobile
   Industry (VDA) 109
Austria 6, 18, 24, 30, 46, 48, 49–53, 72,
   73, 74, 78, 107, 129, 130, 131,
   206, 207, 208, 212, 217, 219, 220,
   226, 227, 228, 230, 233
   Austrian Environment Agency
      (*Umweltbundesamt* – UBA) 50,
      128
   Best Available Technology (BAT) 53,
      84, 195, 197, 198, 199, 204, 217
   business 51, 58, 63, 84, 146, 180, 181,
      182, 200
   Business Chamber
      (*Wirtschaftskammer*) 51, 116,
      146, 180, 181, 197
   Clean Air Act 179
   command-and-control regulation
      116, 197
   companies (or firms) 85, 97, 100,
      101, 144, 169, 181
   competitiveness 116, 145, 146, 180,
      200
   consensus politics 51
   constitution 50, 130, 209
   corporatism 51, 68, 117, 197
   eco-label 83–5, 88, 89, 90, 91, 105,
      208, 213, 220, 230, 231, 232
   ecological modernisation *see*
      ecological modernisation
      Austria
   ecological tax reform (*see also*
      eco-taxes) 145, 146, 147, 155,
      156, 157, 233, 236

eco-social market economy
   (*ökosoziale Marktwirtschaft*) 51,
   52, 146
eco-taxes (*see also* ecological tax
   reform) 133, 134, 144–7, 149,
   155–6, 210–11, 213, 228, 233,
   236
   EMAS 97, 98, 99, 101–2, 103–4,
      208–9, 212, 213, 228, 232
   emissions trading 158, 168, 169,
      170, 173, 174, 175, 176,
      179–82, 211, 222
   Environment Ministry 49, 83, 102,
      147, 173, 176, 199
   environmental follower 83, 101,
      107, 129, 208–12, 220, 230
   environmental groups (*or* NGOs)
      50, 52, 116, 117, 146, 180,
      181, 197, 200
   environmental laggard 101, 184,
      208
   environmental latecomer 53, 116,
      144, 179, 197, 198
   environmental NGOs *see*
      environmental groups
   environmental pioneer 53, 197,
      198
   environmental policy 49, 50, 51,
      52, 84, 117, 144, 195, 197,
      198, 199, 209
   environmental policy plan 179,
      194, 198
   European Union membership 50,
      51, 145
   federal system 49, 50
   government 50, 53, 84, 101, 104,
      116, 147, 236
   grand coalition 51, 146, 157, 199,
      236

274   *Environmental governance in Europe*

industry (or business) 146, 181, 200
ISO 14001 104
Kyoto Protocol target 200
legalistic state 197
organisational structures 49–51
parliament 51, 52
petrol tourism (*Tanktourismus*) 145
policy goals and strategies 52–3
policy instrument patterns 207–12
policy instrument sequencing 212–16
policy style 51–2, 217
political parties 146
provinces (or states) 49, 50, 58, 72
regulations 197–200, 206, 213, 215, 226, 234
social partners (*Sozialpartner*) 52, 117, 146, 180
social partnership (*Sozialpartnerschaft*) 52, 117, 197
union 51, 52, 117, 181, 197
Voestalpine 181
voluntary agreements 108, 116–17, 209, 210, 212, 213, 220, 223, 228, 236
Workers Chamber (*Arbeiterkammer*) 50, 51, 116, 117, 146, 180, 181, 197
working group economic instruments 179
Austrian Business Chamber 116
Austrian Institute for Economic Research (*WiFo*) 145, 180, 236
Austrian People's Party (ÖVP) in Austria 49, 50, 51, 52, 53, 73, 116, 146, 147, 157, 180, 198, 199, 236

Bähr, Holger 26, 27, 28, 30, 237
Bailey, Ian 25
Barroso, José Manuel 68
BP 161, 162, 163, 177, 183, 185

BDI (Federal Association for German Industry) 100, 110, 142, 178
Belgium 98, 108, 134, 153
Bemelmans-Videc, Marie-Louise 11, 26, 30
Binswanger, Hans Christoph 141, 142
Blair, Tony 151
BRICs 238
Brown, Gordon 149
Bruijn, de Theo 26, 27, 30, 115
Bulgaria 134
Bulmer, Simon 40, 44, 83, 208, 230
business 31, 51, 58, 63, 78, 81, 84, 88, 89, 90, 91, 92, 93, 96, 99, 100, 104, 113, 114, 116, 119, 121, 135, 146, 153, 162, 163, 166, 170, 171, 180, 181–2, 183, 196, 197, 200
Business Chamber (*Wirtschaftskammer*) *see* Austria
burden sharing agreement 138, 170, 180
Bush, George W. 160

California 176
Cameron, David 151
carbon dioxide 138, 144, 145, 147, 154, 172, 173, 180, 233
carbon dioxide/energy tax *see* eco-taxes
carrots, sticks and sermons 11, 30
Central and Eastern European States 181
China 86, 88, 175, 238
Christian Democratic Party (CDU) in Germany 56, 110, 111, 142, 143, 144, 173, 174, 192, 236
Christian Social Union (CSU) in Germany 110, 111, 142, 143, 144, 173, 192, 236
Clean Development Mechanism (CDM) 168, 174, 176, 181, 200
climate change 6, 53, 62, 68, 69, 82, 110, 111, 114, 115, 119, 120, 121, 122, 123, 124, 127, 128, 129, 142, 147, 150, 151, 153, 161, 162, 164, 167, 173, 174, 176, 194–5, 210, 221, 222, 226, 239
Clinton, Bill 160

Index

coal 139, 143, 144, 154, 173, 174, 177, 178

coercion (*or* coercive) 11, 13, 27, 30, 33, 39, 40, 44, 107, 160, 175, 182, 211, 212, 215, 221, 231, 234
non-coercive 94, 209

command-and-control regulation 3, 4, 6, 8, 17, 19, 23, 26, 27, 29–30, 33, 34, 46, 52, 55, 56, 57, 61, 70, 73, 74, 110, 112, 116, 128, 130, 131, 189, 190, 191, 193, 194, 197, 200, 203, 205, 206, 223, 235, 237

Commission (of the European Union) *see* European Union

Conservative Party
in the UK 62, 131, 149, 151, 152, 205, 228

convergence 7, 8, 18, 19, 39, 42, 44, 154, 220, 229

corporatism *see Austria*

Council of Ministers *see* European Union

Cyprus 98

Czech Republic 103

Christian Democratic Appeal (CDA)
in the Netherlands 58–9, 113, 137–8, 228

Clement, Wolfgang 172, 174, 178

D66 (Democrats 66)
in the Netherlands 138

Dales, John 32, 158

DEHSt (German Emissions Trading Authority) 179

Delbeke, Jos 152, 167

Department of Energy and Climate Change (DECC) *see* United Kingdom

Department for Environment, Food and Rural Affairs (DEFRA) *see* United Kingdom

Delors, Jacques 153

Denmark 24, 33, 80, 86, 87, 98, 108, 134, 137, 153, 158, 161, 182, 183

Di Meana, Ripa 1

diffusion 41, 78, 85, 114, 160, 182, 189, 210, 238

divergence 7, 18, 41, 42, 43, 44, 129, 217

DIW (German Institute for Economic Affairs) 142

displacement 10, 36, 156, 217, 222, 223, 232

Dolowitz, David 39, 40, 160, 182, 211, 231

drift 10, 36, 217, 223

Eberlein, Burkhard 10, 225

eco-label 18, 27, 29, 30, 31, 56, 65, 67, 71, 77, 78–93, 94, 97, 98, 103–6, 107, 128, 207, 208, 213, 215, 217, 218, 220, 224, 225, 226, 230, 231, 232
Blue Angel (*or* Blauer Engel) *see* Germany
life-cycle analysis 84, 85, 232
Nordic Swan 80, 86, 88, 90, 91

ecological modernisation
Austria 24, 146
European Union 70
Germany 56, 193

ecological tax reform (*see also* eco-taxes) 32, 56, 111, 133, 138, 140–44, 145, 146, 147, 155, 156, 157, 172, 177, 180, 210, 229, 232, 233, 236

eco-taxes (*see also* ecological tax reform) 18, 25, 29, 32–3, 54, 56, 57, 58, 70, 71, 74, 126, 133–57, 161, 162, 177, 200, 207, 208, 210, 211, 212, 214, 221, 222, 225, 226, 228, 231, 233, 234, 236
fiscal incentive 11, 141, 143, 144, 145, 163
hypothecation 140, 141, 147, 156
transparency 136

EMAS 24, 29, 31, 57, 71, 78, 79, 80, 88, 93, 94, 95–9, 100, 101, 102, 103, 104, 105, 196, 207, 208, 209, 212, 213, 218, 222, 223, 224, 226, 227, 228, 230, 231, 232

emission limits 33, 65, 192, 193, 202–3, 204, 206

Emissions Trading Group *see* UK

276　　　*Environmental governance in Europe*

emissions trading schemes (ETS) (*see*
　　also Austria, European Union,
　　Germany, the Netherlands and
　　United Kingdom) 6, 18, 19, 29, 32,
　　33, 71, 111, 150, 154, 158–85,
　　200, 208, 211, 217, 218, 220, 221,
　　222, 225, 226, 229, 230, 231, 233
　　corruption 176, 185, 235
　　doing by learning 163
　　windfall profits 163, 171, 174
EMS (eco-management systems) 30,
　　31, 33, 77, 78, 79, 80, 87, 88, 91,
　　94, 95, 96, 97, 99, 101, 102–3,
　　104, 105, 106, 107, 128, 207–8,
　　209, 211, 212, 217, 218, 223, 225,
　　228, 232
environmental quality objectives
　　(EQOs) 193, 199, 202–3, 204,
　　206, 217
European Environmental Agency
　　(EEA) 32, 108, 116, 175
Environmental Action Programmes
　　(EAP) 67, 69, 70, 85, 95, 125, 153
European Commission *see* European
　　Union
European Community/ies (EC) *see*
　　European Union
European Council *see* European Union
European Court of Justice (ECJ) *see*
　　European Union
European Environment Agency (EEA)
　　32, 108, 116
European Parliament (EP) *see* European
　　Union
European Union
　　BATNEEC (Best Available
　　　Technology Not Exceeding
　　　Excessive Cost) 203, 204, 217,
　　　226
　　Business 78, 88, 89, 96, 104, 183
　　carbon dioxide/energy tax 119, 137,
　　　139, 143–4, 146, 152, 153, 155,
　　　167, 184, 210, 231
　　Commission 5, 32, 67, 68, 69, 71, 73,
　　　74, 85, 86, 87, 88, 89, 95, 96, 97,
　　　108, 109, 118, 119, 121, 124,
　　　125, 126, 127, 128, 132, 137,
　　　143, 152, 153–4, 155, 160, 166,

　　　167–8, 170, 172, 173, 174, 175,
　　　176, 177, 178, 180, 184, 200,
　　　202, 203, 204, 206, 209, 210,
　　　223, 229, 231, 233
　　Directorate General (DG)
　　　Environment 68, 69, 70, 97, 124,
　　　126, 152, 160, 167
　　companies 80, 86, 87, 94, 103, 183
　　competitiveness 95, 153, 202
　　constitution 67
　　Council of Ministers 5, 60, 67, 68, 69,
　　　73, 88, 98, 100, 102, 125, 126,
　　　153, 154, 155, 156, 175
　　Directives 66, 67, 70, 71, 123, 151,
　　　195, 199, 200, 202, 203, 204,
　　　229
　　eco-label 67, 71, 78, 83, 85–9, 91, 92,
　　　93, 98, 103, 104, 106, 128, 208,
　　　213, 218, 224, 231
　　eco-taxes 32, 70, 71, 74, 126, 139,
　　　143–4, 152–5, 207, 208, 210,
　　　212, 21
　　EMAS 24, 29, 31, 57, 71, 78, 79, 80,
　　　88, 93, 94, 95–9, 100, 101, 102,
　　　103, 104, 105, 196, 207, 208,
　　　209, 212, 213, 218, 222, 223,
　　　224, 226, 227, 228, 230, 231,
　　　232
　　Economic and Finance Minister
　　　Council 154
　　Environment Council 126, 168, 176
　　environmental follower 78, 85, 95,
　　　107, 123, 129, 189, 207, 208,
　　　209, 210, 211, 212, 217, 220,
　　　230
　　environmental groups (*see*
　　　environmental NGOs)
　　environmental NGOs (and groups)
　　　73, 82, 86, 96, 97, 100, 125, 126,
　　　183
　　environmental pioneer 95, 107, 152,
　　　167–82
　　environmental policy 24, 25, 27, 28,
　　　48, 66–71, 72–3, 74, 79, 85, 123,
　　　125, 152, 160, 200, 202, 217,
　　　220
　　European Council 68, 69

Index

European Court of Justice (ECJ) 68, 69, 73, 170, 174, 175, 195
European Parliament 67, 68, 69, 72, 73, 88, 98, 125, 126, 128, 153, 167, 168, 175, 184, 201, 229
European Union membership
European Union emissions trading scheme (EU ETS) 111, 115, 154, 159, 162, 164, 166, 167–76, 177, 178, 179, 180, 181, 182, 183, 184, 185, 210, 211, 212, 214, 220, 221, 222, 231, 232, 233, 235, 240
High Level Working Group 203–4
industry (or business) 70, 79, 81, 86, 125, 126, 127, 128, 175
Kyoto Protocol 167, 168, 169, 170, 182, 184, 211
Maastricht Treaty 201
member state 23, 24, 28, 29, 33, 38, 39, 40, 45, 47, 65, 66, 67, 68, 70–71, 73, 77, 78, 85, 86–7, 88, 89, 95, 96, 98, 102, 103, 104, 105, 107–8, 116, 123, 126, 128–9, 130, 134, 137, 139, 152, 153, 154, 155, 157, 160, 168, 169–70, 173–6, 182, 184, 185, 189–90, 197, 200, 202, 204, 206, 217, 218, 220, 226, 227, 228, 229, 231, 232, 233, 235
organisational structures 66–8
policy goals and strategies 70–71
policy instrument sequencing 212–16
policy style 68–9
regulations 70, 200
regulatory state 66, 71, 191, 200, 206, 216, 228
Task Force on the Environment and Internal Market 152
voluntary agreements 108, 123–8, 213, 218
exhaustion 10, 36, 223, 224

Federation of Austrian Industries (*Industriellenvereinigung*) 146, 181
Flemming, Marilies 83

Finland 80, 98, 108, 134, 153
Fischer, Joscka 172
France 65, 86, 87, 89, 95, 108, 133, 134, 135, 148, 153, 154
Free Democratic Party *(Freie Demokratische Partei* – FDP)
  in Germany 53, 56, 110, 111, 142, 143, 144, 192, 236
Freedom Party *(Freiheitliche Partei Österreichs* – FPÖ)
  in Austria 49, 50, 51, 52, 53, 73, 116, 146, 180, 198, 236
free rider (*or* free riding) 117, 118, 121, 124, 125, 127, 129
Friends of the Earth (FoE) 162
  FoE Germany 178

Geel, Pieter van 195
Germanwatch 178
Germany 6, 18, 42, 46, 48, 53–7, 59, 65, 72, 73, 74, 78, 79, 80–83, 86, 89, 90, 91, 96, 97, 98, 99–101, 103, 104, 105, 107, 108, 109–11, 116, 117, 121, 128, 129, 130, 131, 132, 133, 134, 140–44, 145, 146, 149, 153, 155, 156, 157, 158, 160, 168, 169, 170, 172, 173, 174, 175, 177–9, 184, 190, 191–4, 198, 199, 203, 204, 206, 207, 208, 209, 210, 211, 212, 213, 214, 215, 216, 217, 219, 220, 221, 222, 223, 224, 225, 226, 227, 228, 230, 231, 232, 234, 236
  AGE (emissions trading working group – *Arbeitsgemeinschaft Emissionshandel*) 177, 178, 179, 183
  Bavaria 110, 173, 203
  Best Available Technology (BAT) 54, 57, 64, 73, 82, 99, 100, 105, 140, 145, 192, 193, 194, 195, 198, 203, 204, 206, 217
  business 81, 82, 100
  Blauer Engel (*or* Blue Angel) *see also* eco-label 78, 80–83, 84, 85, 86, 88, 90, 91, 103, 104, 105, 208, 218, 224, 230, 232

Bundestag *see* parliament
command-and-control regulations 55, 56, 56, 73, 110, 131, 191–4
companies (or firms) 81, 82, 83, 88, 95, 97, 98, 99, 100, 103, 126
competitiveness 126, 141, 142, 192
constitution 54, 130, 131, 140, 156, 209, 228
eco-label (*see also* Blauer Engel) 56, 78, 80–83, 85, 86, 106, 208, 213, 218, 220, 224, 230, 231
ecological tax reform 32, 56, 111, 133, 140–44, 155, 156, 157, 172, 177, 180, 210, 229, 233, 236
eco-taxes 54, 56, 57, 133, 134, 140–44, 155–6, 208, 210, 211, 214, 233
EMAS 97, 98, 99–101, 103, 104, 105, 208–9, 213, 224, 228
emissions trading 177–9
Environment Agency (UBA) 50, 54, 81, 83, 96, 99, 100, 111, 131, 143, 144, 179, 191
Environment Ministry 54, 55, 72, 81, 99, 143, 215
Environmental Code (*Umweltgesetzbuch*) 192
environmental groups (see environmental NGOs)
environmental NGOs (*or* groups) 56, 81, 82, 100, 110, 111, 142, 177, 178
environmental pioneer *see* pioneer
environmental policy 53, 54, 55, 56, 57, 72, 73, 74, 109, 140, 172, 177, 179, 191, 192, 193, 195, 209, 220
federal system (*or* federalism) 54, 55, 72, 82, 110, 111, 140, 144, 190
follower 177–9, 208, 211, 212
grand coalition 173, 174, 192
Hesse 177
industry (or business) 55, 56, 81, 82, 99, 100, 109, 110–11, 141, 143, 172, 174, 177, 178, 179, 193
ISO 14001 97, 98, 101
IGBCE (Mining, Chemical and Energy Industrial Union) 178

Kyoto Protocol 160, 170, 174
laggard 99, 184, 208
North Rhine-Westphalia 173, 178
organisational structures 53–5
parliament (*or* Bundestag) 143, 173, 174, 179, 184
pioneer 105, 106, 109–11, 128, 129, 140–44, 210
policy goals and strategies 56–7
policy instrument patterns 207–18
policy instrument sequencing 213–16
policy style 55–6
political parties 143, 228
Red-Green coalition *see* SPD-Green coalition regulations
social market economy (*soziale Marktwitschaft*) 55
SPD-Green coalition 56, 110, 111, 142, 143, 144, 157, 172, 192, 236
social market economy (*ökologische und soziale Marktwirtschaft*)
state of law (*Rechtsstaat*) 56, 191
states (*Länder*) 54, 110, 140, 177, 180
unions 55, 100
voluntary agreements 108, 109–11, 213
GHGE (greenhouse gas emissions) 6, 68, 211
Global Climate Coalition 162
Golub, Jonathan 26, 27
governance 3–19, 23, 25, 27, 28, 29, 30, 33, 34, 36, 38, 40, 43, 45, 46–8, 71, 74, 77, 91, 94, 104, 106, 107, 119, 122, 124, 129, 130, 133, 184, 185, 202, 209, 211, 215, 216, 217, 219, 220, 221, 222, 223, 225, 226, 227, 228, 229, 234, 237, 238, 239
coexistence (of governance and government instruments) 10
competition (between governance and government instruments) 10, 11, 14, 26, 28, 221, 225
from government towards governance 7–11
fusion (of governance and government instruments) 10, 17, 221, 225

governance as bridge term 4, 5
governance-cum-government 225, 226
governance theory 4, 5
governance turn 3, 7
governance eclipsed government 220–30
governance versus government 43
hierarchical governance 28, 40
horizontal governance 219
horizontal self-coordination 77
hybrid governance 8, 15, 130, 226
modes of governance 3–4, 7–16, 23, 27, 30, 36, 43, 77, 130, 184, 217, 221, 222
multi-level governance 4
new modes of governance 3, 4, 5, 7, 8, 9, 10, 12, 15, 23, 27, 30, 36, 77, 130, 184, 217, 221, 222
over-theorised 5, 43, 219
self-steering 4, 8, 47, 48, 129, 130, 216, 219
society-led governance 220
soft governance 106
strong governance 130, 225, 226
under-empiricised 5, 219
governing 3–19, 30, 33, 36, 39, 41, 49, 58, 72, 84, 107, 113, 129, 130, 156, 189, 205, 215, 217, 218, 222, 231, 237, 238, 239, 240
co-governing 10
governing as generic term 9
governing by multiple instruments 10–11
hybrid form 18
government 3–19, 23, 25, 28, 29, 30, 33, 43, 44, 46, 47, 48, 49, 50, 51, 52, 53, 54, 55, 56, 57, 58, 59, 60, 61, 62, 63, 64, 66, 68, 72, 73, 74, 77, 80, 81, 82, 84, 90, 91, 92, 93, 99, 100, 101, 102, 103, 104, 107, 109, 110, 111, 112, 113, 114, 115, 116, 118, 119, 121, 122, 126, 130, 131, 135, 136, 137, 138, 139, 140, 141, 1442, 143, 144, 45, 146, 147, 148, 149, 150, 151, 152, 153, 155, 157, 161, 162, 163, 164, 165, 166, 167, 168, 169, 170, 171, 172, 173, 174,

177, 178, 179, 180, 183, 184, 185, 189, 190, 191, 192, 193, 194, 195, 196, 197, 198, 199, 202, 205, 209, 212, 215, 216, 217, 219, 220, 221, 223, 225, 226, 227, 228, 229, 233, 234, 236, 240
better government 5
governance-cum-government 225, 226
government-governance continuum 130
government towards governance 7–11, 17, 18, 29, 33
hierarchical government 47, 219, 226
shadow of hierarchy 4, 10, 107, 130, 221
shadow of the law 55, 110, 129, 192, 221
tools of government (*or* government tools) 7, 8, 9, 10, 11, 12, 13, 14, 15, 18, 19, 23, 25, 28, 30, 43, 77, 130, 131, 184, 217, 222
grandfathering 158, 164, 173, 175
Greece 98, 108, 134
Green Alliance (UK) 162
green consumerism 77, 78
Green parties 157, 228
Austria 52, 83, 146, 236
Germany 56, 110, 111, 142, 144, 157, 172, 174, 178–9, 184, 192, 236
green public procurement 92
Greenpeace 142, 162
Grabosky, Peter 26, 28, 189, 207, 212, 221, 234
Gunningham, Neil 26, 28, 189, 207, 212, 221, 234

Halpern, Charlotte 26, 28
Hansmeyer, Karl-Heinz 141
Heclo, Hugh 37, 44
High Level Working Group *see* European Union
hierarchy 11, 68, 196
shadow of hierarchy 4, 10, 107, 130, 221
Holland *see* the Netherlands

280　　*Environmental governance in Europe*

Hood, Christopher 11, 13, 14, 16, 23, 24, 25, 27
Holzinger, Katarina 26, 27, 30, 33
Howard, Michael 148
Howlett, Michael 13, 14, 42
Hufen, H.A.M. 26, 27, 30, 115
Hundertwasser, Friedenreich 84

India 238
industry (*see also* business) 31, 32, 49, 55, 64, 70, 79, 81, 86, 92, 93, 99, 100, 102, 109, 110, 111, 113, 114, 116, 117, 118, 119, 120, 121, 125, 126, 127, 128, 129, 135, 136, 138, 140, 141, 142, 143, 146, 150, 161, 163, 164, 165, 171, 172, 173, 174, 175, 177, 178, 179, 193, 204, 205, 210, 232
institutionalism 34, 36, 41, 227
Ireland 86, 94, 95, 108, 134, 171, 202
ISO (International Standards Organization) 31, 79, 94, 95, 96, 99, 100, 102, 103, 105, 232
ISO 14001 31, 79, 80, 94, 96, 97, 98, 99, 100, 101, 102, 103, 104, 105, 196, 209, 212, 222, 223, 226, 227, 232
Italy 86, 87, 89, 98, 101, 108, 134, 153

Jänicke, Martin 193
Japan 102, 126
Johnson, Boris 151
Joint Implementation (JI) 168, 174, 176, 181, 200

Kassim, Hussein 14, 237
Kerwer, Dieter 10, 225
Klima, Vitor 146
Knill, Christoph 26, 27, 28, 193
Kohl, Helmut 56, 142
Kyoto Protocol 160–61, 162, 164, 165, 167, 168, 169, 170, 174, 181, 182, 184, 200, 211, 218, 230, 233

laggard 92, 99, 101, 102, 103, 117, 129, 152, 177, 184, 189, 207, 208, 210, 212, 217, 220

Labour Party
in the UK 62, 122, 131, 149, 150–52, 153, 157, 161–2, 171, 181–3, 236
Lascoumes, Pierre 12, 14
layering 10, 36, 131, 221, 223, 224
leadership 73, 97, 113, 129, 142, 195
cost free leadership 74
Le Galés, Patrick 3, 12, 14, 237
Lenschow, Andrea 24, 26, 28
Lloyd, George 147
Linder, Stephen 23, 24, 42
Lubbers, Ruud 59
Luxembourg 108, 134

Major, John 149
Marsh, David 39, 40, 160, 182, 211, 231
Malta 134
Majone, Giandomenico 25, 27, 42, 66, 200
market 6, 11, 32, 55, 77, 78, 79, 80, 84, 85, 91, 94, 104, 105, 106, 141, 151, 158, 159, 164, 176, 180, 182, 231, 232, 233, 236, 240
export market 90, 198
free market 26
free market environmentalism 232
global market 103, 104
market-based instruments 6, 15, 18, 24, 25, 27, 29, 32–3, 43, 52, 55, 56, 62, 65, 85, 121, 128, 133, 146, 147, 152, 154, 167, 176, 184, 185, 192, 200, 221, 226, 235
market and networks 5
market competition 83
market share 83
Single European Market *see* European Union
Mayntz, Renate 36, 44
Meacher, Michael 149
Merkel, Angela 174

National Environmental Policy Plan (NEPP)
in the Netherlands 61, 90, 114, 102, 113, 137, 179, 194, 198

National Allocation Plan (NAP) 168,
169, 170, 171, 172, 173, 174, 175,
179, 183
NEPP+ 61, 114
Netherlands
Agriculture Ministry 58, 115
ALARA 61, 195
Best Practicable Means (BPM) 61,
195
Best Technical Means (BTM) 61, 195
business (*see* companies or industry)
charges (*or* levies) 135–7, 139, 155,
224
coalition 58, 113, 131, 137–9, 157,
165, 233, 236
command-and-control regulations
60–61, 112
companies (or firms) 91–2, 102–4,
112–13, 115, 138, 166, 169, 171,
174, 195–6, 209
competitiveness 137–8, 166, 174
consensus approach in state-society
relations (or stakeholder
consultation) 57, 59, 72,
112, 130, 194, 206, 221
consociational system 59
covenant (or negotiated agreement)
34, 65, 102, 105, 112–15,
129–31, 165, 195, 209, 218, 221,
225, 226, 228, 230, 231, 233
eco-label 89–92, 103–6, 208, 213,
230, 233
eco-taxes 58, 74, 133–40, 155–7,
208, 210–11, 214, 224, 229, 230,
233
ecological tax reform 133, 137–8,
155, 233
EMAS 97–8, 102–3, 196, 208–9,
212–13, 227
emissions trading 138, 158, 164–72,
174–6, 182–4, 208, 211, 214,
222, 233
environmental follower 89, 208, 230
environmental groups 57, 90, 138
environmental laggard 102, 103, 208
Environmental Management Act
1993 59, 60–61, 195, 196, 223

environmental NGOs (*or* groups) 90,
138, 165
environmental pioneer 60, 107, 112,
128, 129, 135, 158, 164, 182–3,
210
environmental policy plan (*see*
planning)
Finance Ministry 58, 137, 165, 172
government 131, 138–9, 157, 164–6,
171, 194–6, 234, 236
industry (or business) 91–2, 102, 113,
114, 135, 136, 137, 164, 165
internalisation 61, 196
ISO 14001 102–3, 196, 209, 212, 227
Kyoto Protocol 170, 174
licensing 60, 112, 194–7
Milieukeur 89–91
Ministry for Economic Affairs 58,
114–15, 165–6, 171–2
Ministry for Economic Affairs,
Agriculture and Innovation 58,
171
Ministry for Housing, Physical
Planning and Environment
(VROM) 57–8, 90, 114–15, 165,
171–2, 194
Ministry of Infrastructure and the
Environment 58, 171
Ministry of Transport and Public
Works 57–8
municipal (or local) authorities 57–8,
113–15, 164–5, 194–6
National Emissions Authority (NEA)
166, 171
organisational structures 57–9
parliament 90, 137–8
planning 59–61, 194
policy goals and strategies 60–61,
140, 194
policy instrument patterns 113,
215–16, 220–21, 224, 226, 234
policy instrument sequencing 215–16
policy style 59–61, 72–3, 130
political parties 58–9
provinces 57–9, 112, 164–5, 194, 196
Purple I coalition 138, 157, 236
Purple II coalition 165

282   *Environmental governance in Europe*

regulations 112, 115, 130, 135, 155,
165, 194–7, 206, 209, 214–15,
223, 226, 234
self-regulation 102
Surface Water Pollution Act 135
target groups 59–61, 112–15,
130–31, 196, 233
Tax Reform Commission 145, 156
voluntary agreements (VAs) (*see also*
covenants) 107–8, 112–15,
129–32, 208, 210–13, 221–5,
228, 230, 233
VNO-NCW (Confederation of
Netherlands Industry and
Employers 102, 165
water boards 59, 114, 135

networks 4, 5, 11, 38, 44, 61, 99, 100
New Environmental Policy Instruments
(NEPIs) 16, 17, 18, 19, 24, 25, 28,
38, 47, 61, 63, 66, 67, 71, 72, 73,
74, 122, 123, 125, 130, 141, 144,
146, 147, 148, 149, 150, 152, 154,
160, 182, 189, 193, 195, 196, 197,
205, 207, 208, 210, 211, 212, 213,
215, 216, 217, 218, 220, 221, 222,
223, 225, 227, 229, 231, 232, 233,
234, 235, 238
Nijpels, Ed 90
Non-governmental organisations
(NGOs) 4, 50, 73, 82, 86, 90, 92,
96, 100, 102, 110, 111, 116, 117,
138, 142, 145, 146, 157, 162, 163,
165, 177, 178, 180, 181, 183, 185,
196, 205
Norway 80, 86, 88, 134
nuclear power 52, 54, 56, 70, 144, 172,
193

Open Method of Coordination (OMC)
5, 40, 71
Organisation for Economic
Co-operation and Development
(OECD) 25, 31–3, 50, 52, 78,
79–80, 81, 86, 87, 109, 127, 133,

135–7, 139, 140, 144, 145, 147,
152, 157, 194–5, 196, 197–200,
238
Osborne, George 151, 159

Padgett, Stephen 39, 40, 44, 83, 208,
230
Pearce, David 63, 148
Peters, Guy 23, 24, 42, 228
policy diffusion 41, 78, 85, 114, 160,
182, 189, 210, 238
policy change 12, 23, 35, 36, 37–9, 42,
46, 196
policy instruments 4–7, 8, 10, 11–13,
15, 16, 17, 18, 19, 23–5, 27,
28–34, 37, 38, 39, 41, 42–5, 46–8,
54, 60, 61, 65, 67, 70, 71, 74, 77–8,
80, 85, 91, 93, 101, 102, 104, 106,
107, 113, 114, 115, 116, 122, 129,
130, 131, 155, 162, 164, 172, 179,
181, 182, 183, 184, 185 n1,
189–218, 219–40
cost effective 17, 24–5, 32, 63, 65,
159, 194, 195, 197, 199, 200,
202, 203, 204, 206, 235
hybrid 17, 104, 207, 216, 217, 221,
222, 227
layering (of policy instruments) 131,
221, 223, 224
optimal design 28, 35, 224
policy instrument patterns 207–18
policy instrument mixes 6, 15, 16, 24,
28, 74, 104, 129, 207, 216, 217,
221, 224, 225, 227, 234, 235
policy instrument sequencing 213–16
hard policy instruments 215, 234
sequencing (of policy instruments)
212–16, 234, 235
soft policy instruments 15, 30, 71, 77,
78, 130, 200, 215
policy learning 6, 18, 19, 23, 35, 36,
37–41, 42, 43, 44, 45, 46, 78, 102,
105, 107, 113, 114, 122, 125, 131,
135, 155, 156, 157, 163, 164, 168,
173, 183, 189, 192, 193, 196, 218,
220, 227, 230, 231–5, 236

Index

policy transfer 18, 19, 23, 26, 38, 39–41, 42, 43, 44, 45, 78, 83, 90, 104, 105, 106, 107, 116, 131, 132, 136, 157, 160, 161, 168, 182, 192, 207, 208, 209, 210, 211, 218, 220, 230–32, 234

political parties 51, 52, 57, 112, 113, 138, 143, 146, 157, 228, 236

Portugal 98, 108, 134

PvdA (Labour Party – *Partij van de Arbeid*)
in the Netherlands 58, 138

regulation 3, 4, 5, 6, 8, 10, 11, 13, 14, 17, 19, 23, 24, 26, 27, 28, 29, 30, 31, 33, 34, 42, 43, 52, 53, 54, 55, 56, 57, 58, 59, 60, 61, 63, 64, 65, 66, 67, 70, 71, 73, 74, 79, 84, 92, 94, 98, 100, 101, 102, 105, 110, 111, 112, 113, 115, 116, 118, 119, 121, 122, 123, 124, 125, 128, 129, 130, 131, 135, 136, 147, 148, 152, 161, 179, 189, 190, 191, 192, 193, 194, 195, 196, 197, 198, 199, 200, 202, 203, 204, 205, 206, 207, 209, 210, 213–14, 215, 216, 217, 218, 221, 222, 223, 224, 225, 226, 229, 232, 234, 235, 236, 237, 238, 239, 240
command-and-control regulation 3, 4, 6, 8, 17, 19, 23, 26, 29, 30, 33, 34, 52, 55, 56, 57, 70, 73, 74, 110, 112, 116, 128, 130, 189, 190, 194, 197, 200, 203, 206, 223, 235, 237
smart regulation 29, 204, 207, 226

Rist, Ray 11, 26, 30

Royal Commission on Environmental Pollution (RCEP) 62, 118, 205

Scharpf, Fritz 4, 36, 44
Schäfer, Ansgar 26, 27
Schmitter, Philip 68
Schröder, Gerhard 142, 168, 172, 174, 178, 179, 184
Schüssel, Wolfgang 146
Schuppert, Gunnar 3
self-coordination 77

shadow of hierarchy 4, 10, 107, 130, 221

shadow of the law 55, 110, 129, 192, 221

Sinclair, Darren 26, 28, 189, 207, 212, 221, 234

Spain 87, 89, 95, 98, 101, 108, 134, 153

Social Democratic Party of Germany (*Sozialdemokratische Partei Deutschlands* – SPD)
in Germany 53, 56, 110, 142, 143, 144, 172, 173, 174, 178, 179, 184, 192

SRU (Environmental Expert Council)
in Germany 54, 141, 177

state 4, 9, 10, 33, 37, 40, 50, 54, 55, 57, 66, 67, 68, 69, 71, 78, 82, 83, 105, 148, 217
continental states 34, 65, 203, 204
corporatist state (*see also* Austria, corporatism) 51
environmental leader state (*see also* environmental leader) 197, 198
federal state (*or* structure) 66, 72, 140, 190, 237, 238
high regulatory state 56, 66, 191, 206
innovator states 210, 231
legalistic state 197
like-minded states 66
member states *see* European Union
pioneer states 128, 152
regulatory state *see* European Union
state capacities 222, 227
state-centred 7
state intervention 8, 55
state-society 46, 47, 48, 57, 61, 99, 111, 131
strong state 8, 56
unitary states 237

Steinmeier, Frank-Walter 172

Stern Report 150

Streeck, Wolfgang 10, 36, 41, 44, 68, 156, 223

suasive instruments 6, 11, 15, 26, 27, 28, 29, 30, 31, 33, 43, 64, 107

subsidiarity 54, 70, 123, 125, 201

Sweden 80, 98, 108, 115, 134, 153

284 *Environmental governance in Europe*

Thatcher, Margaret 73, 236
Thelen, Kathleen 10, 36, 41, 44, 223
Töller, Anette 24
Tömmel, Ingeborg 9, 14, 15, 28
Töpfer, Klaus 56, 142
Transparency International 179
trial and error 37, 63
Trittin, Jürgen 172, 178

United Kingdom (*see also* Britain)
  Best Available Technology Not
      Exceeding Excessive Costs
      (BATNEEC) 203, 204, 217
  BS 7750 94–5, 96, 99, 119, 121, 208,
      209, 218, 230
  business 63, 93, 118, 119, 161, 170,
      171, 208, 229
  City of London 164
  Confederation of British Industry
      (CBI) 118, 150, 161
  Congestion charging 151
  Department of Energy and Climate
      Change (DECC) *see also*
      Environment Ministry 62
  Department for Environment, Food
      and Rural Affairs (DEFRA) *see
      also* Environment Ministry 62,
      92–3
  Department of Trade and Industry 92
  eco-label 92–3, 104, 106, 208, 213,
      215, 217, 220, 230–31
  eco-taxes 147–52, 155–7, 161, 162,
      208, 210, 214, 240
  EMAS 93, 94–5, 97, 98, 208–9, 213,
      230
  emissions trading 150, 161–4, 170,
      182–5, 208, 211, 217, 220, 221,
      230–31, 233
  emissions trading group (ETG) 162,
      177, 183
  Environment Agency 61, 63, 94, 161,
      171
  Environment Ministry 62, 74 n1, 92,
      93, 94, 119, 120, 147, 148, 150,
      151, 161, 163, 165, 171
  Environmental Audit Committee 150

  environmental follower 65, 107, 129,
      205, 208
  environmental laggard 92–3, 117,
      129, 147, 155, 208, 210, 217,
      220
  environmental latecomer 147
  environmental NGOs (or groups) 162
  environmental pioneer 94, 96, 99,
      104, 161, 162, 183, 204, 206
  European Union membership 62
  Fabian Society 149
  fuel escalator 146, 210, 228
  fuel poverty 149
  Green Alliance 192
  House of Commons 122, 150
  House of Lords 92, 118, 147
  ISO 14001 96, 97, 103, 104
  Kyoto Protocol 174
  Marshal Report 161, 163
  National Audit Office 159, 163
  organisational structures 61–3
  parliament (*see also* House of
      Commons *and* House of Lords)
      150
  policy goals and strategies 64–6
  policy instrument sequencing
      212–16
  policy style 63–4
  regulations 63, 65, 204, 206ff, 215,
      226, 234
  road pricing 147, 151
  Royal Commission on Environmental
      Pollution 62, 118, 148
  Treasury 123, 150, 159, 161
  unwritten constitution 63
  voluntary agreements 65, 108,
      117–23, 129–32, 213, 209, 220,
      221

Vedung, Evert 11, 26, 30
Verdun, Amy 9, 14, 15, 28
voluntary agreements (VAs) 18, 26, 27,
      29, 30, 31–2, 55, 56, 60, 65, 67, 70,
      71, 74, 106, 107–32, 138, 142,
      146, 148, 162, 172, 177, 179, 180,
      192, 199, 200, 207, 209, 210, 211,
      212, 213, 215, 218, 220, 221, 222,

223, 224, 225, 226, 228, 229, 231, 233, 236

covenants *see* Netherlands

negotiated agreements (see also covenants) 31, 34, 64, 109, 112–15, 116, 118, 119, 120, 121, 123, 129, 130, 218, 229

self-declaratory voluntary agreements 30, 93, 109, 225

transparency 110, 117, 124

VVD (People's Party for Freedom and Democracy)

in the Netherlands 58–9, 90, 113, 138, 228

Weizsäcker, Ernst-Ulrich 141, 142

WIFO (Austrian Institute for Economic Research 180, 236

Workers Chamber (*Arbeiterkammer*) *see* Austria

World Trade Organization (WTO) 4, 79, 87

World Wide Fund for Nature (WWF) 162, 178